The Meanderings

Of

A One Horse Preacher

The Extraordinary Activity of God

Through an Ordinary Man

By James L. Goforth, Sr.

Dedication

I want to dedicate this book to the memory of my parents Carl and Frances Goforth, and my Father-in-law, Rev. Lester Patterson, and in honor of my Mother-in-law Helen Patterson.

It was their commitment to the Lord, to one another, and to their children that developed Virginia and me into people who learned to love the Lord, their family, and His church.

I also dedicate this book to my wife Virginia and our two sons Rev. James L. Goforth, Jr. and Dr. Thomas B. Goforth, their wives, and our four grandchildren, A.J., Bryan, Emily, and Ashley.

Acknowledgements

I am particularly grateful to my wife Virginia, for the many hours that she spent in proofreading this book.

I am also grateful to my brother-in-law, Dr. Mickey Anders, who graciously consented to edit this book. His expertise is gratefully appreciated.

I am also grateful for the various ones who encouraged me to undertake this project. I will not try to list all of them, but I think they know who they are. Without their encouragement, I would never have been challenged to begin this work.

I am also grateful to all of the churches who allowed me to serve the Lord as their pastor, and to the Adirondack Baptist Association who gave me the opportunity to serve the Lord with them.

Finally and most importantly is the leading of the Holy Spirit, which brought to my mind the things that I believe He wanted to be recorded.

My prayer concerning this book:

I am really a very ordinary man, who never considered that his story was something others would be interested in reading. However, the more I considered it, the more I was encouraged to do it. I was reminded of some very extraordinary activity of God, in which He allowed me to participate. It is my prayer that other ordinary people will read this story and be encouraged that they, too, can be used of God in some extraordinary ways.

The process I used was simply to break my life down in segments and allow the Lord to bring to my mind the things I felt He wanted me to share. That is the process I tried to be faithful in carrying out, and I hope it is what was accomplished. There are many other stories that could have been told, but these are the ones the Lord brought back to my mind.

I pray that in the reading of my story, you will receive some kind of blessing from God. I also pray that you will understand that the activity of God on this earth is designed to be carried to completion by ordinary human beings like you and me. It is really mind-boggling to think that the mighty activity of God on this earth is designed to be activated through imperfect human beings like you and me.

Testimonials

The Lord placed Jim Goforth in my life in 1984, when he became the pastor of First Baptist Church, Rusk, Texas. My wife and I were a young couple with a small child at the time and had no idea that this would be the beginning of a lifelong friendship. Since this time, Jim has had a tremendous spiritual impact on the life of my family. Jim was used by the Lord to instill the value of Bible study, prayer and discipleship in our day to day walk with Jesus. Through Jim's example we learned to trust God in difficult circumstances. That was never more evident than when our twenty-one year old son, Collin, went home to be with The Lord while serving with Mercy Ships in Liberia. Jim had baptized Collin and later would share words of comfort at his memorial service. He simply stated, "There are some things I just don't understand, but I still believe." Heartfelt words from a heart beating for Jesus. That is Jim Goforth! He never turned his spiritual radar to the off position for the sake of comfort, prestige or position. He was, and is, always tuned in to The Lord's voice. From Texas to Ohio, back to Texas, New York and back again to Texas, Jim has always been ready to live up to his name, Go-forth. He is my mentor in the faith and his example of selfless service is a model for all servants of Christ. Thank you, Jim, for taking the time to record your journey and for seeing value in me. Because of my faith in Christ and your encouragement I can state with assurance, I Still Believe.

--Jeff Carroll,
Associate Pastor/Worship & Senior Adults
First Baptist Church Rusk

Jim Goforth has been a godly friend and inspiration for over 25 years. As Church Renewal Director of Texas Baptist Men, I had the joy of bringing multiple teams of lay people to many churches where Jim served in East Texas and New York.

Prayer and Spiritual Awakening have always been the foundation where Jim Goforth served and he always wanted God to be the main attraction. Jim and First Baptist Church, Rusk, Texas, hosted the first *Experiencing God Weekend* in October, 1991. Through a Solemn Assembly held earlier, God was already mightily at work in the church and community. Jim prayed for people to hear and respond to God's voice during the *Experiencing God Weekend*. He had not expected God to speak to him and ask him to leave his comfortable home and pastorate to respond to God's call to a small group of pioneer churches. Jim and Virginia spent the next twelve years as the Director of Missions in the Adirondack Baptist Association in New York where he planted churches, made disciples of Jesus, and mentored pastors. Texas Baptist Men helped the Adirondack Association begin an annual pastor's conference to encourage the pastors and churches.

Jim has countless stories of how God worked in so many ways and places. Some of these are in this book. Read on, be blessed, and give God the glory.

--Don Gibson, Texas Baptist Men

"This is Jim Goforth. He's the associational missionary in the 'North Country'." I was being introduced to some of the leaders in the Baptist Convention of New York as I began my ministry there as Executive Director/Treasurer.

I had managed to keep names and faces pretty well matched but it wasn't until the first week of January of '98 that I really began to know and appreciate this man and his ministry. We had suffered the worst ice storm of the century in the North Country. I had decided to travel there from Syracuse and see for myself. From Watertown to

Plattsburgh and over to Malone it looked like a war zone! My driver and I literally slid into the area where our convention's disaster unit had set up. The scene is better described as organized chaos! Jim Goforth was constantly on one of the few working cell phones. Jim was using his leadership skills to "make everything work" through volunteers who, cooked meals, loaded them on to Red Cross vehicles, steam cleaned cambros and then began the process all over again.

That was the introduction to a relationship that has endured through the years. We are both retired now, but our friendship remains. From time to time but not as often as we would like, we enjoy recounting some of the experiences you will read about in the following pages. I know the man as good friend, fishing buddy, dedicated minister, prayer warrior and faithful personal evangelist.

-- J. B. Graham, D. Min.
Retired from NAMB
Retired Executive Director of the
Baptist Convention of New York

Reading Luke 18 we are reminded to pray with purpose, specifically, persistently and faithfully. Sometimes God poses us questions when we pray, as He did the blind man: "What would you have me do?" Sometimes He pauses, in His God-time that is unrelated to our human time. But we can always be sure that He has an answer ready for us. He is our answer and prayer reintroduces us to Him.

Wisdom that comes from life experience is valuable. Life experience filtered through the truth of the Word is the kind of wisdom that deserves to be passed on, generation to generation. Jim Goforth brings this kind of wisdom. Whether it is through early morning meetings with the Father or believing His answers enough to step out on faith, Goforth has faithfully surrendered for a lifetime.

Throughout his life, he has been willing to take God at His word. At this stage in life he continues to pastor, teach and lead today's generation of believers. Be encouraged by his stories of God's faithfulness.

--Jason Hoffman, Tree of Promise, Rusk

Brother Jim and I are an unusual pair. I am a Catholic dentist and he is a Baptist preacher. But you know what, who cares? He is a close friend and I was there to hold him in my arms when the Yellow Lab we sold him died. Months later, he held me as I cried when my father passed away. But the gift he has in those times is to help you through it with a hug, a smile, and even better....with a story. I have been treating him and his wife in my practice for over twenty years. One thing I can always count on is a good joke or one of his many stories. One day after a particularly hilarious one, I told him, "You need to write these down and write a book some day." Well, I got a call that he had done just that, and could I help with a paragraph in the Foreword section. A paragraph? I could almost write a book. Know this about Brother Jim. He is a Man of God. But he is also a guy who likes to go fishing or to a ball game or to watch his dog run and scratch him behind the ears. I am proud to call him my friend and I am sure you will enjoy the story of his life.

--Jerry R. Ocker, DDS

It is my honor and joy to say a word about my friend and brother, Jim Goforth/alias Joe Gimforth, a result of my inadvertently turning his name around from the pulpit at one of the Lake Placid Maples Conferences.

Patricia and I first met Jim in April, 1991, at a *Prayer and Spiritual Awakening* Conference (PSA) at the Glorieta Conference Center in New Mexico, a year after I had become Henry Blackaby's associate in that office at what is now SBC's North American Mission Board.

Though Jim at the time was pastoring First Baptist, Rusk, TX, it would not be long before he responded to a call from his Master to go north to the mountains of New York State to be Southern Baptist's Director of Missions for the Adirondack Association. It was during this time, when Jim founded the annual fall Maples Conference, that we really got to know and to love him and Virginia.

Over the years we've watched God use, what he calls, "a one-horse preacher," to profoundly impact more lives than some who think themselves hitched to a whole team of horses. God has taken one, who has always considered himself "ordinary," to accomplish the extraordinary for God's glory because God knew he could be trusted not to touch HIS glory.

I recall hearing Major W. Ian Thomas on more than one occasion say: *"I can't, He never said I could. He can, He always said He would."* And God did in the life of our brother, Jim Goforth, who knew from where his strength came. And that's why Patricia and I are proud to call him our "friend."

--Ron Owens, Musician, Author
Retired Associate to Henry Blackaby

I have not read my father's book. It should be an interesting read. But fortunately, I don't need to read a book to know the author. My father has left our family a legacy of faith we will always remember. He was a strict disciplinarian and always expected the best from us. But, he also taught us what it meant to love. I can't count how many times strangers suddenly appeared and there was a family meeting to discuss the fact that we would have a new family member for the next weeks to months. At the time it seemed fun. My brother and I (maybe just I) didn't realize they were a person down on their luck with nowhere to go.

But of all the stories of churches, mission work, community outreach, etc, one scene has stood out in my mind for the past 30 years. It was my senior year in High School. I played for my baseball team. We had our annual Spring Break baseball tournament. Our school could never seem to make the final game of our own tournament. But, this was our year. We beat a slate of good teams and now were on the verge of winning the championship game. We were down by one run with two men on base. I was on deck. We had two outs. All I could think was, "Please let the guy batting ahead of me strike out." I would rather us lose than face the idea of it all being on my shoulders – the hero or the goat. And, of course, the guy ahead of me walked. Now, it was bases loaded, down by one with two outs. I happened to be having a pretty good year at the plate. And…I…strike out!! Ouch! I could not have felt worse. My opportunity to be the school hero came, passed, and now my team was walking off the field dejected. I had let them down. My father had a reputation for being quite vocal at my ball games. If I was not giving my all, I could hear him letting me have it from the stands and he would let me know after the game. But, on this day, my memory is this. As, I walked off the field downcast, my father came up beside me, put his arm around me and told me he was proud of me. That was, that is, my father. He has taught me an important life lesson about the heavenly Father. He always expects my best, but loves me at my worst.

--Dr. Thomas Goforth

I write this on Father's Day 2016. Father's Days come and go. Gifts are given, from handmade crafts, to ties, pens, books, and many forgotten things that fade on refrigerator doors, are buried under dust on a shelf, lost in an attic, or simply thrown away. So what of a little known preacher from Melbourne, Arkansas? Oh he's come a long way from that one horse town. Census found just 567 people there in 1940, just 6 square miles. He came a long way growing up in Houston, Texas. He's come a long way, in school in Louisiana, where he met Virginia Patterson, starting a life together. Mississippi, Ohio,

12

Texas, and New York have been his home ministry fields. He's crossed borders and oceans, North, South, East, and West. Yes, he's come a long way, come to be known by, and known many people, but still a little known preacher.

Father's Days are more about what the fathers give than those often afterthought gifts given to them. So it is true for me. He has given me more than I can give back. He and that little Oklahoma girl, displaced by God's call on her preacher father's life, gave me life in 1964. He gave me love of course. He gave me a love for God. He gave me an understanding of the devastation that sin had wrought on my life. He says I looked at him once while lying in bed at bedtime, when I was about 3 and said "Daddy, am I going to Hell?" I understood my need for Jesus at a young age, that is a gift of God's grace given because my Father preached Jesus' love and justice. My father and my mother taught me to love people, wherever you find them, however you find them, regardless if they love you back. My father didn't teach me how to be perfect because he couldn't, he was far from it, as am I. But he taught me how to say, "I'm sorry. I was wrong. Will you forgive me?" My father taught me how to follow God's call on his life, whether it "made sense" or would "advance his career." My Father taught me how to share my faith. He taught me to love sports, be competitive, hate to lose, but do it graciously, because you will always lose more than you win. He taught me to love an underdog. He taught me how to tell a story. He taught me to make crazy decisions. I guess if I tried to tell you all about our lives' experiences growing up, the 18 years that I was actively involved in his ministry, then there would be no room left for this book. He gave me sporting events, shared ball fields with me, and sat in the stands with me, while we watched my sons. He taught me how to fish, to love golf, and spent 18 years teaching me how to preach the Word of God. He gave me many things.

He gave me my name, James L. Goforth, Jr. Oh, I've been called Jimmy, Jim, Jim Jr, and Jimbo, and a few other names in jest or in jeer. But I'm James L. Goforth, Jr. Oh, you've probably never heard of my name either. That is because I'm a little known preacher too. So, I've tried to give back to him what he gave to me. I write this as a pastor in Germany, serving American Heroes in the cause of freedom. I've preached the gospel, tried to love people, loved one wife, raised two sons, become a father-in-law, and a Granddad, just like him. I've passed on the love for people, love for the gospel, and love for underdogs to my sons. Between us we've preached in the Northern and Southern Hemispheres, Central America, Europe, India, and Africa. Our little family has been on four continents and taken the gospel and love for people everywhere we go. But we remain little known preachers and that's ok.

We are Jim Goforth, and our sons, though most may never know our names, still there are names written in the *Lamb's Book of Life* that are there because we shared the gospel, and God's grace came alive in their hearts. And some day, could be today, we will step across the threshold of a doorway called death. Or better yet, we will hear a trumpet and a shout, and in the time it takes to recognize a face we have never seen before, we will be caught up in the sky. Either way, we will be introduced to the One we have known for years; the One who has known us since before we were born; the One who was slain from the foundation of the earth; the One who was crucified on a hill called Calvary. When we meet him, his approval, his recognition, will be the only one that matters. And he will say, "Welcome home, son, well done, good and faithful servant." Ultimately, we have lived our lives trying to live up to expectations, and find approval, but His is all that matters.

The greatest gift I can give my father is to follow him down the path for the approval of the One who died for me. But for what it is worth, I know and I approve of James L Goforth, Sr. – a little known preacher from Melbourne, Arkansas.

--James L. Goforth, Jr - Father's Day 2016

Table of Contents

Foreword

One of the things I struggled with in deciding to write this book is what do you do with the times when you really messed up in life? If you are going to tell your story, then what do you do about those times in your life that were much less than they could have been? In other words, what do you do with the times when you had sin issues that got your life off track?

If you are reading this, and you have known me for quite a long time, you might be wondering if I intend to tell about those not so good times in my life. After I decided to begin this project, I was really struggling with this very issue. Therefore, I stopped to ask myself how I could be honest about my life and not share those difficult times.

I want to record here what came to my heart one morning while I was writing the things the Lord was bringing up.

No Forgiven Sin in God's Memory Bank

I need to push the pause button for a moment and interject an experience I had after beginning this project. Like most people, there have been those times of sin and rebellion in my life. It appears that this writing is going to end up being a chronological description of the way that the Lord has worked in my life and ministry. That being the case, I have questioned how I should deal with those times in my life, when I get to them in the story. Would it be helpful or harmful to God's intended purpose for this project? Would I be honest with myself and the Lord if I avoided those times?

I got a clear answer from the Lord, when He said, "What sin?" Then God reminded me of the promises of His Word.

"...For I will forgive their wickedness and
will remember their sins no more."
Jeremiah 31:24b

"As far as the east is from the west,
so far has He removed our transgressions from us."
Psalm 103:12

All of us need to remember that when genuinely confessed and repented sin is brought back up in our minds, it is not God; it is Satan.

Satan tries to keep us in a defeated spirit, by telling us that we are not worthy of all that God has for us. So when I asked the Lord about including those times of sin and rebellion, the answer I got was, "What sin?" I was reminded of this wonderful truth about God. He does not have a place in His memory bank where He keeps a record of confessed and forgiven sin. According to the scripture, it is removed from us as far as the east is from the west and He does not remember it against us ever again.

When that truth flooded my soul, I began to weep and shout His praise at the same time. You may need to stop right now and have a personal Hallelujah time with the Lord about His great forgiveness and cleansing of your life. Do not let Satan defeat you by bringing up stuff in your past that God does not even remember, because of your repentance and His forgiveness.

"God is good all the time, all the time God is good."

At Christmas time 2014, I was sharing this experience with my son Tom and my daughter-in-law Karen. When I finished, Tom said, "Dad that would make a great foreword to the book." I told him that I thought that he was right. Therefore, I have added this foreword so that all will know the perspective from which I come as I write this story. If you know me very well, you already know that there have been times of real failure in my life. If you don't know me, then you need to know up front that I am just an ordinary human being, who has struggled with sin issues in his life; but praise God I have been forgiven, because of the blood of Jesus Christ.

I would encourage you to remember that all sin that is confessed to the Lord is also forgotten by our Lord. Praise God!

The Beginning: September 2, 2014

Today I begin a project; I have no idea where it might be headed. I am a preacher and have been one most of my life. I was called to preach when I was 11 years old and preached my first sermon when I was 14. I was licensed to preach when I was 17 years old and a senior in high school. I was ordained to the Gospel ministry, November 7, 1960, while I was a senior in college and shortly after the Baptist Church in Center City, Texas, had called me as pastor. In two more months, I will have been seeking to fulfill that commitment for 54 years.

As I said before, I am a preacher. I have never considered myself to be one who could write things others would want to read and would get anything out of it. For years my wife Virginia has been encouraging me to write my story for the benefit of our children and grandchildren. A few years before we retired, we were attending the annual Southern Baptist Convention. We were in the display area of the North American Mission Board, and I was visiting with Henry Blackaby, who is one of my spiritual heroes. While we were talking, Henry reached out and tapped me on the chest and said, "There is a story in there that needs to be told."

In recent years, various others have commented to me that I should write a book about my experiences in the ministry. Shortly after moving back to Rusk, my dentist suggested to me that I needed to write a book. He said, "I just love your stories." Just recently, I was visiting with a couple of young men that I love and respect, who are both in ministry themselves. We were talking about some of the ups and downs of the lives of ministers, which prompted one of them to suggest that I should write a book.

This probably won't ever become more than something my family and close friends will ever read, but the Lord has put enough stirring in my heart, that I feel I must give it a shot. So for right now, it will be nothing more than a narrative of a story that is in me. It is my story, and frankly, I have never considered my life that exciting. Therefore, I will admit up front that it has the potential of being very boring.

One Horse Preacher

Maybe I should begin by giving you the background for this title that the Lord has given me, "The Meanderings of a One Horse Preacher." The truth is I have owned one horse in my lifetime, which was a gift from a former church member. He gave it to me when I moved from Ohio back to Texas, but that is not the reference from which I have drawn the title of the book. Rather it comes from a very personal and meaningful moment that I had with the Lord, when I was in college.

To know who I really am, you need to know something that even at the age of 75 is painful to tell. It is, however, very much a part of what shaped my own image of myself from the time I was a small boy. Even though I appear to be outgoing, the truth is that I grew up with a severe inferiority complex that was related to the way I looked. I was born with very large ears, which caused my classmates to give me names such as "Elephant Ears" and "Donkey Ears." I finally had plastic surgery when I was 11 years old, but the damage to my self-image was already done. It was not until I was a senior in high school and I heard some high school girls admiring my senior pictures that I first thought that maybe I was not as ugly as I had always thought I was.

I also had another issue growing up. I wanted to be a really good athlete, but I was not. On the other hand, my younger brother Bobby was a star athlete in almost every sport. I was secretly jealous of my younger brother and proud of him at the same time. I felt like I was only known as Bobby's big brother. Our dad had been an outstanding high school athlete, and I guess I felt like it was not fair that those abilities had skipped the oldest son and had been passed on to the younger son.

We both attended the same college. I was there as a ministerial student, he was there on a football scholarship. In fact I was the one that told our college coach about my brother and encouraged them to consider giving him a scholarship. He came to try out for the Basketball Team and while he was there the Football Coach looked at some of his high school game films and offered him a full Football Scholarship.

Although I had already been at the college two years, shortly after Bobby started playing football, I became Bobby's big brother again. I was really struggling with my own identity.

One afternoon I was walking from the dorm over to the practice field to watch my brother practice football. I was literally arguing with the Lord about why He did not allow me to be an athlete like my brother. The answer I got was loud and clear. The Lord said to me, "You have a one track mind; if I had allowed you to be the athlete you wanted to be, you would never have responded to my call to preach." **I knew that was right, and that day I became my brother's biggest fan**. I also recommitted myself to God's call on my life.

So the "One Horse Preacher" comes from that part of who I am. I have a tendency to focus on the one thing that I believe God is calling me to do. By the way, I continue to be my brother's biggest fan. Today, I am proud to be Bobby Goforth's biggest fan. He is a wonderful man of God, who has used sports and coaching as his avenue of ministry for our Lord Jesus Christ. I was recently reliving an experience with my brother that we actually shared at one of his college football games. Howard Payne was playing an away game. I had talked the Band Director Ed Cain into letting me ride the band bus to the game. He said I could do that, but I would have to be willing to help in some way. So I helped with the needed props for the halftime show. During the game I was sitting on the front row of the stands in front of the band, with the director and the twirlers. My brother was playing quarterback and he rolled around to the left trying to find a receiver but could not, so he started running. Every time a defender would come up on him, he would pull his arm up like he was going to throw the ball and they would back off. He ran over 60 yards for a touchdown. By the time he crossed the goal line, I was standing on the narrow rail at the front of the stands cheering for him and some of the twirlers were holding on to me to keep me from falling. I was so proud of him.

I praise God that He helped me to understand that the call on my life to preach was far more important than being an outstanding athlete. I also praise Him that, in that moment, He took all of the jealousy out of my heart toward my brother and made me his biggest fan. You could ask members of churches where I have served as pastor and they would tell you that I probably used more illustrations about my brother than any other subject. I also praise God for my wonderful sister-in-law Patricia White Goforth, who is a wonderful Christian lady. She is one of my personal prayer warriors, and has been a wonderful wife and mother for my brother and their family. My dad said about my mother that she was the solid rock in our family. I suspect that my brother Bobby and their children would say the same thing about Pat Goforth.

As I have moved through this life and ministry the Lord has given me, I have had many moments like the one on the way to that practice field that day, when the Lord has had to get me to refocus. I guess what I hope from this effort is that something I have experienced in my walk with the Lord, will be a blessing and a help to someone else and cause them to stop and refocus on who God has called them to be.

You need to know that I have often said that the only reason I can think that I have any business being in the ministry is that I really love people. I am afraid I don't always come across that way, but I really love people. So wherever these meanderings go, it is out of an act of love for my family and God's people.

So here it goes and I pray that I can tell it the way the Lord wants me to tell it, and in a way that will bring honor and glory to our Lord Jesus Christ. Here is the bottom line truth of the matter. I am just an everyday, ordinary person. There really is nothing spectacular about me. Today I am a man who has just recently turned 75 years of age, and again I say there is nothing really spectacular about my life that would cause anyone to want to pick up a book and read about it. However, the Lord has allowed this very ordinary man to be involved in some very extraordinary activity of God. I am really amazed when I think back about all of the things the Lord has allowed me to be a part of in His Kingdom work in this world.

The truth is that there are far more ordinary people like me out there than there are extraordinary people. Like me, others need to know that God can take the ordinary and accomplish extraordinary things in His Kingdom work. All He needs is our willingness to hear, obey, and follow Him. When ordinary people present themselves to the Lord, He can and will use them to change the world for His Glory and the redemption of men, women, boys and girls.

It is my prayer that at least one person who considers himself or herself ordinary and insignificant will be encouraged by reading this, and know that God takes the ordinary things of life to confound the wise. God has a wonderful plan for every person, and He is able to accomplish wonderful things through anyone who is willing to be used by Him.

Early on in this project, I was visiting with one of my brothers-in-law Mickey Anders, who is an author. He asked me who I was writing this for. I told him I did not know. So if you are reading this, it is for you, and I pray that the Lord will use it to bless your life in some way.

Family

I grew up as the older of two sons born to Carl Robert Lee Goforth and his wife Frances Lydia Evans Goforth. I am James Lonnie Goforth and my brother is Robert Evans Goforth. I was born in the small Ozark Mountain town of Melbourne, Arkansas. I was brought into this world by the brother of my Pappa Evans that we all lovingly referred to as "Uncle Doctor." I was born in August of 1939 and my brother was born in December of 1940.

My dad and mother married 11 days after their first date. Dad was a Baptist, who at best was in a backslidden condition with the Lord. My Mother came from a very committed Cumberland Presbyterian family. My grandfather was an elder in the Cumberland Presbyterian Church. My great-grandfather was a circuit riding Cumberland Presbyterian preacher in the Ozark Mountains of Arkansas.

My Grandfather Goforth was a bridge builder whose crew traveled ahead of the road crews building bridges in the Ozark Mountains of Arkansas and Missouri. This meant that my dad moved often as a boy, which probably had something to do with his lack of commitment to church.

When my parents married, dad refused to go to church with his young wife because, "I am a Baptist and you are a Presbyterian." However, Dad did not know of the determination of this young woman he had just married. Three weeks into their marriage, Frances Goforth came home from church and announced to her young husband, "You are going to church with me next Sunday." When he gave his usual excuse that he could not go with her because he was a Baptist, she announced to him, "I am too; I joined the Baptist Church today and you are going to church with me next Sunday." Praise God for a young wife who was willing to do whatever she needed to do to get her young husband back in church. Dad did get his spiritual life turned around, and when the Lord took him home in 2002, he had been a Baptist deacon for 60 years.

After my mother passed away from injuries from a head-on auto collision, my dad said to my brother and me, "If you don't know, you need to know, that everything we became spiritually as a family was because of the determination of your mother."

Dad moved his wife and two small boys from the Ozark Mountains of Arkansas to Houston, Texas, in 1941, to go to work for Brown and Root Construction Company. He continued to work for Brown and Root, until he went to work for A. O. Smith Pipe Mill that had opened a big-inch pipe mill less than a mile from our home. He worked for that company and those who bought them out, the rest of his working life. So my brother and I grew up on the east side of Houston in a little community known as Greens Bayou and attended the Market Street Baptist Church. We also grew up in the Galena Park School District. That little community, that church, and that school district were major contributors to our lives as boys growing up in a working class family whose dad and mother wanted to raise them right and serve their Lord through His church.

The atmosphere in which we were raised made a strong and lasting contribution to the men that we have both become. The truth is that I would probably be more comfortable writing about my brother Bobby, because I am still his biggest fan. I am very proud of the man he has become.

For those who know me, perhaps I should say something about the evolution of my name. My name is James Lonnie Goforth, and later, after the birth of our first son, became James Lonnie Goforth, Sr. I was

32

named after my two grandfathers, James Lee Evans and Lonnie Goforth. Texas is famous for having boys with a double name and all the way through high school I was known as James Lonnie. When I went off to college, I dropped the Lonnie and was simply known as James Goforth. When I went to seminary, I introduced myself to another man in the dorm as James Goforth and he immediately started calling me Jim and introducing me to others as Jim. My soon to be wife, Virginia Patterson, also decided that James sounded too formal and preferred Jim. I also like the name Jim. Therefore, from seminary days on, I became known as Jim Goforth, or Bro. Jim to the people the Lord has given me the privilege to serve over the years. However, as long as she lived, my mother would say, "I don't know who Jim Goforth is, but I do have a son named James." And I would say to you today that I am proud to be James Lonnie Goforth, the son of Carl and Frances Goforth.

Now let me tell you about my own personal family. At this writing, my wife Virginia and I are in our 50th year of marriage. We were married January 25, 1964. Virginia was born Virginia Ruth Patterson. She is one of 8 children born to Rev. Lester and Helen Patterson. We have two sons, Rev. James Lonnie Goforth, Jr. and Rev. Dr. Thomas Bryan Goforth.

Our son Jim has been a pastor for many years and is currently serving as the pastor of the Faith Baptist Church, Kaiserslautern, Germany, an English speaking congregation that ministers primarily to U.S. military personnel stationed near his church.

Our son Tom served in several church staff positions, including pastor, before he felt led of the Lord to go to Medical School to become a medical doctor. He is currently in Family Practice in New York, New York.

Jim is married to Lisa Gaye Alexander and they are the parents of our two grandsons, A. J. and Bryan. Bryan is married to his wife Maggie Meece and they are preparing for probably foreign mission service. They are the parents of our first Great Granddaughter Lydia Goforth, who was named after my mother. A. J. is in business in Kansas City and is active in church work. Tom and his first wife Shari Shipp are the parents of our two Granddaughters Emily and Ashley. Emily graduated from Brooklyn University with a major in theatre production. Ashley is a student at the University of Buffalo who will probably end up somewhere in the medical field.

Tom is now married to Karen Morice who is also a doctor, working in the field of pain management and physical medicine.

What can you say about someone who has had the grace to put up with someone like me for more than 50 years? That really says it all. Virginia has been there to encourage me, pray for me, and support me every step of the way. About 2 years before I met her, I began to pray that the Lord would lead me to the woman he would have me to marry. Shortly after arriving on the campus of New Orleans Baptist Theological Seminary, I saw her in the cafeteria. I pointed her out to my friend and promptly told him that I was going to marry her. He asked me who she was and I told him that I did not know, but that God had just spoken to my heart and told me that she was the answer to my prayers for a wife. Later I discovered that she felt called to be a preacher's wife when she was 11 years old. We actually met two weeks later and were engaged two weeks after that and then married 3 months later, and now here we are 50 years later, still at it and still trying to serve our Lord.

I am sure stories that relate to various members of my family will be woven into whatever the Lord leads me to tell. But perhaps the above information will help you to understand a little bit about the background from which I come. All of us are shaped to one degree or another by our family background and our family values.

Our family, like all families, has had its share of difficult times. My dad was diagnosed with throat cancer which required the removal of his vocal chords when he was in his early 40's. He lived the last 40 years of his life without vocal chords and yet learned to talk again and continued to work in a plant as a supervisor of others.

34

I have already referred to the fact that we lost my mother as a result of injuries received in a head-on auto accident that she and dad had with another vehicle. Mother lived two weeks. They were two gut-wrenching weeks, but when it came time for her to go, the Lord allowed her to go very peacefully; my brother and I praise God for that. At that time, we thought we might lose our dad also, but the Lord allowed him to live another 13 years. Then dad died of a massive stroke on a Sunday in April 2002.

Virginia lost her dad at the age of 92. We will go to Oklahoma next week to help celebrate Virginia's mother's 98th birthday. She is in amazingly good health, and a wonderful Christian woman. I have been very fortunate to have her as my mother-in-law.

Our family has also experienced the struggles of divorce. Many families can relate to the fact that it is not a good time in the life of any family.

In times of family struggle we determine if we are going to let the difficulty get to us, or if we are going to repent and set our eyes on Jesus. Will we live above the struggles, or will we allow Satan to win and cause us to live defeated lives. We have decided to trust in Jesus in the midst of the struggles and allow him to be victorious. That decision is made by families and individuals and the decisions we make determine if we are going to live in victory in Jesus or allow Satan to defeat us.

The question for any family is not whether or not there will be struggles in their lives, but how they will handle the struggles when they come. That decision is ours and ours alone to handle. In times of struggle, what decision are you making?

My Family and the Church

Without a doubt, the family in which I was raised made an indelible impact upon me and I think, upon my brother as well, about our attitude toward the church in general and the local church in particular.

I have already indicated that when my dad and mother married, my dad was, at best, a backslidden Baptist, and my mother was a very committed Cumberland Presbyterian. My great grandfather on my mother's side was a circuit–riding Cumberland Presbyterian Preacher, traveling through the Ozark Mountains of Arkansas, preaching the gospel of Jesus Christ. In fact, it was this ministry that cost him his life. My Grandfather James Lee Evans told me that when he was a 16 year old boy, his dad had been out preaching in the winter, riding horseback. He said that his father got home late one Sunday night after having been gone three weeks. He said that they heard him holler from outside the house that he needed help. Apparently it had started sleeting and snowing on his way home that night. When he got home, he discovered that he was frozen to his saddle. My grandfather told me that he went out and broke the ice from his saddle, pulled him off of the horse and carried him into the house. He said that he had to pull his overcoat off of him and they stood it up in the corner behind the stove for it to thaw out. My great grandfather caught pneumonia from that experience and died a few weeks later.

My Grandfather Evans was an Elder in the Cumberland Presbyterian Church, a farmer, a teacher, a school principal and a coach. He was probably one of the hardest working men I ever knew.

My Grandfather Goforth was a bridge builder who had a construction crew that went ahead of the road construction crews in the Ozark Mountains of Arkansas and Missouri, building bridges through those mountains. Can you imagine doing that kind of work with the equipment they had in the 1930's? He did some other things too; one of the stories I remember hearing about him is that he appeared in some of the older editions of Ripley's "Believe It Or Not." My grandmother, his wife, was named Mae Flinn. She had a brother-in-law named Earl Battle. At one time my grandfather and his brother-in-law had a general store. Some of the things they sold were antique guns. They had a sign on the front of the store which read, "Get Your Guns from Goforth and Battle." So I guess that sign is our family's historic claim to international fame. I don't know much to write about my Grandfather Goforth. He died when he was 50 something years old, six months before I was born. It must have been very painful for my dad, because he never did really talk about it much. He did tell me one time that his dad probably died of cancer but they did not know what to call it at that time. All three of his sons had cancer. My dad's oldest brother died of cancer when he was quite young. Dad's other brother also died of cancer when he was older. Dad came down with throat cancer when he was 44. He lost his vocal chords, but he learned to adjust, and made a complete recovery. He lived another 41 years. Dad's cancer was more than likely a direct result of the fact that he started smoking when he was 14 years of age and continued to smoke until he was diagnosed with cancer.

I had seen my dad get under conviction about his smoking and quit smoking several times when I was a boy growing up. Sometimes it would last as long as six months, and then he would start smoking again at work and would start again at home when he was smoking so much at work he could not hide it from our mother any longer. Then, according to his testimony, the doctor told him he had two choices; he could quit smoking and live or keep on smoking and die. He had a package of cigarettes in his shirt pocket. He said that he decided that he wanted to live. He said, "I took them out of my pocket and threw them in the trash can in the doctor's office and never even wanted another one the rest of my life."

My dad's determination to overcome his handicap is for me one of the most remarkable stories that I know. I remember when I got the call from my mother that dad had a reaction to the radiation treatment and almost died before she could get him to the hospital. One night after a treatment, his throat started swelling and cutting off his airways. Mother had to drive him across Houston to the hospital so they could give him a trach and get him breathing again. She told me that he and the doctor had agreed that the best thing to do was to remove his vocal chords, and they were going to do that in a few days.

I was in my junior year at Howard Payne College, and my brother was a freshman. Before I went to call my brother out of class to tell him what was going on, I went to see the Dean of the College to tell him that we were going to have to leave, and I did not know if we would be back that spring or not. He was very kind to me and said that he clearly understood how I felt and that he would probably feel the same way. Then he said he wanted to suggest something to me. He said it is only two weeks until our Easter break. He suggested that one of us go and spend the week in the hospital with dad the week before the surgery and come back. Then the other one could go and spend the week of surgery with our dad. Then it would be Spring Break and we would both have a week with him. Then he said that during that time you and your parents could decide what you need to do. He said that if that worked, maybe both of us would only have to miss one week of school, which would go down as excused absence and not have any effect on our standing in school. That sounded like a good plan to me.

From there I went and called my brother out of class and told him what was going on. His immediate reaction was the same as mine. Let's get in the car and go. I then shared with him what the Dean had suggested. He agreed that was a good plan. We only had one more hurdle to get over. Who was going first? You would have to know my brother and me well to know that was not a small hurdle. However, I finally convinced him I needed to go first. I did go to Houston immediately and spent the week with dad and mother while they were preparing him for the surgery. He was in the hospital that entire week before the surgery. One day the speech therapist came in to talk to dad about the process they would use to teach him how to talk without vocal chords. The process was that he would swallow air, stop it in his throat, and belch it back up. While the air is coming back up he would form his lips in the sounds he wanted to make. I was a speech major in college and it sounded really complicated for him. The speech therapist spent a short period of time with him that day and encouraged him to practice the procedure before the surgery. He did that every day that week.

When that week was over, my brother came home on the weekend and I went back to school on Sunday afternoon. He had the surgery the next week, and I got the report that he was doing well. The next weekend I was able to go back because it was Spring Break. I remembered wondering when I went into Methodist Hospital in Houston, how would dad feel and how would I feel when I spoke to him and he was unable to speak back. I walked in the room and spoke to my dad and, much to my surprise, he spoke back and said it was good to see me again. That was four days after the surgery to remove both of his vocal chords. Then I discovered that he had not had any physical therapy. The practice he had done before surgery worked and he was determined that he was going to speak. To begin with, the speech was slow and without much volume, but over time all of that got better. Dad came home from the hospital the week we were home for Spring Break and insisted that we both go back to school. So we went back to school after Spring Break, and both of us had only missed one week of school, which allowed us to remain on schedule for graduation.

Over time, Dad learned to talk so well that if you did not know what had happened to him, you would never have known that he did not have his vocal chords. He went through a hard time at work because of having to talk over all of the machinery in the plant. When dad talked, it took all of the muscles from his waist up to talk. Speech therapy got him what we called his "horn" which had a pipe that fit over the permanent hole in his throat, which was attached to what looked like a pitch pipe, which was attached to a plastic piece on top that he would put in his mouth. He could talk as loud as he wanted with his horn without using all of the extra effort. He would use it at work, and when he talked on the phone. However, there came a time several years later that he quit using his "horn" altogether. I never will forget the first time he visited a church where I was pastor and I called on him to pray from where he was sitting. He could be heard all over the 500 seat sanctuary. I became so emotional; I almost could not continue. There were some complications that came with the surgery, but dad handled them with dignity.

I started this section talking about my family and the church. For some reason this family background seems important to that issue. I guess it was to explain partially why Dad's church background was not as strong as my mother's when they first married. I do know that church and her relationship to the Lord were important to my Grandmother Goforth, but her ties to a church were probably not as strong as they could have been. This was probably because she and her five children were following her husband around with his job during days when transportation was certainly not as easy as it is now.

Dad and mother were married in February 1937. I was born in August of 1939, and we moved from Arkansas to Texas in 1941. Shortly after I was born, dad got his heart right with the Lord and was soon thereafter ordained to be a deacon. In April of 2002, when Dad died, out of curiosity, I called the lady who had been secretary of the Market Street Baptist Church, in Houston where I grew up. I called to see how long Dad had been a deacon. She checked the old records and discovered that he had been ordained a deacon in April 1942. Because they became very involved in the church when I was a baby, we were not sent to church. We were not dropped off at church. We went to church with our parents and worshipped the Lord together as

41

a family. I think there must have been a time when my dad thought that no one could open the church but him, because we were the first ones there almost every Sunday morning.

When I say that we went to church, I mean that we went to Sunday School and worship on Sunday morning. We went to Training Union and worship on Sunday night. We went to RA's and prayer meeting on Wednesday night and stayed for mother to attend choir practice. We went to the church every Tuesday night for church visitation. We attended every service of every revival. When we were growing up, the church always had at least 8 day revivals and sometimes 2 week revivals. I can remember during the fall revival, my dad came to my brother, who was quarterback of the football team, and explained to him that he was going to have to miss his football game on Friday night because the church was holding revival services. In other words, if anything was going on at the church, the Goforth family was there.

I can remember dad working all night on Saturday night because of a breakdown of some sort at the Pipe Mill, coming home about 8:00 or 8:30 Sunday morning, getting cleaned up, and then going to Sunday School and church service. He would come home and get a nap and get back up and go back to Training Union and church service that night. I can remember us having family members visit that we had not seen for years. On Sunday morning dad would say to them, "We are going to Sunday School and church. You are welcome to go with us. If you do not want to go, we will be back after church."

I remember one time my brother did not want to go to Training Union. As he argued with dad about it, he called the name of one of his friends and said that his dad did not make him go to Training Union. Dad's reply was, "Too bad his dad is not your dad. I am your dad and you are going." I have often said that when I was growing up, if I was too sick to miss school or church, I wished I felt good enough to go.

I remember the last year I attended Vacation Bible School; it was the summer before my senior year in high school. I was almost 17 years old and my best friend was already 17. We decided that we were too old to go to VBS that summer. The problem was that our mothers did not agree with us and made us go. So we decided, on the first day, that we would make things so difficult that they would not make us go back anymore. That day we did everything just the opposite from what everyone else was doing. If everyone else was standing up, we would sit down. If everyone else was sitting down, we would stand up. All that our tactics accomplished was getting both of us in trouble when we got home that first day. Guess what? We were back in VBS the next day and every day, and actually enjoyed ourselves, but we tried to not let it show.

We were taught that being faithful to the Lord also meant that you were faithful to His church. That concept was demonstrated to us in the way our parents lived their lives. Although we were not a perfect family, there were certain principles that guided our lives. They were God, family, church, school and work. Basically our family was built around those concepts.

We took family vacations every summer. Dad always arranged our vacation schedule where we could attend church somewhere on Sunday. Believe it or not, if we were driving from one place to another on Sunday evening, dad would stop and we would attend Sunday night service in some Baptist Church somewhere. I can remember one time when my brother and I were visitors in a Training Union class before church somewhere while we were traveling.

I have to be honest and admit that over the years as a pastor, I have not been very patient with some of the excuses that church members give for why they could not attend church services. I am sure my own experience as a child and the example set before me is part of the reason for my lack of patience with most of the excuses I have heard.

Do you know what our experience as children did not do to my brother and me? It did not cause us to turn away from the church as adults and not want to go to church. My experience with adults who don't attend church and use the excuse that they were made to go when they were children is, that they were usually sent to church. They did not attend church with a family unit.

When adults tell me that they are not going to make their children go to church if they don't want to, I usually have a question or two for them. "Do you make them go to school if they don't want to go?" "Do you make them go to the doctor if they are sick, but don't want to go?" The truth is that there are a lot of things that children need to do, but don't want to do. However, we make them do them anyway, because they are too immature to make the right choices about what is best for them. It is called being a responsible parent. It is just what we do, because we love them, and want what is best for them.

My Personal Testimony

I am going to go ahead and share my personal testimony at this juncture. I think it will help all to understand where I have been in my walk with the Lord, and what motivates me most in my present walk with the Lord.

My brother and I literally grew up in and around church life. My dad got his heart right with the Lord when I was a small child, and for the most part, he and my mother lived as very dedicated lay people in the church and were very involved in all aspects of the life of the church. They made sure that my brother and I were involved in all that the church had to offer for its children and youth.

As I have already indicated, my dad worked for Brown and Root Construction Company the first 10 – 12 years after we moved to Texas from Arkansas. The east side of Houston was always home, but we moved several places in Texas for short periods of time as his job would take him there.

When I was 6 years of age, we were living in Orange, Texas. A young man by the name of Jaroy Weber was our pastor. Years later, Bro. Weber would serve as President of the Southern Baptist Convention. It was while we were there that I made a decision and was baptized. I need to say that most of the details I share about that time are what my parents told me happened, because much of it I do not remember.

Our church was in a revival, I wanted to respond at the invitation time, but my dad would not let me for fear that I did not know what I was doing. My parents invited the pastor to the house after church and he led me in a sinner's prayer. The next night I went forward at the invitation time. Someone asked me if I wanted to be baptized and I said yes. I remember clearly the night I was baptized.

When I was 11 years old, I attended RA/GA Camp at Palacios Baptist Camp. It was there at an evening Vesper service, down by the water, that God called me to preach and I responded with a yes. When I returned home from camp, I told my mother that God had called me to preach, and she began to weep. A few years later, she explained why she wept when I told her that God had called me to preach. The night I was born she prayed this prayer: "Dear Lord, if you can see fit to call him to preach, I will try to raise him in such a way that when you call, he will hear and answer yes." My call to preach was the answer to a prayer my mother had prayed 11 years before.

When I was in college, it began to bother me that I could remember everything about the night I was baptized, but nothing about giving my heart and life to Christ. However, pride kept me from telling anyone about my doubts. When I was called to pastor my first church during my senior year in college, I reasoned that God would not allow that to happen if I was not saved. Those doubts arose again more than once while I was in Seminary, but again I found ways to explain away those doubts. It was not until later that I realized that it was pride that kept me from dealing with the real issue in my life.

While serving churches in Ohio, I finally admitted to others my doubts. They tried to help, but also pointed to all of the visible results from my ministry and therefore concluded that I must really be saved. Pride made it easy to accept that, until the doubts would come again.

Finally, my dearest friend in the ministry, Pat Maloney, had moved to a church near me in Central Ohio. When I was going through another time of real struggle in my life, I called him and he came to my house. After a time of visiting with me he said, "Why don't you tell me what is really wrong with you?" I replied, "I don't think I am saved." Instead of pointing out God's working through me, he said, "Well if that is what is wrong, why don't you just get saved. I know you know how; I have watched you tell hundreds how to be saved." It was like I was just waiting for someone to say that it was alright for me to get saved. I raised my eyes to the ceiling and cried out, "O God, save me!" That moment I was wonderfully saved, by the grace of our Lord Jesus Christ.

That was on a Friday afternoon. My wife and I immediately went to visit our Director of Missions Chuck Magruder, to tell him what had happened. He rejoiced with me and gave us some great counsel. On Sunday morning I shared with the church, where I was pastor, what had happened and asked them to authorize our Director of Missions to baptize me that night. Even though there was much discussion about what happened to me, it was a wonderful day and the church asked me to stay on as their pastor. The night I was baptized, 3 other adults were saved and I had the joy of baptizing them after I was baptized.

Over the years, I have had people ask me how I could explain other people getting saved when I preached, when I was not saved myself. The truth is, I can't explain it, except God promised to honor His Word, and I was preaching His Word. When people heard the true gospel and accepted the gospel, God gloriously saved them.

An important thing happened about three weeks after I was saved. I got a call from a dear friend of mine who had been a pastor in Ohio and now was the Director of Evangelism for the Baptist Convention of Ohio. He said he had called because of something he had heard about me. I asked if he had heard that I had been saved, and then told him it was true. He said he rejoiced with me, although he was surprised because my ministry had been so evangelistic.

 He did say that he had one question he wanted to ask me. Then he asked me, "What changed?" because Scripture says that we are changed when we are saved. As it turns out, that was an easy question to answer. Before I was saved I could not open scripture and get a sermon from scripture on my own. All of my ministry I had used the sermon books of others. I had even come to believe that God gifts some men to write sermons and others to preach them. Week after week, I would preach the sermons that others had written. On the Monday morning after I was saved, I was in my office and was going to do some sermon preparation. I turned my chair to my bookshelf to find me a sermon book. As I reached for one, I decided to read scripture for a while first. I opened the Bible and was amazed as the Bible came alive for me. I grabbed a pencil and paper and in the next 30 minutes, the Lord had given me my first sermon. It then dawned on me what had been wrong over the years. The Holy Spirit could not reveal scripture to me because the Holy Spirit did not live within my heart. It was important for me to be asked a question about what changed, because it was a significant change in my life that demonstrated that my salvation was real.

I don't want anyone who has been genuinely saved to doubt their salvation. However, if there are any doubts about the genuineness of your salvation, you can know for sure that you are born again. I would encourage you to settle it once and for all. However, because of my own experience, one of the driving factors that motivates my life and ministry is that everyone knows that they have been "Born Again." John said, in I John 5:13, "I have written these things that you may know that you have eternal life."

When you think about ordinary people and how God might use them, the greatest example might be the "12" that Jesus called. For the most part, they were probably considered, by the people of their day, ordinary people. Then one of them became a traitor. It is very remarkable, when you think of all of the extraordinary things God has accomplished through ordinary people.

As I write this, it sounds like a theme is developing. **Look what God can do through ordinary people like you and me.** Maybe that should be the sub-title to these meanderings, "Ordinary people being used of God to accomplish His extraordinary purposes." Think about it. If any

48

good has been accomplished through any of our lives, it is because we have allowed God to work through us to accomplish His purposes.

Those Who Have Influenced My Life

As I look back on my life, I recognize, as I am sure almost everyone does, that there have been positive and negative influences in our lives. Hopefully, we can look back and know that there have been more positive than negative influences. Praise God, I can honestly say that there have been more positive influences than negative. So I want to mention some of them.

Carl and Frances Goforth

I praise God for the family the Lord allowed me to be born into. Dad and mother were far from perfect, but they were as real as any two people knew how to be. Their lives were an open book. What you saw, was what you got. They taught my brother and me basic Christian values as they understood them. Their values may have seemed narrow-minded to us at times, but the message that came from them was consistent. One of my dad's favorite sayings was, "As long as you live in my house and put your feet under my table, you are going to abide by my rules whether you like it or not." That pretty much became the philosophy by which I raised my boys, and in listening to my grandsons talk, that is pretty much the philosophy by which they were raised.

I never did know my Grandfather Lonnie Goforth; he died before I was born. However, I knew my Grandfather Lee Evans well, and I suspect that is exactly the way he raised his children.

What I am trying to say is that I grew up in an environment of strong discipline. At times it may have seemed extreme, but it was consistently the same. For the most part, my life has been better because of it. Not only was discipline a strong characteristic in our home, but also there was a high regard for the truth and integrity. My dad was a man of his word. I have seen my mother go back into a store when she was short changed by a few pennies. I have also seen her go back into a store when she was given a few pennies or more too much in change. Because of that influence, it amazes me that a cashier is amazed when you call it to their attention that they have given you too much change.

They taught us to be faithful to the Lord and to His church. They did not send us to church. They took us to church. We were involved as a

51

family in the life of the Lord's church. It never occurred to us to question what we were going to do or where we were going to go on Sunday.

As a family, we often took family vacations that involved sleeping under the stars on a cot in a camp ground or state park. However, on Saturday, dad would go find us a motel for the night so that we could get cleaned up and go to church somewhere on Sunday. We would even stop on the road at church time on Sunday night and go to church somewhere. Some would probably think of that as being radical. For my parents it was a way of life. Dad did his best to arrange our trips where we could be somewhere to go to church when it was church time on Sunday.

I have already mentioned how my mother prayed the day I was born that the Lord might see fit to call me to preach. My parents were always supportive of the ministry to which the Lord had called me. There were times when they could have wished it was not so far away from where they lived, but I always knew they were praying for me. In fact, I had more than one of their pastors tell me that they were very open about who their favorite preacher was. He was their son. I owe a debt to parents who loved me and encouraged me and sought to point me in the right direction.

Bobby Goforth

We were normal brothers growing up. Sometimes we fought like cats and dogs. It seemed that every time we fought, I was the one who would end up doing something that would cause a severe problem for both of us and me in particular. One time our parents were down the street visiting neighbors and we got into a pillow fight in the living room, with our first ever TV turned on. There was a vase of fresh flowers in water sitting on top of it. It was me who swung my pillow, Bobby ducked, the pillow slipped out of my hands, and went flying across the room. The pillow hit the vase of flowers, knocking them over, and the water ran down into the picture tube and burned out the picture tube. Oh, did I mention that we had owned the new TV two days? Needless to say there was a severe price for us to pay and then a second price for me to pay when dad found out I was the one who swung the pillow. As you can imagine, there are many of those kinds of stories. However, let us move on to why Bobby has been an influence in my life.

When Bobby was the Head Coach and Athletic Director at Buna, Texas, I had an opportunity to visit there and attend church with my brother on Sunday. After church I was visiting with the School District Superintendent. During our conversation he had this to say about Bobby, "I want you to know that if we did not win a single football game, Bobby would be worth every dime we pay him because of the positive influence he has on the lives of our students." I suspect that you would find a lot of that sentiment in every place where he has coached, well, maybe not the statement about never winning a football game. We are, after all, talking about Texas High School Football. If you are not from Texas, then you may not understand that Friday night in Texas is a culture all its own. I do know that the sentiment about his influence on the lives of students would be repeated over and over in the places where he has coached. Coaching was more than a job for him. It was and is a calling. He has come out of retirement again and again to be a coach because of his love for football, but mostly because of his love for making a difference in the lives of young people. Bobby and Pat have three wonderful children who I have loved dearly all of their lives.

There is one memory that Bobby and I made together that sums up the man that he is. Many years ago I was serving as pastor of the First Baptist Church, Pickerington, Ohio. Pickerington, at that time, was a small town 20 miles east of Columbus, Ohio. I had gone there to be their first pastor when the mission was 6 months old and had 3 members. The Lord blessed and we began to grow. Before long we were able to buy 6 acres of property to build our church building. The men of the church built the building, probably a story I will share later. We had started the building in the fall of the year with the men of the church working on Saturdays. My brother had brought his family up to visit us for Christmas. At church on Sunday, Bobby heard one of our men expressing concern that they had only had time the day before to nail down the 4 corners of all of the decking on the roof before it got dark. We had a heavy snow over night and the men would not be back to work on the roof until the next Saturday. They were concerned that the decking would warp before they could get back to it. Our family plans on Monday were to take the family to Canton, Ohio, so that they could visit the Pro Football Hall of Fame. When we got up Monday morning, Bobby said to me, "Maybe we better skip the trip to the Hall of Fame and go nail down that decking on your church roof." Even though they were leaving to go home the next day, he insisted that we should go work on the church building. So we went down to the church, swept the snow off of the 40' x 80' roof, and spent the day nailing down the decking. While we were working, Bobby said to me, "Imagine this the WMU ladies back home are studying about missions, and the heathen coach is actually doing missions." I laughed so hard I nearly fell off of that roof.

Bobby's life has been a steady, strong example of a positive role model for others. This has been particularly true with the many students he has coached and taught in the public schools for so many years. He has been an inspiration to me.

Mamma Mae Goforth

I never knew my Grandfather Lonnie Goforth; he died before I was born. As long as I knew her, my Grandmother Goforth lived in the little town of Cushman, Arkansas. She lived in a small house on the highway, right across the street from the General Store that her son-in-law Charles Sims owned and operated. My Uncle Charlie was a unique character himself and kind of a Mark Twain type of author and story teller. You could literally see through the spaces in some of the wood panels of Mamma Mae's house. It was a place I loved to go visit as a child. She never threw anything away. I loved to rummage through her stuff. She had two, two-hole outdoor toilets in her backyard, and she papered the walls of one with pages from old magazines and the other one with pages from the Sears and Roebuck catalogue. You could go in one and see all of the old news from Life and Look magazines, and you could go in the other one and look at all of the things you wished you had ordered out of the Sears and Roebuck catalogue.

I remember one day when I was staying with her; she stumbled around the house all day talking about how bad she felt. Then in the late afternoon she saw a lady she knew across the road at my Uncle's store. She said, "That lady owes me $2.00," and she took off in a dead run across the highway to catch up with her. She got her $2.00.

My Uncle Charlie wrote me a letter one time about the Federal government coming into Cushman and deciding that everyone who did not have inside bathroom facilities was underprivileged. Therefore, they gave them all $1,000.00 to have an inside bathroom with toilet facilities installed. My uncle said that he knew that there would be a demand for a product that he had only carried in small amounts in the past, so he made a large order of toilet tissue. To his surprise, it was not being purchased in the quantities he had expected. So he said he asked one lady (my grandmother) why she was not buying the toilet tissue. He said that her reply was, "You don't think I am going to do something like that in the nicest room in my house do you?"

I guess my grandmother's one vice was that she dipped snuff. She left a trail of snuff everywhere she went. So if she came and spent any time with you, you spent a lot of time cleaning the snuff stains from all of the sinks in your house.

My grandmother loved life. I loved to hear her laugh. She loved her family. She loved the Lord and she loved her church. I think she must have kept pestering the pastor of the Baptist Church in Cushman until he invited me to come and preach a revival for them in July, just before I started to seminary.

This was just shortly after she had gotten her new bathroom. It was hot summertime and I was taking a bath every day, before I got dressed to go to the church. After a couple of days she asked me if I was going to take a bath every day. I told her yes, and then I realized that maybe she was afraid I was going to run her well dry. I asked her if she was worried about the well running dry from filling up the bathtub every day. She said no, but she was worried about how much her electric bill was going to be because of all of the time the well pump was running to fill up the tub. On the last night of the revival, before we went to church, she told me that she had not put her love offering in yet, because she thought I ought to get at least $100.00. She said she was going to wait until we got home that night to give me hers. When we got home, she asked me how much they gave me. I pulled the check out of my pocket and it was exactly $100.00. When I told her that, she just said, "Oh that's good," and went on about her business.

Virginia and I went to Arkansas on vacation the summer after we were married. While we were at her house, she took Virginia into the room where all of the stuff she had accumulated over the years was and gave her a set of dishes that were unopened, in the original box. Years later we started using them some. Virginia and the boys were washing the dishes after a meal. They noticed on the back of one of the plates that it said that the gold trim on the dishes was 24k gold. Needless to say we quit using them on a regular basis. She had probably gotten them years before with some mail order coupons.

One thing that stands out to me about my grandmother is what a strong woman she was. She was a relatively young woman when my grandfather died. She did not remarry. Her home was always open to her family. At least that is the impression that I had. I am sure that if you were to talk to all of her grandchildren, they would all have one or two favorite Mamma Mae stories.

Pappa and Mamma Evans

James Lee and Exie King Evans were my grandparents on my mother's side. I am named James Lonnie Goforth after my two grandfathers, James Evans and Lonnie Goforth. Although most years we were only able to visit them once a year, we always went back to Arkansas during dad's vacation to visit our grandparents. I am grateful that my parents saw the need for my brother and me to have regular visits with our grandparents. My mother's parents lived up the road from Cushman in Mt. Pleasant, Arkansas. We also enjoyed spending time there. Mother's two youngest sisters were still at home when we were boys. I think we probably embarrassed them from time to time when we came. We seemed to think that we could just take over the town when we got there.

My grandfather was a hardworking strong Christian layman. He was a very active layman in the Cumberland Presbyterian Church. He was a farmer, teacher, and coach. He was also a very diehard, old time Arkansas democrat. I remember saying to him one time, "Pappa you are so against the Republicans that if Jesus Christ Himself were the candidate of the Republican Party, you would not vote for him." Without batting an eye he said, "I won't have to worry about that, Jesus Christ has too much sense to ever be a Republican."

Mamma Evans was a hardworking, stay at home mother and wife as was typical of the day and time in which she lived. She loved her family and she loved doing for them. She particularly loved cooking for her family. She milked the cow twice a day, carried the raw milk in, and let the cream rise to the top overnight. The next day she would churn her butter, make homemade ice cream, and many other wonderful things.

She spoiled her two oldest grandsons, and Bobby and I enjoyed every moment of it. She was a strong Christian wife, mother, and grandmother. I am quite sure that my brother and I learned much about family values from them. Their lives were a solid example of the way you should live your life.

One of my fondest memories of time I spent with my grandfather was the week that I preached the revival in the little Baptist Church in Cushman, Arkansas. My Pappa Evans drove over every night from Mt. Pleasant to attend the services. You could tell that he was quite proud of his oldest grandson. I had some wonderful adult conversations with my grandfather that week, and probably learned as much about what really made him the man that he was than at any other time in my life.

That week was a very special week that allowed me to spend some real quality time with my Grandmother Goforth and my Grandfather Evans while they were still in fairly good health. It was shortly after that visit that I moved from Houston to New Orleans, to begin my seminary training.

Warren Watson

Warren Watson was my best friend's uncle. He and his wife Doris did not have any children of their own, so they treated several of us boys like we were theirs. Warren was a deacon in the Market St. Baptist Church, but he was far more than that to a group of about 10-12 boys. He was our Sunday School teacher. We were 12 years old and were proud of the fact that we had run off just about every Sunday School teacher we had from the time we were about 6 years old. At 12, we had just run off another teacher. We were sitting in our classroom, quite proud of our accomplishment, when in walks Warren Watson. He did not say a word; he just proceeded to take off his belt and spank every one of us. Then he said, "Sit down and be quiet while I teach you the Bible." Warren loved us and he loved the Word of God. He was our Sunday School teacher from that day until we graduated from high school.

I have always remembered the last piece of advice he gave us on our last Sunday with him before we all went off to college. He said, "Boys, you are going to come across people who are a lot smarter than I am." Then he held up his Bible and said, "However, measure everything someone tries to teach you by the truth of the Word of God. You stick with the Word of God and you will be ok." That was great advice that has rung true in my heart over all these years. Warren was a simple, ordinary, working man who worked in the Paper Mill. He loved his wife, loved his church, loved the Word of God, and loved a group of boys, and faithfully taught them the Bible every week.

Rev. Thomas B. Guinn

Rev. Thomas B. Guinn is the man I consider to be my "father in the ministry." He was my pastor during most of my teenage and college years. I remember Bro. Guinn as a man of great conviction and a strong preacher of the Word of God. He was not necessarily the kind of man that you might think would have great appeal among the youth in the church, but he did. I think the reason for that was that he was someone who knew what he believed and why he believed it. He preached the whole counsel of God without apology to anyone.

Bro. Guinn came to be our pastor when I was in high school. I already knew that God had called me to preach. Later in my life, when I began to pastor churches, I realized that I was performing many of the duties of a pastor in the same manner I had observed him perform them. He was such a strong preacher of the Word of God that I invited him to come and preach revivals in almost every church where I was pastor.

One of the great pieces of advice that he gave me was when I was a seminary student. My wife and I were in our second year of marriage with our first child, and I was also pastor of a small, but growing, church. I was finding it hard to balance marriage, learn how to be a parent, pastor a church, and also carrying a full load of classes at the seminary.

I had invited Bro. Guinn to come and preach a revival for our little church. I was sharing my frustration with him about trying to do justice to my seminary training and pastor the church at the same time. I think I really wanted him to tell me that school work should not come before my church work, which would give me an excuse to quit school. Instead he asked me a question. He said, "Do you believe that it is God's will for you to be the best trained preacher you can possibly be?" My answer was yes. He said, "So do I, therefore, at this

62

point in your life if you have to choose between the church and your seminary training, you need to resign the church and give full attention to your seminary training."

That was not the answer that I wanted to hear, but it was the answer I needed to hear. At that point in my life and ministry, the most important thing that I needed to be doing was preparing for the long haul of whatever ministry the Lord had laid out for me in the future. I was able to learn how to balance my time and continue to pastor that church and do justice to my seminary training. I praise God for a man who told me what I needed to hear at a very important juncture in my life.

Bro. Guinn has been in heaven several years now, but his influence on my life will last as long as I live. I pray that in some small way I have had a similar impact on someone's life.

Dr. J. Patrick Maloney

Pat Maloney became my dearest friend from seminary days. We laughed together; we cried together; we played golf together; etc. I think in many ways he was like another dad to my boys when they were young. Pat was the kind of man that you either liked or you didn't. He was very vocal about what he did and did not believe. He was a brilliant man, and yet a very simple man.

Pat had lived a very rough life, and was not saved until he was a man. However, when God saved him, He got every ounce of him. He was a very energetic man who had a passion for the Word of God, and a passion to see people come to know Christ as their personal Savior and Lord. He was a powerful preacher of the Word of God. You either accepted him for who he was or you really did not like him very much. I guess it was all of the above that really drew me to him.

Pat was already doing his work on his PHD in Theology at New Orleans Baptist Theological Seminary, while I was working on getting my Masters Degree. He was the grader for more than one of my professors. He and I were both pastors of small churches in New Orleans and I think that it was that relationship that initially began to draw us close to one another.

We played golf at least once a week while we were in seminary. Within our two families, our golf games became legendary. I don't know how he stole the affections of my younger son Tom, but Tom was always pulling for him to win. Golf was something we both enjoyed, but it was also a great get away from the pressures of seminary life and the work in our churches. There came a time when, once a year, we played the Goforth/Maloney Annual Golf Tournament. On that day, no one else was allowed to play with us, because we did not want any distractions from the seriousness of the matter. On that day, it did not matter what your score was, as long as it was at least one shot better than the other. The winner that day got to take the trophy home for the next year and had the bragging rights for the year. I am afraid that I must admit that the trophy resided in his office much longer than in mine, and it was very disconcerting when my younger son would give him a victory high five when he won.

In all seriousness, very few people played a more important role in my development as a young minister and developing theologian, than my dear friend J. Patrick (Pat) Maloney. He was the one that was with me the day I got saved. He is the one that asked me that day what was really wrong with me, and I replied, "I don't think I am saved." He did nothing more or less than say, "If that is your problem, why don't you just get saved. I know you know how; I have watched you tell hundreds how to be saved." Those words were the release from bondage of being a lost pastor that gave me the freedom to call on the Lord to save me. Praise God, on that Friday afternoon, November 19, 1978, at 2:30 PM, God saved me, and He used my friend Pat Maloney to bring me to that moment.

Pat was 11 years older than me and was my spiritual older brother. He loved me just like I was, and I loved him just like he was.

Evangelist Rick Ingle

I first met Rick when he was the pastor of my home church, Market Street Baptist Church, Houston, Texas. It was the Christmas season of 1970. We had been in Niles, Ohio, since the summer of 1969. My dad told him we were coming to visit them, and Rick asked me if I would preach on a Sunday night. My dad had already told me that he was a really good preacher and I valued my dad's judgment when it came to the ability of men to preach.

As Rick and I visited together, I invited him to come and preach for me at Central Baptist Church, Niles, Ohio. We made arrangements for him to come in late April, early May of 1971.

By the time the revival time arrived, the Lord had already led him to resign and go into full-time evangelism. When he came to Niles, Ohio, he told me that it was his first revival experience in the Pioneer Mission areas of Southern Baptist work in the USA. He really enjoyed the week, and it created a spark in him which would mark the last 20 plus years of his ministry. I will say more about that later.

When Rick came to Central Baptist Church, Niles, Ohio, our average attendance was about 100. During that week of revival, there were 120 public professions of faith recorded. It was at that time the largest number of conversions recorded in a single church revival in the history of the Baptist Convention of Ohio. It probably still remains among the most recorded in a single church revival in the history of the Ohio convention.

After that, Rick preached revivals in every church where I was pastor. When the Lord left me in one place long enough, he preached twice in those churches.

Rick had a major impact on my ministry and my approach to evangelism. Rick had a powerful testimony that he shared and the Lord used how he was saved out of a life of crime, drugs, and alcohol. I was beginning to be asked to preach revivals in a lot of churches in Ohio. I remember saying to Rick that I wish my testimony was as powerful as his. He quickly responded back that my testimony was more powerful than his. Because he had been pastor of my home church, and dad was one of his deacons, he knew some things about my testimony. He said that he wished he had a testimony where he had a Christian father and mother who raised him in the church. He said he wished he had a testimony that did not include crime, drugs, and alcohol. Then he encouraged me to develop my testimony and begin using it in revival services. He said that the reason my testimony was more powerful than his was, because it was an example of the power of the Holy Spirit keeping a person out of a life of crime, drugs, and alcohol. He said it was an example that a person could be saved from a life of crime, drugs and alcohol, rather than having to be saved out of that kind of lifestyle.

I took Rick's advice and began to share about growing up in a Christian home that was not perfect, but had a Christian father and mother who did the best they could do in training their children in the ways of the Lord. When I discovered later in life that I had not really been saved at an early age, the Lord was able to use that on numerous occasions to allow church members who knew they were not saved to have the courage to admit it and trust Christ.

As I said earlier, that first revival Rick preached for me in Niles stirred an interest in his heart in preaching Pioneer Mission revivals. He preached for me in three more churches in Ohio during the time I was there. When the Lord moved us to Texas, he preached in both of the churches where I was pastor, before moving to New York. Rick preached in some of the largest churches in the Southern Baptist Convention, but he really enjoyed his ministry of evangelism in small churches.

For more than 20 years, during the latter years of his ministry, his focus had been on God's call on his life to Pioneer Evangelism. He told me that the Lord told him to go to the small churches and that he was to pay his own travel expenses, pay his living expenses while with the church, and not accept any love offering. I know that there were a number of people who supported his ministry, which helped him with this special calling on his life. Praise God for those people who believed in his ministry, which allowed him to do what the Lord had called him to do.

I can tell you that he was obedient to that calling for the rest of his life. He came to the Adirondack Baptist Association and spent all summer preaching revivals in our small churches. There were at least 3 music evangelists who would go with him, and they would go with him under the same arrangements. His wife Betty came with him for the summer. I remember going to one of the revival services and Betty came to me and said that they had a problem. Someone had given them a check for $100.00. She said they could not keep it, but she did not want to hurt the person's feelings. She gave it to me and asked me to use it in the association.

At the end of the summer Rick and Betty and Music Evangelist Phillip Willis stayed two more weeks and did the preaching and singing for our Youth and Children's Camps. Although they were 70 years old, our children and youth loved them.

A couple of weeks after the end of the summer, I had a man come to me and say the Lord had been generous with him and he wanted to share it with Rick. He gave me a check for $2,000.00 to send to Rick. I sent Rick the check. When he received it, Rick called me. He wanted to know if the check was given to me while he was still in New York. He said that if that were true, he could not accept it.

When I told Rick that the check was given to me after they were gone, he said that he could accept it. Then he said he wanted to tell me something. He said it took them two weeks to get back to Texas after the two weeks of camp. He said by the time he got home they had replaced the brakes on their truck and all of the tires of their RV trailer and some of the tires of the truck had blown out. He said he spent $2,000.00 on repairs on the way home. Praise God for the way He provides for our every need, when we are faithful to Him.

Over the years, he went back to several of the churches in the North Country to preach revivals. At least one music evangelist would go with him. Their desire was to bring evangelistic crusades to churches who could not otherwise afford to have such meetings. In fact he and Phillip Willis were back there less than two months before he died. His footprint will be on the ministry of many of the churches of the North Country until Jesus Christ calls His Church home.

Because of my relationship with Rick, I had the opportunity to meet and work with several of the Evangelistic Musicians who worked with Rick from time to time. I particularly have appreciated the close friendship that developed with Phillip Willis. He has been with Rick in several revival meetings and has stayed in our home on numerous occasions. He, like Rick, just became a part of our family. I think Phillip may be one of my favorite singers of gospel music. I have worn out several of his CD's in my vehicles over the years.

I am writing this on October 14, 2015. I received word this morning that Rick went home to be with the Lord from complications from injuries received in a serious auto accident almost two weeks ago. His wife Betty was with him, and also has serious injuries, but it looks like she is going to make it. My son Jim and I agree; if it was time for him to go, what a great way to go, to get to preach one more revival meeting as the last thing you would do on this earth at age 86. I PRAISE GOD, that I had the privilege of being a friend and co-laborer with Rick Ingle.

I had scheduled Rick and Phillip to be with me for their third revival meeting at Camp Ground Baptist Church, Alto, Texas, in February 2016. After Rick went home to be with the Lord, I asked Phillip to keep the revival on his schedule. I am sure Rick would have wanted us to do that, but more important, I became convinced the Lord wanted us to do that.

Luke Garrett

Luke Garrett is one of the finest gospel musicians that I have ever known. His vocal ability is as good as it comes. I first became acquainted with his ministry when Perry Eaton and I had taken the youth from FBC, Rusk, Texas, to the Texas Baptist Youth Convention. He was one of the soloists for that convention. As soon as I heard him sing, I told Perry to do whatever he had to do to get him to our church. When we got back from that youth convention, Perry made contact with his manager to schedule a concert. When Perry told me how much it was going to cost to get him for a one-night concert, I told him that we could not do that. Perry was a very persistent young man and he told me that he was going to find out how to communicate with Luke personally. Later he came back to tell me that he had made contact with him and that he had agreed to come for a love offering and travel expense. That was the beginning of what has become a lifelong friendship.

Later we invited Luke to come back and do the music for a County-wide Youth Revival. I remember one morning I picked Luke up to take him to lunch. I asked him what he had been doing that morning. He told me that he noticed that the Rusk, Texas, phone book was not very thick. Therefore, he decided he would spend the morning calling people in Rusk and inviting them to the revival service that night. I asked him how far he got and he told me he called everyone in the phone book. We had him back for another revival and during that time he became very close to Virginia and me and our sons Jim and Tom. Jim was in the process of developing his first Christian music recording. Luke agreed to do a duet with him on that cassette. That cassette was completed shortly after the accident which resulted in the death of my mother and a lengthy stay for my dad in the hospital.

Jim dedicated that tape to the memory of my mother and in honor of my dad.

We left Rusk and moved to northern New York. During those 12 years, we just about lost contact with Luke. Shortly after we moved back to Rusk, FBC, Rusk, had Luke for another concert. Tim Timmons, the Music Minister at Rusk, invited us to have dinner with he and his wife and Luke after the concert. During that dinner, Luke told me that he had felt that the Lord wanted the rest of his ministry to be spent in local churches. I told him that I believed the Lord would bless that. Later Luke asked me if I would be interested in scheduling him in local churches. I agreed to do that. I did that for a little over a year. We were both surprised to discover that very few churches were scheduling concerts as a part of their ministry. I was especially surprised that churches were unwilling to include a gospel concert in their calendar, when they could get someone like Luke, for a love offering and travel expenses. We both decided that this was probably due to the financial situation our nation was in during the early years of the 2000's. The last concert I actually booked Luke for was the Southern Baptists of Texas Evangelism Conference. He did an amazing job during that conference and was a blessing to all who attended. We had already agreed that I would not be scheduling him anymore after that conference. We both agreed that although our arrangement had not gone as we had hoped at least we went out with a bang.

We have maintained a good relationship with one another. He has been in our little church at Camp Ground several times. I took a group from Texas to lead a prayer seminar in my son Jim's church in Germany. Luke went with us to provide the music for that seminar. I have told him that I expect him to sing, "Then Came the Morning," at my funeral. In fact, I was telling my son Jim that I expected him and his brother to sing, "He's Alive," at my funeral, and Jeff Carroll of Rusk, to sing, "Beulah Land." Jim said, "Dad, what makes you think Luke is going to drive from Oklahoma to sing at your funeral?" My answer was, "Because he loves me and I asked him to do it."

What I think about most when I think about Luke Garrett is not his amazing singing ability. It is his humility, and his genuine desire to serve his Lord. "Luke, I am so grateful that I can call you my friend."

Our plans are not always God's plans, On June 11, 2016, my wife and I were driving back from Tyler where we had been visiting with one of my best friends who is critically ill. My cell phone rang and I noticed immediately that the call was from my friend Tim Timmons. I assumed he was calling to ask me what I knew about the condition of the man we had just visited. When I answered the phone, Tim said, "Jim, have you heard about Luke Garrett?" I told him no, then he told me that Luke had a heart attack the night before and had passed away. To say that Virginia and I were stunned, would be a huge understatement.

My tribute to my dear friend Luke Garrett:

I know that I am only one of so many that probably cannot be counted, whose lives were impacted in a positive way by the life, ministry, and incredible talent of Luke Garrett. The most important thing to say about the talent that God gave to Luke is that Luke gave it back to his Lord and Savior Jesus Christ.

I have already mentioned the ministry opportunities that Luke and I had together earlier in my ministry, when I was pastor of First Baptist Church, Rusk, Texas. Our church fell in love with him, and they were happy to have him anytime he could work us into his schedule.

The opportunities we had to have him in our home, after we moved back to Rusk from New York, really gave Virginia and me the opportunity to get to know the heart of the man. I can say that, as great as his talent was, the most impressive thing about Luke, to me, was his heart, and his deep love for his Lord. Thank you, Luke, for allowing my family to become a part of your life. We are better because our lives crossed paths with yours. When you left this world so unexpectedly, one of the Lord's truly committed servants made his way into the eternal reward for all those who love Him.

I could mention many others who have had a profound influence on my life, but that in itself would take way too long, and I would surely miss someone. So for all whose paths have crossed mine over the years, and you took the time to care about me, and seek to meet a need of one kind or another, "Thank you."

Our Sins, Repentance, and God's Memory Bank

I could wish that my life had not had so many misdirected times, but I praise God that in the midst of weakness, He continued to be patient with me and love me anyway. God's love and forgiveness is truly amazing. His patience with us, while He is bringing us to where we need to be, is equally amazing.

The Journey

Where do I begin? I guess I should begin with an acknowledgement of how amazing it was that the Lord allowed me to continue to serve in His churches for 18 years before I was genuinely born again. For God's grace to be so patient with me is absolutely amazing. I have been asked many times how I can justify that so many people became Christians under my ministry, when in fact I was not saved. The truth is I don't know. The best answer I have is that it is not something I was doing on purpose. For a long time, I did not know what was wrong; I just knew something was wrong. People were saved because I was preaching the Word of God. God promised to honor the preaching of His Word.

What is even more amazing is that some of the extraordinary things that God allowed me to be a part of in His Kingdom work happened before I was genuinely saved. That is really amazing. Don't ask me to explain it beyond what I have already said, because I cannot. All I know is that, "I once was lost, but now I am saved." Praise God.

Howard Payne College

It would be safe to say that the Lord was definitely in my decision to attend HPC. At the time I graduated from high school, most Baptist young men in Texas, who felt called to ministry, were making the choice to attend Baylor. I had a pastor who had attended Howard Payne and he encouraged me to visit there before I made my choice. I did make that visit and it just felt like the right place for me. One of the things that attracted me was that it was a much smaller school and I felt it would be easier for me to fit in to the environment there.

When I entered HPC, I had just turned 18 and was still very immature. It was my first time away from home and my first time to be making all of the decisions about what I would be doing from day to day. Learning to make the right decisions, even about such things as how often to go to class, did not always come easy for me during my early days in school. Those bad decisions just about cost me my college education before it had a chance to get started.

Jack Riley and Roy Kornegay

Fortunately for me, a couple of upper classmen who were ministerial students, took me under their wings and helped me develop the discipline needed in order for my college experience to be all it could be. One of them (Jack) asked me to be his roommate my second semester of my first year. Because of my immaturity, I thought that he wanted to be my roommate because I was such a great guy. I later found out that the two of them had seen me as someone with a lot of potential who was about to blow it. They decided that one of them had to take me on as his personal project. They flipped a coin and the loser became my roommate. Jack took me under his wing and did two very important things for me. He helped me develop good study habits and he made sure I went to class. He actually set up a study schedule with me and he and I would be in the room studying every day during that time. Roy served as the encourager to Jack to not give up on me. In fact, when I got my grades for the first semester, which included 4 D's, I threatened to leave school and join the army and Jack refused to allow me to leave the room until we had talked about other alternatives. That was when our study plan was devised. The result of that effort was that nine weeks later, when grades came out again, those 4 D's had all become B's, and I was on my way to becoming a real college student. I am eternally grateful to those two men who decided, in the midst of their own college journey, to invest themselves in my life. I have since had the opportunity to express my gratitude to both of these men, who have faithfully served the Lord for many years.

Although I preached my first sermon when I was 14 years of age, and had several opportunities to preach while I was in high school, my spiritual journey into ministry really began as a student at Howard Payne College in Brownwood, Texas. It was there that broader opportunities for service were available. It was while a student there that I served the First Baptist Church of Albany, Texas as their Minister of Music. It was about an hour and a half drive from the school. Usually I would leave early Sunday morning and come home late Sunday night. I served there my junior year and through the summer before my senior year. I had a wonderful time with that church and they were very good and patient with me. However, the Lord had called me to preach, and there was a growing desire to pastor a church, so I told the pastor I needed to resign and make myself available to serve as a pastor. He encouraged me to stay on until I had been called by another church, but I felt that I needed to make that break to demonstrate to the Lord how serious I was.

The next week I went in and talked with one of my Bible professors about the desire of my heart. He told me that he would let me know if he heard of any opportunities. Three days later he called me and asked me if I would like to go preach for the Center City Baptist Church, Center City, Texas, as a potential candidate to be their next pastor. I did go to preach for them, and I became their pastor in September 1960. I served them throughout my senior year at Howard Payne. The church was about a 45-mile drive one way from school and I would drive up on Sunday mornings, spend the afternoon with a church family and drive back to college on Sunday night. There were two different families that had a room for the pastor and once or twice a month I would go on Saturday so I could do some visiting on the church field. In the spring, I had my first baptism experience in a creek, and a rather large snake tried to become a part of the proceedings. Fortunately, I was unaware of it and he swam harmlessly away. As I look back on that experience, I am amazed at how much patience those people had with their young preacher who was trying to find his way, and probably did not know nearly as much as he thought that he knew. In fact there is no doubt that he did not know as much as he thought he knew. But praise God, He blessed the preaching of His Word and people were saved.

It was at Howard Payne that my Bible professors challenged me to begin to dig into the Word of God. It was there that I finally began to mature a little bit physically and spiritually, although that process was probably far slower than it should have been. Many classmates and professors made a lifelong impression on my life. I praise God for the experience that He allowed me to have in college. Howard Payne made many valuable impressions on my life that have served me well to this very day.

After College

When I finished college, I did not feel like I was ready to go to seminary. I came home and lived with my parents. Through an unusual set of circumstances, I ended up getting a teaching job in the school system where I had graduated from high school. I taught at the Galena Park Junior High for two years. My father in the ministry, Thomas Guinn, was a pastor in Baytown, Texas. His church was sponsoring a mission in the Trinity Bay area and they called me to pastor their mission, The Tri-City Beach Baptist Mission. Both of these were good growing experiences for me.

During this period of time in my life, I had a great experience regarding the saving power of God for all people. The men of my home church, the Market Street Baptist Church, invited me to go with them to a Men's Rescue Mission in downtown Houston. They asked me to be the preacher that evening. The Mission was a place where men who did not have a place to spend the night could come and get a meal, a shower, clean clothes, and a place to spend the night. The only requirement was a willingness to attend a worship service after dinner.

I preached that night on our need for repentance and God's willingness to forgive. As I was preaching, I used an illustration I had never used before. In describing God's willingness to forgive those who genuinely repent, I said that even if you had committed murder and came to the Lord in genuine repentance, He would forgive you

81

and save you. When I extended the invitation at the close of the message, a man came forward from the back of the room. He wanted to know if I meant what I said. I told him yes I meant it all. Then he wanted to know if I really believed that God could forgive someone who had committed murder. I told him yes. Then he told me that he had just gotten out of prison in Huntsville, Texas, where he had spent the last 15 years, after being convicted of second degree murder. Then he began to weep and tell me that he was guilty. He told me that he had taken another man's life. He said that he had decided that he could never be forgiven,

I held that man's hand as he prayed for forgiveness and prayed to receive Jesus Christ.

That experience made a powerful impression on my life as a young preacher. If we will just preach Jesus Christ, through the work of the Holy Spirit, He will do the rest.

Seminary Days

While I was teaching school, I was also able to fulfill my call to preach. This became a very comfortable time in my life. I was single, living at home, no serious financial obligations and getting to do all the things I enjoyed doing. In the spring of my second year of teaching, I had a school board member let me know that they had renewed my contract for 3 years. It would have been easy to settle in to that and never go to seminary, but I knew the Lord wanted me to continue my training. The next day I took my letter of resignation and gave it to my Principal so that there would be no turning back from my commitment to enroll in seminary the next fall. I began looking for the school the Lord wanted me to attend.

When I visited New Orleans Baptist Theological Seminary, I had a visit with the Dean of the school, Dr. Kennedy. He made a statement that settled the issue for me as to where I would go. He said, "We believe that a student can get a quality education here and while he is doing that, he can minister in the city of New Orleans. This experience will equip him to serve the Lord anywhere in the world."

Seminary days were life changing for me in many ways. I met my wife Virginia in the early weeks of that first year and we were soon married. Our first son James Jr. was born during my second year of school. So in August of 1963, I left Houston as a single young man, pulling a 6' U-Haul trailer with everything that I owned in it. By the end of December 1964, I had a family, was pastor of a church, and

almost halfway through my seminary training. By the way, that 6'
trailer would not even hold all of the Nativity scenes Virginia has
collected over the years, and that is not an exaggeration. I think at
this writing there are over 300 and counting. Every year is an
interesting experience to watch her pull out all of the nativities and
begin to decorate our home for the holidays. It is something she truly
enjoys. She never gets tired of taking people on a tour of our home at
Christmas to show and tell them about each piece. She will give
detailed information about each nativity (where it is from and who
gave it to her).

Field Missions at New Orleans Baptist Theological Seminary

Every student at NOBTS was required to participate in the Field Missions Program. Theology students had to do it for 2 years and Religious Education and Music students had to do it for one year. There were a variety of ministries throughout the city of New Orleans from which a student could choose. These ministries included things such as street preaching, jail preaching, hospital visitation, ministry on ships that were docked at port, and various orphan's home ministries.

Participation in this program of the seminary became a major part of my training. In fact, I was asked to be the student assistant to the professor in charge of this program the last year and a half I was in school. I was personally involved in street preaching, jail preaching, and hospital visitation. I helped establish the Seamen's Ministry through the New Orleans Baptist Association.

The first year I was in school, there were a group of us that went to the First Precinct Jail, downtown New Orleans; every Sunday afternoon we preached in the jail. Each one of us would have a cell block. A cell block consisted of a row of 8 – 10 individual cells. We were let into the cell block and would walk up and down the hall preaching to those in the individual cells. After preaching, we would go cell to cell to see if anyone wanted to talk to us. I had many good experiences, but I remember one in particular. There was a young man from East Texas. When I got to his cell he was weeping. I found out that he was a Baptist preacher's son who had run away from home. That day he gave his life to Christ. He asked me if I would write his dad and tell him that he had become a Christian and that he was sorry for hurting him. He said that if he wrote him he did not think his dad would believe him. It was with great joy that I wrote his dad and gave him the good news about his son and told him when his son was getting out of jail.

There was one women's cell block at that jail, and none of us wanted the assignment of preaching in that cell block. Therefore, we developed a rotation system so that each man would know when it was his week to be with the women. The women were always meaner than the men and would do all kinds of things to try and distract us while we were preaching. In spite of the difficulties, God was able to do some good things even in those circumstances.

Jerry Hines was my roommate before Virginia and I married. He and I would visit the Oschner Foundation Hospital on Wednesday afternoons. We were allowed to visit patients who had listed a Baptist preference, but if there was someone else in the room that wanted to talk to us, we could do that. We met a young man from Central America named Carlos Escobar. He was from a wealthy family and he was very sick. He was in the hospital for months. Over a period of time, Carlos finally warmed up to the gospel and one Wednesday afternoon Jerry and I had the privilege of leading Carlos to Jesus Christ. That was many years ago. I don't know if he is still alive, but I do know that I will see him again one day in heaven.

I don't know that what I believe was much different when I left seminary than it was before I came. I do know that I was far better equipped to express what I believe. So I praise God for my seminary experience and for all those professors who had a positive influence on me.

In relating my seminary days, let me share this experience, which might help some young preacher who is where I was. I was in my second year of seminary training. By then, Virginia and I had married, we had our first son James, Jr. and I was pastor of a small but growing church across the river from New Orleans. I had invited Bro. Thomas B. Guinn, the man I considered to be my "father in the ministry," to come and preach a revival for us. During the week he was there, I shared with him the difficulty I was experiencing as the pastor of this church, because of all of the time my seminary classes were taking away from time I could spend with the church. I asked him what I should do. I think I was hoping he would tell me it would be alright to quit school and spend all my time with the church. He asked me if I believed that the Lord wanted me to be the best trained preacher and pastor I could possibly be. I answered him, "Yes." He said, "Then you must accept that God's primary will for your life right now is your seminary training." He went on to say that if there was too much conflict between the seminary work and my church, I should resign the church. Needless to say, I continued my seminary training and gave the church as much time as I could. That was some of the best advice I ever received. I needed to be reminded that I needed to look at the long term benefits. As I look back, almost 50 years later, I am so glad I took that advice.

Church Growth

It is true that, everywhere the Lord has allowed us to go, the church has experienced at least some measure of growth during our time there. Any preacher that has any sense at all will know that all positive things that happen during his ministry are a direct result of the moving of the Holy Spirit in that church.

I took God's calling on my life seriously and wanted to learn everything I could about how to grow one of the Lord's churches. Therefore, as a young minister, I went to as many conferences as I could that I thought would help me learn how to do my ministry better. I did receive much helpful information, and also discovered that some of those trips were not the best use of my time.

The other night, after I had begun this project, I found myself asking the question to myself, "Is there something that has remained the same over all of these years that might have contributed to any success that might have been achieved?" To my surprise, the answer was an easy one.

One thing that has remained the same to this very day, even at the age of 75 as pastor of a small rural congregation, is that we have developed a strong identity with the community where we were. Wherever we moved, there was the attitude that, if the Lord left us there for the rest of our lives, we would be happy with that. In fact almost every Pastor Search Committee I have ever dealt with has asked me the same question, "How is your wife going to feel about moving?" My answer has always been the same, "She won't like it, because she does not like change, but if we move to your church, she will not want to leave there either."

Not only has every where we moved become our home, but we also became involved in the life of the community as quickly as possible. That was true when I was pastor in "Hog Chain" Mississippi, and it was also true when I was pastor in Columbus, Ohio. We got involved in all of the activities of the schools where the students from our church attended. That was true even when our own boys were too young to go to school. It was also true when we went to Pickerington, Ohio, to become the first pastor of the Baptist Mission there, which had a membership of 3 adults.

I discovered that the sooner I found ways of identifying with the community where the Lord had placed me, the more effective my ministry in that community would be. Identifying with the community did not always mean the church where I was pastor would have remarkable growth. It did, however, mean that it gave me a larger platform for ministry than I would have had otherwise.

Because the Lord led us to spend many years, particularly our younger years of ministry, in non-traditional Southern Baptist areas, I quickly discovered that you had to earn the right to be heard. I also learned that you could be a very strong conservative preacher of the gospel and still be respected by most people, if you were consistent and not a bully about what you believed.

In almost every community there are two ways that you can quickly become involved in the life of the community. One is the local Ministerial Alliance. You will read later how I was first encouraged to become involved in the local Ministerial Alliance. I learned that, with the right attitude, there is much good that can be done for a community by a group of ministers who have theological differences, but who desire what is best for their community. The other way is through the local school system. One of the things that I have always done is introduce myself to local school officials and let them know

90

that I am available to help. Then you could just about count on it, if there was a school event going on, we were there. I can promise you, that does not go unnoticed by school officials and students.

Let me give you some examples of that. A number of years ago, I had recently retired to Rusk, Texas. I was attending a high school basketball game. A student came up and sat down beside me. He said that he had noticed that I had come to all of the football games that year. Then he told me that he was going to be the quarterback next year and wanted to know if I was going to come watch him play. As far as I know, I had never had a conversation with him before. I assured him that I would. I developed a very close relationship with this boy his last two years in school.

I was sitting in my doctor's office one morning, an African American man came up and introduced himself to me. He said that he had noticed that I attended all of the ball games. Then he said he wanted me to know that it meant a lot to his son for me to be there. After a track meet a lady came up to me and wanted to know if I had a grandchild on the track team. A lady from my church told her no. Then she wanted to know why I came every week. Before I could say anything, the lady from my church said, "Because he loves them."

For several years now the coach has allowed me to feed the football team pizza after practice one day and share a devotional with them. We have also been doing that with the cheerleaders the last few years. I was at a football game recently. At halftime I saw a group of the boys who had graduated the year before. I stepped into the group of young men and began talking to them. Immediately one of them said, "I want some pizza." I told them we could have a pizza reunion if they wanted, and I would buy the pizza. Then one of them said, "We can come out to your church and have it there."

As I thought about this thing that has remained consistent throughout my ministry, I asked myself the question, "Where did I learn to do that?" I could not remember a specific moment when in some conference, this was emphasized, although I am sure it must have been at some point in time. But I think the truth is that you are either a people person or you are not. I have often said that I can only think of one quality that I have that would justify the Lord calling me into the ministry. That quality is that I really love people, and I know that characteristic came from the Lord Himself.

If you genuinely love people, they will be attracted to you and to the message that you preach. That love is demonstrated not by what you say, but by what you do. Love is not something you can fake. You either really love people or you don't.

Sunrise Acres Baptist Church
Marrero, Louisiana

I had been in seminary about a year and had not had an opportunity open up for me to serve a church. I went to the Association Missionary and told him if he could just find me a place to preach, I was willing to go anywhere. About a week later he called me and said that if I was really willing to go anywhere, he had the place. He sent me out to the Sunrise Acres Baptist Church, Marrero, Louisiana. They had 10 in the morning and invited me back that night and there were 20 that night. The next week the Association Missionary called me and asked me if I wanted to go back to that church. He said, "I think they are either going to vote to call you as pastor or vote to close the church. They did vote to call me as pastor, and in a few weeks we moved into the parsonage. We stayed there about 2 years and the church grew to a little over 100. We were living in their parsonage when our first son James, Jr. was born. When you turned off of Jefferson Highway onto Barataria Blvd., there were only two Baptist churches. Sunrise Acres and then, if you drove almost down to the end of the road to Lafitte, there was the Barataria Baptist Church where my father-in-law Lester Patterson was pastor.

One of my fun and comical experiences while pastor at Sunrise Acres was an overnight trip I made with one of our men to the off-shore drilling rigs where he worked. I went out with him that night to fish and do some crabbing. The fishing was poor, but we filled up several baskets with the crabs we caught that night. The plan was that I would bring my family to his home the next afternoon to eat boiled crabs with him and his family. We got there at the appointed time, went to the back yard where the boiled crabs were spread on the picnic table and sat down. When we all started to eat, we realized that there had been an oil slick around the drilling rig the night before and the crabs tasted so oily that we could not eat them.

In September 1965, Hurricane Betsy left the Gulf of Mexico and roared up the mouth of the Mississippi River, destroying almost everything in its sight. The change of direction of the hurricane happened so quickly that there was not time to do much more than hunker down and hope for the best. The parsonage at Sunrise Acres was a typical construction for that area; it sat up on blocks. I remember when I arrived home from school that evening, Virginia's family who lived in Lafitte, right down on the Bay, were there and wanted us to go with them. From my previous experience with a hurricane in Houston, I felt that it was too late to try to evacuate, and so I decided for us to stay at home and hope for the best. Our oldest son Jimmy was 9 months old. We watched that night as our next door neighbor's garage folded up like an accordion. All of the shutters on our house were blown off. Our garage was moved about a foot off its foundation, but praise God, our house withstood the storm.

Ironically, our little church building was not in the best shape, and I was secretly hoping that the storm might destroy it and the insurance would help us get a new one. However, after the storm was over and I went to inspect the church building; there were only minor damages. The insurance did allow us to make some needed improvements, but that old building was still standing tall.

First Baptist Church, Westwego, Louisiana

After leaving Sunrise Acres Baptist Church, we went to First Baptist Church, Westwego, Louisiana, which was only about 10 miles away. This was in February 1966, during my last semester of seminary. Their sanctuary had been destroyed during hurricane Betsy, 6 months earlier, and the rubble of the sanctuary was still on the ground. The church did have a new two story Education Building and they were having worship services in the second floor Fellowship Hall.

I had two big issues facing me. I was in my next to last quarter of school at NOBTS, nearing graduation, and I had never led a church in a building program before. I made what I felt like was the best decision for me and the church and I dropped out of school in the Spring Quarter of 1966, with plans to start back to school and finish in the Fall Quarter of 1966. I felt like if I could give all of my effort to getting the building program going, that by the fall it would be far enough along that I could start back to school and give the attention I needed to give to graduation from seminary. As it turned out, the Lord blessed. He gave us a good architect and a good contractor and the construction and completion of the building went on schedule. In the fall I was able to start back to school and I finished my work at NOBTS. Praise God.

A few years ago I was invited back to First Baptist Church, Westwego, for the 30th Anniversary of the completion of that building. This was

95

one year after Hurricane Katrina, which was the strongest hurricane to come through New Orleans since Hurricane Betsy, and it did even more damage in the area than Betsy did. The sanctuary we built was standing tall after Hurricane Katrina. I shared with the church what both the architect and the contractor shared with me time and time again when the building was under construction. I would ask them why they were doing something a certain way and they would say, "Because it is going to take something a lot stronger than Betsy to blow this one down." I did not know how to build that building, but God put two men in my life who did, and who were determined to do their work right.

One of my fond memories about that church is related to a young man who had moved down from North Louisiana. He was as country as he could be. He married the niece of one of my deacons, who had also moved down from North Louisiana. We needed to divide a boys Sunday School class and this young man came and volunteered. I did not really think he was qualified, but I did not have a good reason to tell him he could not do it. His class started growing. His teaching skills left a lot to be desired, but his class just kept on growing. One day I asked him what he thought was the secret of the growth of his class. He said, "Oh, I don't know, preacher, I'm not a very good teacher. Maybe it has something to do with the fact that every Saturday morning I go pick up all of them and take them to the park and play ball with them. Then when we finish, I take them to McDonald's and buy them a hamburger before I take them home." I stood there speechless, what this young man had just told me was that every week, he demonstrated to those boys that God loved them. You would not be surprised to know that all of the members of his class became Christians.

While we were at Westwego, the Lord gave us H.C. (Bro. Big) and (Mamma) Flurry. Everyone called him Bro. Big because he was 6'7" and weighed 325 pounds. He was a giant of a man, but he was a gentle giant if there ever was one. Everyone called her Mamma because she was everyone's grandmother. She was 4'10" tall. They

96

were quite a sight. She was small in stature but a spiritual giant. Bro. Big was one of our most faithful deacons. He was a real friend to his young pastor. He carried a cane fishing pole strapped to the top of his station wagon, just in case he decided to stop to do some fishing at one of the many creeks that ran from the Mississippi River out to the bays of south Louisiana. He and I did a lot of visiting together. It was not uncommon for us to stop at McDonald's and get a milkshake while we were out. He would always say, "Don't tell Mamma or she won't let me have anything to eat for a week." You see, he was diabetic. One day we were at his house and he was determined to have a bowl of ice cream. I said to him, "Big, you are going to die," and he said, "I know it and so are you, but I am going to die enjoying myself."

We had just finished our new building and it was dedication Sunday. A neighbor had left his broken down car in front of the church all week. The chief of police told me to leave a note on it asking them to move it by Sunday morning, and if they did not, to call him. On Sunday morning the car was still there, so I called the chief of police and he had it towed away. That afternoon, just before the dedication service was to start, the owner of the car found me and was giving me a hard time. Bro. Big came up behind him, put his hand, which was as big as a catcher's mitt on the young man's shoulder, turned him around and said to me, "Do what you need to do, preacher, I will handle this matter." I walked away and the issue was apparently resolved.

I had started a men's prayer meeting before the service on Sunday morning; Bro. Big and another deacon, Bro. K. J. Murray, were the only two men who came on a consistent basis. When I left the Church to go to the Mt. Moriah Baptist Church, near Brookhaven, Mississippi, these two men decided to continue to meet for prayer before church. The second Sunday after I left, Bro. Big was not feeling well after the prayer meeting. At 9:30 AM, he asked his wife to drive him home. By 10:00 AM, he was in heaven. That night after my Sunday evening service was over, and I was home, our phone rang. It was Bro. Big's daughter. She said, "Bro. Jim, I need you to sit down; I need to tell you something." She then told me what I have just described about his death. After I got my composure, I asked her why she had not called me that morning. She said she wanted to, but her mother would not let her. She said, "Mom said, 'He has two sermons to preach today and there is nothing he can do here today anyway. We are not going to bother him until he finishes his responsibilities for the day.'"

Wow!!! God has put some amazing people in my life, people who taught me how to put the needs of others before my own needs. I haven't always done that as well as I should, but I praise God for those He has placed in my life who demonstrated, by their lifestyle, how to put others first.

One of the things that I am already discovering about this book, or whatever it ends up being, is that it is probably more for me than it is for anyone else. Already the Lord is reminding me of life experiences and people that the Lord placed in my life, for example, the architect and contractor for our new Sanctuary. I remember that the architect had never designed a church before, and he told me up front, "I am going to give you my very best effort. This will open up a whole new field for me." The same was true about the builder, he had never built a church before and he wanted to use our church as a showcase of what he could do in building churches. The three of us worked together as a team during that whole project as if we had been together for years. It was a really amazing experience and we became close friends during that time. Because of the relationship between the three of us, we got much more for our money than we might have expected. You might call that an extraordinary thing, and almost 39 years later that church still has a wonderful House of Worship. The architect's name was Thomas J. Gilbert and the contractor was Bill Wells, owner of B & W Construction Company.

I guess one of the great lessons I learned while at Westwego, and actually during the entire time spent in the New Orleans area, was how to witness to people who had grown up in a different church background from mine. For example, one of the questions I learned to not ask was, "Are you a Christian?" Almost everyone would answer yes, but the truth was that very few had a clear biblical view of what that meant. The question I learned to ask people was, "Have you ever had a personal experience with Jesus Christ?" If they said, "yes," I would ask them to tell me about it. What I learned was that those who have not had a personal experience with Jesus Christ, don't know how to make up one, and they will usually ask you what you mean. Being critical of someone else's religion will not have any positive result in bringing them to salvation. Being able to share with them from the Word of God how to have a personal experience with Jesus Christ will cause many to want to have that experience.

Mt. Moriah Baptist Church, Hog-Chain, Mississippi

I only served as pastor of this church for 15 months before the Lord moved us to Ohio, where we served in various places for 12 years. As I reflect back on the short tenure of some of the churches I served, it sometimes concerns me about the length of service. Several years back my son Jim asked me if I felt I had left any of the churches that I served too soon. My answer to him was that you cannot go back and question those decisions. What I did know is that, to the best of my knowledge, I was following the Lord's direction in each move that I made.

Then in a lighter vein he asked me why my tenure was so short while he and Tom were still at home and had been significantly longer after they both grew up and left home. I laughed and told him that I appreciated that observation. I never had considered before that the two of them were the reasons I couldn't keep a church very long.

Mt. Moriah Baptist Church was located in a rural area near Brookhaven, Mississippi. Our actual mailing address was Bogue Chitto, MS. However, everyone knew the community where the church was located as "Hog-Chain," a name that had been given to it years ago by a railroad conductor who had to stop his train almost every time he went through the area to wait on a chain of hogs crossing the tracks. It was just a few months after we moved to this church that our second son Tom was born at King's Daughter's Hospital in Brookhaven, Mississippi.

As is obvious, our first son was named after me. I trust that has not been too big a burden for him to bear. As we discussed what we would name our second child, if the child were a boy, there was not any combination of our two fathers' names that we liked. Therefore, rather than name him after one of them, we looked for other options. By this time in our marriage, Virginia was aware of how much of a blessing Rev. Thomas B. Guinn had been to my life. We then agreed that, if our second child was a boy, we would name him, Thomas Bryan Goforth. We did not tell Bro. Guinn until after he was born; then I had the joy of calling him and telling him about his namesake that had just been born on May 9, 1968. Needless to say, he was pleasantly surprised.

As I think back upon the things the Lord allowed me to learn during those days, there are actually four things that stand out in my mind.

First, I had never lived in a rural area before, and except for my first church, while a senior in college, had never served a church on a full-time basis as their pastor. So there was much to learn about living alongside and serving people who lived in that kind of setting.

Second, in the 15 months that I was pastor of that church, I preached 16 funeral messages. So there was much that I learned very quickly about ministering to grieving people. The pastor, who is willing to give of himself to grieving families, develops bonds with them that are never broken. I learned the truth of what one of my college Bible professors meant when he was asked, "What do you say to a grieving family?" His answer was, "You have said everything you need to say when you walk in the door." It is not some magic formula of words that a pastor can say to a family. It is the fact that he is there and that they know that he really cares about them, and that he is going to bear the burden with them.

Third, it was my privilege to start a Sunday School class for single young adults. We started with just a few, but grew to a class that averaged 15-20 every Sunday. That class was a real source of joy during the time we were there.

Fourth, I learned that even in a small rural church you could develop a strong ministry to the young people in the community. It really began almost by accident, when I started a Youth Choir and became the director myself. It grew to a group of over 20 and they really began to sing very well. I remember thinking that I wanted to do something special for them. Most of them had never been out of that county and, for sure, out of the state of Mississippi in their lives. So I planned a Youth Choir trip to Houston, Texas. I arranged for them to sing in the church where I grew up; then I took them to AstroWorld.

The next fall, I got a letter from an English professor in a Junior College in the area where many of our students attended. It started out by saying, "I had never heard of Hog-Chain, Mississippi, before, but now I will never forget it." She went on to say that she had several students from our church in her classes. She had given them an assignment to write an essay on what had made the greatest impact on their lives and why. She said she wanted me to know that every one of them had chosen to write about our church and what it had meant in their lives.

Several years ago, we were traveling from Texas back to New York. We purposely took a route that would take us through that area, hoping we would get there in time to attend their Sunday morning worship service. It had been at least 25 years since we had been there. After the service was over, we took a picture with those who were in attendance who had been in the church when we were there. There were 21 people in the picture with us. It was a joyous experience. Several weeks later I got a letter from one of the young women in the church, who had been a part of that youth choir. I want to share a portion of it with you to demonstrate how even the smallest things we do for others in the Lord's name are lasting.

"Dear Bro. and Mrs. Goforth,

It was wonderful to see you at Mt. Moriah again a few weeks ago! Here are the photographs I took that day. They were placed in the foyer for a couple of weeks and everyone enjoyed seeing them, and commented again about how good it was to see you and how much you both had meant as our pastor and friend.

I have been reminded of the youth choir trip to Houston, Texas. That was unquestionably, the highlight of my youth experience. It meant a great deal to me then; it was the first time most of us had been that far away from Bogue Chitto! I enjoyed staying in the home of another youth, and going to the Astrodome and AstroWorld. The best part of the trip, for me, was getting to play a "big organ" in a "big church" for our youth choir to sing – Wow – I still remember those butterflies in my stomach. They felt more like California Condors! But doing that, and in some measure, being successful at it, gave me the confidence to continue to be available as an organist and pianist. Although my ability is still sometimes inadequate, my availability placed me as pianist at Gramercy Baptist Church in Louisiana for a year, at Meadville, MS. Baptist as organist for 16 years, at Concord Baptist for 3 years, and now back at Mt. Moriah as pianist and organist for 10 years.

Looking back, I can see more clearly how much your encouragement and support meant to me. I can more fully appreciate your efforts – so much above and beyond what you were required to do as a very young pastor of a growing church – to also be youth director and youth choir director. Now it would take at least 3 people to do what you did then!

Even if this comes very late, it couldn't be more sincere – Thank you! Thank you both!"

I have not shared this letter in order to receive personal praise for only being obedient to what the Lord told me to do. I have shared it to remind all of us that, when we are seeking to be obedient to the Lord, He uses that in a positive way to make impressions on others that end up making a difference for a lifetime.

I remember when we got to the Market Street Baptist Church, which was not big in Houston, but was huge for a group of kids from Mississippi, she sat behind the organ and looked at the biggest key board she had ever seen and said, "Bro. Jim, I can't play this." I simply said to her, "Sure you can." I had no idea that this encouragement and experience would lead her to a lifetime of Church Music Ministry.

Praise God that he helps us to know what to say even when we do not know what the end result is going to be.

On to Ohio

There was a time when we felt like the Lord might be calling us to Foreign Missions. In fact, we even started the initial approval process with the Foreign Mission Board, while I was still in seminary, and Virginia took some missions classes with me, just to be ready, if that was where the Lord was leading. One of my professors at New Orleans Seminary knew of my interest in missions and recommended me to an Association Missionary in the Steel Valley Baptist Association in Ohio. The Ohio Baptist Convention was still considered Pioneer Missions by Southern Baptists at that time. The Associational Missionary Ross Hughes made an initial contact with me and began corresponding with me shortly after we moved to Mississippi. I remember well the information from him that first got my attention. He said, "If they started one church a month for 20 years, it would take that long to have one SBC church for every 20,000 people. Lincoln County, Mississippi, had a total population of 20,000 people and we had 20 SBC churches just in that county. When I first began to pray with Bro. Hughes, I assumed we would be going either to start a new mission or to a recently started mission.

Bro. Hughes encouraged me to begin the approval process with the Home Mission Board so that he could apply for Church Pastoral Aid for me, when the time came for us to move to Ohio, and more than likely pastor a new mission. He had the Home Mission Board send me all of the paper work, and I did fill it all out and send it back to them. I was very comfortable with the idea of being the pastor of a new mission. As it turned out, things did not work out that way.

Central Baptist Church, Niles, Ohio

I was called as pastor of the Central Baptist Church, Niles, Ohio, which was the strongest church in the association. At that time, the Steel Valley Baptist Association was the newest association in the Ohio Baptist Convention. I became the second pastor in the young history of Central Baptist Church in Niles, Ohio. I remember thinking how good it was going to be to go to a church that did not have many years of history and tradition to deal with every time you tried to do something.

My first lesson at Central was that the second pastor is the worst one to be. Every time I tried to do something that was different from the first pastor, it was interpreted as me believing that the first pastor did it wrong. I could not even make changes in the bulletin format without someone thinking it was a slap in the face of the first pastor. Since that was not my intention, I probably did not handle some things well and probably over-reacted to other things. In spite of the blunders, the Lord blessed in numerous ways. One year we were third in the State Convention in baptisms, with 103 baptisms. Bro. Rick Ingle had recently resigned his church to go into full-time evangelism. In fact, the last church he served as pastor was my home church, Market St. Baptist Church, Houston, Texas. Rick preached a revival for us that resulted in 120 professions of faith in Christ. This was in a church whose average attendance was about 120. It was, at that time, the largest number of conversions in a local church revival in the history of the Ohio Baptist Convention. We also started 4 missions during those two years. Two were across the border in Pennsylvania, one in Warren, Ohio, and one south of Niles about halfway between Niles and Youngstown.

We had two students from Southwestern Baptist Theological Seminary who came and spent their Easter break with us and did survey work in areas where we might have the need to start a new mission. As they left each day, I told them, "Don't promise anybody anything without talking to me first." This was the week before Easter Sunday. About the middle of the week, they came home at lunch time to tell me that there might be a problem. They said they had found some folks that morning interested in starting a Baptist church in their community and we promised them we would have church somewhere this Sunday. This was in McDonald, Ohio. After getting over the initial shock of realizing that I had two days to find a place where we could have church on Easter Sunday, I began to make some calls. I found out that in Ohio, in 1970, churches could not be denied the use of the public schools if they were not already in use. I went to the office of the school district and made arrangements to use an elementary school, which was near the area we had surveyed.

On that Easter Sunday morning, I took some of our lay people along with the two students from the seminary, and we had church. Then they had Sunday School while I came back to preach the Easter service at Central Baptist. We had about 20 from the community that came. One of those two seminary students went back to finish school and then returned as the first pastor of the Salt Springs Baptist Mission. Until he got back, I continued to go out and preach and then come back to Central Baptist while some of our lay people stayed and conducted Sunday School.

Later I became impressed with a corner lot that had a side road which butted into the main road (Salt Springs Road). I found out who the owner was and went to see if there was any interest in selling the lot. When I asked the elderly lady about buying the property on the corner, she told me, "No." When I started to walk off the porch, she asked, "What did you want to do with that property?" When I told her that we wanted to build a church there, she invited me into the house. She asked me if I was really interested in building a church there, and I told her we were. She began to weep. She told me that her husband had been dead about one year. She told me that they were Presbyterian and that they had always dreamed there would be a church on that corner. She said, "If that is what you want to do with that corner, then I will sell it to you." She asked me how much land we needed and I told her 3 acres and she agreed.

Later that summer, and before we were able to close on the property, she agreed to allow us to have a Vacation Bible School on the property. It was the first of August and the grass and weeds had not been cut all summer. The grass and weeds were about waist deep. We decided to use the weeds as walls and cut circles for the classrooms and cut hallways between them. Then we put canopy tents over each classroom. I had a problem, I was the only one who had the time to go out and cut the weeds and all I had was a 20" gas powered push mower.

I was out there, in the August sun, trying to cut the weeds. The man who lived across the road was standing in his yard watching me. Finally he came over and asked me what I was doing. I was tired and hot and I probably snapped back at him, "I am trying to cut the weeds." To which he replied, "Trying is a good description, you will never get it done with the equipment you brought with you." Then he wanted to know why I was trying to cut the weeds and I told him we were going to have a VBS for the children of that community. Then he said to me, "Preacher, if you will show me what you want done, I will bring my tractor over and do it for you. You need to go home before you burn up your mower and die of heat stroke." I showed him what I wanted done and I did go home. He called me later to tell me he was finished. I went out to find four nicely cut circles, with hallways mowed between all of them. Three of the circles were for the age group classes and one was for our refreshment area. We set up our canopies over them and that week we enrolled over 50 children in a

VBS in what had been a pasture. Later I found out that the man from across the street was a Catholic, who also allowed us to come into his home one night a week and have a week night Bible Study for adults.

A few months later, I had the opportunity to lead Victor, an alcoholic husband of one of the ladies in the mission, to Christ. I certainly did not know at the time, but later the Lord would call him to preach and he would pastor that mission for a period of time.

By the way, let me say a word about that Association Missionary Ross Hughes. In the two years I was in the Steel Valley Baptist Association, I learned more about local missions, and the value of having a church as near where people live, than at any other time in my ministry.

I also learned, while at Niles, the value of seeking to work as much as possible with churches of other denominations. So I will share some of those experiences before closing the chapter on my ministry in Niles, Ohio.

I had not been at Niles very long when I received a phone call from the pastor of the First Christian Church inviting me to attend the local Ministerial Association Meeting. I told him that I appreciated the invitation but that I probably would not join their organization. He was very insistent; so I finally told him that they would probably be better off without me, because I would probably be too conservative to suit them. Then he asked me, "If you are not willing to be a part of us, what right would you have to be critical of anything that we do?" I told him I would think about it and call him back. He told me that they would really like to have my opinion as a part of their group. I later called him back and agreed to attend their next meeting. That was a very good decision for me. It opened up doors of opportunity for me that would never have been opened otherwise. I became a very active member of that association of interdenominational clergy. I found that I was never asked to compromise my convictions and, at the same time, I had a voice of influence in the community that I would not have had any other way.

The Catholic Church had recently allowed its priest to be a part of such organizations. The two largest churches in town were the Catholic churches. A few months before Thanksgiving, the priest at St. Stephen's Church called and asked if I would be the preacher for the community Thanksgiving service, which was going to be held at his church. It became a topic of great interest around town that the Southern Baptist pastor was going to preach at one of the Catholic churches. The church was full that night and everything went very well.

Later the priest at the other Catholic Church became president of our organization. He invited us to move our meetings to his Manse and allow his staff to cook the meal for us. At the first meeting, I was the only one that did not drink wine with my meal. Toward the end of the meal I told them that I would not be attending anymore meetings. Pastor Nick (I would not call him Father, and he understood why) asked me why and I told him because of the wine that was being served with the meal, and since I was the only one who did not participate it would be better for me to just not attend. He immediately apologized and said that he should have known that I would have been offended by the serving of the wine with the meal. He urged me to continue to attend and promised that it would never happen again, and it didn't.

Chapel in the Mall

Perhaps the greatest example about the value of gaining the respect of, and learning to work with, other ministers in your community, came in an unexpected opportunity that came our way. A large shopping mall had recently been built in Niles, Ohio. Niles is located between Warren and Youngstown, Ohio. We discovered that a well known, wealthy family was the major financial backer of this mall. This family, which was from Pittsburgh, Pennsylvania, was perhaps best known as the owner of an NFL franchise.

A representative of that family came to the Niles Ministerial Association with a proposal. It seems that a member of the family had been on a flight recently and was seated next to Norman Vincent Peale. He was talking to Rev. Peale about the new shopping mall that his family had just completed in Ohio. Norman Vincent Peale suggested to him that they consider putting an Interfaith Chapel in the mall. The family liked the idea, but did not know how to bring it all together. They approached our Ministerial Association and said that if we would staff it with volunteers, they would put in it whatever we needed. We told them that we would be happy to do that, but that they must trust us to operate it in the way that we saw fit. We also told them that we wanted final say on everything that went in the chapel and specifically emphasized to them that we were a Christian Ministerial Alliance. They agreed to our requests and the remodeling of a section on the second floor of the mall began. As it drew near to completion, a time was set for the official Dedication Ceremony, and the opening of the chapel was set. I was asked to participate in the Dedication Ceremony, which was going to be televised on one of the local television networks, which was also owned by this family.

From time to time I would stop by to see how the chapel construction project was going. About a week before the Dedication Ceremony, I stopped by. Much of the furniture had arrived. I noticed on the pulpit that there was a large round disk. It had praying hands in the middle and surrounding the praying hands were the symbols of the five major religions of the world. I could not believe what I saw. I immediately went to the mall office and spoke to the manager of operations for the mall. I told him I wanted that disk taken off of the pulpit in the chapel and he told me he could not do that because the owner of the mall himself had ordered it to be put on. I told him I did not care who ordered it; the agreement with us was that nothing would be placed in the chapel without the approval of our Ministerial Association. He insisted that he was powerless to do anything about it. Therefore, I told him to remove my name from participation in the Dedication Ceremony, and that I for one would have nothing to do with the operation of the chapel, because it had ceased to be a Christian sponsored chapel and had become a world religions chapel.

Later that day I got a call from Pastor Nick, who was still president of our association. He had gotten a call from the Mall Manager and wanted to hear my perspective. So I just repeated to him what I had told the Mall Manager. I told him, if the rest of them could stand behind a pulpit that had the symbols of the five major religions in the world on it, that was up to them. I just could not do it. He then told me that he would call me back within the hour. When he called back, he asked me if I could meet him at the mall office the next morning at 10:00 A.M., to see if we could get this resolved.

I met him the next morning at the mall office. The Mall Manager met us in the reception area to tell us that there were others waiting to meet with us in the conference room. To my surprise, Pastor Nick said to him, "You need to understand that you need to find a way to satisfy Rev. Goforth in this matter. If you do not, you lose him, and you also lose the entire Niles Ministerial Association. We are a single unit and we stand united together." When we went into the conference room, we found the attorney for the family of the owners, and the Rabbi of the Jewish Temple where the family attended, waiting for us. The meeting started with the attorney reminding us that they had put up all of the money for the construction of the chapel and he did not understand why I was making such a big deal over one thing that they wanted. I reminded him that they were the ones who came to us and asked us if we would provide the volunteer staff, if they built the chapel. I also told him that we told them up front that we were a Christian Ministerial Association and would have to be free to operate from that perspective. I also reminded him that they had promised not to put anything in the chapel without our approval. At that point the Rabbi spoke up and wanted to know why I was so offended by the disk with the symbols on it. I told him that I did not mean to be rude, but frankly, even the symbol for the Jewish faith offended me, because the New Testament teaches me that Jesus Christ came into the world to be the promised Messiah. He died on the cross for all mankind and the Jewish faith denies that Jesus Christ is the true Messiah. They continued to try to convince me that this was not a big deal; I kept insisting that it was a big deal for me because my Bible teaches that Jesus Christ is the only way to eternal life. For that reason, I refused to stand behind a pulpit that contained the symbols of four religions that declare that mine is false. Therefore, the best thing for everyone was for me to just bow out. As I started to leave, Pastor Nick reminded them again that, if they allowed me to walk out, they were losing the entire Niles Ministerial Association. At that point, the attorney asked me how I felt about the praying hands. I told him I had no problem with the praying hands. He then told me that all of the symbols of the major religions were screwed onto the disk, and wanted to know if I would be satisfied if all of the symbols were taken off and they just left the praying hands. I told him that would work for me, and that is what happened. The Dedication Ceremony went well, and we ended up having a good ministry there for several years.

When we had finished that meeting, I told Pastor Nick how much I appreciated his support. He said to me, "I am embarrassed to admit that I don't think I would have taken that strong a stand on my own, but I am grateful you did." Even though he and I had some strong theological differences, we developed a strong bond; this allowed us to accomplish some things together that we could never have accomplished separately.

Because of the experience I had in Niles, Ohio, I have sought to be a part of the Ministerial Association everywhere we have served. That has proven to be a positive part of who I have been and who I continue to be as a preacher of the Gospel of Jesus Christ. I am grateful that the Lord taught me as a young preacher that I can be strong in what I believe, and at the same time find ways to cooperate with those who may not believe exactly as I do. I have tried to live by the principle, "There is a right way and a wrong way to be right." I haven't always accomplished that, but when I do, I generally get more accomplished for the Kingdom of God.

I was only at Central Baptist, Niles for two years; part of the reason for that was young enthusiasm combined with a lack of maturity as a pastor. As I look back over my ministry, one of the things that I regret is that, far too often, I made immature decisions that created relationship problems. This probably could have been avoided with some more mature patience on my part in dealing with people. I was somewhat forced a few years ago to take a look in the mirror through one of my pastors in New York. One night he said to me, "I am getting tired of being called their young inexperienced pastor." I responded by saying, "Let's examine that statement; one, you are 27 years old, so you are young; two, this is your first church to serve as pastor and you have been here 3 months, so you are inexperienced." Then I said to him, "Just hang on, you are going to get older; then you will wish you were young again. If you will be patient with your people, you will be able to stay long enough to get some experience."

Unfortunately he did not take that advice any better from me than I probably would have when I was his age. For some people, this writer included, the only school that makes a lot of difference in them is the "School of Hard Knocks." However, one of the things we cannot do is go back and relive the past as if it had never happened, seeking to

117

correct the mistakes of the past. We can, on the other hand, have open minds and hearts and learn from past experiences. I suspect that much of my learning, both positive and negative, has been from past experiences. I keep on reminding all of us; most of us are just ordinary people, living out the lives the Lord has given us to live. As we are walking this journey called life, the Lord will intervene from time to time and allow us to be involved in some of His extraordinary Kingdom Work. Praise God!

James L. Goforth, Jr.

It was while we were at Niles that our oldest son James, Jr. (Jimmy/Jim) came to know Jesus Christ as his personal Lord and Savior. Jim, as you can see, has gone through a transition in his name as well. Jim was born while I was still a student at New Orleans Baptist Theological Seminary, and the pastor at Sunrise Acres Baptist Church, Marrero, LA. When we moved to Ohio, Jim was four and half years old. We had been in Niles only a short while when Jim came forward at the invitation time. When I saw him coming, it irritated me, because Jim was constantly doing something at what seemed to be inappropriate times for me.

Examples:

- The ushers missed him one Sunday, so he waited until the offering plates were brought back to the front; then he got up and brought his offering to the front.
- It bothered him that I would not call on him to lead in a public prayer, so one Sunday he just started praying out loud while the other prayer was being offered by one of our men.
- Just a few Sundays before the Sunday night in question, I was dealing with a young woman who had come forward at the invitation time. I suddenly looked down and he was standing between us trying to hear what was going on.
- Once he told someone that I took a bath with a woman at church, referring to a lady I had baptized.
- He was constantly doing things on the spur of the moment whenever the idea came to his head.
- One Sunday morning in Sunday School (he was 5), in response to the question, "How do you feel about Jesus?" Jim said, "I

feel sorry for him; He had two dads to put up with and I am having a hard enough time with one."

So needless to say, I was somewhat put out when my young son came to me at the invitation time. I said, "What Do You Want?" He said, "Dad, I want to be saved." Again, needless to say, my whole attitude changed, but I was having a hard time wrapping my mind around the idea that a 4 year old boy knew enough to make that decision. I did pray the sinner's prayer with him. We talked about it again after we got home and he told me that he had actually prayed to receive Christ in bed the night before. He had all of the right answers, but Jim was very bright and had literally been in church all of his life. I had his Sunday School teacher and another lady in the church talk to him the next week, and both of them came away with the impression that he knew what he was doing. So I decided to just leave it alone and wait to see what he would do next. The next Sunday night he came forward again at the invitation time. My thought was that I was right because he was going to try to get saved again. With a much more gentle spirit than the previous week, I asked him why he was coming. He said, "Dad, you remember last week? You remember I got saved last week. I was just wondering if you are going to let me be baptized like the Bible says I should."

I decided that the best thing for me to do was to accept his profession of faith as valid and baptize him. I believed that if he really did not know what he was doing, the Lord would reveal it to him in the future. It was my responsibility, as his dad and pastor, to encourage him and allow him to do what he believed the Lord would have him do.

Jim will be 50 in December of this year (2014). He would tell you that he has never doubted that he was genuinely saved at the age of 4 ½. He was later called to preach when he was 11 years of age, when we were in Pickerington, Ohio. Jim has served the Lord in many capacities over the years. He is a very gifted musician. Not only does he have a wonderful voice, but he is also a gifted writer of words and music. However, his main passion has been and is preaching and teaching the Word of God. He has served churches in Texas and Missouri as pastor and is currently serving in one of the most strategic locations in the world. He is the pastor of the Faith Baptist Church, Kaiserslautern, Germany. His church ministers primarily to U.S. Military families who are stationed on bases near his location. There are almost 70,000 U.S. Military stationed within a 30 minute drive of his church.

There is much turmoil in the world here in the fall of 2014. The U.S. Military is being called into action in many of these places to combat the turmoil. Many of those who are being called into action are the families that Jim and his church serve. It is difficult to have him so far away from home. We don't get to see one another nearly as much as we would like, but I am honored that the Lord has chosen to place our son in such a strategic location. He has an opportunity on a daily basis to minister to people who are putting their lives on the line for the cause of world peace. I am also grateful that the Lord gave him Lisa, who has been his faithful companion and supporter and ministers alongside him on a daily basis.

When I think about Central Baptist Church, Niles, Ohio, one of the fondest memories is that this is the place where my oldest son began his spiritual journey. When Jim walked the aisle of that church at 4 ½ years of age, I could not have imagined all of the things that would transpire in my life and his in the next 45 years.

Salem Baptist Church, Columbus, Ohio

I had only been at Central Baptist, Niles, about a year when the Pastor Search Committee from Salem Baptist Church, Columbus, Ohio, came to hear me preach. They invited me to come and preach for the church in view of a potential call to be their pastor. I told them that I really did not feel like it was time for me to leave the church where I was. I found out in the discussion that I was the first one they had come to hear. I told them that, if the Lord continued to impress them about me, they could feel free to contact me again at a later date. Several months went by and I was visiting with the State BSU Director, who was a member of that church. He reminded me that the church was still looking for a pastor and he thought they were still interested in me. I told him he could tell them I would be willing to talk with them again, if they were still interested.

They did contact me in the spring of 1971. I agreed to come and preach a revival for them and see how the Lord led. We had a really good revival. At the end of the revival the Search Committee recommended to the church that they call me as pastor, and I felt led of the Lord to accept. So in the summer of 1971, Virginia, the boys and I moved to the north side of Columbus, Ohio. I had no idea what was about to happen in the next few years.

First Overseas Preaching Experience

I had not been in Columbus very long, when I got an invitation to join an Evangelistic Crusade Team going to the southern part of India. My friend Pat Maloney had been with this group before and encouraged them to invite me. The church agreed for me to go and also provided some financial assistance and I borrowed the remainder of the money needed. There were about 28 who went on this preaching crusade. The plan was that the evangelist who had planned the crusade would preach a crusade in a major city in southern India and the rest of us preachers would preach in some of the surrounding villages at the same time.

The plan was that we would fly into New Delhi and stay in the Ashoka Hotel for three days of sightseeing and orientation for the crusade. This hotel was a very large International Hotel. Those days went very well. For those of us who had never been out of the U.S.A., it was a very eye opening experience to see some of the most spectacular structures of ancient history and, at the same time, to rub shoulders with poverty like we had never seen before. Our team leader tried to prepare us for what we would see, but no words could really prepare you for the reality of what you were seeing before your very eyes. You wanted to take all of the money you had and give it away. However, I realized that if I just gave everybody $1.00 of what I had, I could not scratch the surface of the great need that was there. However, the Lord reminded me of the disciples' experience with the lame beggar at the Temple gate. Peter said to the beggar, "Silver and gold I do not have, but what I do have I give to you; arise and walk," and the beggar leapt to his feet shouting and praising God. Acts 3:6. At that moment, I needed to be reminded that I had not come to India to pass out dollar bills. I came to India to preach the Gospel of Jesus Christ.

Pat Maloney and I were rooming together while we were in New Delhi. On the last night there, we decided to go somewhere in the hotel we had not been before to have some dessert. Before we left the room, we prayed that the Lord would allow us to be a blessing to someone that night. We entered one of the restaurants and asked if they had any dessert. He said they had some pudding with rum sauce, but that was all they had. I told him no thanks because of the rum sauce. As we started to leave, he said they had some fresh mangos and that he could peel and slice some and put them over ice cream. We said, "That would be great."

After we were seated, we also ordered a coke. He brought us our coke and as he was coming back with our mangos and ice cream, we were having a blessing for our dessert. He served our food and started to walk away. Then he came back and said that he wanted to ask us a question. He asked, "Are you Southern Baptist?" When I told him we were, he exclaimed, "I knew it, I just knew it. Only a Southern Baptist would refuse the pudding with rum sauce and then pray over a coke and a bowl of ice cream." Then he said, "Billy Graham is a Southern Baptist; he is a great man." We discovered that Billy Graham had preached a crusade in New Delhi the year before and had stayed in that hotel. This man had watched how consistent Billy Graham was in the way he lived his life.

The young man sat down and visited with us for nearly an hour. We discovered that he was already a Christian, but according to his testimony, was living in a backslidden condition spiritually. He prayed with us and rededicated his life to the Lord. He told us that he was married and had 9 children. He said that when he got home from work that night, he was going to get his family together and apologize to them for not being the spiritual leader in the home that he should be. Then he promised us he was going to have his family back in church on Sunday.

I have thought about that moment in time many times over the years. The truth is that we could have eaten that pudding with the rum sauce on it without it hurting us, but we would have missed the opportunity to be a blessing to that man. Without knowing who it was, he was the one we prayed for before we left our room that night. That prayer would have gone unanswered and we would have never known. Little things can be big when accomplishing the work the Lord has for us.

The next day we made our journey on several smaller planes to the southern part of India. There we found the local Christians, who had been planning for the crusade for many months, waiting on us at the airport. It was a very warm greeting and in a short period of time, I felt I had known them all of my life.

I soon found out that there had been a change of plans for me. One of the members of the crusade planning team had moved north to the city of Trichur in Kerala state. He had talked the local pastors there into having a crusade and I had received the assignment to be the preacher. In less than 24 hours, I was on a train early on Sunday morning to travel to Trichur to preach the crusade there. I was the only American to make this journey and traveled with a man who spoke broken English. We traveled by train most of the day to reach Trichur, a city of about 60,000 people, to begin the crusade that evening.

When we arrived in Trichur, I was taken to the Central Hotel, which was to be where I would stay for the week. The crusade was to begin that Sunday night and services would be held nightly through the following Saturday night. It was the third week in August 1974. I remember it well, because I had my birthday during the week of the crusade. Some found out about my birthday and planned a birthday party for me at a children's home that I visited. They had made me a birthday cake and the children sang Happy Birthday to me and each one gave me a big birthday hug. So, I celebrated my 35th birthday with my wonderful new friends in India.

To my surprise, many of the people of Trichur spoke some English. This certainly made it easier for me to communicate during the course of the week. I had forgotten that India had been a British Province until 1947. Many of the advertising signs were still in English as well as their Indian dialect. I think I was the only American in the city that week. My skin complexion is fairly dark, and I noticed that I looked a lot like the young men there. I also noticed that most of the young men had a moustache so I decided to grow one for the week.

The Central Hotel was an interesting experience in itself. The grounds had a concrete wall completely around them. There was a large 2-story building in the middle of the property. This is where they did all of their cooking and washing, etc. The guest rooms looked like small huts surrounding the main house. There was another house over to the side; this was the home of the owner of the hotel and his wife. I was introduced to the owner and his wife and was told that he would drive me to the crusade each night. Their religious faith was Hindu. Then I met the young man who would be my personal valet all week. I was told that, if I needed anything, to call him, which meant standing outside my door and calling out his name. He brought my breakfast, lunch, and dinner to my room. I told him that I did not want to eat in the evening until after the service, so he would bring me my evening meal when I got back to the room at night. They grow a lot of tapioca, in that part of the world, and I really like tapioca pudding. The first night there was a large green ball of tapioca pudding with my meal. It was the worst thing I had ever tasted, and I only took one bite. My young man was hurt, because he had made it just for me. Instead of being honest with him, I told him I was too full to eat it. You guessed it; the next night I had another bowl of that pudding, which was about the size of a softball. I decided I would flush it down the toilet to keep from hurting his feelings. When I dumped it into the toilet, it hardened almost like concrete. It took me most of the night to flush it down the toilet. One of my favorite things about the Central Hotel was one of my regular morning visitors. Every morning, when I came out to sit on the porch, there would be a small monkey on the wall by my room. He would stay for about 10 minutes before he would leave. It was like he was showing up to say good morning to me. It was an enjoyable way to begin the day. Then there was the little zoo just down the road from the Hotel. Among other things, it had a glass enclosed case which held a live 15' King Cobra. They said his bite could kill you in 5 seconds. I did not need to see that snake but once.

Everyone at the hotel was very gracious to me and treated me with great respect and dignity. The owner and his wife would sit out in the car during the crusade and wait for me each night. There were speakers on the outside of the building, so they heard my message each night. At various times throughout the day, he would ask me questions. One night they brought a friend and his wife with them. The four of them sat in the car during the service. About halfway through my message I saw the wife of the guest standing in the doorway of the church. After the service that night, we all went to the home of the owner of the hotel for dinner. While we were waiting on dinner, the wife of the guest asked her husband if she could speak to me. He then asked me if it was alright for her to speak to me, and I told him yes. She said she needed to ask me if I could explain what had happened to her that night. She then told me that when I prayed the sinner's prayer of confession and repentance, she prayed with me. Then she took her hand and began to beat upon her chest and say over and over again, "Something happened to me right here. I have a strange new feeling right here," as she continued to pound upon her chest and weep tears of joy. This was a Hindu lady who heard the Gospel for the first time in her life and the truth of the Gospel rang true in her ears and she trusted the Christ she had never heard of before as her Lord and Savior. It was with great joy that I was able to share with her that she had just received Jesus Christ as her personal Savior and Lord. I told her that I probably would never see her again on this earth, but one day we would meet again in heaven. Without a doubt, this was one of the most meaningful experiences of my entire life and ministry.

I am getting ahead of the story, so let me take you back to that first Sunday night of the crusade. The crusade was held in a CSI (Church of South India), which was a branch of the Anglican Church of England or would be similar to the Episcopal Church in America. It was not the typical church that you would think would be hosting an evangelistic crusade. The church building itself would seat 2,500 people. I met that first night with the pastors of the cooperating churches to discuss how the services would go. I shared with them that I would be giving people an opportunity to respond to the message at the close of each service. They told me I could not do that. I then told them that my church and I had spent a lot of money for me to travel halfway around the world to preach the Gospel and that I was not going to do that without giving them an opportunity to respond to the Gospel. They told me that the problem was that an invitation had never been given and the people would not know what I was wanting them to do and would not respond. Then they told me that I was the visiting dignitary in their city that week, and if I asked them to do something and they did not do it, I would be publicly embarrassed, and they would not come back the rest of the week. I told them that I did not know about any of that; I just knew that when I preached Jesus, I needed to give people the opportunity to respond to Him and that I would do that and trust the results to God.

They had secured a young Assembly of God layman by the name of Bobby to be my translator for the week. While we were talking, someone came in to tell them that Bobby was sick and would not be there that night.

These preachers became very nervous and did not know what they were going to do. When I suggested that one of them serve as my interpreter, they all declined. Finally one of them mentioned a Heart Surgeon, who had gone to medical school in New York City, was in attendance. They went and got him and brought him in. Then they all left me with this 84 year old, still practicing surgeon, who had gone to medical school in New York City in the 1920's. They had not told him why he had been brought back to me. When I explained that he was to be my interpreter for the night, I thought he was going to have a heart attack. He then said to me, "I can't do this, I have never interpreted for anyone in my life." I then told him I had never preached through an interpreter in my life. Then I told him, "It looks like you and I are the best God has got for tonight. Let's pray and go out and do our best." I prayed, and then I will never forget the simple prayer that old doctor prayed. He prayed, "Dear Lord, You know that I am not much, but this preacher tells me I am the best You've got tonight, so I will give it my best." The prayer was so humble, simple, and at the same time powerful that I just stood there for a few minutes soaking in what I had just heard come from the mouth and heart of that old doctor.

The building was filled to capacity that night. There was a lot of singing and the Bishop of the CSI Church of that area was there to bring greetings. When he spoke, I only understood two things. He said my name, and he said Billy Graham's name in the same paragraph. I remember thinking, "I don't know what he said, but at least I am in good company." I was very nervous and had not understood anything that had been said. I remember praying, "Lord, I really need to know that you are here. Could you do something that would make me know for sure that you are here?" Just before I was to get up to preach, the musician stood once more and in broken English he said, "To honor our American guest, let's sing one more song in English." He had them turn to a hymn in their hymnal and all 2,500 of them, in their broken English, sang, "There Is Power in the Blood."

I said, "Thank You, Lord," and that old surgeon and I got up and preached our hearts out. By the way, I had been told before the service that if I did not preach at least an hour and a half the people would think that it had not been worth their effort to come, because most of them walked anywhere from 5 – 15 miles one way to get there. That first night, when I gave the invitation, 50 people got up from where they were sitting to come and stand before me to give public testimony that they had just prayed to receive Jesus Christ as their Lord and Savior. Praise God!!! Before the week was over 300 people made public professions of their faith in Jesus Christ. Praise God for what only He can do. One of the thoughts that came to my mind during the week was how, when God called William Carey to India, he was there 7 years before he saw his first convert. I just knew that he was rejoicing in heaven over the response to the preaching of the Gospel of Jesus Christ.

My interpreter, Bobby was able to be there Monday night and was there the rest of the time. After the service on Monday night, some university students came to Bobby and had him ask me if I would do a Bible Study at 7:00 AM the next morning before they went to school. I was glad to do that, but did not think there would be much of a response at 7:00 AM. I was surprised the next morning when about 300 students showed up for the Bible Study. I did 45 minutes of Bible study and then gave them some time to ask questions. They could understand my English, if I spoke slowly, but it went more smoothly, if Bobby translated for me. He and I really became a team quickly and worked together well all week. When I was preaching, he would preach as hard as I did. During the question and answer time in the mornings, the students would ask a question; he would interpret it to me. I would give the answer; then he would interpret it back to them. One morning a young man asked him a question and he just spoke directly back to him and then went on to the next question. When we were alone, I asked him about the question and he would not tell me what it was. I asked him what it was that he said to him in response to the question. He said that he responded by saying, "It takes an intelligent person to ask an intelligent question and that was a stupid question." He did not want me to know what the question was, so I just left it at that.

The young women who came to the Bible Study would not ask questions during the time they were there with the young men. However, one morning several of them came to me after the session and wanted to ask me a question. They wanted to know how American young women felt about the Dowry System of marriage. That is a system where the parents of the boy and the girl agree on the marriage, while the children are small, and the girl's parents begin developing a dowry of gifts that will make their daughter acceptable at the time of the marriage. I told them I did not know any American young women who would agree to that kind of arrangement. I think that caused some of them to want to move to America.

There were those who made sure that I saw some of the local sights during the day. According to local history, the disciple Thomas visited this ancient city. One of the most enjoyable parts of my days was the time I spent with University students who stopped by my hotel to ask questions about the Bible Study that I had led earlier that day. I was told about the middle of the week that the communist party actually controlled the power system. When they heard about the large crowds that were coming to the crusade, they made the decision not to turn on the street lights at night in hopes that it would discourage people from attending the crusade.

I mentioned earlier that I had my birthday during the week of the crusade, and that I was given a birthday party by the children of a Christian Children's Home. I remember that we had cake and juice and small bananas. It was heartwarming to have those children sing Happy Birthday to me in their broken English. What really surprised me was that they had somehow gotten the word out around town to come and honor their guest preacher from America on his birthday at the service that night. As I have already said, the church building had a seating capacity of 2,500. On the night of my birthday, all of the seats were filled. People were standing around the walls, and they told me that the crowd was in rows three deep all the way around the church. It was estimated that between 3,500 – 5, 000 were in attendance that night.

The services were advertised as starting at 7:00 PM. Their definition of the service was a few hymns, but primarily the preaching of the Word of God. However, the people loved to sing, so they started arriving around 6:00 PM, and the Music Leader would start leading them in congregational singing. They would do that for about an hour. After that, I would preach 1 ½ - 2 hours and by the time the invitation was over, it would be about 9:30 PM. Most of the people would then walk 5 – 15 miles one way back home. Many of them would not get home until midnight or later, then would get up and go to work the next day, and be back at the church by 6:00 or 6:30 PM the next night. This week made an impression upon me as a young preacher that I have never been able to forget. If it had not been for my wife and two young sons being in the USA, I could have just stayed.

I have had many wonderful overseas preaching experiences during my ministry. However, I will have to say that this first trip set the bar high for all future trips.

I guess I would be remiss if I did not mention my trip back to join up with the rest of the team. My crusade in Trichur closed on Saturday night so that I could get back and participate in the closing rally where everyone else had been. So, early Sunday morning they put me on a train, in a private car, and my two traveling companions rode in the open car behind me. My private car was private until the train made its first stop, at which time I was joined by a man, his wife and baby, who had a dirty diaper. By the time I had to change trains, there were about 12 of us in my compartment. It was August, no air-conditioning, and someone closed the window. Two men were smoking cigars, and I think I was the only one who had taken a bath anytime recently. When I got off of that train, I was so sick; I thought I was going to die. Of the two men traveling with me, one spoke good English; the other did not. The one who spoke good English told the other one to take me to get me something to eat. I told him I was sick and did not want anything to eat, but he was determined to get me something to eat and took me to an eating establishment. I finally convinced him of how sick I was and he jumped up and ran out. He came back with the largest white tablet I had ever seen. He told me, "My friend the pharmacist said, 'You take this; you will feel great.'" I did not know what it was, but I was so sick I did not care. In about five minutes I was feeling great. I guess I took some high powered dope, but at the time I did not really care.

When we got back to the train station, we found out that my train had been cancelled because the tracks were flooded. It was the beginning of the Monsoon season. So he decided to put me on a bus. I got on a school bus type bus that soon became packed, which included a man and woman and their child in the seat with me. Fortunately, I had gotten in first, so I was by the window. While we were waiting for the bus to leave, the little boy next to me stuffed himself with all kinds of cookies and candy. When the bus finally started moving, we had not gone very far when he threw up all over my suit coat sleeve. I took that coat off and hung it out the window the rest of the way. At this point, I was traveling alone and just praying that I would get where I was headed. Late that afternoon we did arrive at the hotel where the rest of the team was staying. I think the activity of that day had me somewhat shell-shocked, and for about 30 minutes I ran around the hotel finding people I knew and hugging them. Interesting as it may seem, that train ride also became a fond memory of my trip, because it gave me the opportunity to see how the people of India lived out their lives on a daily basis.

I am so glad that I am writing these things down. After all these years, I can still see the faces of many of those people. I can hear that old surgeon's prayer ringing in my ears, "Dear Lord, I am not much, but this preacher tells me I am the best You've got tonight, and I will do my best." I can see myself standing on that platform and hearing those Indian Christians singing, "There Is Power in the Blood." I can still see that Hindu woman who had just heard the gospel for the first time tell me that she prayed the prayer with me, and now, could I explain the wonderful feeling she had as she pounded on her chest.

I have not thought about that young man who served as my personal valet at the Central Hotel for a long time. But it was obvious that he got great joy out of serving a man he had never met before and would never see again.

Oh, I can see and hear that waiter in the Hotel in New Delhi, come back to our table and tell us he wanted to ask us a question. Then he wanted to know if we were Southern Baptist, and when I said yes, he exclaimed, "I knew it, I just knew it, only a Southern Baptist would refuse the pudding with the rum sauce and then pray over a bowl of ice cream."

I wish I could genuinely say that would be true about all Southern Baptists. However, I want to get in a little plug for Southern Baptists. We are far from what we ought to be, but praise God, we do have a reputation for being a denomination that knows what it believes and is not ashamed to stand up for what it believes. I am one of those who is opposed to our changing our name, for the very reason I have just mentioned. I have served in various places around our nation, and I have not found my identifying myself with Southern Baptists as being a hindrance to doing the Lord's Kingdom Work. In fact, I have found it to be an asset. When people find out that I am Southern Baptist, they already have a pretty good idea about my belief system and my approach to ministry. It took me a while to figure out that I don't need to spend my time trying to make a Southern Baptist out of everyone. I just need to be the most faithful believer in Jesus Christ I can be, serving Him through Southern Baptist Churches.

Happy in God's Calling

There was a significant period of time in the early years of my ministry when I struggled with what shape God's calling on my life would take. There was a period of time when I thought that it might be to Foreign Missions. This was most true in the early years of seminary, which were also the early years of our marriage. Virginia and I were married in January of my second semester of seminary. We talked about it quite a bit and her response was as it has been with every decision I have made about my ministry, "God called me to be a preacher's wife; I am married to you, and I am going wherever the Lord leads you." While in seminary, we even started the initial application process with what was then the Foreign Mission Board. The requirements of the FMB did not require Virginia to be a seminary graduate, but we were told that, if she took some seminary courses, it would be helpful to the process. Therefore, she did take a few classes with me particularly in the field of missions. That process really never did go any further with the FMB than the initial application and a few conversations with FMB Field Representatives. It was, however, my interest in missions that caused one of my professors, Dr. Thomas Delaughter, to recommend me to a Pioneer Missions friend of his in Ohio. This friend was Ross Hughes. Ross Hughes was known in Ohio as Mr. Missions. When he contacted me, he was serving as Association Missionary with the Steel Valley Baptist Association in Northeast Ohio. When Ross first contacted me, I had just moved to the Mt. Moriah Baptist Church in Mississippi. I told him that I just could not consider making a move so quickly. He sent me a vast amount of information about the need for more churches in Northeast Ohio. I kept all of that and would reread it from time to time. After I had been in Mississippi about a year, I called him and suggested that we might need to begin to pray about us moving to Ohio. I really thought that, if we moved, it would be to start a new mission. Ross suggested that I go ahead and start the approval process with the Home Mission Board to speed up the process, if and when the time came for us to move. I did that. As it turns out, I did not go to a new mission, but to the largest church in the association. An interesting side note to that whole situation is that about 3 months after we had moved to Niles, Ohio, I received a forwarded letter from the Home Mission Board telling me that I had not been approved for Church Pastoral Aid on the Pioneer Mission field in Ohio. I showed that letter to Ross Hughes and he said that, apparently, the Lord had approved me anyway. I was able to help start other mission churches while in Niles and other places and help the pastors get financial aid from the HMB. Another interesting side note is that several years later, when I became the first pastor of the Southern Baptist Mission in Pickerington, Ohio, I was approved by HMB for church pastoral aid.

While I was at Niles, I began to have a strong desire to be a full-time evangelist. There were times when that desire was almost all I could think about. In my second year at Niles, I was close to resigning and announcing that I was going into full-time evangelism. Virginia suggested that I get some advice from others before making that decision. So I wrote four friends and asked for advice. Those friends were: my best friend from seminary days, my father in the ministry, a full-time evangelist friend, and our state Director of Evangelism in Ohio. None of these men really knew one another. The Lord led all of them to say almost the same thing. Basically, they all said, "If the Lord is calling you into full-time evangelism, you will begin to get so many requests for revivals that you will not be able to accept all of them and fulfill your responsibilities as a pastor." That was not happening. I accepted their advice, but to be honest, I was not very happy about it.

We moved to Salem Baptist Church, Columbus, Ohio, in June of 1971. In the winter of 1972, I attended our Ohio Baptist Convention Evangelism Conference. I remember that conference, and the impact that it had on my life and ministry. The impact that it had was not the typical thing that you might think would happen in the heart of a young preacher at an exciting Evangelism Conference. The very first

137

afternoon of the conference, I found a seat, sat down, and began to look at the program. I saw the name of an evangelist that everyone would know, if I called his name. He was to speak that afternoon. He and I were near the same age and had grown up near one another on the east side of Houston. We did not know one another very well, but I knew some of those who were closest to him very well. At this point in his ministry, he had already begun to preach some city-wide crusades. As I think about what happened in my heart, it is almost too embarrassing to admit, but that experience became a vital part of who I became and, for that reason, it is worth telling.

I began to argue with the Lord about what He was allowing that preacher to do and yet He would not allow me to do what had become the desire of my heart, which was full-time evangelistic preaching. I said some of the dumbest things to the Lord that afternoon, such as: "I don't even want to do city-wide crusades, I just want to preach in churches." and "I've heard him preach, I can even preach better than he can." and "Why are you allowing him to do what he is doing and won't allow me to do what I want to do?" All of this was going on in my heart during the time before he was to preach. The time on the program for him to preach had arrived. When he got up he said, "Something strange is going on in my heart; I have a message that I am to preach, but there seems to be a more personal message that God has for someone here today. So before I get to the planned message, here is what the Lord is leading me to say. There is someone here this afternoon who is unhappy with the gift the Lord has given you, and you want Him to give you my gift. The Lord has told me to tell you that, if you don't get happy in the gift He has given you, He will take that away and not let you do anything for Him." I felt like suddenly a spotlight was shining on me and that everyone in that room knew that he was talking to me. In fact, I fully expected that he would turn in my direction, point at me, call my name, and say, "The Lord is talking to you." If the Lord could tell him everything that was on my mind, He could certainly have given him my name at the same time. I really don't know what his other message was about, because I spent the rest of that time getting my heart right with God. The next

138

Sunday morning I stood in the pulpit at Salem Baptist Church, proud to be their pastor. In fact, the Lord led me to share with them the experience I had at the Evangelism Conference, and to let them know that I considered it an honor to be their pastor.

Interestingly enough, during the 12 years we were in Ohio, the Lord did allow me to participate in a number of significant revival campaigns in local Southern Baptist Churches across the state. There were never enough requests during any particular year that would cause me to neglect the main thing God had called me to do, which was to be a pastor in one of His churches. Later in my ministry, God did call me to spend 12 years as Director of Missions of the Adirondack Baptist Association, in New York, but I have never gotten away from His primary calling on my life. Toward the end of my ministry in New York, I was meeting with the Association Steering Committee. They asked me this question, "If the Lord were to let you do what you really want to do before you retire, what would it be?" My answer to them was, "It would not be this job." Then I told them that, "If the Lord let me do what I really wanted to do, it would be to pastor one of His little churches somewhere that would allow me to love on them and they love me back, and give me the freedom to preach God's Word without compromise." The Lord has given me the desire of my heart as I am now nearing the completion of 8 years with the Camp Ground Baptist Church, Alto, Texas.

Amazing New Ministry

I had no idea when the Lord was dealing with me about the call on my life what He was about to do in the life and ministry of Salem Baptist Church, Columbus, Ohio. I had a layman, Jim Russell, in our church who had been trying to stir an interest in my heart about our church developing a Bus Ministry. In the winter of 1972, I became aware of a Bus Ministry Conference that was going to be held at Walnut Street Baptist Church, Louisville, Kentucky. Jim encouraged me to attend. One of Virginia's sisters and her husband, Mickey and Sarah Anders, lived in Louisville, where he was a student at Southern Baptist Theological Seminary. Because we could stay with them at no cost, and Virginia could visit with her sister, I decided to go to the conference. I confess that I did not go with a great deal of anticipation of gaining much worthwhile information. However, I very quickly discovered on that first day of the conference, that the Lord had me right where he wanted me. There was much that I was going to learn, and perhaps, I would receive the biggest challenge I had faced so far in my young ministry.

I call it an amazing new ministry, not because the concept of Bus Evangelism Outreach was new, but because it was new to me. I had some experience with the church owning a bus and using it to pick up children for Sunday School and church, but had not had the experience of using that kind of outreach as a major church growth plan.

The first afternoon of the conference, a pastor from Des Moines, Iowa, shared his testimony of how the Lord used this kind of outreach to have a successful Church Bus Ministry that would lead to real church growth. I remember that he said that, in order to have a successful bus ministry route, you needed a team of three: the bus

140

driver, the bus captain, and a teen-age worker. I remember thinking that as soon as the Lord gave me those workers, I would consider beginning such a ministry. While these thoughts were going through my mind, he said he had all of these workers with his first Bus Ministry Route. He was the bus driver, he was the bus captain, and since he was twice the age of any teenager in his church, he had two teen workers. At that point the Lord began to deal with my own willingness to get involved in such a ministry. He had explained that to have a successful ministry those who worked on the bus route must be committed to visiting their route every Saturday morning.

He then explained that we would probably need at least $1,500.00 to buy a used school bus, repair it, and paint it for our use. Salem Baptist Church, at that time, was barely able to pay my salary and our other basic bills. So, I then said to the Lord that as soon as he provided the money to buy the bus, I would consider leading the church to become involved in such a ministry. At that point, the Lord reminded me that I had recently bought a new car and that I could sell that car and buy me an older one, which would give me enough money to make monthly payments to buy a bus for the church. As the conference moved forward, it was obvious that the Lord was leading me in the direction of leading our church to begin a Church Bus Evangelism Ministry. Therefore, I had a private conversation with the pastor from Iowa about how to do it right. He suggested that I take 3 months to get the church ready before we actually began. That sounded like a good plan to me.

We left Louisville, Kentucky, after lunch on Wednesday to drive back to Columbus, Ohio, so that I could be there for prayer meeting. It was a cold Wednesday night in February. We met in the overflow section of the sanctuary so that we would not have to heat the whole building. A group of about 20 showed up that night. I shared with them the experience I had in Louisville and how God had been speaking to me. What I soon discovered was that while the Lord was speaking to me in Louisville, He had been speaking to many of them and preparing their hearts for the word their pastor was going to bring back to them. Just before prayer meeting began, the man that had encouraged me to go to the conference told me that he had been looking for used school buses, just in case we needed them, and he had found two.

After I shared my heart that night, an 18 year old young lady, named Julie, who had grown up in the shadow of our church and had only been saved a few months, spoke up. She said that she had asked the Lord to show her how she could minister to the children in her community. She said that she would be willing to join this effort. An older man spoke up and said that he had told the Lord, if he could give him a good reason to quit smoking, he would. Then he told us how much money he could contribute every month toward the purchase of a church bus by not smoking. A young man spoke up and said he had been saving money to take a vacation to go out to California and visit family. Then he said, "The trip can wait. I will give the money I have saved, to buy a bus." One by one, almost everyone there either made a commitment to work in the ministry or give toward the buying of the bus. I found out later that one lady made a commitment that night that she would give any unexpected income for the next six months to this ministry. When she went to work the next day, she found out that she was getting a raise that she did not know about. She gave the first six months of that raise to this ministry. By the time I left the church on Wednesday night, $80.00 a month had been committed, toward buying a church bus. I suggested to the group there that we might want to meet back for a breakfast meeting Saturday morning and see where the Lord was leading us. When I got home that night, I called the pastor over in Iowa, who had suggested that I take three months to prepare the church. I told him what had happened that night and asked him what he thought I should do. He said, "I think you should forget everything I have told you, follow the leading of the Holy Spirit, and start."

The next morning I went to the bank and asked to borrow $3,000.00. The first $1,500.00 would be used to buy the first bus, and the balance would be used to purchase the second bus, when we got ready for it. The bank agreed to loan us the money. When I asked him how much the monthly payment would be, he said, "$80.00." The Lord had already given us what we needed to get started.

The last Saturday morning in February 1972, about 10 -12 of us met to have breakfast and discuss what to do next. They did not know that I was going to suggest that we start that day. The church already owned an old van; we figured we could pick up children in the van until we could get a bus. It was below freezing that day and we went door to door in Salem Village, which was the neighborhood right behind the church. I remember a man and his wife, who had no children, invited us in and gave us some hot chocolate and visited with us about what we were doing. Not long after that, this couple gave their lives to Christ, and they were baptized into our fellowship.

When we finished the day and counted the number of promised riders, it was close to 40. Our van was a 15 passenger van. So the next morning, I sent the van and three more cars out to drive in a caravan and pick up all who would actually come. I remember waiting anxiously at the front door of the church when the caravan arrived. They had picked up 34 first time attendees to our church. I was happy beyond measure. The next week we did buy our first bus and had it painted; that was one of the stipulations in Ohio those days. You could not buy a school bus and leave the color school bus yellow. We discussed the color with the commercial painter who was going to paint our bus. We wanted it done by a professional, because we wanted it to look sharp. He told us that he had just received the contract from Coca Cola, to repaint all of their trucks with a new color that he was calling Coca Cola truck red. He said they did not have an exclusive contract on the color and he would like to paint it that color. We liked the idea, and it really came out well. In the next two years, we had a small fleet of red school buses running all over the north side of Columbus, Ohio. People did not even need to read the sign on the side of the bus, to know who it was. All of our buses, except one, were repainted this color. The second bus we found had been bought by a Boy Scout Troop. They had fixed it up, repainted it, and it really looked nice. There was just one problem with the color of the bus. When we went to transfer the title, it identified the color as burgundy. I told them I wanted that changed to purple. We did not want a burgundy Baptist Church Bus. Therefore, it suddenly became a purple bus and the pastor was happy.

Something I probably ought to interject at this point was the cost of the buses we bought. With the first $1,500.00 we bought 4 buses; with the remainder of the $3,000.00, we bought 6 buses for a total of 10 buses. It was remarkable where and how we found all of the used school buses. At the height of the ministry we had 10 bus routes and we owned 12 old school buses. So we always had two as spares, if one would not crank on Sunday morning. Without a doubt, the most awesome thing about those buses were the men who kept them running. Most of them were men who had come into the church as a direct result of our bus ministry reaching their children, and, eventually, their whole families. The pastor in Iowa told me that I would learn how to do some selective praying just so we could keep the buses running. I found out what he meant when I began to pray that the Lord would send us a truck mechanic. Not long after that, the engine in one of our buses burned up. We bought a rebuilt engine, for almost nothing, and used two of our other buses for him to rig up a hoist. With the help of the other men in the church, he pulled the old engine and installed the rebuilt engine in the church parking lot. In the winter time, about 5 or 6 of these men would come to the church about 10:00 PM on Saturday night and crank all of the buses that were going to be used the next morning. They would let them run 30 – 45 minutes. They felt this gave them a better chance of the buses starting on Sunday morning. Then on Sunday, when these men would see someone who had ridden one of their buses give their heart to Christ, they would grin from ear to ear. As I look back on this time and remember these men, I am amazed. They were, for the most part, all hard working, blue collar men. They worked hard at their jobs all week and then they would give their Saturdays either to be out visiting on a bus route or working on a broken down bus so it would run the next day. Most of them started their Sunday mornings very early, because they were the drivers for the bus routes. For many of them, that meant that their Sunday morning at church did not end until about 1:30 – 2:00 PM, when they brought their buses back to the church after taking all of the children home.

It is an interesting story just to know where we got all of the buses. As I have already said, I was told to expect to pay about $1,500.00 per bus. So we borrowed $3,000.00 to have the money to purchase two buses. Most of the first 12 buses, we eventually bought, were purchased from that $3,000.00. The first two buses, we bought and had painted for $900.00. We found the rest of the buses in various ways. We heard about a gas and oil construction company that was selling some equipment at an auction, which included some buses that were used to take work crews back and forth to the job sites. One bus that we looked at would not start, but otherwise was in good shape. We got some jumper cables to see if maybe it was the battery, and it was. We turned the engine off quickly and waited for the auction to begin. We bought 3 buses that day for $600.00. We heard that a large Independent Baptist Church in Cincinnati was going to sell some of its older buses. I took three men with me, and we drove the 100 miles from Columbus to look at those buses. We bought two of them that day for $550.00. We made the decision to buy one of them after it was almost dark, because the engine sounded so good. It was a 1956 Dodge bus. We drove it right behind my car all the way back because there was an electrical short and the headlights blinked all the way back to Columbus. I nicknamed that bus, "Blinky." The next day when we got a good look at it, we discovered that the bottom half of the body was severely rusted from one rear wheel cover around to the other. In fact a small part was rusted loose and flapping in the wind. We had a man in our church who worked for an air conditioning duct business. His boss donated some galvanized duct material. Some of our men cut out that whole bottom section of that bus from one rear wheel well to the other and riveted this galvanized steel onto the bus, trimmed it out, and repainted it. That old bus was the most reliable one we had for starting in the dead of winter. We heard about a school district down on the Ohio River between Ohio and Kentucky that was going to have a sealed bid auction on some of their old buses. I drove down there with one of our young men who had recently been saved. I think we got 3 buses out of that sale and spent less than a $1,000.00 for the three. It just seemed that when there was the need for another bus, the Lord would provide in ways that we could not have imagined.

Another awesome thing happened early in this ministry. We had been praying about having something to feed the children when they got on the bus, because many of them would come to church without any breakfast. So we started a fund to buy enough donuts for each bus. One Saturday afternoon, one of my bus captains called me to tell me that the daddy of one of her riders was manager of a Dunkin' Doughnut Shop, and if I would come and talk with him, he would give me his day old leftovers. I was a bit skeptical, because I knew that we needed 12 – 15 dozen doughnuts, but I went and talked to him. He assured me that he could do that, because they advertised that their doughnuts were fresh every day and all I had to do was come pick them up the next morning. I told him I needed 17 dozen. He told me he would have them ready. So the next morning I got up early enough to go get the doughnuts and get them back to the buses before they left. When I got there, he had 17 dozen on the counter waiting for me. Then he said, "Reverend, these are fresh doughnuts. I figured if the children were going to get up and go to church, I could at least give them a fresh doughnut to eat on the way, and there are a few extras for you." You will not be surprised to know that this man became a Christian. Every Sunday morning for almost three years I would go to his store and pick up the fresh doughnuts. The number needed got up to over 20 dozen before we finished.

Where were we before we began a very aggressive approach of outreach to the unsaved and to the unchurched? We were averaging about 65 in Sunday School with a Sunday School enrolment of 262. After we began our Bus Evangelism Outreach Ministry, in three weeks time, our Sunday School attendance went from 65, to110, to 175, to 219. It was absolutely amazing how Sunday School teachers who had been used to having 3 – 5 in their Sunday School class, were able to handle such a rapid increase in their attendance, and did so without any complaints. I remember our 5 year old kindergarten class, in particular, went from an attendance of 5 to 19 in three weeks with one worker in the class and not one complaint from her. Well, we surely must have already had facilities that were ready for such rapid growth. What we had was a sanctuary that would seat 250 with a 50 seat capacity overflow area at the back that was closed off with folding walls, and really was never used. In addition to that we had a kitchen/classroom, and 8 more small to normal size rooms, which included the nursery. Two years later the Sunday School enrollment had grown from 262 to 1,150, and the average attendance in Sunday School was over 350.

We did not have enough money to go into an immediate building program and that would not have solved our immediate space problems anyway. What we did was to adjust the space we had, as much as possible, and all of our Sunday School teachers learned to make do with inadequate space that would be used for many other things than just their Sunday School class. We had one Sunday School class that met in the front of the sanctuary, another one that met in the back of the sanctuary on the other side. We had one class that met in the choir loft, and two others that met in the two baptismal dressing rooms. Someone suggested that we would have probably had one in the baptistery, but it was full of water almost every week. We also had another class that met in the overflow space, but we had to move them fairly soon so that we could use that area to greet people who were coming in for church who had not come for Sunday School. Our building sat on a narrow 3 acre plot of ground. We had quite a bit of empty property behind the building, but the very shape of the property gave us some challenges as we began to think about expansion and improving our parking facility. It would be inaccurate to say that we did not have some naysayers, especially among some of the original members of the church. However, God was doing such a remarkable work that their complaints were pretty much drowned out by the sheer force of the activity of God at work among us. In the next 2 ½ years, over 700 people made public professions of faith in Christ in our public worship services. For 2 years straight there were people being saved every Sunday, and most of the time it would be multiple conversions.

I remember one Sunday, after we had moved into our new building; we did not have any professions of faith in the adult/youth service. I remember feeling somewhat disappointed. I went back to check and see how things went in the Children's Worship Service. They had just finished, and I discovered that they had 25 public professions of faith that morning. By the way, you may notice that I keep referring to the children's service as the Children's Worship Service. Some churches use the terminology "Children's Church." We avoided that term because we were one church having worship in two different locations at the same time. That was an important distinction for us. All who made decisions (Adults, Youth & Children) were counseled in their homes before they were presented to the church for baptism and church membership. This meant that much of my personal visitation ministry, during the week, was to counsel those who had made decisions in our worship services. This gave me a great opportunity to get to know the parents of the children who rode our buses to church. I always tried to make these visits by appointment. That accomplished two things for me: 1. It saved me a lot of time of trying to contact people and find that they were not at home. 2. It let them know that I cared enough about their schedule to make an appointment with them. So one of the assignments my secretary had the first part of the week was to begin making these appointments for me.

I had an interesting experience in some of the subdivisions where we had bus routes. If I had several visits to make on the same street, I would park my car and walk from house to house. When the children who rode our buses would see me, they would start following me. When I would go inside, they would wait out on the sidewalk for me to come out, and then they would follow me to the next house. They would shout out to people walking or driving by, "This is our pastor!"

That always made for a warm fuzzy feeling in my heart. It seemed that this was especially true in the communities where most of the children were African American. Being a pastor is the greatest job in the world, and you even get paid to do it. Sometimes the pay is not much, but I found that it was always more than I deserved. I also found that the Lord always found ways to meet every need that I had, and He continues to do that.

How Did This Ministry Work?

This did not happen in a haphazard way. I have already talked about going to a "how-to" conference to learn how to do it right. There was at least one Bus Ministry organization that had developed out of a large Baptist Church in Nashville, Tennessee, that was developing a lot of helpful materials for churches. I picked the brain of everyone I could find that seemed to be doing it right. I wanted us to do it right. One of the criticisms of some of the large Independent Baptist Churches that had very large Bus Ministries was that they were only doing it to pick up children to pad their attendance. I am not sure that criticism was justified in most cases, although there were some who may have used it in that way.

I hope that you have noticed that I have used the terminology of Church Bus Evangelism Ministry. I wanted it to always be the objective of our church that we were not just interested in bringing a bunch of children to church, but we were interested in evangelizing the whole family. I constantly reminded our bus workers that the greatest compliment to them was, when one of their children quit riding their bus, because they were now coming to church in the car with their dad and mom.

We did have a very specific plan of action that was partly gleaned from others, and partly developed on our own. We began with a bus route that was right in the back door of the church and our second route was the next area that was closest to the church. We believed in beginning in our own Jerusalem. In fact, the truth is that we really did not have any idea that it would spread as much as it did, and that, eventually, we would have one route that was 17 city miles one way from the church. Our intention was to try to reach the area where we were. We had two target areas near the church, the one being in

Salem Village, which was right where the church was located, and where the church got its name. The other was in an area nearby where a church member lived who was very interested in the ministry and willing to work in it. Other routes developed from church members having a burden for the area where they lived and were willing to become a part of a team who would work that area every week. So, what began from a consecrated effort to reach one subdivision, grew to 10 bus routes that covered much of the north side of Columbus, Ohio. This ministry really grew out of the burden that the Lord would put on the hearts of our church members. What began with a group of people going out into the community in the immediate vicinity of the church, soon developed into a full-blown ministry with all of the positions, except that of the pastor, being held by volunteers. In fact, although it became a very large ministry, there was never a staff position created to oversee this ministry. There is no telling how many hours each week the volunteers would give to this ministry.

We really did not have the money to finance this ministry, even though gas was much cheaper back then than it is now, old buses used a lot of gas, and most of them required work of one kind or another from time to time.

I mentioned that there was a ministry in Nashville, Tennessee, that had developed and provided, many needed supplies for a bus ministry. I had seen some cardboard bus banks in their catalogue. I ordered a good number of them and challenged as many of our people as would, to give a penny a week for the number of riders on one or all of our buses. We had a board, much like a Sunday School attendance board, that hung in the sanctuary. Each week we would indicate how many had ridden on each bus. You would not believe how the Lord multiplied that penny per rider idea to help finance the weekly operation of the bus ministry. One Sunday morning, a man told me that his young daughter had started coming in every night where he emptied the change out of his pocket, and getting all of his

151

change and putting it in her bus bank. He just laughed while he was telling me that story.

I also got another idea from the pastor from Des Moines, Iowa, about how to finance this aggressive, new for us, Bus Evangelism Ministry. Early in this process at Salem Baptist Church, I made another financial challenge to the people in a Sunday morning worship service. I asked them, if they had any money come in during the next six months that they did not now know was coming in, would they consider that a gift from God and give it to the Bus Evangelism Ministry. Several people made that commitment that morning. It was amazing, week after week, how various ones would share that God had given them a certain amount of money that they had not known about, and now they were giving it to this ministry. The details of one story are particularly interesting. On Monday night after the Sunday I had issued this challenge, I got a call from one of the ladies in our church. She said that when she got to work that morning, her boss called her into his office. He called her in to tell her that he was giving her a raise in her salary. She said she could not help but weep. Then she told her boss about the commitment she had made at church the day before, to give any money she did not know she was going to get, to her church for six months. She thanked him for the raise and told him that the first six months of that raise would go to support a ministry in her church. She said she called me because she could not wait until the next Sunday to tell me what the Lord had done. For the next six months, she gave every penny of that raise to our Bus Evangelism Ministry. With commitments like that, there is no wonder that the Lord really blessed our efforts. As I look back upon all that happened to allow that ministry to flourish in such a dramatic way, it continues to amaze me. When I reflect on it, I praise God for the faithful lay people that allowed God to use them to cause all of those things to happen.

The success of Sunday, all happened on Saturday. We began Saturday morning by coming to the church at 8:00 AM. We would fix all of our bus workers a full breakfast. Then we would have our team meeting.

They would share praises and struggles from the previous week and we would spend some time discussing how to overcome the struggles. I shared a brief devotional with them each week. Then before they left to go out and visit door-to-door on their bus route, each bus captain would share a goal of how many riders he or she wanted to have on their bus the next day. We would get in a circle, and have prayer before we left the church. We required them to spend a minimum of two hours knocking on doors and inviting people to ride their bus to church the next day. As our ministry grew, most of our teams had 2-3 people that would visit every week. They would leave the church between 9:30 and 10:00 AM, and visit at least until noon. I know that my own wife Virginia was a bus captain, and most Saturdays she did not get home until about 5:00 PM. We would fix them a big breakfast so that they would not get hungry at noon and go looking for something to eat. I am convinced that this, meeting together every Saturday morning before the teams went out, was absolutely critical to the things they were able to accomplish that day, and to the spirit they had when they went out. I remember one Saturday I was at the church about the middle of the afternoon, when one of my bus captains came by the church. He said he needed to apologize because he had only made one visit that day. The first visit of the day was to the home of some children who were regular riders. Their daddy was at home and wanted to talk to him about spiritual things. He spent most of the day with this man and the bottom line was that he and his wife were both saved in their home that day. The next morning they got on the bus with their children and came to church and they both made a public profession of faith that day. I baptized them soon after that.

I don't know where I got the information, but it sounded good enough for me to use. The information was that, on a regular basis, you could find more families at home on Saturday morning than any other time of the week. The reason we would not go out until about 10:00 AM was to honor the early Saturday morning time of the family. Our workers would visit all of their regular riders every week. Then they would dedicate some time each week to try and enlist new riders.

One of the things that we learned very quickly was, that it was hard to tell a parent on Saturday what time the bus would be by on Sunday. The reason was that the time schedule would change depending on how many children you were picking up. So we learned early on to say, "We will call you at least 30 minutes before the bus arrives tomorrow to let you know what time we will be by." We found another advantage to that was that it sometimes woke parents up soon enough to have them ready. If they said, "Don't call", we did not call, but most were happy to get the call. This also became another way to get some people involved in this ministry who would not go out and visit on Saturday. Every bus captain had someone he or she would call on Saturday and give the list of names of riders and what time to call them the next morning. So while we had the one bus team member headed to the church and preparing to go out, there was another team member who was calling the children to tell them what time the bus would be by. We also learned, when giving the time, to use odd numbers instead of even numbers. For example, instead of saying the bus will be by at 8:10, the caller would say, "The bus will be by at 8:11 to pick up Johnny and Suzy."

We also had other outreach ministries going on at the same time. I had ladies who would scan the papers for announcements about births, deaths, marriages, and new move-ins to our area. I had written appropriate letters for each situation. These ladies would find these announcements and send an appropriate letter from their pastor to the family. Every now and then we would have someone visit the church I had never seen, and they would say, "I got a letter from you this week. Thank you." We also had visitation teams that went out and visited prospects on Tuesday night. There was a time when, between all of our outreach activities, we were averaging 1,100 – 1,250 contacts every week. The growth was an intentional effort on our part to be obedient to the Great Commission.

Our bus workers were constantly coming up with promotion ideas for us to have a greater attendance. One Saturday, one of our young ladies came to me with an article about a pastor who swallowed a live goldfish, when they had 700 in Sunday School. She wanted to know when I was going to do that. At that time the most we had ever had was 400, so I said, "When we have 700, I will do it too." She never did let that die. We never did actually have 700, but on one of our high attendance emphasis Sundays, I thought this was going to be the one. So I went to the pet shop to buy the goldfish. I told the store owner I wanted one goldfish and I wanted the smallest one he had. He wanted to know what I was going to do with one small goldfish. I told him he would not believe me if I told him. When I told him what I was going to do with it, he just said that if that was really what I was going to do with it, he would just give it to me.

By that time in the life of our church, we had built a large multi-purpose room on the back of the building. One of the ways that we used it on Sunday mornings was for a Children's Worship Service for all of the children, at the same time we were having worship for the adults and youth in the sanctuary. We did not have 700 that day, but we did have 501, which was our largest crowd yet, so I decided to go ahead and swallow the goldfish. We did not have anywhere, inside the church, large enough to hold 501 people. After church, I had everyone go outside and I stood on the hood of one of our buses so everyone could see, and swallowed that goldfish. It turned out not to be such a big deal. On that same Sunday, we had 25 people saved. We never did anything just to get a lot of people to come to church; our goal always was for people to be saved.

What did we do about the lack of space to adequately care for everyone at the same time? We adjusted and used the same space twice every Sunday morning until we were able to build additional space. There was a rent house next door to the church. The owner would not sell the property to us, but he would rent it to us. So we rented the house and the youth would meet in the house for Sunday School and the adults and preschoolers would meet in the Sunday School space we had in the existing building. During the Sunday School hour, the children would all come to the sanctuary and we would have a worship service for them and their teachers. When the

Sunday School hour was over, the children would move to the house and the back of the existing building and the youth and adults and older preschoolers would come to the Sanctuary. The movement part between services could get a bit tricky, because of so many people moving from one place to the other in such a small area, but somehow it all worked.

When we were finally able to build the addition onto the back of our existing building, we built a completely open multi-purpose building that had three primary purposes. It was the Sunday School space for our children. We had portable walls that we rolled into place to create Sunday School rooms. When a Sunday School class outgrew its space, we just rolled the walls out a little more. Those walls were then rolled against the outside walls after Sunday School and the chairs set in rows for the Children's Worship time. We bought a pulpit and communion table to make it look as much like a sanctuary as possible. The third use for this room was a much needed Fellowship Hall.

The construction of that building was an interesting experience in itself. One of our men was a housing contractor. We decided that we could be our own contractor and hire the work that we could not do ourselves. However, with those that we hired for various parts of the construction, we asked them to give us their list of materials they would need, and when they would need them. We would then buy the materials and have them delivered to the job site. By doing this, we did not have to pay sales tax on the materials, which saved us 7% on the cost of all of the materials. Also by serving as our own contractor, we saved another 20% that a contractor would have charged to do his work. We started the construction during the winter and during a time when there was a major energy crunch in America. The city of Columbus was issuing almost no new permits to tap into their natural gas utilities, and many businesses were receiving notices that their energy supply might be rationed. So when we put in our heating and air conditioning system, we put in one that could run on natural gas or propane, but we, initially, hooked it up to our existing system. The footers for the slab were poured in a snow storm in

February. It was too cold to pour the floor, so the basic outside structure was built on the foundation footers with plans to come back later and pour the floor. We got the walls up and the roof on and then there was a late winter rain storm and blew water through the opening for the windows and doors which had not yet been installed. Because the ground was frozen, the rain put about 8" of water inside the building, which froze overnight. We could have had an ice skating rink inside the building. After we got the windows and doors in, it was still too cold for the ice to thaw. So I was told on Sunday that we had to get some heavy plastic nailed to the exposed eaves of the roof line so that we could turn on the furnace. Since I was the only man that did not have another job during the week, I told them I would do it. It was so cold the day I was doing it that, at one point, I not only drove a nail through the end of my glove, but also through the end of my thumb without knowing it, until I tried to pull my hand away. I did get the job done though and we turned on the heat. It took two weeks of the heating system running 24 hours a day, to thaw out all of the ice. Our church had been on a $47.00 per month contract. That month our gas bill was almost $400.00. I just knew that the city was going to come out and make us disconnect the new building from their system, but they never did. So for years, we had a propane tank that sat alongside the building that we did not have to use. Needless to say, the men of our church gave me a hard time about nailing my thumb to the roof. I simply replied that I had been willing to shed my own blood to get that building built. I also reminded them that they had hired a preacher, not a carpenter. One of our men said to me, "Jesus was a carpenter." I told him that Jesus was not available to drive nails that day.

The Children's Worship Service was led by a team of volunteers that felt led to lead the worship for the children. The same person did the preaching every week, and he involved the other members of his team in various ways. An offering was taken and an invitation given at the end of the message, just like in the service for youth and adults. Our guideline was that, if you were in fourth grade or younger, and did not have a parent in the service, you had to attend the children's

157

service. For our families that had younger school age children, we left the decision to them about which worship service their children would attend. I remember that my own boys preferred to attend the children's service because it was more geared to their age group. (I swallowed my pride and allowed them to do what was best for them.)

At least once a month, during the music part of the adult/youth service, I would go back to the children's service and speak to them for about 5 minutes. This gave the new bus riders that month, the opportunity to meet the pastor and hear a word from him. I remember when I first approached the man to be the leader of the Children's Worship Team. His response was that he did not think that he wanted to be out of the regular service all of the time. I then asked him if he would be willing to lead a team, a month at a time, every three months. He agreed to do that. He then started, while I began looking for two other teams. Two weeks later he came to me and said that I did not have to be in a hurry to find other teams. He said that he would get to worship with the adults on Sunday night and Wednesday night anyway. Two years later, he and his team were still serving that first month.

Random Stories Related to the Ministry at Salem Baptist

One of our families lived in a subdivision about 17 miles away. Their subdivision had transitioned from an all white community to a mostly African American community. There was a teenage boy named John, who lived with his blind grandmother, and really was the one who took care of most of her needs. John began coming to church on a regular basis with our church family. Then one Sunday morning he walked the aisle and made a profession of faith in Christ and said he desired to be baptized. I made arrangements to baptize him the next Sunday. If you had asked me at that point in time, I would have told you that I had long since dealt with prejudice and that I was no longer inflicted with the prejudice that I knew while I was growing up.

During that week before I baptized John, I was driving on a city street in Columbus, when another driver made a dangerous move in front of me that could have resulted in a bad accident. He just happened to be black. I was surprised at the thoughts that went through my mind that probably would not have been there had he been white. After I got over my anger, I really did not think about that incident anymore, until the Lord brought it up Sunday morning, as I was preparing to baptize John. As John was entering the baptistery, the Lord spoke this to my heart, "Are you really going to baptize him and become his pastor, while there is still prejudice in your heart?" By the time John got all the way into the baptistery, the Lord and I had done business and he had removed the rest of the prejudice that was in my heart. Praise God!!!

The church family that lives in that area first started bringing several children to church in their old station wagon. They came to me and wanted to know if they could get a bus and start a real bus route over where they lived. I knew that there was a Southern Baptist Church very near where they lived. I asked them if that church was trying to reach their subdivision. They said they had lived there several years, and no one had ever knocked on their door to try to find out if they went to church. So we agreed to get them a bus. Within a matter of a few weeks we had about 25 black teenagers that were coming to Sunday School with about 25 white teenagers. That is when I discovered very quickly that racism in America was not just a problem in the South.

It was an amazing thing to watch unfold. When we only had a few cute little African American girls who were all dressed up to come to church, all of our people began to talk about how we were a church that was not prejudiced. Then when this large group of black militant teenagers began coming, and we put them in Sunday School with a group of white racist teenagers, it was a whole different story. Now some of our white people became very pious about these ungodly black kids that were ruining our church. That attitude was also before we had our first racially mixed couple begin to attend the church, and before some of the parents of the black children started getting saved and coming to church.

One Sunday morning after church, a lady came to me with a cardholder that had been yanked off of the pew. She asked me what I was going to do about it. I told her I was going to get me some screws and glue and see if I could put it back. Then she wanted to know what I was going to do to the one who did it. I asked her if she saw the incident and saw who it was, and she said, "No, but I am sure it was one of those black kids." She suggested that we needed to stop all of them from coming. I told her that I was going to try to find out who did it and explain to him or her (black or white) that you did not act that way in church, but I was not going to stop anyone from coming.

Two of the long time members of the church came to the treasurer to tell him that they were going to withhold their tithe until we quit bringing those destructive black kids to church. By the way, both of those white men grew up in the North. My treasurer told me that

160

they were the two largest contributors to our church. He said he did not know if we could survive without them. I asked him if he thought those men had more resources than God and he said, "No." I told him that, if we would do the right thing, God would provide and he agreed. We did eventually lose those two men and some others, and in the process, we became one of the five fastest growing Southern Baptist Churches in Ohio.

At the height of our growth, about half of our attendance every week would be African American and half Anglo. It is important to understand that we did not start our bus ministry, or any particular bus route, for the purpose of integrating the church. The efforts that were made were out of our desire to reach as many unreached people with the Gospel as we could possibly reach. This was also the motivating factor in our church recreation program which had men's, women's and youth softball teams entered in summer church softball leagues and a men's and young men's basketball team, which participated in the fall and winter in a church basketball league.

There were older teenagers and young men and women who participated in our recreation program that probably would not have started to come to church for any other reason. I think, particularly, of one young man who had been in all kinds of trouble, and he wanted to play on our basketball team. In order to do that, he had to come to church at least every other Sunday. I remember the Saturday that we beat the best team in the league to win the league tournament. Several hours after the game was over, this young man who had been a drug addict stopped by my house just to tell me how much he loved me. The next day he became a Christian. This group of young men that played softball and basketball with me had a nickname for me. One summer they bought a birthday cake and brought it to church the week of my birthday. The inscription on it was "Happy Birthday, Revy Baby." Some of our adults thought they were being disrespectful, but they were not. That was the nickname that some of the older teenagers had given to me. It was their way of letting me know that they loved and respected me, and had also accepted me into their inner circle. So they always referred to me as, "Revy Baby."

The Race Question

The truth is that the race question was as big an issue in the minds of many in Columbus, Ohio, in the early 1970's, as it was in most of America. Not only was it a big issue among Anglos, it was also a big issue among African Americans. Every time a child would make a decision to receive Christ in our church, I would go, as soon as possible, to visit with that child and his or her parents about the decision, and the possibility of baptizing the child, if the decision seemed to be real. When I would go into the home of an African American family for the first time, I could feel the tension coming from them. It was never asked, but I could see them wondering what my real motive was. I understood that feeling and understood that I had to earn the right to be accepted by them. I did that by simply being as genuine as I knew how to be.

I remember visiting in the home of 9 year old Mark, after he had been saved in VBS. His dad was a business man, and he was very suspicious of my motives. He told me that he did not think that Mark was old enough to understand the decision he had made. I told him that I respected his opinion, and I wanted to be as careful with his son as he was. I then asked him if he had talked to his son about the decision and he said, "No." I then asked him if he would do that and get back with me. Without saying another word, he got up and went upstairs. I visited with his wife until he came back down. When he sat down, he told me that he had just talked to Mark, and he asked Mark if he wanted to be baptized and Mark said, "Yes." Then he told me that he asked Mark why he wanted to be baptized and he said, "Mark said, 'Because I have been saved and I love Jesus and I want to serve Him until I die.'" Mark was baptized the next Sunday. Ron (Mark's dad) and his wife began attending our church and his wife joined our church. Just a little over a year after Mark was saved, I led Ron to the

Lord and he was also baptized into our church. Later he became our first African American Sunday School teacher, and I considered him to be one of my best friends. I remember one Sunday morning we were preparing to leave church, as I was shaking hands with Ron, he said, "Bro. Jim, I am going to have to teach you how to give a soul handshake." He then proceeded to teach me what he called a "soul handshake." That lesson has served me well over the years, as I have had the opportunity to participate in countless "soul handshakes" with African American men. It is fun to watch their face as they are wondering if I know the next step. I have discovered that there have been one or two variations added to it, but by and large it has remained the same. I am often asked how I learned to do that, which gives me the opportunity to relive that moment years ago when my friend Ron taught me how to relate to African American men and young men without saying a word.

There was a 5 year old black child that rode my wife's bus to church. He and his family lived in some apartments just a couple of blocks from the church. In the summertime his dad and mom started coming to church. His dad wanted to play on our softball team and started to church for that reason. He and I were having a conversation after a softball game. He said that he wanted me to know that our church was having a real impact on his son. He said that one Sunday afternoon he said a curse word and his son said, "Daddy, Jesus doesn't like it when you talk that way." He said that on another Sunday, they sat down for lunch after his son got home from church and when he started to eat, his son said to him, "Daddy, aren't you going to thank God for the food? When we have cookies and juice at church, we always thank God first." You won't be surprised to know that it was not long after that experience that this man was saved and baptized.

14 Year Old James

James was 14 years old when he began riding the bus to Sunday School. James came with a real attitude and was just waiting for someone to say or do something he did not like. On his first Sunday, I broke up a fight between him and a white boy out in the church parking lot. The next Sunday, he threw a shoe at a lady who tried to get him to be quiet and listen during church service. The next Sunday, this same lady sat beside him and when she tried to get him to pay attention during church, he pulled out his switchblade knife, popped it open, and threatened to stick her with it. About two months later, James became a believer in Jesus Christ and I had the joy of baptizing him. James became as different as anyone could when he became a Christian. One Sunday he came to me and asked me if I had seen on the news the night before about the gang that had robbed a store and had shot the manager of the store. I told him that I had seen that. Then he began to cry and he said to me, "That was the gang I ran with before I started coming to church, and it was always my job to carry the gun." Then he said, "If you had not loved me, I would be in jail this morning for armed robbery and attempted murder." From that day forward, I never wondered again what an expression of Christ-like love could mean to someone else. How did James know that I loved him? It was not because I grabbed him and hugged him and told him that I loved him every time I saw him. It was more gut real to him than that. It was because he knew that I had genuinely accepted him and wanted the best for him, which included him learning how to have some self-discipline in his life. I have often thought about James over the years. I don't know what became of him, but I do believe he was genuinely saved and therefore, I will see him again one day in heaven.

One of the neat little stories is that one Sunday an African American boy with the last name of Goforth came to our church. I introduced him to our boys as their long lost brother. As far as I know, we could not find a relationship. But I do know that the Goforths in North America come from two backgrounds, British and Native American. My heritage is Native American and I suspect the same was true of this young boy.

It was a wonderful time in the life of this church when, for the most part, everyone was welcomed. Everyone was seen as a person who needed a personal relationship with Jesus Christ. The Lord had brought this boy, born in Arkansas and raised in Houston, Texas, a long way.

What Were My Children Getting Into?

Every Sunday there was mass chaos at Salem Baptist Church because of the limited space and the large number of people that were trying to get from one place to another. One Sunday morning between Sunday School and worship time, I was standing in the hall. I saw a new man and his wife come in. I went over and introduced myself to them. He said, "My name is Jack, my children rode one of your buses to church this morning. I felt like I owed it to them to come one time to see what they were getting into." Well, he found out; within three months, he, his wife, and their three children had been saved, baptized and had become active members of our church. Jack became such an active part of the fellowship that, when the Lord moved me on to another church, he was elected Chairman of the Pastor Search Committee. Almost 20 years later, the Lord called us to go to northern New York to be the Association Missionary for the Adirondack Baptist Association. When we left Rusk, Texas, to begin our journey to New York, we planned our trip with the hope that we would arrive in Columbus, Ohio, in time to worship with one of the churches there where I had served as pastor. We did arrive just in time and decided to attend Salem Baptist Church, because it was the quickest to get to off of the interstate. We came in just before Sunday School was over and there was a class meeting at the front of the sanctuary. Jack was teaching the class when we walked in; he looked in amazement and said, "There is the man I have just been telling you about." As it turned out, the Sunday School lesson that day had been on personal evangelism. When we walked in, he had just finished telling the class about the day I had led him and his wife to accept Jesus Christ as their personal Savior.

After the service that day, the pastor's wife, who had been a young person in the church when we were there, introduced me to her children. She introduced me to them by saying, "I want you to meet the man who led your granddad to faith in Jesus Christ." When we continued our journey that afternoon, it was with a warm, fuzzy feeling in my heart. I remember thinking that the only thing that I did of any consequence 20 years ago was to help someone else come to know Jesus Christ as their personal Savior. Both of those men are in heaven today and one day, we will be reunited for all eternity.

Vacation Bible School

The Bus Ministry and Vacation Bible School went together like a hand and a glove. As I think about the commitment of our people for VBS, it is as amazing to me as those men who worked so diligently on our buses. In looking back, I find it hard to believe that I even asked them to do what I did. In the early 1970's there was still a two week curriculum for VBS. I asked our church about doing a two week VBS and they jumped right in and agreed to do it.

In two weeks time we enrolled over 700 boys and girls in VBS, with an average daily attendance right around 400. We had to do a lot of improvising to find classroom space for that many, even though we had completed our new building by then. We had classes that met under shade trees, and buses became classes after they emptied them of the children who had come that day.

The VBS was held in the evening and almost everyone who worked in VBS also had a daytime job before coming to VBS. For those who not only worked in VBS, but also were a part of the bus ministry, night usually did not end until 10:30 – 11:00 PM, and they did that for two solid weeks. Needless to say, the Lord honored that; many children were saved, and we were able to reach many of their parents with the gospel.

I had to expel one 11 year old boy from VBS for dropping his jeans in a mixed class. I called his mother and told her that he could not come back to VBS, and why he couldn't come back. She was very apologetic, but understood. Later that week she called me and wanted to know if he was also expelled from Sunday School. She said she really wanted him in our Sunday School, and because she worked on Sunday, riding our bus was the only way he could get there. She told me that she could guarantee me that he would never do what he did again. I assured her that he was welcome back in Sunday School. Not long after that, the boy became a Christian.

Our sanctuary would be packed every day at the start of VBS and I was having a real discipline problem with some of them. One day I told them that if anyone misbehaved the next day, I was going to take them to my office and spank them. I came into the sanctuary the next day, and one boy, in particular, was really acting inappropriately. I took him to my office and spanked him with my belt on his baggy jeans. The baggy jeans made it sound like I was really spanking him hard, and his screams really made it sound like I was giving him a hard spanking. When I brought him back into the sanctuary, every child was sitting down, and you could have heard a pin drop. Later that day, when I got some time, I called his mother to tell her what I had done. She too was embarrassed, but thanked me for caring enough to want her son to behave in church. I guess I would be sued and go to jail today, but it was a different time in America, when most parents really wanted their children to behave.

As I look back on that time, none of us had an idea that we were doing anything extraordinary. We were just trying to be obedient to what we believed the Lord had given us to do.

One Man's Spiritual Journey

Herb was the dad of the young woman Julie that I mentioned earlier. Sometime after Julie had become a Christian, her parents also became Christians and were baptized into our church. One of the things that I did with our new Christians was to lead them through a new member's class, using a book written many years before by Joe T. Odle on What Baptists Believe and Why We Believe It.

I was in Herb's home one day and he was asking me about the part of the Church Covenant that said, "I will abstain from the sale of or use of alcoholic beverages of any kind." He asked me to show him in the Bible where that was specifically taught and I told him that I could not. However, it was our belief that because of the problem alcohol had become in our society, a Christian's testimony was better when he or she chose to abstain from all use of alcoholic beverages. He did not drink a lot, but did on occasion, and did not believe it would hurt his testimony. He had a large and apparently expensive wine collection on shelves in the den of their home. Nothing I could say would convince him that his testimony would be stronger without the use of alcohol of any kind. I decided to just leave it alone.

Herb was a Boy Scout Troop Leader. He had a neighbor who worked with him in the Boy Scouts. His name was Lawrence. Herb had been trying to get Lawrence to come to church with him without any success. During the summer, their Boy Scout Troop had been asked to handle the parking for the annual picnic for a large company in Columbus. It was a hot August day. During the day, someone brought cokes out to the boys and cold beers to Herb and his friend Lawrence. Herb took the beer and began to drink it. Lawrence said to him, "I thought you said you had become a Christian; why are you drinking that beer?" Herb poured out the rest of his drink and apologized to

Lawrence. I arrived at Herb's home late that afternoon to find him pouring his wine collection down the drain; his alcoholic neighbor was watching him, and begging him to give it to him. Herb turned to his neighbor and said, "If it is not good for me, it is not good for you either." He then told me the experience I have just related. Later he was able to win Lawrence to the Lord and he and his wife became a part of our church.

Herb volunteered to take half of our 3rd and 4th grade boys Sunday School class that had grown to an enrollment of 74. So when Herb took the class, he had about 32 enrolled in his class. Because he had never studied the Bible very much, he would take his Sunday School Leader's Guide with him to work so he could study his lesson during his lunch break each day. He had read in the Leader's Guide that a Sunday School teacher should visit all of his class members at least once each quarter. He wanted to be a good Sunday School teacher, so he decided he had better do that. You will not be surprised to know that his Sunday School class grew rapidly. His 4th grade class had grown to over 70 enrolled in his class, with an average attendance of about 40. WOW!!!

Thomas Bryan Goforth

Our younger son Tom made a profession of faith during a revival, while we were at Salem Baptist Church. Tom was 5 years old at the time. I guess because of the experience I had with his older brother, I was more prepared to accept his decision and did not question him as much as I had his brother. I remember that, before Tom made his decision, if I called on him to pray at the dinner table, his prayer would always be, "Thank you God for the food. Amen." Then I remember calling on him to pray at the dinner table after his profession of faith. He prayed for everyone he could think of who was sick and everyone he could think of who needed to be saved. For me, this was the assurance I needed that he had really been saved.

Years later, I was pastor of First Baptist Church, Rusk, Texas. Tom was in his first year of college. I had asked him to come home and preach one night during a revival at FBC, Rusk. Tom had attended Rusk High School his last two years of high school. That night he shared with us an experience he had the summer before his senior year in high school. He had participated in the Texas Baptist Youth Choir tour. Shortly after the tour was over, he received word that a girl who had become a really good friend, while he was on the tour, had died in a water skiing accident. That experience caused him to examine his own spiritual life. He then shared that one night after he went to bed, he actually prayed to receive Christ as his Savior.

I had noticed during his senior year, that he appeared to be a lot stronger spiritually. I had interpreted that as a personal renewal of his faith in Christ. That night, although it was over a year later, he felt the need to share with the church and his family about his conversion experience. Then he closed by turning to me and indicating that he needed to be baptized. It was a glorious night and God used that testimony to touch many of his former classmates.

Pickerington Baptist Chapel
Pickerington, Ohio

One of the churches in the Capital City Baptist Association had started a mission on the far east side of Columbus, Ohio, in Pickerington, Ohio. Pickerington was a small city of about 5,000, about 20 miles east of downtown Columbus, and just a few miles south of Interstate 70. The mission had been in existence about six months. I knew that one of the laymen in our church was feeling that God might be calling him to be a pastor. I called Chuck Magruder, who was our Director of Missions, to recommend this man. As soon as I told Chuck that I had called him to recommend someone to be the pastor of the mission in Pickerington, he interrupted me and said, "What about you?" I said, "What?" He said, "What about you as the pastor of that mission?" I responded with an emphatic no. He then told me that he would not listen to any recommendation from me until I had prayed about it myself. I told him I would pray about it, but I was sure I was to stay where I was. After several restless days and sleepless nights, I called him back to tell him that we needed to get together to talk about the possibility of me becoming the first pastor of the Pickerington Baptist Chapel.

After spending some time in Pickerington, and visiting with the pastor of the sponsoring church, I felt led to accept the call of the sponsoring church to become the first pastor of the mission in Pickerington, Ohio.

With a great deal of sadness, we announced my resignation as pastor of Salem Baptist Church, in order to accept the call to Pickerington, Ohio. I began my ministry as pastor of Pickerington Baptist Chapel the first Sunday of November 1974, which was also the 14th Anniversary of my ordination to the gospel ministry. When I accepted the call to pastor the mission in Pickerington, there were 3 adults who had already officially become members of the mission. Because both of our boys were already church members, this is the only time in my ministry when my family of four more than doubled the church enrolment. I had a meeting with them, and some others who lived in the area, who had expressed an interest in a Southern Baptist Church. There were about 15 people who attended that meeting, who actually lived in the area where the mission would minister.

The mission was meeting in the basement of a home that had been converted into a Real Estate Office. We agreed that night that we needed to find another place to worship, and that we needed somewhere that would give us a physical presence in Pickerington.

They authorized me to begin to look for something. My first impression was to go to the school to see if they had any facilities that were available. I visited with the superintendent and told him about our need. He said they did not have any appropriate space that was not already being used. Then he hesitated and said, "I do have one space but I am sure it is too big for your needs." I asked him what he was talking about and he told me that he could show it to me, because it was in the same building we were in. We left his office and walked about 50' and opened the door onto the stage of the 700 seat Gymnatorium. It had been built in the days when schools would build an auditorium which also had a stage that was also a gym floor and the school would get two buildings in one. While we were standing there, he wanted to know what I was thinking. I told him I was just wondering what it would be like to preach in this building with it full. I asked him if he would rent us this building and if so, for how much. He said that if I really wanted it, we could have it for $25.00 per week. I signed the contract that day. I also asked him about using some of the classrooms that were in the attached building for Sunday School. He said we could have them for an additional $1.00 per room. So I made arrangements for us to have three classrooms (one for nursery, one for children, and one for the youth). We only had one child who was already committed to the mission, but several of the families that had met with us had children and youth. The adults met at the front of the auditorium. So every time we needed to add a Sunday School class, we had a whole building full of classrooms and it would cost us an additional $1.00 per week to start the new class and have a place for it to meet. We also met there on Sunday evening. By the way, I did get to preach in that building full. One year the high school seniors invited me to preach their Baccalaureate Service.

We found a beautiful old house with a lovely yard that all of us loved. It was available to rent immediately. There was only one little problem with the house. When it rained, the basement would fill up with water. One time it almost covered the heating system and almost came up to the first floor; but it met our needs in getting us a place to live on short notice. Later we found a new house that was under construction, and we were able to buy our first home. While the home was being finished, we became friends with the builder and were able to get some things added that we wanted, as he was completing the house. He actually lived close to where we would soon live. One of the interesting things about where we lived is that our house was just off of the road we traveled on into town almost every day. On that road, not far from our house, was one of the still functioning covered wooden bridges in Ohio. The boys enjoyed going down and riding their bikes across the covered bridge, until one day, when a fully loaded cement mixer truck decided he could save some time by crossing the covered bridge. He got about halfway across, when the bridge gave way and he ended up nose down in the creek. Unfortunately, the state of Ohio decided to replace the bridge with a modern concrete bridge rather than repair the old bridge. That was a sad day for all of us who lived in the vicinity of the old bridge.

We found an empty house trailer, with some parking area in downtown Pickerington. We rented that and used it as office space for me and a place where we could have Wednesday night prayer meeting. So we were off and running, and almost every Sunday, our attendance began to grow.

In January of 1975, I was called in by the superintendent, and was told we could not meet there any longer. The problem was that the school had been put on a natural gas ration program because of the energy crunch. Therefore, they would not be able to turn the heat up for us on Sunday and take the chance that they would run out of gas for the school days. He said that they were just going to keep that building heated to a bare minimum. I told him that would be better than our meeting outside somewhere. So we continued to meet there during the winter of 1975. Many Sundays it would seem colder inside than it was outside. I remember one Sunday, one of our ladies came out after church and said to me, "I have on a wool pantsuit, long john underwear, this blanket wrapped around me, and I am still almost frozen." In spite of those conditions, we were having additions to the mission almost every Sunday. We were able to meet in the school on Sunday until we bought property and built our first building.

The trailer did serve us well for good exposure, while we were getting established in the community. However, there came a time when we decided, that the money we were using on that facility, could be of better use by putting it in the building fund. So we moved the office to our home and started rotating from one home to another for Wednesday evening Prayer Meeting.

Very soon, we began to talk about what our permanent name should be. Although there was another Baptist Church in the area, no one had taken the name, First Baptist Church. I suggested that we should take that name because it has such high recognition among Baptists. We did decide that we would take the name, First Baptist Church, Pickerington, Ohio. It was a good choice for a name. It made us readily identifiable to new residents who were already Baptist.

We put up a sign with our name on it at the office space we had rented. We also made some stand alone café type signs and put them out at each end of the street where we met on Sunday.

I probably should mention that, although at least two churches where I was pastor had started new missions, I had never been the pastor of a new mission. Therefore, I found myself doing my work as if we were a fully organized church. Unintentionally on my part, that created some tension between me and the pastor of the Mother Church. There came a time when he needed to come and talk to me about the importance of keeping him and his church informed on what we were doing. It was an uncomfortable meeting for both of us, but it was a meeting that I needed. I needed to be reminded of the importance of keeping our Mother Church informed, and the need to seek their approval of major decisions that we made.

There is one other thing that I need to say about an action the Mother Church made, which contributed greatly to the good start that we had. They gave us three of their best families for six months. They were there at every service, and some of them taught Sunday School until we could develop some Sunday School teachers. They also brought their tithe with them for the entire time they were with us. This was a very unselfish attitude on the part of the pastor and people of the Mother Church. They wanted to make sure they did everything they could to help ensure the success of their mission.

The Capital City Baptist Association was a strong Association of Southern Baptist Churches; Columbus was where the offices of the Baptist Convention of Ohio (Southern Baptist) were located. Pickerington was located only 20 miles east of Columbus. However, almost no one in that city of 5,000 knew anything about Southern Baptists. There is a movement among some Southern Baptists that the best way to grow a Southern Baptist Church is to keep identity with Southern Baptists unclear, and in some cases, to not even use the name Baptist in the name of the church. I have a very strong opinion on that subject. First, I believe that it is less than honest to not be very clear who we are and who we relate to as a church.

Second, I do not believe that it is what is in our name that enables us to reach people. Rather, it is how we go about ministry that draws people to our churches. Third, if we do not clearly identify who we are, there is the possibility that the time comes when we don't really know who we are. I have discovered that in very non-Southern Baptist areas, such as Ohio 30 – 40 years ago, and New York in recent years, our name has not been a hindrance to our ministry. In fact, many in other denominations have come to appreciate the positions that we have taken on moral issues which conflict with biblical teaching.

When we moved to Pickerington, I spent a lot of time just letting people get to know us. I wanted them to know that we were not some weird group that they had to fear. I very quickly became involved in the local Ministerial Association. We became an accepted congregation in the community, not because of our name, but because of our actions. We used various ways to become actively involved in the community.

We also decided, soon after I became pastor of the mission, that as soon as we could find some property and at least put up a sign that indicated the future site of First Baptist Church, the better we would be. We felt that such a move would say to the community that we were not just some little "here today, gone tomorrow" group that was meeting in one of the schools. So the church gave me permission to begin to look for property.

There was a fairly new small shopping center on the main road that led from Pickerington out to Interstate 70. This road was traveled more than any in our area. I immediately turned all of my attention toward trying to find property on this road and as near to the shopping center as possible. Every effort I made failed.

Later one of my members called to my attention some property that was not far from downtown Pickerington, on a road that led out of town in the other direction. He also called to my attention that plans were in the making for several subdivisions to be built out in that direction. I was able to make connection with the owner of the property, who was not necessarily interested in selling any property, until he found out why I was interested in buying it. He gave it some thought and agreed to sell us 10 acres. We could not afford all 10 acres, but he did sell us 6 acres with a first option to buy the other four. Our 6 acres had 650 feet of frontage on the road. I will talk about the construction of the building later, but let me just say that before we could finish our first building, four subdivisions had already been completed in the general area, where there were only open fields when we bought the property. Everyone, who came into town or to the schools from that general area, had to drive right past our property.

Early in the summer of 1975, we had a large sign painted which read, "Future Site of First Baptist Church, Pickerington." We mowed an area around that sign and had Wednesday night prayer meeting in the open air on that property during the course of that summer, unless of course, it was raining; that only happened a couple of times. We made a big event out of the sign planting. We met as far away from the property as we could. Put the sign in the back of a pick-up truck and formed a parade of cars behind the truck blowing our horns and getting as much attention as we could. We then drove the sign to the property and planted it that day. After planting that sign, we dedicated that property to the glory of God, for the purpose of proclaiming the gospel of Jesus Christ.

Later, the Pickerington Little League Association came to me and wanted to know if we had any intention of having any recreation facilities on the property. I told them that we would eventually build a softball field at one end of the property. They were in need of additional baseball fields. They said they would build the baseball field at their expense if we would guarantee that they could use it for at least five years. We wrote out a contract for usage that was agreeable to them and to us, and they then built the field. It became another way of our identifying with the community and we also got a field that was much nicer than we would have been able to afford.

The Core Membership

It was remarkable to think about some of the families that began to align themselves with us. Three of our early families to become members were all builders by trade. One man was a building contractor that had built two of the large shopping centers in Columbus. His son, who was also a builder, also joined the church. Then another man and his family became members. He was a home builder and he designed most of the homes he built. These men became crucial when the time came for us to build our first building. There were also some very accomplished business people who became a part of us in the early days. God gave us a core of very capable people who had varied backgrounds. All of them contributed to the early growth of the congregation, and to the willingness of the community to accept us as a viable congregation in the community.

About a year and a half after I became the pastor, we had a constitution service to move from mission status to a fully organized church. We organized with almost 200 charter members. This action was taken with the blessing of our Mother Church, The Capital City Baptist Association, and the Convention of Baptists in Ohio. We immediately aligned ourselves with both of these organizations, as well as the national Southern Baptist Convention.

First Vacation Bible School

I made connection with a church in Clarksville, Tennessee, that wanted to come to Ohio on a mission trip. The church sent their Youth Minister up and I spent a couple of days with him looking at the area and finding a place where they could stay. At this point in our ministry, we were still meeting in the school, and so the best plan for a VBS seemed to be to conduct several Backyard Bible Clubs in the various communities where we had members. So the plan was to conduct four Backyard Bible Clubs in subdivisions in the Pickerington area. We had people who lived in three of the four subdivisions who were already members of our mission and were willing for the Backyard Bible Clubs to meet at their homes. In the fourth subdivision we did not have anyone from that area who attended our mission. However, we did find a lady, who was not connected to our church, who was willing to have it at her home.

A church staff member from the church in Clarksville came up to look over the area several months before they would actually come back on the mission trip. During the time that he spent with me, he asked me how many would participate. I told him I would be thrilled if we enrolled a total of 100 in the 4 Backyard Bible Clubs.

We found a large building owned by a local service club that had kitchen facilities, bathrooms, and a large open area. It was located on several acres that also had a nice size pond. We were able to rent this facility for the week. They cooked their meals there. The boys slept there, and we had group meetings there daily. We found better sleeping facilities for the women and girls.

The lady who agreed to allow us to use her home for one of the Backyard Bible Clubs told me that I needed to be aware that the sub-division's Swim Club would be holding swimming classes everyday that same week and that we would not have many to attend. I told her we would just take what we got and be grateful. We ended up having 100 enrolled in that one Backyard Bible Club alone.

In the sub-division where we did not have anyone attending our church, we found a Catholic lady who was willing to have the Bible Club meet at her home. We did not know that on Sunday afternoon, before the Bible Clubs began on Monday, she went to every home in her sub-division, with a handmade brochure, inviting the children to attend. We ended up having 35 enrolled in that Bible Club.

By the time the week of Backyard Bible Clubs had come to a close, we had enrolled over 200 in our first VBS. Needless to say, both we and the mission team from Clarksville, Tennessee, were overjoyed. On Sunday night we had our VBS parent's program and well over 200 people attended. That first VBS gave us the jump start to our ministry that we really needed. It showed us that God could do a great thing in our midst.

It was a great combination of a Youth Mission Team, their sponsors from Clarksville, Tennessee, and those who had already become a part of the Pickerington Baptist Mission (First Baptist Church, Pickerington). They were all willing to do whatever needed to be done in order to teach the Bible to the children in our community, and to make connection with their parents. We were not trying to pull families from other churches; rather, we were trying to find those families who did not have a regular connection with a local church and make a connection with them.

Every day was an interesting experience. The four Backyard Bible Clubs were held at a specific home in four subdivisions that had already been designated as places where we might find prospects for our church. The members of our mission did all of the leg work that had to be done every day to make the Bible Clubs successful, and the Youth Mission Team and their sponsors from Tennessee did all of the teaching and recreation activities. For refreshments we served snow cones at each location. A local grocery store provided all of the ice we needed from their ice machine. Each day I would go to the grocery store and get the ice and bring it back to the location where we were renting a building for the week. We would run the ice through a snow cone machine and put the amount in each cooler that they would need for that day, then I would deliver the ice to the four locations. While I was there, I would make sure that I met those who were new that day.

I mentioned earlier, that we had rented a service club building for the week. Not only did the boys sleep there, but meals for the mission team were also cooked there. We would all meet there after the Bible Clubs were over, and have a reporting time while we were having lunch. I also mentioned that there was a large pond on the property. As the attendance began to grow, the youth wanted to know if their Youth Minister and I would be willing to be thrown in the pond on the last day, if the enrolment went over 200. On the last day, the enrolment reached 210. The youth had a great time taking us out and tossing us into the pond.

It was a wonderful week that made a powerful impression on all of us, as to what God could do through us, if we were just willing to be used. That week also taught us, as a new congregation, that there was nothing we could not do as long as we knew that God was in it. That was a lesson that served us well for years to come.

Trust God to Provide

On the Sunday morning at the close of that first Vacation Bible School, the pastor of the church from Clarksville, Tennessee, had come in and he preached a message on faith. While he was preaching, the Lord spoke to my heart and asked me how much faith I had. Basically he asked me if we had enough faith to begin construction of our first building and believe that He would provide the resources to finish it. I knew that we had $3,500.00 in our building fund. After church that morning, I asked the Chairman of our Building Committee, who was a contractor by profession, what it would cost us to dig the foundation and pour the floor. He said about $3,000.00. I spent considerable time that afternoon in prayer. That same Sunday evening, I shared the message I believed that I had gotten from the Lord about starting the building and trusting Him to provide the resources to finish it. The church was in complete agreement that we should do just that. We were still a mission of another church at that time, so I called their pastor the next day to tell him what we wanted to do and assured him that we had no plans to borrow any money that would then become a liability of theirs. We received permission to continue with our plan.

I mentioned earlier that three of the first families to join the mission were all builders by trade. One had built two large shopping malls in the Columbus, Ohio, area. One was a home builder who designed his own homes and said he had always dreamed of designing and building a church.

On the Wednesday night after the Sunday we had voted to start, we had prayer meeting in the home of one of our members. I had been home from prayer meeting about an hour when the phone rang. It was the home builder in our church. He said he had a question to ask me. He said that most of the people, who were at the prayer meeting that night, were still there, and they had gotten into a discussion about adding a basement to the building. He said that we could double our space for $3,000.00. He said he had already called a man who dug basements and he could begin the next morning. I told him that was not the way we did things. I told him that we would have to have a business meeting first. He wanted to know why, since most of the members were still there, and they were all in favor of doing it. I told him that we would have to raise the money first. He then told me that the money had already been raised by those who were still at the prayer meeting. Then I asked him if a certain man that I considered to be very conservative about such matters was still there. He said he was not, so I told him that he should call him first. He said they had already called him and he had wondered all along why we were not adding a basement but had not said anything, because he was not on the Building Committee. I had run out of reasons why they could not start, so I asked him what the plan was. He said he was going to be on the property at daylight the next morning and lay out the stakes for the basement and that the one that would dig the basement would be there by mid-morning.

I can tell you that I did not sleep much that night. It was a combination of enthusiasm on the part of the people, and a realization that we had done more than just state our faith that it could be done, that kept me awake. We were now putting those words into action. We started that first building about 10 months after I had accepted the call to be the pastor of a mission with 3 members. We were getting ready to build a 40' x 80' building with a 300 seat sanctuary and a full basement, and we were not borrowing any money from anybody. At the time, we had about 45 members and about 70 who were attending Sunday morning services that were still meeting in the school.

I also got to the church site not too long after daylight the next morning; our man was already there laying out the stakes so that the one digging the basement would know where to begin. I waited a little while and then I called our Director of Missions and the Pastor of the sponsoring church and told them they might want to drive over and see what was going on. So that Thursday morning, the work began on the basement that the church voted to include in the building plan, using the money that had been raised the night before, after Prayer Meeting. The original dimensions were 40′x80′ for the building, so what we ended up with was two floors that were both that size.

One day, while we were still in the process of completing the basement, I got a call from W.C. Dudley. He was the Mid-West United States Representative for the Church Loan Division of the Home Mission Board. He told me that he was in Columbus and had heard about our building project and wanted to come out and see what was happening. I encouraged him to come on out. As we stood there, while they were digging the basement, he said to me, "You know you will not get through with this project without needing some money from me. You also know that I cannot loan you any money without the approval of the Church Architecture Department of the Sunday School Board. You also know that they hate basements, and they will never approve this plan." I told him that we fully intended to be able to build the building without borrowing any money. However, if we did come to that place, I would cross that bridge when we got there. I will talk about the way the money was raised almost on a weekly basis at a later point. The time did come when we used up all available resources and did need to borrow money from the Home Mission Board. We were about 80% complete when that happened. I called Mr. Dudley to tell him I was making contact with the Architecture Department of the Sunday School Board, and that I would get back with him when I had finished that process. He just laughed and told me that he was sure I would not get their stamp of approval on the plans for two reasons: first, because we came to them after we had started and nearly completed the project, and second because one floor of the building was a basement.

I called the Church Architecture Department and made an appointment with them, and I drove from Columbus, Ohio, to

Nashville, Tennessee, for that appointment. I made the appointment for the first thing on a Tuesday morning and drove to Nashville on Monday and spent the night so I could be there early. I did not know how much time I was going to need to get them to approve our plans, but I knew that I would take all day, if necessary.

As the architect started looking at the plans, he was impressed with the overall layout of the building. However, at the far end of the building, where he saw the stairs to the second floor, he took a red pen and drew an emergency door to the outside. After he did that, I realized it was time for me to do what I knew I was going to have to, eventually, do, and tell him about the basement. So I told him that the building he was looking at was now 80% complete, and that we had hoped to complete the building without having to borrow any money. However, that was not possible, and we had started an application process with the Church Loan Division of the Home Mission Board, and I was sure he knew they could not grant us a loan without the approval of his department. Then I told him that the floor he kept referring to as the first floor was, in fact, a basement and that he had just drawn a plan for us to cut a hole in an eight foot high, poured concrete wall which was already there. I then told him that I knew that we should have come to them for advice before we started, but we were just trying to be obedient to what we believed the Lord wanted us to do when we started. I also told him that I knew they hated basements, but it was the cheapest way for us to get twice the space we would have otherwise had and this seemed to us to be the best route for us to take. I told him that in Ohio, basements were a standard way of getting additional space. Because of the severe winters we had, all structures had to dig down four feet to get below the frost line for the foundation and you could go four more feet and have another whole floor the same size as the one above it.

So I told him that I was prepared to sit there and let him fuss at me all day, if it would make him feel better. I was, however, not prepared to leave his office without his stamp of approval on the plans. He looked at me and said, "You are really serious aren't you?" I assured him that

I was. I then told him I was not trying to be ugly with him; I just needed him to know that our people had made incredible personal sacrifices for us to get to the place where we were, and we really needed his help. He looked at our plans again and wanted to know what areas were not already complete. I told him that most of the interior walls of the ground floor were not yet installed. He did make some helpful suggestions that we did use, then he stamped and signed our plans. I had a copy of the plans with me for him to keep and I had another copy to send on to the Home Mission Board. I mailed that copy before I left Nashville.

I used a phone there at the Sunday School Board, and called W. C. Dudley at the Home Mission Board in Atlanta. I told him I was in the process of mailing the approved plans to him, and that he should get them in a few days. At first, he did not believe I had told them that one of the floors was a basement. I finally convinced him that I had and that the word basement was even written on the floor plan. He was astonished. Later he reminded me that this was the second time I had come to him for money after we had started a church building. He said, "Jim, don't you know that it is normal to seek a loan before you start a building rather than in the middle of the process?" I assured him I knew that, and I would try to be more normal next time. He laughed and said that the problem was, that I just did not have a very normal approach to anything. Over the years, when I would see him at various meetings, he would tell others that I gave him more grey hair than almost any other pastor he knew, but that I always seemed to be able to get things done. I guess the truth is, I never was very good at coloring inside the lines. It has always been my approach that, if the Lord wanted you to get something accomplished, He would honor your efforts, as long as you were doing it for the right reason, and seeking to bring honor and glory to His Kingdom.

That really has been my rule of thumb for doing things. How can I best do this and bring honor and glory to my Lord Jesus Christ and His Kingdom? I wish I could say that I have always accomplished that goal, but I can say that has always been my desire.

Most of the work was done by the men of the church on Saturdays. The work began in late August of 1975, continued through the winter, and into the next year. We worked almost from sun rise to sun set every Saturday, except for a three week period of time when the County Building Inspector drove by, saw what we were doing, and shut us down until we got a building permit.

I had asked our men about getting such a permit. They were sure that we were so far out in the country that the Building Inspector would never come by, and if he did, would not require one from us. However, with the winter months rapidly approaching, we found ourselves shut down from future work on the building, until we could get a building permit. As quickly as I could make an appointment with the Building Inspector, I did so. I told the builders in our church, particularly the one who had built two of the largest shopping centers in Columbus, Ohio, that I thought it would be best if I went to talk to him by myself. I told them that I thought that the argument that we did not know any better would be more believable from the one who really did not know any better, and maybe I could appeal for mercy.

So that is the approach that we made, and I spent all of the time dealing with the Building Inspector. The outcome of my first meeting with him, when I was as contrite as I knew how to be, was that I came away with a list of things that I needed to present to him. For those of you who know me, you may be surprised to know that I can really be contrite, when I really have to be.

The main thing that I needed was to have plans and specifications signed by a licensed architect or structural engineer. The house builder in our church, who was the one who designed the building, was neither of the two. He did not have to be in order to build private homes. In his defense, because we were building a church, he did not think that the same rules would apply that applied to commercial buildings.

A local Southern Baptist attorney had a friend in Dayton, Ohio, who was a strong Christian, and was a structural engineer. I went to see him; he agreed to take our plans, draw something that looked more professional, and write the specifications. When I finished putting together everything the Building Inspector had asked for, I made another appointment with him. What I neglected to say about the building was that, at the time we were shut down, the outside shell of the building was already up, including the floor for the first floor of the building.

When I went back to see the Building Inspector, I discovered that he had been out and had gone through the building with a fine-toothed comb. One of the things that he said to me was that the building code called for an eight foot ceiling, and that he was sure that after we got the sheetrock on the basement ceiling, we would not have more than 6'5" clearance. I assured him that my builder had assured me that we would have a 7' clearance in the basement, and that he knew of buildings in the county that had 7' ceilings which had passed inspection. The Inspector looked at me and said, "Reverend, I am trying to work with you, but when you are finished, if that ceiling is 1" under 7'clearance, you will have to tear it out and start over. The next time I met with the Building Committee, I was able to present them with the building permit, but I also gave them the warning I had received about the basement ceiling. The truth is that when we put up the ceiling drywall, we really had to screw it down tight in order to get the 7' clearance.

One of the things that I felt strongly about was identifying with the local community while we were constructing the building. I went to the local hardware store and told the owner that, if he would give us a good price, I would buy everything from him that we needed, and that he could supply. He did make us a good offer, and throughout the construction, we bought from him all of the practical construction supplies we needed. It was also a blessing to us, because his business was only about a quarter of a mile away. Because I was the one on Saturday with the least amount of building skills, I was usually the "gofer" when we needed supplies on Saturday. There was one very humorous experience one Saturday that had to do with my lack of knowledge of building terminology. I was told to go to the hardware store and get 5 pounds of 16 penny nails. So off I went to the hardware store which, by the way, was the local gathering place for the men to get together and drink coffee and solve all of the world's problems. I went in and was looking around at the nails. The owner came over and wanted to know if he could help me. I told him I wanted 5 pounds of those nails that cost 16 cents. That seemed to get everyone's attention, because everyone quit talking and looked at me. Then the owner asked me what exactly they had told me to come and get, and I told him, 5 pounds of 16 penny nails. While everyone was laughing, he told me that was the size of the nails. The only thing you can do at a time like that is just let everyone have their laugh. By the way, when I started to leave, I invited everyone to come to church the next day. I told them that I knew a lot more about the Bible than I did about construction terminology.

Because one of our men had built two shopping malls in Columbus, he had bought millions of dollars of building materials from suppliers all across the area. The Lord used those connections to enable us to build our building at a much lower cost, than it would have cost otherwise. In those days, a turnkey construction job would cost $40.00 a square foot. When all was said and done, we built the building for $11.00 a square foot. Almost every week I was going somewhere to pick up something that was being donated to the church, things such as: exterior and interior doors, windows, light fixtures, etc. One of our builders was remodeling a school. His bid included getting rid of everything they were replacing. He called me one day and told me he had six pianos that he had to get rid of and he wanted the church to have first choice. This enabled us to have some extra pianos in our building that we would not otherwise have had. There was another time when, on their secular job, they were remodeling a school, including their cafeteria. They were putting all new furniture in the cafeteria. That school gave us as much furniture as we needed for our fellowship hall from the furniture they were discarding.

How the Money Was Raised

How did the money come in for the building of our first building? When we started, we had $3,500.00 in our building fund. It was estimated that it would cost $3,000.00 for the foundation and floor. So we voted to start and trust the Lord for the rest of the money we would need. Then, as I have already shared, it was decided after Wednesday night prayer meeting to add a basement to the plan, and those present that night pledged an additional $3,000.00 for the cost of the basement.

Now, here is the way we raised the rest of the money until we got the building 80% complete and borrowed $40,000.00, to complete the building. On Sunday morning the Chairman of the Building Committee would come to me and tell me how much money we needed to buy the materials that would be needed to do the work that was scheduled for the following Saturday. I then would tell our Music Director, who was also the Church Treasurer. During the worship service the Music Director would announce to the people how much money was needed before the following Saturday to buy the building materials for that day. He would then say to them that we needed to raise that amount of money before we left that day so that the materials could be ordered. Every Sunday, within 10 minutes after the service was over, the Music Director would come to me and tell me that he either had the money in hand or that it had been promised to him. I would then tell the Chairman of the Building Committee that we had the money and would announce to those that were still hanging around, which was almost everyone, that we would be able to work the next Saturday. That is exactly what took place week after week while we kept on building the building the Lord had led us to build.

One week I was in the local bank and the bank President said that he would like to talk to me. He asked me if I knew what our church members were doing in order for us to be able to build our first building. I told him that I only knew that they were being very generous. He said he wanted me to know just how generous they were. He then told me that some of them had completely emptied their savings account and then had set up an open-ended loan. The reason they set up open-ended loans was so they could borrow as much as was needed in order for the church to build its first building. It was an extremely humbling experience for me to hear of the unselfish witness our people were having in the community where we served. I just looked at him and told him what a great group of people they were. I told him they were doing this because they were simply seeking to be obedient to their Lord.

I did not have any way of following up on what happened to the personal finances of those people, and I would not have anyway. However, I do know this; you cannot out give God. Without knowing any specifics, I know that the Lord rewarded every one of those families for being obedient to the Lord. Another thing that I know is that they were teaching their children a wonderful truth about being obedient to God. I know that just from what I have seen in the lives of our children when they became adults, some of the most powerful teaching that we do with our children is not with our mouths, but with our deeds.

It Happened on Saturdays

When I was talking about the success of the Bus Evangelism Ministry at Salem Baptist Church, Columbus, Ohio, I made the comment that the success of Sunday really happened on Saturday. The same could be said about this building project. The bulk of the work happened on Saturday. Basically all of our men had full-time jobs and could only work on the weekend. From time to time there would be a job we had to hire someone to do and that would be done during the week. About the only one who could work during the week was me and sometimes I could not do things right even with supervision. Eventually, there came a time when there were a few things they could let me do during the week. For example, when we put the plywood down for the floor on the main floor of the building, they let me do the bulk of the nailing during the week. They put the flooring down and nailed the four corners, then during the week, I finished nailing them down. Our Building Chairman said to me that it would be alright, whatever it looked like because they were going to cover it with carpet. Once I heard one of our young men say that he knew for sure that his pastor did not cuss, because of all of the times he had seen me hit my thumbs and fingers with a hammer without cussing.

There was one other job that I was allowed to do during the week; I did it with a young veterinarian in our church. When we dug the basement, it was the time of year when it was too cold to pour the concrete floor. They went ahead and brought in the pea gravel that would be under the concrete, and continued with the building, with the plan to pour the concrete in the spring. One Sunday our building chairman came to me and said that we had a problem. We had too much pea gravel in the basement, which would make the floor too high, which would mean that we would not be able to have the 7' ceiling we had promised the Building Inspector. He said that we

196

needed to get an inch and a half of the gravel out. Because the basement was completely enclosed, there was only one way to do it, with a shovel and a wheel barrow. The building was 80' long and the only exit outside was at one end of the building. So for a solid week, the young veterinarian, Tom, left all of the vet business to his wife, and he and I hauled gravel out of an 8' deep basement. Down at the end where the stairs to the outside were going to be, we made a ramp and we would push the wheel barrow up that ramp and dump it, then start over again. Come to think of it, no wonder I have had so much back pain as an old man. As we worked our way from the far end of the building, the builder would come every evening when he got off from work and level the gravel and shoot a grade to show us where to pick up the work the next day.

When I think about the various things that we did in order for the building to be completed, I am amazed. What I just described to you may sound like something you would never do. We did not think about it like that. When an obstacle got in our way, we just did what we had to do to overcome that obstacle.

One of the funny things I think about, when I think about those Saturdays, was lunch time. One Saturday we were sitting in one of our church buses eating lunch, with the bus motor running so we could get warm. The ladies who were preparing lunch that day decided that, because it was so cold, some homemade soup would be good, and it was. However, our builder was the kind of guy who at least had to have some meat on a sandwich. He felt like that stuck with him better throughout the day. He came to me and said that we had the soupiest women he had ever met, and he wanted someone making sandwiches every week. "Our soupy women" became the joke of our men.

One day, in particular, that I remember was the day we put up the walls to the main floor. We knew that was going to be the project that day and had asked everyone to come as early as possible so that hopefully we could get it all done that day. We would build a section of wall studs on the floor of the building and then pull it into place

197

and bolt it to the foundation. Then we would nail some support beams to it and start on the next section. As it got almost dark, I really became concerned that someone was going to get hurt. We had completed one end and both sides. I suggested that we anchor them the best we could and call it a night. I told them that they could not see what they were doing and someone was going to get hurt. One man asked if they wanted to finish before they went home and they all said, "Yes." They then laid down their tools and went and got in their cars and pulled them around to that side so that their car lights would enable us to see what we were doing. Then they finished building that last set of wall studs and pulled them into place. When that wall went up, a shout of joy went up from a group of worn out men. They did a few things to anchor the whole thing in case of a heavy wind. We then knelt inside those walls and thanked God for a wonderful day, and everyone went home tired but happy. When the people came to church the next day at the school, almost everyone had driven by the church building site on their way to church. Needless to say, there was great enthusiasm that morning.

The next Saturday, a crane was rented for the day along with its operator, and all of the roof trusses were put in place that day. When that was completed, there was enough daylight left to nail supports to the trusses, so that the wind would not damage them. That Sunday there was a lot of enthusiasm at church because the building was beginning to take shape and you could sense that everyone believed this was really becoming a reality. You could also sense that same kind of feeling in the community.

I have already mentioned that my brother and his family came to visit at Christmas the year we were building the building. My brother overheard our builder expressing concern that the roof decking that had been put on the day before, had only been nailed down at the corners. It had snowed during the night, and he was fearful that the decking would buckle before we could get back the next Saturday to nail it down. Our family plan was that we were going to drive to Canton, Ohio, the next day so that my brother and his family could visit the Pro Football Hall of Fame. When we got back home from church, my brother suggested that he and I go the next morning and nail down the decking before we went to Canton. I told him there was a good possibility that we would not finish in time to drive to Canton before the Hall of Fame closed for the day. I knew they were going to have to start back to Texas the next day, but he insisted, so I called the builder and told him what we were going to do the next day. It did take us longer than we had hoped. Because of the snow on the roof, we had to be very careful. We would sweep the snow off of a section, nail it down and go on to the next section. Neither one of us slid off of the roof, although we came close a couple of times.

One of the amazing things to me was how many men kept coming back every Saturday. I think one of the main reasons was that we had such knowledgeable builders who were in charge, and there was one who was recognized by everyone else as being in charge. Every Saturday, when we got there, he had already taken the time to lay out the schedule of what needed to be done that day, and everyone just plugged in where they felt their skills could best be used. There were a few like me, who just tried to stay out of the way and do whatever we could do to be a help and not a hindrance.

When we got to the place where we were doing inside finish work, and the heating system had been installed, we started meeting at the building on Wednesday night. We would have a short Bible Study and Prayer Meeting, and then, as many as could, stayed as long as they could to work on the inside. At this point everyone, men, women, youth, and even older children, found things they could do.

Obviously there are many stories that could be told about various little incidents that came up during the year we were building our first building. However, the thing that keeps coming to my mind is that "the people had a mind to work," and work we did, week after week for almost a year. There were times when people rubbed one another the wrong way, but all of those were insignificant.

What I do know is that the common goal of getting that first building completed, and the sacrifices that were made both physically and financially by almost every family, drew them together in an unusually tight bond. It was a joy to behold and an honor to be called their pastor. It seemed that everyone found some way that they could make a positive contribution to what was going on in the life of the church.

Wonderful Activity of God

While the building was still under construction, the church was still growing. Men, women, boys, and girls were being saved. People were leaving their nice, comfortable homes and driving up to the school to come to a church, which they knew would not be heated. Almost every Sunday in that old cold Gymnatorium, people were being saved, and others were joining the fellowship of the church. One corner of the balcony is where I took a man and led him to the Lord after church. A few weeks later I took his parents up there and led both of them to the Lord. On Sunday, that old school building became "Holy Ground." We were one of the fastest growing Southern Baptist Missions in Ohio, in an environment that you would not think would be conducive to church growth.

My wife had started a much smaller scale Bus Evangelism Ministry than we had in Columbus; nevertheless, it was also successful in reaching people with the gospel. We bought two old school buses that went in different directions from the church every Sunday. It was the Bus Ministry that caused us to find the first Black families that had moved into our community. Their children first rode the bus to church, but in time we were able to reach the parents in both families. The husband of one of those families went by the name, Tom. A couple of years after they joined the church, Tom became our treasurer. The first time he signed my pay check he signed it with the initials D.R., instead of Tom. I asked him where he got Tom out of D.R. He said to me, "My mom named me Doris and when you are a boy in South Louisiana with the name, Doris, you get a nickname in a hurry. Tom also became a close personal friend.

When the children of the other family started riding our bus, I went during the week to visit the parents and discovered that the mother was Anglo and the dad was African American. The husband had to work late that night and I did not get to meet him. I remember, as I was inviting her to church, I was also wondering how they would be received by our people. I am happy to say that they were received warmly into our fellowship. Later I had the privilege of baptizing her and both of their children, and the husband moved his membership into our fellowship. He had a beautiful tenor voice and would sing for the church services from time to time. Their son was about the same age as our son Tom and the two of them became very close friends. He would either come to our house or Tom would go to his. Virginia and I became very close to this family. I baptized Linda when she was 33 years old. One year later she was diagnosed with double breast cancer. I preached her funeral when she was 35 years of age. I think this may have been one of the hardest funerals I ever did.

Linda had confided in me that from the time they married, she had never felt completely accepted by anyone, until she found our church. She said that she really did not feel accepted by the black community and she knew that she was not accepted by much of the white community. Though the time that this family was in our lives was brief, it was a great time of growing for me and for my family. I believe that my two sons may be the two least prejudiced men I know anywhere. I think part of the reason that is true is, because of what they experienced in our home growing up. Virginia and I made a lot of mistakes with our boys; I praise God that He helped us teach them how everyone is to be treated, and they are much stronger than I am.

I don't even know how to describe how much I learned to love this family. During the time that she was sick, I don't know how many times her husband and I just sat and cried. He and I became like brothers in so many ways. We were, of course, spiritual brothers, but we became so much more. As it became obvious that she was probably not going to survive, I made regular trips to visit them in the hospital. At that point I had moved to a church near Dayton, Ohio, so I was no longer their pastor, but they were my dear friends. So I would drive from Medway, Ohio, to Columbus, Ohio, about once a week to visit her and seek to encourage him. So, for me, preaching her funeral was a very emotional experience. It was also a difficult time for our son Tom, who had to watch one of his best friends lose his mother when he was just a boy.

I praise God for what he has done in my heart over the years and, in particular, what he has done in my heart regarding racial questions between people. I am particularly grateful that, during the time that my own attitude toward others who were different from me in some way was growing and changing for the better, that the Lord shielded our sons and allowed them to just see everyone for who they were and not for the color of their skin, or anything else that might make them different from us.

One of the toughest hurdles for me personally was interracial marriage. The relationship I have just described, that was developed while we were at Pickerington, did more to change my view point on that issue, than any other experience that I have ever had. All of the reasons that I had given myself for not accepting an interracial marriage as legitimate in the eyes of the Lord, were blown away as I got better acquainted with this couple. They and their two children were as happy a family as I have ever known. This was particularly true after she became a Christian and the whole family became involved in the life and ministry of our church. I will never forget the Sunday morning that he sang the special music for our worship service for the first time. He sang the Lord's Prayer a cappella. I was amazed at the beautiful high tenor voice that came out of this Air Force officer. I was blessed beyond measure, not by the flawless way that he sang, but by the spirit in which he sang. When he finished, you could have heard a pin drop on the carpet in that sanctuary. In that moment, God did something special in our congregation, and from that moment forward, they were no longer seen as an interracial couple; they were seen as a vital part of our congregation. It was one of those moments in time, when the Lord stepped into our midst, did something wonderful, and you were just glad you were there.

Frankly, like a lot of other things, I had not thought about that family and the impact they made on my life as a relatively young pastor, until I started this project. If nothing else good comes out of this writing experience than the Lord reminding me of the things that He did in my past to make me at least a little more like Him, then it will have been worth all of the effort.

Today, there is an interracial couple here in Rusk, that although they are much younger than us, I consider them very close friends. Without a doubt, the relationship I had with that couple in Ohio, 40 years ago, had much to do with the expanding relationships that I have today.

One of my most unusual experiences with a Pastor Search Committee came while I was at Pickerington. One Monday night during the summer, our phone rang. The call was from the Chairman of the Pastor Search Committee from a church in Galion, Ohio. He had called to tell me that my name had been given to them and they felt impressed that I was to be their next pastor. They wanted to come hear me preach the next Sunday. I told him that I had no indication at all that the Lord was finished with me where I was, and I was not interested. I also told him that for that reason I did not want them showing up in our church and creating some unnecessary tension in our church. He finally promised me that they would not come the next Sunday, but encouraged me to pray about it because they felt so strongly about it. I promised him that I would pray about it, but was fairly sure I already knew the answer.

The next Monday night my phone rang again. It was the same man who called the week before. He called to tell me that they were so convinced that I was to be their next pastor, that they did not even need to come hear me preach. He then invited me to come and preach for their church as a candidate to be their next pastor. I tried to tell him that was not the way churches did it. He was persistent, and so much so, that it caused me to wonder if I was closing a door that the Lord was really trying to open.

I then made a suggestion to him. We had already planned a week of vacation. We were borrowing a pop-up camper from one of our church families, and were going up to Lake Erie to camp out for a week. This church was located about halfway between where we lived and Lake Erie. I told him that I would agree to come and just be their supply preacher for the day, but I did not want the church to know that the Pastor Search Committee was considering me as their possible next pastor. He agreed to that; he promised me that they would keep their considerations away from the church. We arrived on Sunday morning and I was to preach Sunday morning and evening, then we would make our way on up to Lake Erie the next day. During the announcement period on Sunday morning, it was announced that I would meet with the search committee that night before church. At that meeting they tried to get me to allow them to present my name to the church that night for a vote. I refused to do that, but promised to pray about it throughout the week, and they could call me when I got back home the following Saturday night.

They did call me the following Saturday night and asked for permission to vote on me the next day. I told him no, but I also told him that I would drive back up there on Tuesday night, meet with them one more time, and then give them a final answer. That night I had a hard time sleeping. I got up and began to pray. I don't like to use what I call "Fleece Praying" often, but I do when I feel that it is necessary. It was the third week in August. I prayed that the Lord would do something so dramatic in the services the next day that I would be absolutely sure if I was to stay or go. On that third Sunday morning in August, a Sunday when the attendance was usually down, I walked into the sanctuary for the worship service and the house was full. There were well over 300 in attendance that day. When I gave the invitation that morning, nine people came to receive Christ as their Savior, and six more moved their membership to our church. I went home that day rejoicing that I knew the Lord had told me I was to stay right where I was.

I called the Chairman of the Pastor Search Committee and told him what had happened. I told him about the way I had prayed on Saturday night, and then I told him what had happened on Sunday morning. I asked him how he thought I should interpret what had happened. There was a long silence on the other end of the phone. He then said that he did not know how they missed it, but it sure did look like the Lord was telling me to stay where I was. I thanked him for the honor they had given me and assured him that I would be praying for them.

Petition

I had another first and thankfully only experience of its kind in my entire life and ministry. It was Memorial Day, and we had our annual Church Picnic and had spent the day playing softball and fellowshipping with one another. I had noticed that several of our people who normally came to those kinds of functions were not there, but did not think a lot about it. We had been home for less than 30 minutes, when the phone rang. It was one of our deacons. He told me that he and another deacon would like to meet with me at the church, and they wanted to meet right then. I agreed to meet with them. I told my wife where I was going, and that I was concerned that they were not up to anything good.

I went by one other church member's home and asked to borrow his portable tape recorder. I told him where I was going and that I wanted proof, after the fact, of whatever would be said during the meeting. He then suggested that he go with me to serve as an observer of what took place. This man was a very good personal friend of mine and a man with a lot of resources at his disposal. On the way to the meeting he encouraged me to keep my cool whatever might happen. He also told me not to worry about my job, and said that if they were trying to fire me, he would form an evangelistic association the next day for me and I would never miss my salary.

When we got to the meeting, I explained to the two deacons that my friend was there as an observer, but if this meeting was not about me and my job security, he was prepared to go home. They were caught by surprise by him being there but did not say that he should go. They then presented me with a petition that they had spent that day going to people's homes and having them sign. The petition read, "For the good of the church, we the undersigned ask our pastor to resign."

There were about 30 names on the petition, including both of their names. So I asked them if this was how they had spent the day, while most of the church family was enjoying our annual Memorial Day picnic; they told me it was.

I asked them the grounds upon which this request was being made, and they asked me what I meant. I then told them that they only had two reasons that could be valid for them to make such a request. The only thing they could think of to say was what the petition itself said, "for the good of the church." When I asked them to be more specific, they could not. I will say that I was not surprised with some of the names that were on the petition, but there were others that greatly surprised me.

After about an hour of discussion, it was obvious that we were not getting anywhere. I then told them that I was very concerned about how a move, such as this, would affect all of the young Christians in our church. Most of our church members were new Christians. This meeting with them was being held on Memorial Day, Monday night, and they wanted me to resign effective Wednesday night. I reminded them that I had a wife and two boys to support, and they were giving me a two-day notice that I should vacate my job and lose my ability to support my family. I then told them that, if they would give me time to leave with dignity, I would leave. I explained to them that leaving with dignity meant allowing me the time to find another church, and that process could take several months. When I said that, I thought my friend, who had told me to keep my cool, was going to explode. He said, "Wait a minute, I think I just lost my pastor and I didn't even get a vote." Then he said he could go out and get a petition with many more names than were on that one, which would say that if the pastor left they were leaving also. This opened up another whole area of discussion that took a great deal of time.

The bottom line was that they decided to let the church discuss it on Wednesday night. I was not sure that was a good idea, but decided to allow it. On Tuesday night, one of the two deacons came to me and apologized and asked that his name be taken off the list. His grown son also came and did the same thing. By Wednesday night, several people had already contacted me and asked that their names also be removed from the petition. I discovered that it was really two women who had stirred this whole thing up. One repented and the other left the church angry.

Several months later the Lord did lead me to another church; however, I am sorry to say, I left without making an effort to make things right with those two women. What they did was wrong. However, Scripture does not allow you to hold a grudge, even when you are the one who has been wronged. I will have more to say about the subject of restoring relationships later.

Knowing God's Will

Several years ago my son Jim asked me if I believed I had ever made a mistake in any of the moves I made from one church to another. I told him that I believed that was almost an impossible question for me to answer. All I knew to go on was that I made the best decision I knew how to make at the time, and genuinely believed it to be the right decision.

I do remember two times in the leaving process at Pickerington that I believe the Lord kept me from making the wrong decision. I use the term, leaving process, because I believe there comes a time when the Lord starts preparing you to wind down your ministry in one place, in preparation for His next assignment.

It was shortly after the petition incident that the Lord began to prepare my heart. First, I was contacted by a church in Fairborn, Ohio. That contact led me to accept an invitation to spend a weekend with them and preach in view of a call as pastor on Sunday morning. For the most part, the weekend went very well. Then I preached on Sunday morning to a packed house, gave the invitation, and 8 people responded to receive Jesus Christ as their Savior. I left there that afternoon, convinced that, because of what I had just experienced, I was to be their next pastor.

I was leaving from there to drive to the Southern Baptist Convention in Atlanta with my family and a pastor friend and his wife. The search committee was very excited and was sure there would be a very positive vote that night. I told him I would stop on our journey and check with him about the vote. I did stop about 8:30 PM that night to call the chairman of the committee. Before he said a word, I knew something had not gone well. The bottom line was that there were

100 people there to vote and the vote was split exactly 50 – 50. I was confused, but the good news was that I still was in a place that I loved.

Shortly after that, I got a call from a small church in Depew, New York, which is just outside of Buffalo, New York. I found out that my Director of Missions had recommended me to this church. My close friend in Pickerington was President of a Fortune 500 company in the Buffalo area. When I told him what I was considering, he got excited, because he had wanted to talk to me about starting an industrial chaplaincy in his plant in Buffalo. I did go and spend a weekend with this church. The weekend went very well. I preached in both services on Sunday with the understanding that they were going to vote on me at the close of the service. At the last minute they decided to delay the vote until the following week. Had they voted that night to call me, I probably would have accepted the call.

I was somewhat confused about what had happened, until I received a call from the Pastor Search Committee of the Medway Baptist Church, Medway, Ohio. They told me that they had been praying about me for weeks and wanted to come hear me preach the next Sunday. The next day I called them back and gave them permission to come. I then called the church in New York and told them what was happening and told them I did not want them to go ahead with the vote on me on Sunday. However, I got a call from New York on Sunday afternoon to tell me that they had gone ahead and voted to call me as their pastor and that the call was a unanimous call for me to be their next pastor. I had to tell him I had just accepted the invitation from the church in Ohio to come, in two weeks, to preach for them as a candidate to be their next pastor. I assured the church in New York that I would be praying for them, but I was sure I was not to be their next pastor. The church at Medway, Ohio, did call me and that will be the next stop in this journey. The church in New York called me several times to see if I would change my mind. The last time they called, he asked me, "Are you sure you are not to come here?" I told him that I was so sure, that the moving van was literally at my house while we were talking, to move us to Medway, Ohio.

So three times in the five years I was at Pickerington, the Lord kept me from making the wrong choice. The first time, the Lord confirmed that I was to stay instead of go. The other two times, although it was time for me to go, the Lord kept me from going to the wrong place. Both times, had those churches called me, I would have accepted, and both times, I would have been wrong. There is at least one huge reason that the Lord sent me to Medway, and I will share it in that segment.

Discipleship

Before I leave this segment in my life, I need to talk about one of the most life changing experiences I ever had, and it happened while I was at Pickerington, Ohio. I had been the Chairman of Evangelism for Capital City Baptist Association for five years. It was that time of year when I needed to make my annual report to the association on evangelism activity in the association for the past year. I decided to do something different than I had done in the past. Instead of just reporting on people that were being saved and baptized, I decided to try to find a way to find out how we were doing in conserving those who were being saved.

I used the records of our association and chose 10 churches to use as a plumb line. Two of the 10 churches included two of mine, the one where I had been pastor, and the one where I was now pastor. I looked first of all at how many people those 10 churches had baptized over a 5 year period of time. As a way to gauge how many of those we had won were now growing in the Lord, I looked at how much the average Sunday School attendance had grown in those same churches over the same period. What I discovered was astounding. Those 10 churches had baptized over 2,800 people during that 5 year period of time. However, when I looked to see how much the average Sunday School attendance had grown during that same period of time, I discovered that the growth was only a little over 100 in total attendance in Bible Study in those same 10 churches over that same 5 year period of time.

Having 2,800 people saved and baptized into the fellowship of those churches is a good number, however, the records showed that nearly 2,700 of them were not even enlisted in a regular Bible Study program. In other words, we were doing a lousy job of discipling those we were winning. I promised the Lord that, if He would show me how to be an effective discipler of His people, I would begin to make sure that those we were winning were also becoming mature Christians.

While I remained at Pickerington, I used whatever I could find that I thought might be helpful. We even developed some things of our own. The main thing was that we were at least beginning to try to correct practices of the past. About the only thing that I had done at Salem was a New Member's Class on "What Baptists Believe." It certainly was helpful for them to understand what we believe and why, but there were no tools in this study that allowed them to grow as Christians.

Medway Baptist Church, Medway, Ohio

I did not know it at the time, but this place of service would prove to be a brief stop in our journey. Although it was for only a short period of time, there was a very specific purpose, for me and for the church at Medway, for me to be there. There was a great group of people there that I came to love very quickly. They were very thoughtful of us as a family in many ways.

The ministry at Medway was a good one. The church was fairly strong, in fact probably stronger than any church I came to at the beginning of my ministry there. I would say that my time there was characterized, for the most part, by strong support from most of the leadership and the congregation.

Our boys were getting to high school and middle school age. They both seemed to be fitting in with the other youth in our church, and were making their own mark on their identity at school. Jim was doing well on the High School Soccer Team and was about to become the kicker on the High School Football Team. Tom was doing well in football and was also playing some basketball.

MasterLife Seminar

It was during this time that I received a brochure from our State Church Training Director about a seminar for some new discipleship material known as MasterLife. It looked like what I had been praying for and looking to find. I called our State Director and asked him what he knew. He did not know a lot but felt it was something worth looking into. He said that a church could not get the material without someone from the church going through the week-long training seminar. He then told me that there was a seminar coming up soon in Houston, Texas. Because my parents lived north of Houston, I knew that I could go and stay with them. The only thing the trip would cost me was an airplane ticket, so I decided to go. The conference started on Monday evening and went through Friday noon. I decided to stay over the weekend in order to spend some time with my parents and go visit my brother.

My plan was that I would go back to Ohio and introduce this material to our church and also be a resource person for our State Convention in this new discipleship material. I did not know, until after I had arrived, that my mother had called my brother's pastor and asked him if he knew of any churches in Texas he could recommend me to for consideration. That is when I found out that my brother's pastor had made arrangements for the Pastor Search Committee of First Baptist, Rockdale, to come and hear me preach at First Baptist, Caldwell, on Sunday night. I told my mother that she was going to have to call the pastor and cancel that, because I was sure my ministry was not over in the church in Ohio. She told me I would have to call him myself. So I called the pastor at Caldwell and told him I appreciated him being polite to my mother, but that she had made this request without consulting me and that I had no feelings that I needed to leave where I was. He then proceeded to tell me that he had made the arrangements with the church at Rockdale because he felt led of the Lord to do it and not because my mother had asked him to do it. Then he said, if I wanted it cancelled, I would have to do it myself. He spoke with such conviction that I decided to go ahead and keep the appointment. I called my wife and told her what was going on so that she could begin to pray about it.

Meanwhile, I was in the midst of what would prove to be one of the biggest life-changing experiences of my life. The MasterLife Seminar was led by Avery Willis, the author of the material. Avery would go on to lead many of these seminars; this was the second one he ever led. The material was literally hot off of the press. The seminar started Monday afternoon. We had another session Monday night. Then there were morning, afternoon, and evening sessions Tuesday – Thursday and a closing session on Friday morning. Since it was about an hour and a half drive from my parent's home to the church where the seminar was being held, there was very little time for me to visit with my parents during that week.

I was receiving just what I needed. Along with the material that was being taught, there were little signs hanging on the walls all over the room. One sign caught my attention and grabbed my heart. It said, "You have to be what you teach." Since that week in the spring of 1981, that has become the motto for my life. I don't always live up to it as much as I should, but the desire of my heart, ever since that day, is "to be what I teach." My wife made me a cross stitched sign that still hangs over my desk to this day, reminding me that "I have to be what I teach."

I did go that weekend and preach for the search committee of First Baptist Church, Rockdale, Texas. When I met with them after the service, I told them about the week I had just experienced. I told them that they needed to know that whether I stayed where I was, or moved somewhere else, what I had just learned and experienced would be a major part of my ministry. The bottom line is that they did extend a call to me to come and serve as their pastor, and I felt led to accept.

217

The church at Medway already had a revival scheduled in the spring of 1981; I really felt that we needed to go ahead with that revival. Also, I felt I should let the boys finish out the school year in Ohio, because it was so close to the end of the school year. So we worked it out with the church in Texas that we would not come until June, which meant that I went about a month before announcing my resignation in Ohio, in order for things to stay as normal as possible for as long as possible.

Financial Responsibility

One of the things that I did not know about the Medway church was that it was seriously in debt with numerous small bills that amounted to well over $15,000.00, and there did not seem to be any urgency about getting those bills paid. We were so far behind in payments to the Sunday School Board for literature that we could not order any more literature without the check coming with the order. I had tried over and over to talk to the church leadership about this, but just was not getting anywhere.

On the last night of our Spring Revival, I felt the Lord leading me to do something. I motioned for Virginia to come to the front. I told her that I believed that the Lord wanted us to take $1,000.00 out of our savings account and give it to the church to go toward the paying off of bills. I also told her that I believed the Lord was telling me that we could not take any more salary from the church, until they were caught up on the bills. She told me to do whatever the Lord told me to do. At the close of the invitation, I shared with the church what we were giving and that I could not accept any more salary until the church was caught up on its bills. I then placed my check for that week in the offering plate.

One of my seminary friends was preaching that revival for me. When I took him to the airport the next day he said, "Jim, you know that you cannot out give God. I want you to call me when God gives you that money back and tell me how he did it." I assured him that I would do that.

On Monday night, the Church Council called me into a meeting. They wanted me to know that I had to take my salary. I told them that what I had to do was to be obedient to the Lord, and He had told me that I could not take any more salary until they caught up on their bills. I then told them that they would still owe me, but that it was better for the church reputation for them to owe me than to owe the world. Even if they never were able to repay me, it was still better to owe me than to owe the world. When they kept insisting that I had to take the check, I told them that, if they made me take the check, then I would have to give it back to them. It would then become a contribution from me, and they would not owe it. They insisted that I take my weekly check anyway.

When I got home that night, I told Virginia what had happened and what I had to do the next day. She then asked me what we were going to do for grocery money. I told her we would use the money we had in savings from the sale of our house in Pickerington, which we had hoped would go toward our oldest son's college expenses when he graduated from high school. That is a whole other story that I will get to later.

The next day I went to the church and got one of the church deposit slips to fill out so that I could give my salary for the week back to the church. I was totally unprepared for what would happen to me at the bank, when I actually deposited my entire salary for the week back in the church account. As I gave the deposit to the teller at the bank, I literally shook from head to toe, as the words from the model prayer came to my heart, "Give us this day our daily bread." I suddenly realized that I had put myself in the position where I was totally trusting God, even to feed my family that day. It was one of the high spiritual moments of my life.

I am sure that the bank teller did not know that anything unusual was going on, which was as it should have been. But without a doubt, I was having one of the truly high personal spiritual moments of my life. I was truly learning what it meant to trust God for everything. He was going to demonstrate to me that he could truly meet every need that I had. I left that bank knowing that I had been in the very throne room of God. The next several weeks, as my ministry at Medway was winding down, was an interesting time for me and an awakening experience for the church. Later on in my ministry, the Lord would use this experience to help me in trusting Him financially about other matters.

The next Sunday morning, the church treasurer tried to give me my weekly check. I asked her if we were caught up on our bills and she told me no, but that we were down to $3,500.00 in back bills. She said that she was sure that the way money was coming in to get us caught up on our bills that it would happen soon, and I should take my check. I told her that if she insisted that I take my check before the back bills were all paid, I would have to do what I had done the previous week. I told her I was not trying to be difficult; I was just being obedient to the Lord. She said that she did not want me to give my whole check back to the church again, so she would not make me take it. The next day I went to the bank and withdrew the amount of my salary from our savings and put it in our checking account so we would have the money we needed for that week.

The next Sunday morning our treasurer tried to give me my check, and before I could ask she said, "We are down to $1,500.00 still owed in back bills so would you please take your check?" I told her I could not. She smiled at me and left my office. That Sunday night, at the close of the evening service, our Church Treasurer got up and started to the front of the sanctuary. She had a smile on her face and a check in her hand. When she got to the front, she handed me my pay check. She said, "Pastor, you can take this because we are now caught up on all of our back bills." The congregation broke out into applause. I then told them that I was very proud of the way they had responded to the challenge to get caught up on their bills. It was a very good moment in the life of the church, and as I have already said, it was a great learning experience for me in trusting in the Lord for everything that I need.

I was able to move on to the Lord's next assignment for our family, with the knowledge that although our ministry at Medway had been brief, it had been effective. A good number of people were saved and baptized into the church, and they had a new understanding of what it meant to be financially responsible for the church and its ministries.

First Baptist Church, Rockdale, Texas

We went to Rockdale in the spring of 1981, to preach in view of being called as their next pastor. Although I had begun that process in an unusual way, by the time that weekend was over I was convinced that we were meant to move there. According to their church constitution, they could not take the vote until the following week. We went back to Ohio with assurance from the church leadership that there would be a very strong, positive call the next Sunday morning. The following Sunday afternoon the Chairman of the Pastor Search Committee called me to give me the results of the vote. The Church constitution required a 70% yes vote in order to call a pastor. The vote was 75% yes. I was disappointed. I was hoping the vote would be over 90%. I told him I would have to pray about it and I would call him back as soon as possible with my answer.

While I was praying about it, I decided to call the Chairman of the Deacons and find out what the feeling was among the deacons. He told me that the deacons were 100% in favor of calling me as pastor, and they were hoping I would accept the "call." Knowing how the deacons felt and how I felt, I decided I could accept the call, even though the vote was not as strong as I had hoped it would be. I then called the chairman of the committee to tell him I would accept the "call" of the church to be their next pastor. I told my wife when I got off of the phone that the chairman of the committee sounded disappointed when I told him I would accept the call. As it turned out,

I think he was disappointed that I was coming as their next pastor. In fact, soon after I arrived he quit coming to church. He never did tell me what the problem was between us and I decided not to try to find out.

The Baptist General Convention of Texas had developed a partnership with the Brazilian Baptist Convention. An Evangelistic Crusade was being planned for Brazil, and Texas was providing Evangelists for the Crusade, our association had offered to pay my way, if I would go as one of the evangelists. I agreed to do that. Later the Lord impressed upon me that I was to take my wife and boys with me. Jim was preparing for his senior year in high school, and Tom was getting ready for the ninth grade.

In order to be able to do what I knew the Lord wanted me to do in taking my family with me, I had to borrow a significant amount of money. That was not a hard decision to make because of the knowledge that God wanted me to do it. I am also confident that the experience I had already had at Medway, Ohio, concerning trusting the Lord for daily needs, made it an easier decision. We had just bought a new car. I had a smaller car that was a few years old, so we sold the new car in order to have the money needed to make the payments on the loan for the mission trip. Just prior to our leaving on the mission trip, our sons were involved in an accident in my older car which totaled that car. The only vehicle still in the family was a much older car that I had sold to our oldest son for his first car. We used that vehicle to get us to the airport in Houston for the trip to Brazil, and decided that we would not worry about another vehicle until we got home.

In retrospect, I have no regrets in the decisions that we made. I believe that trip was a major stepping stone to the kind of men our sons have become. God used all three of my family members in an amazing way on that trip.

When we returned home, I had to deal with the reality that I was pastor of a fairly large church, and I did not have any means of transportation. I walked back and forth from home to the church for several days, but I had no means of transportation to visit hospitals, etc. One of our older church members called me and told me that he had an old car in his garage that he would be happy to make available to me. I took him up on his offer and drove that old car for several weeks. Through the settlement with the insurance company on the wrecked car, we were able to purchase another vehicle and the Lord provided what we needed to pay for the mission trip loan. By the way, that mission trip to Brazil was worth every dime I spent for the lessons learned by my sons about sharing their faith in another culture. The large number of Brazilian people who were saved, also made it a very worthwhile trip.

We had experiences there in less than two weeks that could not have been duplicated in the USA in years. From witnessing to the Governor of the State, to sharing our faith on the streets by using a bi-lingual testimony and gospel tract, to preaching and singing to a packed house through an interpreter, and then seeing the aisles of the church flooded with people giving their lives to Christ, it was a worthwhile trip. It was topped off by my ninth grade son Tom, weeping on the plane because he did not want to go home. When I asked him why he was weeping, he said, "I don't want to leave. There are plenty of people in Texas to tell others about Jesus, but not that many here."

I had one other meaningful financial experience while pastor at Rockdale. Our association had decided to have a county-wide evangelistic crusade. Through a close friend, I was able to secure outstanding athletes, who were also dedicated Christians, to share their testimony each night of the revival. There were two businessmen in my church who had committed to raising the money in order to make it possible to bring in these sports personalities. Just a few weeks before the crusade, I found out that they had done nothing to raise the money they had promised to raise, and had no intention of living up to their commitment. I was absolutely convinced that the plan that we had was of the Lord and that it would help to draw a crowd to hear the gospel every night. Therefore, I went to the bank and made a personal loan in order for us to be able to keep the financial commitment we had made to those who were coming in to minister with us.

We had a great week. The 1,000 seat tent was filled every night, and several hundred people came to salvation in Jesus Christ. I had just concluded the closing service and the people were beginning to leave. Our evangelist for the week rushed to the microphone, got everyone's attention, and got them to sit back down. I had told him earlier in the week what I had done about the loan to take care of the commitment we had made to our special guests each night. The evangelist then told the people that there was one more offering that needed to be taken that night. He told them what I had done and challenged them to give sacrificially to pay that loan. When the money was counted the next day, there was more than enough to pay off the loan, so we added the balance to the love offering for the evangelism team. Once again the Lord provided when I was faithful to him. That kind of sounds like a pattern of life that a person can use as a guide for life and the decisions we make.

I will always be grateful for the lesson I learned while at Medway Baptist Church, in Medway, Ohio. The lesson about giving and trusting God the day I stood in that bank, and gave my whole weeks salary back, served me well in those two experiences in Rockdale. It is a lesson that has continued to serve me well throughout the remainder of my life. Praise God for lessons learned. He is always sufficient for every need.

It was at Rockdale that I began MasterLife Discipleship Training as a major emphasis of my ministry. I had 8 people in my first group, and those 26 weeks of study together were absolutely life-changing for all of us. We became a very close-knit group of people. The things that we learned were more than just what we got out of the material itself; the bond that developed between us was more than we could have imagined. I still have a certificate "from my first MasterLife group" framed and hanging in my office. I will always treasure the memories that I have from that very first group. I remember when we had our spiritual gifts retreat at the conclusion of the 26 week study, one of our ladies made a dramatic discovery in her life. At the close of the retreat each member of the group was sharing something they had experienced. The wife of one of our deacons shared that she had been saved for 40 years, had been a Sunday School teacher for 20 years, and when she came on the retreat, she actually believed that she did not have any spiritual gifts. She paused and began to weep. Then she said, "I have five," and she began to name them and tell how God wanted to use them in her life. I was overjoyed and sad at the same time, as I thought about the fact that it took the church so long to teach this lady these wonderful truths. From that moment, I had a new mission in life; I needed to help the church discover that it is gifted, and how God wants to use those gifts in His Kingdom Work.

There was a very trying part of our time in Rockdale. It had to do with our oldest son and the way that he was treated by some of his classmates. Rockdale, in those days, was a place where being popular and a part of the "good ole boys" were very important. The free flow of alcohol among high school students and sexual immorality were very prevalent among most of the students. Our son Jim had some very strong convictions and was very vocal about them, maybe at times more than he should have been, but none-the-less, he was unashamed to stand up for what he believed.

As a result, he suffered what I called at the time, religious persecution for his beliefs. I still think that is an appropriate description for what he faced. There is no need to go into all of the details, but there was a period of time during his senior year, that almost every day, when he came home from school, there had been something new happen. I found myself having a feeling of personal guilt growing in my heart, because I felt responsible for putting him in such a situation.

In the spring of his senior year in high school, we had planned a revival with a strong emphasis on reaching young people with the gospel. The Lord opened up the doors of heaven and poured out His Spirit on that revival effort. The revival had originally been scheduled for Sunday – Wednesday. It was going so well that we decided to extend it through Friday night. There were 79 people who trusted Christ as their Savior that week; most of them were young people. The Sunday that followed those revival services was Easter Sunday. There were so many who had been saved and were ready to be baptized on that Easter Sunday, that I did not preach. We celebrated the resurrection of Christ in the baptistery as person after person gave their testimony and were baptized. The list of those who were baptized included Sunday School teachers, deacons, the wife of my Music and Youth Minister and even he came forward to acknowledge that he had been saved in high school after he was baptized as a boy, so he was also baptized that morning.

Included in the group of those who were saved that week, were 13 members of Jim's senior class. Many of them gave testimony of the fact that the way Jim had handled himself through their persecution of him had something to do with them becoming Christians. He had the privilege of leading his classmates in a weekly Bible study during the summer before they all went off to school, and he has maintained contact with some of them throughout the years since their graduation. Praise God!

From a Blessing to a Ministry

My seminary classmate Benny Jackson was the evangelist for the revival at Medway Baptist Church, Medway, Ohio, when the Lord led me to give my salary back until the church got caught up on its back bills. When I took Benny to the airport the day after the revival was over, he told me, "You know that you cannot out give God. Let me know when the Lord gives that money back to you."

Shortly after we moved to Rockdale, Texas, I was visiting the hospital in Temple, Texas. I knew that a long time friend, Dr. Bobby Parker, was the President of the University of Mary Hardin-Baylor, in Belton, Texas. I decided to go to the school and try to visit with Dr. Parker, whom I had not seen for 20 years. He was in and had time to visit with me.

I became acquainted with Dr. Parker when I was a student at Howard Payne College. When I was a freshman, I got reacquainted with Bunny Martin, whose dad had been pastor of my home church when I was a small boy. Dr. Parker was serving as the Dean of Students at HPC and he and his young family were living in an apartment on the first floor of Taylor Hall, where I lived my first three years in school. Ed Cain was a Music Professor Band Director and the Dean of Men. Mr. Cain was single and was also living on the first floor of Taylor Hall. These three men had been playing "42" regularly. Dean Cain's partner had graduated the spring before I entered HPC. I was invited to join this foursome and become Dean Cain's partner. For the next two years we played regularly before the three of them moved on. Bunny graduated and Dean Parker and Dean Cain moved on to other jobs. Needless to say, we became very close during those days. There were about 10 students in the dorm that Dr. and Mrs. Parker saw as their boys. The day I walked into Dr. Parker's office at UMHB, I had not seen him in at least 20 years.

We spent some time getting caught up on what had been going on in our lives. Then he asked me to tell him about my family. I told him about my wife and my two boys and that my oldest was a junior in high school and had been called to preach. He then told me that although the Lord had not called him to preach, God had put him in a position where he could be a blessing to preachers and their families. He said that he guessed our son would want to go to Howard Payne like I did. Then he said, "If he would like to come here, I will help him." We visited a little while longer and I prepared to leave. Then he told me he wanted to explain what he meant by helping our son, if he decided to come to school there. He said that what he meant was that, if he decided to come to school there, he would pay his way. To say the least, I was stunned. I told him how much I appreciated the offer and that I would share it with my son.

When I got home, I shared the news with Virginia and then sat down with Jim that night and shared the news with him. I assured him that it was his decision to make. Later I took him to Belton to visit UMHB, and early in his junior year in high school, Jim made the decision to attend UMHB. I called my evangelist friend to tell him how the Lord had repaid me for being obedient to him with our money. He was happy and stunned that it was in such a significant way.

Jim was able to influence several of his classmates to also attend UMHB. One of his classmates played on the men's basketball team and another classmate played on the women's basketball team.

One of the greatest stories was with another classmate that had hoped to attend another school. Her name was Lisa. Lisa is Hispanic and no member of her family had ever attended college. Our younger son Tom had been out on Sunday afternoon and had visited with Lisa who was working at the Sonic. She shared with him that she had just gotten the word that she had not been accepted at the school where she had applied. Tom came home and told me that I had to get her into UMHB. I went down to the Sonic with Tom to talk to Lisa. I asked her if she would be willing to go to UMHB, if I could get her in. She said she would, but did not know how she could afford it. I told her we would worry about the money later. By the way, did I mention that it was the second week in August?

The next morning I called a friend in administration and asked him about getting her enrolled. He put me on hold for a few minutes; he came back on the phone to tell me that there was one bed left in the freshman girl's dorm. I told him to hold that space and I would bring her up the next day. The school had a policy that they would match any scholarship a church would give to a student. I got the deacons together on Wednesday night, and we gave her a $750.00 scholarship which the school matched. I also made contact with the Mexican Baptist Convention of Texas and they also gave her a scholarship. Lisa had become a Christian during a spring revival at our church her senior year. She was an art major and got a scholarship from the Art Department of UMHB after she got there. During her first year, she redesigned the school logo. A couple of years later I was there for the Homecoming Basketball game, when she was crowned Homecoming Queen. I was standing courtside with Dr. Parker when she was crowned. He looked at me and said, "There is one of your kids that is doing really well." Many years later we were driving through Rockdale. We stopped at a locally owned Mexican Diner. As it turned out, the diner was owned and operated by Lisa's family. When they realized who we were, they were overjoyed. They told us that Lisa worked and lived in the area. They called her and she came to see us while we were there. Once again it was such a joy to see how well things were going in her life, and to know that we had a small part in making some big things happen in her life.

While Jim was in school, he worked with the president's office in recruiting and PR for the school. Dr. Parker created what he called the Junior Presidential Scholarship. It would be for very qualified students who would commit to UMHB during their junior year in high school. Over the years, many very deserving young men and women have been the recipients. I was able to recommend this scholarship to several students, who were in churches where I was pastor.

During the time that Jim and our other son Tom, who also attended UMHB, were students there, I had many opportunities to work in various phases of the life of the university. I became particularly close to many of the members of Jim's class and had the honor of preaching the baccalaureate message at their graduation ceremony.

During the remainder of my time at Rockdale and while we were at First Baptist Church, Rusk, Texas, I had the privilege of helping a good number of students fulfill their dream of going to college. In fact one year I was visiting with Dr. Parker, in the spring of that year. He gave me several blank scholarship certificates that he had signed. He told me to take them home and pray about what to do with them, and give them to any students I felt were qualified and might come to UMHB if they had a scholarship. He left the amount of the scholarship blank and told me to fill in that line for each student. I actually gave several of those to Rusk High School seniors that year. This is actually a ministry that I continue to enjoy to this very day. I love young people and have believed that one of the greatest things I can do for them, after their salvation, is to help them become as trained as they can possibly be for the rest of their lives. (Just last year, 2014, it was my privilege to help a very qualified young lady from Camp Ground Baptist Church to secure a scholarship to Jacksonville Baptist College.)

During this same time frame, Dr. Don Newberry, who had been one of my classmates, had become president of Howard Payne University. Because of our friendship, I also had the opportunity to help a good number of students attend Howard Payne. So because of long time relationships, the Lord made it possible to present two Christian universities to students as potential places for them to continue their education. This was something that I really enjoyed doing and still enjoy doing today. It is really a labor of love. A college education is not a cure-all and guarantee to a successful life, but it sure does give a young person a good starting point.

232

After I returned from New York, I was having a conversation with a young man that I will probably discuss again later. He was only 5 years old when we left to go to New York. He had recently graduated from high school and was attending Junior College. In a casual conversation he said that he had always wondered if he could play college football. I asked him if he was serious enough that he would be willing to move to Brownwood, Texas, and attend Howard Payne College. I told him I was sure I could get him a try-out on the football team. He said that he would. When the time came for him to make the visit, I was unable to go. However, the Pastor at FBC, Rusk, who had also attended Howard Payne, agreed to take him out there. Not only did he find out that he could play college football, but he became a starter his first year. He graduated from HPU in three years. After his graduation, one of his high school classmates, who had played Junior College Football, got a scholarship to a school in Missouri. Because he still had a year of eligibility left, he went up there and played with his old high school quarterback. In one game they both set school records for most touchdown passes thrown and most touchdown catches. He is another one of those ordinary people that has allowed the Lord to do extraordinary things in his life.

There was another young man in Rusk, who was an outstanding athlete. When he was near graduation, for some reason, no one seemed interested in helping this African American young man get a scholarship to play college football, so that he could afford to continue his education. This was in spite of the fact that he had been a good student as well as a good athlete. I talked to him and then I called the President of Howard Payne and told him I had another young man I was going to bring out there. I took Wesley Foreman out to Howard Payne. He did receive a full four year scholarship. He was an outstanding student and athlete in college, while on a pre-med course of study. Every time I would see President Don Newberry, he would ask me if I had any more students like Wesley that I could send their way. After graduating from Howard Payne, he went to medical school at the University of Texas. Now, Dr. Wesley Foreman practices medicine in Austin, Texas. I recently ran into an African American

Baptist Minister in Rusk, Texas. He looked at me for a moment and then he said, "Don't I know you?" Then he said, "You are Rev. Goforth, you are the one that got my nephew, Wesley Foreman, a college scholarship. Our family will never forget what you did for him." I just touched Wesley's life a little bit, and God has used him as a Doctor to touch untold numbers of people. Praise God!

I have made a lot of mistakes in my life. However, I hope people will remember that I really love children and young people and want to see them achieve all that the Lord has in store for them.

Perry Eaton

When I became the pastor of First Baptist Church, Rockdale, Texas, I had been the pastor of Southern Baptist churches on a full-time basis since 1968. However, I had never been pastor of a church where we had another full-time staff member besides me. I had had several people who served in a part-time position on the church staff, but I never had even a secretary who served on a full-time basis. FBC, Rockdale, had a full-time secretary and had voted to call a second full-time staff member for the first time in the history of the church. They had voted to seek a full-time Minister of Music and Youth. Although they had selected a search committee, they decided that they would wait until a new pastor came on the field before they began the search process.

I was personally very grateful that they realized the importance of the new pastor having a major role in the selection of the second staff member. It was, of course, the right decision for them to make. Therefore, I began meeting with and praying with the Music and Youth Search Committee on a regular basis shortly after arriving on the scene. As we began to talk about attributes that we would be looking for, I remembered something from a Pastor's Retreat that I had attended in Ohio. I had invited my friend Jimmy Draper to come to Ohio and lead our pastors in a retreat. During a question and answer session, Jimmy was asked what he would look for if he was hiring his first staff member. He quickly replied, "A Music Minister who could sing in such a way that it would stir the hearts of the people before I preach."

I told the committee that, among other things, we really needed to find someone who could sing. Not long after that, one of the ladies on the committee told me about a young man she had been told about who would soon be graduating from the University of Mary Hardin-Baylor. His name was Perry Eaton. I discovered that he was a member of the University Basketball Team. His plan was to teach and coach after college. He is the son of a Southern Baptist pastor.

I drove to Belton and spent an afternoon visiting with him. He agreed to pray about the matter, and acknowledged that he had some feelings that the Lord might be leading him into full-time church ministry. He had made a music cassette and gave me a copy of it. When I played it and heard him sing for the first time, I knew that I had found our man. It was not long after that when he was called as Minister of Music and Youth at FBC, Rockdale, Texas. That began a ministry together that I am sure ended up being far more than either one of us knew it would be at the time.

Even though both of us had literally grown up in the church, we soon learned that we had a lot to learn about working together to lead a church to become all that the Lord would have it to be. I will not go into the struggles of learning to work in harmony with one another for the good of the Lord's church. Let's just say there was a learning curve that had to be experienced. However, I will say that, during that learning curve, there always remained respect for and love for one another that allowed us to overcome all obstacles through the power of the Holy Spirit.

I said two things to him early on that I did my best to honor. First, I told him that I was not interested in doing his job; if I was going to do his job, I did not need him. Second, I promised to always support him to the church. If I disagreed with him, it would be in private. I probably could have done those things better at times, but I really tried to honor the personal commitment I had made to him.

The Lord developed a very special relationship of trust and respect for one another that He was able to use, as we ministered together in two different churches (FBC, Rockdale, Texas, and FBC, Rusk, Texas). When I moved from Rockdale to Rusk, it was two years before the

Lord put us back together, but that did happen and we had five more years of ministry together before the Lord called me to New York.

It would probably take another book to talk about all of the things that the Lord allowed us to experience together. Needless to say, Perry was a wonderful part of my life and ministry. I think we would both agree that we complimented one another's ministries, and we were both better because of the other.

Perry worked hard to learn how to be at his best in the Lord's work. In the fields of Music and Youth ministry, he was constantly working at becoming better at what he did. I remember when he came to Rusk; I told him that he was going to have to work hard at improving his skills with the choirs, because that would be expected at Rusk. He did exactly that. In the fall of the year, it would not be uncommon for me to come into the church building and hear music blasting in the sanctuary. I would go in and find him sprawled on the platform with the Christmas Cantata in front of him. He would be listening to the CD on our sound system. He would do that every day until he knew it, and was ready to introduce it to the choir.

Another instruction I had given him at both churches was that, if he had to make a decision between being at the church or at an event at the school, I wanted him to be at the school. I remember one spring at Rockdale; I was at a High School Track Meet. I was sitting next to one of our deacons. Perry came on the field wearing some red coaching shorts and his college practice basketball jersey. The school colors at UMHB are purple and gold. He was wearing the jersey with the purple color on the outside to go along with his red coaching shorts. My deacon made a disparaging remark about the way he was dressed. I told him that he was not dressed for us. He was dressed for the students, and I was good with that. As you might imagine, he was soon surrounded by high school students.

One of the practical ways that we complimented one another was that I have not ever been good at telling people no. At Rusk this was becoming a huge problem because so many people were making requests for time during the Sunday morning worship service, that we were having a hard time having the time we needed for real worship and proclaiming of the gospel.

I approached Perry and told him that I wanted to redefine his job to include him being the Leader of the Worship Services. I told him that meant he would be the one to make the decision on what happened during the worship service. I told him that my only concern was that he would give me time to preach. He agreed to take on this responsibility, which took a major problem off of my shoulders. He developed a policy about what could be considered as part of the service, and when he would need to know about that request. One Sunday morning I had a person come to me, who had gone to Perry at the last minute wanting to add something to the service, and he said no. That person wanted me to override his decision. I refused to do that, which did not make the person happy, but people did start doing better planning and our worship services became more meaningful.

Though we do not see one another often enough, there continues, to this day, a close personal relationship between the two of us. I have great love for this man of God.

Preparing for Change

During the time we were at Rockdale, Virginia and I were invited to participate in a number of MasterLife Conferences. This was during the time when the Sunday School Board was still requiring that someone in a church be trained before that church could purchase the MasterLife material. I thought that was a good thing. That meant that there was someone in that church who was serious about discipling God's children, and they understood the commitment that was needed to participate in the MasterLife study.

At one particular conference that Virginia attended in East Texas, which I could not attend, she came home telling me about a Director of Missions in Tyler, Texas, that she had met. He had told her that he wanted me to send him my resume. For whatever reason, I told her that if he wanted my resume, he could ask me for it himself. He and I finally met and he asked me if I would send him my resume. I told him that I would.

 After the church in his association became interested in someone else, he began sending my resume all over North and Central Texas. Every time he would send my resume to another church, he would send me a copy of the letter. I had gotten several such letters and had not felt anything particular about any of them and did not hear anything from most of them. However, one day I received a copy of a letter he had sent to the Pastor Search Committee of First Baptist Church, Rusk, Texas. I had never heard of Rusk, Texas, before, but I had a strange feeling that something was about to happen. When I went home for lunch that day, I told Virginia I had gotten another one of those letters and that she should not be surprised, if we moved to Rusk, Texas. She wanted to know where that was and I told her it was somewhere in east Texas.

Later that week I received a phone call from the Chairman of the Pastor Search Committee from Rusk. He told me that they wanted to come hear me preach the next Sunday. I have already mentioned the County-wide Evangelistic Crusade we had while I was at Rockdale. At the time I got the call from Rusk, I told him about the crusade and that in fairness to everyone, I could not be distracted in our efforts to prepare for this crusade. I told him that I could not even talk to the committee until after the crusade was over. I thanked him for calling and told him that, if they needed to go in another direction, I would understand. On the Friday night, which was the last night of the crusade, I received another phone call from Rusk. The chairman of the committee from Rusk was calling. He said that if he remembered his information correctly, our crusade was over that night. He then asked me if I would be preaching in my pulpit Sunday. I told him yes and he said, "We will be there."

That next Sunday, the search committee from FBC, Rusk, did show up. I was surprised to discover that I had known two of them most of my life. They were actually the aunt and brother-in-law of one of my brother's best friends when we were growing up. They decided they wanted to come back a second Sunday. I overheard one of the ladies in our choir say, "I recognize those two bald-headed men; they were here last Sunday." Then she said to my wife, "That is a pulpit committee; we need to just have prayer and go home."

That afternoon the committee visited with me for a second time. When they had finished their questions, they wanted to know if I had any questions. I told them I only had one question, and that only two members of the committee could answer the question. I directed my question to the two members of the committee who had known me all of my life. I reminded them that they had not seen me since I was in high school. I wanted to know if I would still be James Lonnie to them, or could they now respect me as an adult and their pastor. This was an important question to me, because this family represented three deacons in the church, Sunday School teachers, and WMU leaders. One of the family members looked at me and said, "If that is

all you are worried about, you don't have anything to worry about."
She was right; that family was very supportive and they remain some
of my best friends to this day.

First Baptist Church, Rusk, Texas

In May of 1984, Virginia, Tom, and I went for a week-end visit with the First Baptist Church of Rusk, Texas. We attended a number of functions that were planned for us that weekend, and then I preached in both services that Sunday. After the Sunday evening service, the three of us went to the church office while the church was voting whether or not to extend the call to me to be their next pastor.

There was a good crowd there that night and I was hoping for a unanimous call. When the committee came back with the report of the vote, the vote was 232 yes and 19 no. The committee was excited about the vote. I told them that I had hoped for a unanimous call. One of the members of the committee said that, if I came as their pastor, I would soon discover that only19 no votes with 250 people voting was about as unanimous as I would get. I told them that I felt strongly that the Lord wanted me to come, and I accepted the call. Normally I would have gone home and given the church a two week notice. However, I knew that our Vacation Bible School at Rockdale was only a few weeks away, and I felt I needed to wait until after VBS to resign and then give them a two week notice. So I suggested that my beginning date with Rusk should be the first week of July. The church agreed, and that is what we did.

It was a long six weeks back in Rockdale, trying to keep things halfway normal until after VBS, and then experiencing the trauma that always goes with leaving a place of service. As you might expect, word began to leak out that I was probably leaving. I had to spend time avoiding questions before the time when I would resign. I finally went ahead and resigned a week earlier than I had planned, and stayed a week longer than I normally would have in order to help the church at Rockdale complete some projects that needed to be completed before I left.

We moved to Rusk the first week in July 1984. We were in services for the first time on Wednesday evening, July 4, 1984. This was the first time we had made a move minus one of our family members. Jim had finished his first year of school and was Music Minister at a church in Belton, Texas. He was living at home and driving to Belton, which was only 50 miles away. However, we were now going to be almost 4 hours away. He had a full scholarship at the school, but that did not include living in the dorm during the summer. We had a small camping trailer that he felt like he could live in for two months. So I pulled it up to an RV Park in Belton, paid the two month's rent on the campsite, and for the first time, moved off without one of our sons. That was easier to talk about doing than it was to actually do, but we did it, and it all worked out. When school started, Jim moved back into the dorm. I went and picked up the travel trailer and brought it home. By the time the next summer rolled around, he and Lisa were planning their wedding for that summer and he had rented an apartment just off campus for them. So for the first time, one of our sons was not an intricate part of our lives and ministry on a church field. Jim became loved and respected in Rusk, but the church did not have an opportunity to get to know him on a daily basis.

We had an interesting arrival in Rusk. We had two vehicles and Tom had recently bought his own car. However, he had not been driving for very long, and had never driven by himself for an extended period of time on the road. He convinced us that he could do that and so we started out with me driving the lead car, Tom in the middle, and Virginia in the last car. We arrived in Rusk after dark. We had just gotten into the city limits, when I noticed that a police officer had pulled Tom over. I knew that we were not speeding. I stopped and went back to Tom's car and Virginia pulled in behind him. I interrupted the officer and asked him what the problem was. He wanted to know why I thought it was any of my business. I told him because he had pulled over my son and I wanted to know what he had done. He then told me that he was swerving a bit and he stopped him to see if he had been drinking.

I assured him that he had not and that we had been traveling together for several hours and I was sure that he was just tired, but I knew he had not been drinking. He then wanted to know who I was and what we were doing traveling through Rusk in three cars. I told him that I was the new pastor at First Baptist Church, and that we were just moving to town. Needless to say he was embarrassed and apologized. He then told me that from time to time young people would drive from Rusk over to Palestine to drink alcoholic drinks and would come home somewhat under the influence of alcohol. We have laughed about that incident several times as a family over the years.

Church Staff

I have already talked about the Lord bringing Perry Eaton into my life while I was at Rockdale, Texas. I would like to talk a little bit about the learning process of learning to work with a church staff, when you have spent so many years of your ministry as the only full-time paid staff member of a church. I will also share about the people the Lord allowed me to work alongside. When you are the only full-time paid staff member of a church, it does not take long to figure out that the success or failure of the things that are happening in the church are going to fall directly on your shoulders. When you add to that the fact that you are a type A personality, you are almost guaranteed a situation where that one staff member is going to keep his hand in everything that is happening. The truth is that most of the activities that have been generated in a one-staff member (pastor) church were his ideas to begin with. Therefore there is a lot of built-in feeling of responsibility to make the things work that you have led the church to do.

When I came to Rockdale, I had a full-time paid church secretary and a part-time custodian. Within months after I arrived, we hired the church's first full-time Minister of Music and Youth. So just like that, I went from being the one who was professionally responsible for everything, to having shared responsibility

When I came to Rusk, there was already a full-time secretary, a full-time custodian and an Interim Minister of Music and Youth. The church would begin the search for a full-time Minister of Music and Youth when the new pastor got his feet on the ground. A couple of years into the ministry at Rusk, we hired an additional part-time secretary which soon developed into an almost full-time job. So now, I had to learn to share responsibility with four people. On the surface that was exciting; underneath it was very scary. I had been in church all of my life. I knew that when things were not going well in any area of church life, the church was going to hold the pastor responsible. Type A personalities also have a tendency to believe that no one can get done what you want done, the way you want it done, better than you. So to turn anything over to someone else is a major adjustment. Yet here you are with these other staff members that are being paid to do a job, and your job may hinge on them doing their job effectively.

If I was really going to be an effective pastor to the churches in Rockdale and Rusk, which were two of the largest churches with the largest ministries and budgets that I had ever pastored, I had to learn to work with a church staff and let them do their jobs. That was a huge learning experience for me; I hope I learned to do it fairly well without causing those who worked alongside me undue consternation. Hopefully, we were all doing the things we were doing for the glory of God and to see His Church and Kingdom advanced.

When I came to Rusk, Steve Slover was serving as Interim Minister of Music. Steve had been serving a church in Houston and had resigned to go into Music Evangelism. He had moved back to Rusk because Rusk is home for him. The church had called him to serve as Interim Minister of Music as his evangelism ministry was getting started. It was becoming obvious that he was not getting a good start into full-time evangelism. He was doing a really good job with our Music Ministry. After I had been in Rusk about two months, I felt impressed to ask him if he would consider becoming our full-time Minister of Music and Youth. He told me that, if I felt good about it, he would be happy to do it. Actually I think what I asked him one morning was, if he would be interested in having the word "interim" taken off of his title? So for the first two years of my ministry at FBC, Rusk, Steve Slover and I served together. All of us are stronger in some areas than others. Steve's strongest area of interest was Music, and his long-term goal was to serve in a church where he could be just the Minister of Music. My advice to him was that to accomplish that goal he should go on and get his seminary training. He began pursuing a way to do that and the Lord moved him on after two years.

We began the search for a new Minister of Music and Youth. In my heart, I knew that I would love for us to call Perry Eaton to come and serve with us. He and I had already learned how to become a team at Rockdale. I just really liked the idea of calling someone who I already knew. However, there were several obstacles to overcome. The first was that Perry had already moved on from Rockdale to a church in Memphis, Tennessee; I would need to know if he had any sense that the Lord might be leading him away from there. The second was that we had elected a Music and Youth Search Committee and I felt I needed to honor the integrity of that process.

To take some pressure off of the process, and to keep our music ministry going, I approached Craig Anderson about becoming our Interim Music Minister. Craig was still working with his dad at the time. He prayed about it and agreed to take on that responsibility. As many know, that led to a redirection of Craig's life and career, and for many years now, the Lord has been using Craig and Kim very effectively in full-time Music Ministry. Most of those years have been spent in a very strong church in Arizona.

God's Vision for my Ministry in Rusk

In coming to Rusk, the Lord gave me a clear vision of what my ministry was to be. The goal the Lord gave me was that, within 5 years, a significant number of the members of the church would have discovered that they had been gifted by God for ministry; they would have discovered what their gift or gifts were; they would be trained to use those gifts to the fullest potential. They would actually be living out their lives on a daily basis in the way God had gifted them for service.

As I write that goal down again, it really sounds like a mouthful, but the truth is, that is actually the goal the Lord gave me. Therefore, that is the direction that I immediately began to try to lead the church. I am sure that I had made it clear that discipleship was going to be a major emphasis of my ministry. I am equally sure that very few had any idea what that really meant.

I am going to make an assessment of the condition and attitude of First Baptist Church, Rusk, realizing that some who were in the church at that time may read this and may not agree with the way I saw the spiritual condition of the church. FBC, Rusk, was filled with a lot of good people who loved the Lord in their own way and loved their church. They attended the church. They supported the church with their finances, and they were very tight about how those finances were used. Maybe conservative would be the way many would have expressed their view about the church finances. One of the most difficult times of the year was at the time of budget adoption. If the new budget reflected a substantial increase of any kind, there was a fear of the unknown.

The church was very comfortable with doing church the way they had been doing it for many years. They liked good strong biblical preaching, but they did not want to be drawn out of their comfort zone. Therefore, the goal the Lord had given to me was foreign to the understanding of many, if not most, in the congregation. Let me acknowledge that I was unprepared for receiving severe criticism for spending so much of my time discipling people. However, there was a small but significant group in the church that really had a desire to grow spiritually.

MasterLife and the Life Training Courses

Shortly after we arrived, the first of July 1984, I put out a sign-up sheet for MasterLife, which I would begin teaching in September. In just a week's time, there were 34 who had signed up for the course. I was the only qualified leader besides my wife and she had already felt a strong calling to the youth of the church. The course was best taught in groups of 8-12, which meant I would have to take on 3 of these classes at the same time that I was trying to get a handle on being the pastor of the largest church I had ever pastored.

I took a Wednesday night Prayer Meeting hour the last week in July to describe how difficult this study would be. It was 26 weeks of intense study. I told them that it would mean that I would have to find the time to lead three groups for two hours at a time each week. I told them I was willing to do that, if they were really serious, but if they did not want to make that kind of commitment, they needed to come and remove their name from the list, and I would understand. I left the list on the communion table and got busy and forgot about it until just before I left to go home. I went to get the list to find out how many names had been crossed out. To my surprise, no names were crossed out and ten more had been added. Now I had a list of 44, which meant 4 groups.

When I came to the office the next morning, our Interim Music Minister said that, if he had stayed at the church in Houston where he had been six more months, he would have been certified to lead a group. I asked him if he was willing to get certified and he said he was. I quickly got on the phone and made arrangements for he and his wife to go to Glorieta the next week to receive the training needed. A couple of hours later, George and Tommie Nielsen came by and also expressed a desire to help. So, Steve and Kay Slover and the Nielsens headed out the next week to be trained, and in September we began. Each of these families led one group and I led two groups. Of the 44 that started, 36 went all the way through the training, so we were off to a running start.

One of the things that is missed by some, when they do MasterLife, is something they recommended at the beginning of the development of MasterLife. It is a Spiritual Gifts Retreat at the close of the full study of MasterLife. The material that was recommended and that we used was "Discovering Your Spiritual Gifts and How to Use Them in the Church." It is material that is not even in print anymore, but is one of the best things ever produced in Southern Baptist life. It helps God's people understand that they are spiritually gifted, and that those gifts come from God to enable them to do the ministry He has called them to do. It was a part of our discipleship curriculum that when you signed up for the 26 week study of MasterLife, your study was not complete until you participated in the Spiritual Gifts Retreat. The retreat consisted of 8 hours of study, which started on a Friday night and concluded by mid-day on Saturday. The very last thing that would happen at the retreat is that, one by one, each participant identified at least one spiritual gift they had and how God intended to use that in their own personal ministry. It never failed, that was always an awesome time for each member of the group and the larger group as a whole.

We always included all of the MasterLife groups in this one retreat. That made it possible for those who had been in different groups to get to know those who had just spent the last 26 weeks the same way they had. They would come back on Sunday fired up and ready to go. We usually turned that Sunday night, after the retreat, over to those who had just spent those 26 weeks in intense discipleship training. Usually from their sharing came the ones for the next year who wanted to experience for themselves what they had just heard.

I had a friend who was on the staff of the University of Mary Hardin-Baylor, Belton, Texas, who was also the Minister of Education at FBC, Belton, Texas, when my two sons were in school there. He had started

MasterLife at FBC, Belton. One time when I was on campus he approached me to tell me that MasterLife was not making the impact on his church he had hoped it would. I immediately asked him how the Spiritual Gifts Retreats were going, and he did not know what I was talking about. He had missed that recommendation altogether. I told him that was his problem. He was developing and discipling people, but then was not helping them plug into their own personal ministry.

I suggested to him that he pick a Friday night and Saturday and work hard at getting all who had participated in MasterLife over the past couple of years to participate. I told him I would come with my volunteer Discipleship Director and we would lead them all through this study. He did that and we had over 100 from his church who participated in the week-end. Later he told me that his church had been transformed.

God's timing is absolutely amazing. It was just a couple of years after we began MasterLife at FBC, Rusk, that the Sunday School Board began developing the "Life Series" of discipleship courses. Our State Convention's Church Training Director contacted me about our church being one of the pilot churches in Texas for the "Life Series." He said that would mean that, every time a new course of study came out, it would be made available to us and they would train leaders from our church in these various studies. Then he said, "We will want to keep track of how they are impacting the life of your church."

Do you remember that I said that 36 of the 44 who started MasterLife the first year completed that course? Those 36 people became the core group that were leading small groups in discipleship training of one kind or another almost every day of the week. They would meet in homes and at the church, whenever a small group who was interested in the same thing would decide they could get together.

Let me give you some examples of how, what God was doing in our church, mirrored the materials that were being written and developed and made available to the churches. Without a doubt, the one course of study that impacted people, as much and for some more than MasterLife, was and still is to this day, "Experiencing God." I will say more about that later. Just as God began to burden some of our members about an organized Prayer Ministry in the church, "The Disciple's Prayer Life" by T. W. Hunt came out. Some were beginning to feel the need to learn how to be better Christian parents about the time "Parenting by Grace" came out. Virginia led some of our parents through that study. We were beginning to have more and more people making decisions for Christ on Sunday.

We became concerned that not enough time was being taken with those who were coming to make decisions, to help them clearly understand the decision they were making. It was something that one man could not do effectively by himself during the invitation. You guessed it. A study was produced designed to help people counsel those who came forward at invitation time. One man saw this as his ministry. People would receive the training, and then become counselors of those who made decisions during the invitation. I would generally receive those who came forward to hear their decision. I would then turn them over to our Witness Counseling Director, who in turn would turn them over to a counselor. They were then taken to a room behind the sanctuary where more detailed counseling, about the decision they were making, could be done. If sufficient counseling could be done before the invitation was over, they were brought back to the sanctuary so that their decision could be shared with the church. If that could not be accomplished, then whatever time was needed was spent with them and their decision was made public at a future service. This was probably one of the most significant, immediate ministries, that was developed out of our Discipleship Ministry. Weekly you could see the value of this ministry.

I skipped over the prayer ministry of the church pretty quickly. However, just about the time that we began to get serious about becoming a praying church, the prayer study was out and available to us. Two volunteers became the volunteer directors of the prayer ministry.

There are three things, in particular, that I remember about the developing of our prayer ministry. First, a junk closet was cleaned out and a beautiful little prayer room was developed in that space. It was literally a junk closet. Later I said that I wished I had taken a before and after picture of that little room. It would have been a perfect illustration of where we were spiritually as a church before people started getting serious about their walk with the Lord. It was a picture of how far the church had come spiritually, after so many started getting serious about their own walk with the Lord. The walls were redone and painted and one of our deacons made some beautiful crosses for the back wall. The one window in the room was taken out and two of our ladies made a stained glass window. I will never forget the look on their faces when that window was installed. Others gave money and carpet and appropriate furniture was purchased.

Second, a ministry of prayer was begun for the Sunday Morning Worship Service, while it was going on. Various groups of two signed up to be in the prayer room during the morning worship service. They had a copy of the bulletin and literally prayed for every phase of the service while it was going on. One of those, who was on the schedule on a regular basis to pray during the morning worship service, told me that it was one of his most rewarding prayer experiences. At the conclusion of the service, he would go out a side door of the building and go around to the back of the sanctuary to see the answers to prayer that happened during the invitation time. Almost every Sunday morning there were various decisions that were being made, as the Holy Spirit of God moved upon the service. The prayer room was located at the bottom of the stairs from the choir entrance onto the platform of the sanctuary. There were times when I was preaching that it felt like the power of those prayers was moving right up those stairs and into the sanctuary. The power of the prayers being offered during the worship service was almost like a mighty, rushing wind of the Holy Spirit.

Third, was the development of my own personal prayer life. I began meeting with a man in the church almost every morning of the week at 6:00 A.M. Out of that time, a group of men began meeting every Thursday morning, for an extended time of prayer, before they went to work. Because I was at the prayer room almost every morning, it was not uncommon on any given morning for different ones to drop by and spend some time in prayer with me.

I could feel and see new positive relationships developing between me and various ones in the church, as we began to pray together. God began to do a new and powerful thing in our lives. I remember one morning, my prayer partner and I had been there praying for a short while when two high school young men showed up. They had stopped by to pray with us before they went to school. They were burdened about some of their classmates and wanted to pray with us for them before they went to school. One morning a young business man in the church showed up, just to pray with us about some things that were on his heart. I don't know of any better way for people to get to know and understand one another, than to spend time in prayer together.

In a very real sense, the prayer room helped me develop wonderful relationships with many in our church. These relationships probably could not have become as meaningful as they were any other way. All of my life I will cherish many of the wonderful things that I saw the Lord accomplish in that little prayer room. There was nothing magical about the room. It was what took place inside the room that made such a powerful difference in so many of our lives, and I believe, in the life of our church.

It is exciting to know that, after almost 30 years, there is still a small prayer room at First Baptist Church, Rusk, where God is still accomplishing some wonderful things. I praise God for those who have kept that vital ministry going for so many years. Only when we get to heaven will we know the complete story of the victories that have been won through God's people on their knees before Him in prayer.

One of the most significant things that happened during our ministry in Rusk was the growth in the number of active young couples in the church. Larry and Dianne Sinclair agreed to take the Young Adult Couples Sunday School Class. They started with about three couples. Over a period of several years that class grew into a Sunday School Department of about 70 enrolled. Many of the couples that got involved in that class also got involved in the discipleship ministry of the church. On a yearly basis, when we were in need of Sunday School workers and other areas of ministry, most of the time we found them in that Young Adult Sunday School Department. How did such growth happen? It was through the caring outreach of Larry and Dianne. Every Sunday they would check the visitors' cards that had been placed in the offering plates. If there had been visitors in the worship service on Sunday, who would be in the age group they taught, the Sinclairs would visit them the next week.

About the same time, JoEd Anderson started a Men's Sunday School Class with just a few names of men who were not coming to Sunday School. Before long, that class had grown to about 30. That happened the same way, the teacher of the class giving himself to those men.

Looking Back

Looking back is always an interesting experience; you almost always have 20/20 vision when you have the option of looking back. When I look back at Rusk and the decision we made to leave FBC, Rockdale, Texas, there are some very mixed emotions. When we moved back to Texas after 12 years in Ohio, I really thought that we would be in Rockdale a long time, but for whatever reason, things just never did seem to gel for us to have an extended ministry in that town. At least it was my impression that an extended ministry in that town was not going to happen.

For whatever reason, we just never did seem to be able to get on the same page with most of the leadership of the church. There seemed to always be a struggle any time we tried to get something going. When we made the decision to leave Rockdale and come to Rusk, I was overwhelmed how disappointed most of the people in the church and even in the city seemed to be when they learned we were leaving. I told them that, if they had treated us with such love during the previous 3 years as they did the 3 weeks after I resigned, it would have been much harder to leave.

Because of the outpouring of love we received the last three weeks we were in Rockdale, we moved to Rusk believing the Lord had called us, but with great fear and anticipation about the calling I knew the Lord had placed upon my life to disciple His people. I came to Rusk wondering how truly supportive the people would be in another First Baptist Church in a small Texas town.

When we arrived on the scene, the church leadership had done a wonderful job of preparing the church and the city for our arrival. We were really made to feel special, not only by the church, but by the city as well.

One of my goals for years had been that the Lord would allow me to pastor a church somewhere with the possibility of that city becoming better because that church was there. In some respects that was already true about FBC, Rusk, Texas. It was already an influential institution in the city and the pastor already had a place of respect in Rusk. However, my observation about the city was about the same as my observation of the church. A lot of really good people lived in Rusk, Texas, but beyond attending church on a fairly regular basis, there was not a great deal of spiritual maturity in the city.

The attitude of the church and the city toward me and my ministry was, in my opinion, "We will do our best to let you do whatever you want to do, but don't expect a lot of involvement on our part. We are too busy to get overly involved in church beyond supporting it with our attendance and money."

The Lord had long before convicted me of the responsibility that He had given me to disciple His people and to get them involved in ministry on a daily basis. Shortly after arriving in Rusk, I stood up to preach on a summer Sunday morning. Even though it was summer, the church was just about full. I said to them that I wanted them to know what I saw when I looked out upon them.

That summer Sunday morning I told the church that what I saw was a lot of beautifully wrapped gifts that never had been opened. Then I explained to them that everyone who was there that morning, who was already a Christian, had at least one spiritual gift. I explained to them that spiritual gifts are given to believers to enable them to accomplish the task that the Lord has for them as believers. I went on to tell them that most of them probably had more than one spiritual gift, but that I knew for a fact that all believers have at least one spiritual gift.

Spiritual gifts are given by the Lord Himself to His children to enable them to accomplish the work He has given them to do. Then I told them that the goal the Lord had given me as their pastor was:

First, to help them know beyond any doubt that they were born again believers in Jesus Christ;

Second, to help them know that they were called to and gifted for ministry;

Third, to help them to discover their own spiritual gift or gifts;

Fourth, to help them know how to use their spiritual gifts;

Finally, to help them get out there in the world every day, using the gifts the Lord has given them, in the ministries He has given to them.

I wanted them to know that day, that was the direction the Lord had given me for my ministry, and I was going to be faithful to the Lord in doing what He had called me there to do. I did not always do everything in the best way it could have been done. I made my mistakes from time to time. However, as I look back, I can honestly say that during my entire ministry at FBC, Rusk, Texas, my priority was winning people to Jesus and training them to become all that God wanted them to be. My plan for accomplishing that was through my preaching ministry and discipleship ministry.

Preaching Ministry

I remember one experience I had with the Lord late one Saturday night. I was in my little study on the third floor of the old building, working on my sermons for the next day. I had had one of those weeks that pastors have from time to time. It had been a very busy week. So here I was at 10:00 P.M. Saturday night trying to get my sermons prepared for the next day. I was worn out. As clear as a bell, the Lord spoke to my heart and said, "What in the world are you doing?" I replied, "I am trying to get my sermons ready for tomorrow." The Lord replied, "Trying is a good word for you to use; you are so tired that you can't hear me speak." Then He said, "You will be speaking to 400-500 of my people tomorrow who have come to hear a fresh Word from Me. However, you are so tired, if I gave it to you, you would not hear it."

That night I asked the Lord to forgive me, and the next morning I muddled through my sermon and then shared my experience with the Lord. I asked them to be considerate of my sermon preparation time. I promised them and the Lord that, with His help and their help, I would never stand before them again without first spending enough time with the Lord to have a fresh Word from Him when I stood to preach. As I look back on those years, I can honestly say that I kept my word to them and unto the Lord. I was surprised at the eager way that they received the news that their pastor was going to spend enough time with the Lord to get a fresh Word from Him for them. That experience revolutionized my preaching ministry. I have never gotten over that experience of knowing that God's people deserve to hear a fresh Word from Him when they come to church. When I spent the time to get that word from God, I then trusted His Holy Spirit to help me get it out the way He put it in, and trusted that the hearers would get the message also. When I did that, it was up to God's people to decide what they were going to do with the message that had come from God.

It needs to be said that I was at the church late on that Saturday night working on sermons for the next day, not because I had been lazy all week. In fact just the opposite was true. I had been very busy with "Pastor Work," things that were good. These things were time consuming. They took away from the time I needed to be spending with the Lord, getting ready to deliver His message to His people. One of the things I realized that Saturday night was that I was the only one in the church who had been given the assignment of sharing the Lord's message with His church. Others in the church had vital roles, but only the pastor had been called to stand before all of the church every week and proclaim God's message to them. I had to make choices between spending my time doing good things and spending my time doing the best thing.

I believe that, through the preaching ministry of the church, the Lord has the opportunity to set the agenda for that church, if the pastor will keep his spiritual heart and ears open to the things God is saying to him. Most of the time, God is not able to communicate with the heart of the pastor unless the pastor is willing to take those times when he steps back from everything else, and just spends time listening to the Lord. I believe that, when a pastor is in harmony with the Lord and spends time with Him, God speaks to His church through His chosen servant who is serving as the under-shepherd of that church. That does not mean that the Lord does not speak to others in the church, but, ideally, the Lord's direction for a church will come through the pastor. That does not mean that the pastor is superior to others in the church. It simply means that he is being obedient to God's calling on his life. Unfortunately, there are some in the church who do not understand that concept. If the pastor is a strong leader and takes his work seriously, they accuse him of trying to run the church. To some degree they are right. When a pastor takes the proper approach to the work God has called him to do, he is trying to give the church the spiritual leadership he has been called to give.

Then he deserves to be supported unless it should ever prove that his motives are wrong.

So, back to my preaching ministry at FBC, Rusk, on that Sunday morning I told them I needed their help. I needed them to honor the time that I needed to spend alone with the Lord in preparing to have a "fresh Word from God" every time I stood before them. I told them that if they called to speak to me and they were told I was in my study, they would need to decide if what they had called me about was so urgent that I should be interrupted to deal with it at that very moment, or if it was something I could call them about later. I assured them that if they were calling about an urgent matter, I did want to be interrupted from whatever I was doing. To my surprise, the church liked what they had heard and, for the most part, all in the church were willing to honor my request. When I was in my study, if someone came by to see me or called, the church secretary would say, "He is doing sermon preparation, should I go get him or can he call you later?" That worked very well because I honored my commitment and the people were thrilled to know that when they came to church for worship, their pastor would have a fresh Word from the Lord for them. I think it would be safe to say that the preaching ministry became one of the strongest ministries in the church. This was true because of the commitment by the pastor and the church to make it what it should be.

Years before, I had a preacher friend in Ohio that had challenged me to consider doing my preaching preparation for a year. I resisted at first because it sounded like too much work, although I used other excuses. Finally when we moved to Rockdale, Texas, I decided to give it a try. I had purchased a small camping trailer before we left Ohio. I took it out onto some private, remote property and spent 4 days working on my sermons for the next year. What I came home with from that first trip was the sermon title, scripture text, key verse, and main purpose for each sermon for the entire year. I did that retreat in early November for my preaching ministry for the next year. I remember in August of the next year, I came out of my office after the morning worship service, and one of our young men was standing there with tears in his eyes. He said, "Pastor, that sermon dealt with exactly what I was going through this week." All of a sudden a wonderful truth came to my mind. I said to him, "Isn't it remarkable that last November, when the Lord led me to preach this sermon this week, it was because he knew last November what your experience was going to be this week, and He led me to preach a sermon to meet your need this week. I was amazed and he was amazed. I don't even remember how many times since 1981, that I have had the same kind of experience with someone. I do remember the last one. It was this last week, February 8, 2015, when I was told the same thing after the service by a man in our church.

While I was at FBC, Rusk, I would begin reminding the people about my yearly Preaching Planning Retreat about two months before the retreat and asked them if they would begin praying for me and for the sermon planning process. I asked them to specifically pray that the Lord would lead me in the direction He wanted the preaching ministry to go in the coming year.

My pastoral preaching for years has been to preach verse by verse through books of the Bible. Normally I would preach through one book on Sunday morning and another on Sunday evening. If I knew that I would be beginning a new book at the beginning of the new year or sometime during the new year, I told the people they could give me the name of a book they would like for me to pray about whether or not the Lord wanted me to use as the next book through which I would preach. Every time there was opportunity for the people to make recommendations, I would get several suggestions, and the Lord led me to use several of those suggestions.

I would choose a retreat site that was no more than an hour from home. I would leave on Sunday night after church and be back in time for prayer meeting on Wednesday night. That may not sound like a lot of time, but I would literally work 16 -20 hours a day and take naps when I needed to do that. When I would get back to the church on Wednesday, I would bring the sermon outline notebook into the prayer meeting and ask the people to pray that the Lord would use the messages for the coming year, the way He intended. I believe this helped create an understanding that I was not just standing up and preaching something that I had come up with, but rather I was standing week after week to proclaim the Word of God.

No pastor has all of the skills he needs in every area of responsibility that becomes his, but I believe that most church members will overlook other shortcomings in their pastor's abilities, if he is consistently feeding them from the Word of God. When a man stands week after week to preach before the same group of people, it will become painfully obvious, if he is not spending adequate time with the Lord in preparation to proclaim God's message.

No one else in the church has been given the specific assignment the pastor has been given, to feed the flock of God. I have already talked about the fact that every believer in Jesus Christ has been given spiritual gifts in order to perform the ministries the Lord has given them. He even gives some lay people gifts in preaching the Word of God. The Word tells us that He calls some to be evangelists and some to be pastors and teachers. The role of a full-time evangelist is a valid ministry role. Even that is not the same as the role of the pastor. The Pastor is to labor, week after week with the same group of people, proclaiming the Word of God, and growing up the people of God through the teaching and preaching of the Word of God.

The role of pastor/teacher may not be as glamorous as some other ministry callings, but there may not be a more vital role in the life of the church than men who have heard the call from God to serve as pastor/teacher of His churches. Of all of the things the Lord has allowed me to do, none is more fulfilling than getting a message from God for His people, and then allowing His Holy Spirit to deliver it through me. I have tried, the best I know how, to take that role seriously. I have tried to remain committed to having a fresh Word from God when I stand before His people to proclaim the Word of God.

Discipleship

I had started to get more personally involved in discipling the church while I was at FBC, Rockdale, Texas. I had made some efforts in other churches, but had not gotten really serious about it until MasterLife became a part of my life and ministry. I had hoped to introduce MasterLife at Medway, Ohio, but then the Lord moved us to Rockdale right after I became certified to use the MasterLife material. I had the privilege of having my first MasterLife groups at Rockdale. This was the most powerful ministry experience of my life up to that time.

When we moved to Rusk, there were a group of people who were ready to grow in their walk with the Lord, and MasterLife was just the tool they needed to begin to grow. The timing of the things that happened next could only have been orchestrated by the hand of God Himself. As we took each new group, who had completed MasterLife through the Spiritual Gifts Retreat, I had a whole new group who were equipped and now ready to be used of the Lord.

In God's timing, the Sunday School Board began to turn out a whole series of Life Courses. The Church Training Director for the Baptist General Convention of Texas called me and asked me if FBC, Rusk, would be willing to be a Life Pilot Church in Texas. What this meant was that each time another new Life Course came out, we were willing to teach it in our church. I agreed that we would do that. Almost every time a new study came out, it met a new need that we had in our discipleship ministry.

One year we had so many people involved in discipleship training that we were listed in the top 25 churches in the Southern Baptist Convention in numbers of people earning discipleship training awards. It was not about earning awards; it was about preparing God's people to be on mission for Him.

Without a doubt, the study that capped off everything else we had been doing was "Experiencing God." Our Discipleship Director could not wait to get back from Glorieta after he had been introduced to "Experiencing God." It took him a while to get me to sit down with him long enough to introduce this study to me. When I began to grasp what this study was about, I was overwhelmed. In the next couple of years this study revolutionized our church.

Don Gibson, from Texas Baptist Men, recommended to Claude King that "Experiencing God" be introduced to churches in a weekend setting like the Lay Renewal Weekend. Claude agreed and suggested that he have the first one in Texas. Don called me and asked if we would like to host that first Experiencing God Weekend. We did that in the fall of 1991. That was just before Virginia and I moved to New York. That weekend also prepared our church for our moving to New York as missionaries.

God's Touch on Lives

Something, that I later discovered was not a normal situation, began to happen in the life of First Baptist Church, Rusk, Texas. On a fairly regular basis young people and sometimes young adults came to the altar at the time of invitation to declare that God was calling them into some kind of full-time ministry. Over the almost eight years I served as pastor of FBC, Rusk, over 30 different people made a decision of that sort. They are now serving all over the world. I cannot think of anything that is much more fulfilling than to know that the Lord has taken the message He has given to you and touched somebody's heart to call them into Christian service. The only one that would top that is, when the Lord uses the message He gave you to call someone to repentance and faith in Jesus Christ.

I have had the joy to observe many of those same young people grow into strong and faithful servants of Jesus Christ. I have even had the joy of working alongside some of them in ministry. What a wonderful and rewarding experience.

Invest Your Life

Being a pastor is not a job. At least, if you are a successful pastor, it is never viewed as a job. Being a successful pastor is not defined by the size of the church that you serve. Being a successful pastor is defined by a pastor's faithfulness to the place the Lord has given him to serve. Perhaps I should say something here just to get it out of the way. You will perhaps have noticed that, when I talk about the role of pastor, I always use a male reference. That is because I believe that the Bible places that restriction on that role in the church. If you have a different interpretation of Scripture that is between you and the Lord, but for me, the teaching is clear and so I will stick with what I believe the Bible teaches rather than worry about being politically correct on this issue. You also need to know that I do not believe that women are second class citizens; I believe they play a vital role in Kingdom Ministry in the Lord's Church.

For me, being a pastor means that I invest my life into the lives of the people the Lord has given me to serve. I don't know any other way to be a pastor. You can be a preacher and not invest yourself into the lives of your people. You can be an evangelist and not invest your life into the lives of the people. You can even be a teacher of biblical facts and not invest yourself into the lives of the people. But I do not believe that you can truly be a pastor without investing your life into the lives of your people.

Let me give you an example of what I am talking about. I had not been in Rusk long, when I discovered that one of our older and very well-respected deacons was going to Houston for heart surgery to repair some surgery that had been done 10 years before. I got up very early on the day of the surgery to drive to the south side of Houston, Texas, to the Medical Center where he was going to have the surgery; then he would come home in a few days. When I arrived at the hospital, I discovered that they had just postponed the surgery, because overnight he had developed some inflammation somewhere in his body. There was concern that the surgery would just make matters worse, so the plan was for him to remain in the hospital. They would do the surgery as soon as the problems had been resolved, and he was otherwise healthy enough to do the surgery.

The deacon and all of his family expressed appreciation for me coming and suggested that I return to Rusk. I told them I was going to stay until he had the surgery. I knew it would be at least a day; therefore, I went across the street from the hospital to the Holiday Inn and made reservations. My only problem was that I had not come planning to stay all night. Therefore, off to Wal-Mart I went to buy me some basics for my unplanned stay in Houston. I called my wife and told her what was going on and told her I would give her a daily report. I called my secretary and told her the same thing and that I would at least be back to preach the next Sunday.

It was four days before the infection cleared up and they were able to do the surgery. The family was very appreciative of me being there, but they were also concerned that I might get in trouble with the church for spending so much time with just one family. I told them that I was telling the church by my actions how I would treat their families, when they had a crisis. Every pastor has to decide for himself where he places his priorities. For me, one of my highest priorities has always been to be with families as soon as I know they have a crisis and to stay with them through the crisis.

By the way, at the next deacons' meeting I was asked about the time I spent with this family. However, the question I was asked was, "Who paid your expenses while you were there?" When I told them I did, they told me to submit those expenses to the church and I would be reimbursed. Then they instructed me to get a corporate credit card so that I would have an immediate way of taking care of my expenses in the future.

When you invest your life into the lives of your people, it is both a rewarding and painful experience at the same time. You laugh when they laugh, but you also cry when they cry. You are there for the things that are important in their lives and you never consider it an intrusion into your life, because they have become a part of your life.

Mission Trips

Mission trips became an important part of the ministry of FBC, Rusk, Texas. Over the years I have had several personal opportunities to be involved in mission trips outside of the USA. When we were in Rockdale, Texas, I had the opportunity to take my family and a young man, who was living with us at the time, on an evangelistic mission trip to Brazil. However, the circumstances never were quite right to get the church involved, not only in sending, but also in going, until we came to Rusk.

When I began talking about mission trips, a great deal of interest was expressed by a number of people in the church about going. There were also some who could not go, but would give us money to spend on needs that might arise while on the field. So I began to look for possible opportunities not only to go myself, but also to take members of the church.

Belize, Central America

Green Acres Baptist Church, Tyler, Texas, had been taking regular trips to Belize for several years. I was able to arrange for us to go with them on one of their trips and take on one of their projects for that trip. I was able to put together a team of 8, and we were assigned to Punta Gorda. It was located in southern Belize, which is right down on the bottom of the country where you could see the Dominican Republic just across the bay. Green Acres had a young lady, Mary Lou, who lived there and worked with the little Baptist Church they had started.

We flew into Belize City with the group from Green Acres and then 7 of us flew in a single engine plane from Belize City to Punta Gorda. One of our team members, Doc Martin, worked elsewhere the first part of the week and joined us later. The plane could not carry us and our luggage and supplies for the mission trip, so we went on one plane and they sent our luggage and supplies on a later flight. We taxied out to one end of the runway with the tail of the plane hanging out over the water and just missed the palm trees at the other end of the runway as we took off. In midflight, our son Tom pointed out the shadow of the plane in a circular rainbow on the cloud below us. He said he was taking that as a sign from the Lord that we were going to get there safely, and we did. We breathed a sigh of relief when our luggage and supplies arrived a few hours later. We were met by our American hostess and local pastor, Tony, on the airstrip, which we named the Punta Gorda International Airport. We were then taken in the back of his orange pickup to our hotel, which we referred to as the Punta Gorda Hilton. The room that Virginia and I slept in all week was an enclosed part of the front porch, which was right across the street from a bar that stayed open most of the night and played very loud music.

Inside, on the first floor, were the other bedrooms. The community wash basin, showers, and toilets were at the end of the hall. That made for an interesting experience to get used to during the week. There was sight privacy, but no noise privacy. In our group were my wife and I, our son Tom and his friend Jerry Johnson, one deacon and his wife George and Tommie Nielsen, and Richard Johnson from our church. Another deacon, Doc Martin, who was a Veterinarian, worked in another place the first part of the week with farmers and their animals. At the end of the week, he joined us on our assignment.

Our assignment for the week was that we did VBS in the morning, visitation and various activities in the afternoon, and revival services at night. We had a good number of children that came to the VBS. The revival services had overflow crowds every night. There were a number of children, youth, and adults who were saved during the week, which made everything worthwhile.

 It was a very hot time of the year and you might literally drink 6-8 cokes a day and sweat all of them out of your system. One of the ways to stay, somewhat cool, was to go down to the water and walk out on the pier and enjoy the breeze blowing off of the water. The ladies began to notice that if they walked out on the pier, they needed to make sure they were wearing slacks instead of a dress, because the local boys would jump in the water and swim under the pier and look up through the cracks in the boards.

We found out that Mary Lou, the lady from Texas, had a fishing village she would go to for Bible Study. You could only get there by boat. I made arrangements for George Nielsen to preach one night, and she got a man who had a 20' boat to take her, Tom and Jerry, and me to this fishing village. It was about a two hour boat ride on the Caribbean Sea to get there. They fed us a wonderful lobster meal that evening, and we led a Bible Study that night. A man and his family of about 20 – 25 people lived there. It was a section of land where about 100 yards had been cleared between the sea and the jungle and you could only get there by boat or hiking through the jungle. Their houses were built about halfway between the sea and the jungle.

That afternoon, Tom had an encounter with a man that I am convinced was demon-possessed. Tom handled himself very well with him. The people were very polite to us and I think two people were saved after the Bible Study. I did not know what our sleeping arrangements were going to be until after the Bible Study.

When we had finished, the head of the family pulled some rolled up sleeping mats out of the rafters of his house and gave each of us one. He then told us there was a school building just a little ways down, and we could go down there and spend the night. The only light we had was our flashlight. We got to the school, which was a big, open room upstairs. When we opened our sleeping bags, Tom said he felt something on his arm. I shined the flashlight on him and there was a large scorpion on his arm just above his hand. I quickly knocked it off and killed it, but we soon discovered that all of the bedrolls were filled with small scorpions. Needless to say, between the heat and the scorpions, we did not get much sleep that night.

The next morning the young man came back with his 20' skiff that had two 20 horse power engines on it, to take us back. On the way back, a storm came up on the sea and we were right in the middle of it. I was sitting on the bench seat of the boat, literally, looking up at the waves we were going through. The driver of the boat asked me if I wanted him to pull into harbor. I told him to do what he thought was best. He pulled, no more than a quarter of a mile out of the storm, into a little cove and beached the boat. We stood on the shore as a light rain fell and gave us the shower we needed. He climbed a tree and picked some coconuts and we drank the coconut juice, and watched the storm pass over. I thought about the song "Till the Storm Passes Over." We were certainly in a safe harbor, created by the Lord Himself, waiting for the storm to pass over. We were refreshed by the showers that fell from heaven and refreshed by the juice that God had made. It was one of those special moments in life that only the Lord could provide. After the storm was over, we got back into the boat and made our way back to join the rest of our team. We all had a wonderful experience that week and were blessed by the commitment of the small band of believers we found there.

Rio de Janeiro, Brazil

I think I learned, through what was at the time the Foreign Mission Board of the Southern Baptist Convention, that Dr. Wayne Dehoney and his church from Louisville, Kentucky, were leading an evangelistic crusade in Rio and were looking for other participants. I called them and discovered that they did, in fact, need some additional teams. I came up with 10 people who wanted to go. We were given the assignment of two churches. This meant that we would provide the evangelist, musician and other lay leadership to work in these two churches during the crusade.

I had told the Crusade leadership that I had other members of my team who could preach if they were needed. I also told all of my men to go prepared to preach at least one sermon. When we arrived in Rio and were in line checking into our hotel rooms, I was pulled out of the line by the crusade leader. I was asked if I had team members who could preach in other churches and I said yes. Then I was told that two of the evangelists had not been able to come and they were in need of evangelists for two additional churches. I went ahead and told them we would accept the additional assignments.

I told all of our team to take their luggage to their rooms and then come to my room for a team meeting. I reminded them of the instruction to be flexible. I told them about the additional assignments, and began to give them their new assignments. Randall Jinkins, who had already preached quite a bit, was assigned to a church as their evangelist. Richard Johnson and Thomas Parsons, who had never preached before, but were told to have one sermon ready, were assigned to another church to preach every other night of the revival. Jim Boone was assigned to another church with Tom Goforth and Shari Shipp. My wife Virginia and I, and Doc and Kay Martin were in another church. So instead of our team of 10 leading revival services in two churches, we led revival services in four churches.

Those who were given new assignments had one day to make adjustments and get ready to serve. There were some nervous moments, but all served without complaint and served our Lord and the churches in fine fashion.

The Lord used each team to lead many people to a commitment to Jesus Christ as their Lord and Savior. Each night, when we all got back to the hotel from our church assignments, we would get together and share the blessings of the day. It was a glorious celebration of what the Lord had done.

One of our laymen, Randall Jinkins, ended up preaching an entire crusade on his own in a mission church. This mission was holding their services in a very interesting place. They were meeting in a building, which was also a house of prostitution. I think the owner of the business lost some of his employees that week, because they became Christians. Praise God!

Because I was only in one church, I can only share personal experiences about that church experience. It was a wonderful week. My wife sang each night, some songs in Portuguese and others in English. We had other lay people, Doc and Kay Martin, who gave their testimonies and worked with the children and youth. One of the neat stories happened the first day of the revival in the first service. Juan de Baptista was saved; in other words, John the Baptist became a Christian. We were all particularly impressed with the music program at the church. They had a young man, who was an outstanding musician, who worked with their choir program. He gave personal voice lessons to all of his adult choir members. He also had the most disciplined children's choir I have ever seen.

The church would seat about 400 people, and there were overflow crowds at every service. On the closing Sunday night they moved the service outside to the church courtyard. The city street was also closed off for the service. They estimated that there were over 1200 in attendance that night. None of us will forget the close of the service when the whole crowd got out white cloths, waved them in the air, and sang to us in broken English, "Till We Meet Again."

Mission to Mexico

Then there was our involvement in Mexico, primarily in the Monterey, Mexico, area. In 1988 a devastating hurricane hit the northern border of Mexico and moved through the Monterey area killing many and wiping out thousands of low income family homes. One of our Hispanic churches in Palestine, Texas, where Dexton Shores was the pastor, had people who had come from the affected areas. They discovered that for less than $500.00 U.S. currency, small 3 room homes could be built for these homeless people. At our three annual meetings of the Dogwood Trails Baptist Area, over $20,000.00 was raised to fund this project. We had been told that the government had taken a large segment of land on the outskirts of Monterey and had blocked it off in small parcels, and were allowing the homeless to build some kind of shelter on it that would get them out of the weather before winter.

We took a small group down to scope out the situation and provide some clothing for those who needed it. When we arrived, we discovered that the land had already been divided up, and shelters of one kind or another had been built on it. We met with our Foreign Mission Board appointed missionary to the area, and some local church leaders, to find out how we could best help. We were told about an area about 20 miles northwest of Monterey that needed a lot of help, including families that needed shelters. We did some investigation and decided to concentrate our help in the village of Villa de Garcia, where there was a fairly new Baptist Mission that had been started.

We then went back home to gather building teams to go back and get as many shelter type homes built as possible before winter. There was a team of 8 men from FBC, Rusk, who went on that first trip. There were also men from several other churches who sent men on that trip. Our total number of men was about 20.

One of the neat things about these mission trips to northern Mexico was that we could drive, which saved a lot of money. It was about a 10 hour drive. So we could leave one day and drive to the border. We would spend the night in Laredo, cross the border at Nuevo Laredo, and then make our way on down to the Monterey area. In those days crossing the border into Mexico was a much safer and easier process than today. It was an interesting personal experience for me. Although I had grown up in Texas, I had never been to Mexico until this trip to build shelters. I don't think that any of us imagined what would develop from this effort to provide shelter for families who were left without a home after the hurricane. When it became obvious that much more than we had imagined was developing, a committee from the Dogwood Trails Baptist Area was elected to coordinate our efforts. I was asked to serve as chairman of that committee. I soon learned that, although our Director of Missions was very supportive of the effort, he had no real interest in traveling to Mexico to do the necessary planning with the leaders there. So I found myself making regular trips to Monterey, and the surrounding area, making sure that all necessary planning was being made for the various mission trips that developed over the next three years.

Now let's get back to that first trip to Villa de Garcia to build shelters for families that had been left homeless. One day I was approached by some ladies from the Baptist Mission. They told me about some remote villages out in the mountains that had been severely damaged by the flooding that followed the storm. They told me that no one had tried to help these people. I gathered up some of the clothing that we had brought with us. With two local ladies and a translator, we headed out in one of our church vans. The roads had been so washed out by the flooding that they were almost nonexistent. Two hours later we arrived in the first village. We got the clothing out and I watched as the people went through the clothing in a very orderly fashion. I watched as one man about my size tried to find something but could not find anything to fit him. I had worn a flannel shirt like a jacket over my other shirt, so I took it off and gave it to him. You would have thought I had just given him a large amount of money.

281

While the clothing distribution was going on, a woman approached me with her three small children. She asked me if we had any food. She told me that she had no food and that she had not been able to feed her children for three days. She said, "If you are hungry enough, you will eat anything, even rice with worms in it. I did not have any food with me, but I promised her I would be back.

We made the trip back to town. I pulled the men from our church off of the work site and told them what I had found. One of the men looked at me immediately and said that he assumed we were going to go buy some food and take it to them. I told him I had hoped that was the response I was going to get. We went to the store and bought some large bags of rice and beans and then we headed out again over those very rough roads. This particular village was one of about 100 people. Before the sun went down that day, we were able to provide food for each family, and also leave them a copy of the Word of God in Spanish. As far as I know, I was the first evangelical Christian minister to ever visit this village.

Over the next year, the people gave us a small parcel of land upon which we built a small church building for the new Baptist Mission. I think most of the adults, who lived in the village, became openly professing Christians. We were able to support the ministry of the mission pastor in Villa de Garcia so that he was able to go out there on a regular basis to lead a Bible Study.

We also found two other remote villages and were able to provide them with immediate help. We were also able to go back later and have VBS and revival services in those villages.

It soon became obvious that a much larger opportunity was opening up for us through our relationship with our SBC Missionary, who was assigned to that area. We began to discuss the need for some sort of formal agreement between the Monterey Association and the Dogwood Trails Baptist Area. I learned that the Monterey Association began at the Texas/Mexico border and went south of the City of Monterey. It was a large geographical area with more needs than you could even begin to try to list. I mentioned the idea of the partnership with the leadership of the Dogwood Trails Baptist Area. They were very excited about it. The leaders in Mexico were equally excited about the possibilities. After much discussion between all parties involved, (The Dogwood Trails Baptist Area, The Monterrey Baptist Association, The Foreign Mission Board of the SBC, and the Mexico Baptist Convention), an agreement was reached on the scope of the partnership, and the work was begun.

The men who went on that first trip would be disappointed in me, if I did not share about our experience with the Monterey Police after the first day of work in Villa de Garcia. Although we were working in Villa de Garcia, we were staying in a hotel in downtown Monterey.

When we left to go back into Monterey, it was already nearly dark. It had been a really long day. We had driven from the border at Laredo and had gone directly to Villa de Garcia, and had spent the day working. It had already been a 12 hour day when we started back into Monterey. There were three vans of volunteer workers. I was the only one who knew how to get to our hotel. I told the other two van drivers to stay close to me, and I thought we would be ok. I was watching the other two vans to make sure they were staying up with me and, near the hotel, I made a wrong turn. I thought I could go up and turn around and be right back where we needed to be. That was a bad assumption. When I realized where I needed to turn, I made a left turn where a left turn was prohibited and the other two vehicles followed me. Keep in mind that all drivers in Monterey break driving laws of one kind or another all the time. However, we were pulled over by the local police. They took my driver's license and then wanted me to give them $15.00 for each van. I told them I would give them the money, if they would write me a ticket. He refused to write me a ticket. So I am standing in the middle of the street demanding a ticket and the police officer is demanding $45.00. Finally, I showed him the business card of the hotel where we were staying. He put his young assistant in the van with me to get us back to the hotel. This young man had my driver's license. When we got to the hotel, he and

I got out and the others drove the vans to the back of the hotel. When we got in the lobby, I thought the clerk at the desk would be able to help me; however, he did not speak English, and the young police officer also did not speak English. I was trying to make the young man understand that if he would just give me a ticket I would give him the money. Soon this young police officer was surrounded by 15 Texans in the lobby of the hotel. I finally asked him to give me a receipt, hoping he would understand that. I later found out that I was asking him to give me a prescription. Finally, I demanded that he give me a receipt. He looked at all of the Texans around him, gave me my driver's license back and left.

By now it was very late; I was frustrated, and all of us were very tired. I told the men what time we would be leaving the next morning, and we all went to our rooms. I was sharing a room with a pastor friend. When we got to the room, we were discussing the things that had just taken place. He said that he was sure that, when that young officer got back to his superior, he was going to be very upset that he did not have the money. Then we talked about the horror stories we had heard about Mexican jails. As we were turning out the light, he said, "I hope you don't end up in one of those jails tonight." Then there was a loud knock on the door to our room. My heart jumped up into my throat. I went over to the door and quietly asked who it was. It was Randall Jinkins from our church. He wanted to know what time we were leaving the next morning. I jerked opened the door, and told him to go to bed. Later I explained to him the conversation that had gone on just before he knocked on my door. We have laughed about it many times over the years, but in the moment it was not funny to me.

I did not realize at the time, but we were really on the cutting edge of the idea that Southern Baptist churches could send volunteers on short term mission trips to other countries of the world. A representative of the Foreign Mission Board came to East Texas to visit with me about this project. He shared with me that there was some concern at the FMB about the long term effects on our SBC churches sending teams in to do short term mission projects. FMB was concerned that these projects might harm the support the churches were giving to the work that the FMB was doing with career missionaries. I assured him that it was not having a negative effect in our church, and that, in fact, just the opposite was true. Now that there was a greater awareness of the need, our people were more generous in their financial support of the FMB.

It was very important that all parties involved have a clear understanding of what the partnership would involve. This was important so that there would be no misunderstanding of expectations by anyone after the partnership began.

After we reached an agreement about the scope of the partnership, it was important for all parties involved to make an official commitment. We were coming close to the time for the annual meetings of the three associations which made up the Dogwood Trails Baptist Area (Cherokee, Henderson, and Saline Associations). Our Director of Missions Charles Russell felt that it would be helpful if I would attend all three of these meetings. He felt that I could best answer whatever questions might arise about the proposed partnership. I did attend those three meetings and the partnership was approved by all three associations. The partnership had already been approved by the Dogwood Trails Baptist Area Committee and some funds had been put in the area budget for this project. Then I needed to attend the Annual Meeting of the Monterey Baptist Association. Dexton Shores and I made our plans to attend that meeting. I felt that it would be helpful if I made my comments in Spanish, if possible. I wrote my presentation in English and Dexton translated it for me into Spanish. On the flight from Houston to Monterey, I practiced until he felt that I had it down pat.

The night of their Annual Meeting there was a large crowd. After being introduced, I read my presentation to them in Spanish. Everything went really well during the meeting, and the association in Monterey also agreed to the partnership. It did not occur to me that, as a result of my presentation, everyone there was going to think that

I could speak Spanish. When the meeting was over, Dexton and I got separated. He was not available to translate for me. So I just stood there and nodded my head and said "Si" to everything that they asked me. When we finally got back to our hotel room that night, I told Dexton that I did not have any idea what kind of things I had committed us to do, but I guess he would soon find out. Fortunately, I did not commit to anything we could not deliver.

Without a doubt, one of the most precious experiences for me, in all that we did in Mexico, revolved around one man, Lupe and his family in Villa de Garcia. On our first trip to Villa de Garcia to build shelter type homes for those who had lost everything, we worked through the Baptist Mission that had been established there. The home of one of the members became our base of operations. The ladies of the church would cook our lunch and evening meal, and we would eat in and around their home. Their home was within walking distance of all of the houses we were building on that first trip. I became friends with the man of the house who was a police officer in Monterrey.

We went back to the same general area the following summer to conduct VBS and show the "Jesus" film in various locations in the evening. On the last night of that trip, he got an interpreter so that he could tell me something. He told me that, when we first came, he was not a Christian, and that he had never seen anyone do anything for anyone without expecting something in return. He told me that he was also an alcoholic and a gambler, and that, every payday, he would spend all of his paycheck on gambling and alcohol and would be gone from home all weekend. When he came home, he would be broke and his wife would have to work odd jobs to buy food for their family. He said the pastor had said they could not have the Bible Study in their home anymore because he was an embarrassment to the church.

Lupe told me that, because of the witness he had seen in our lives, he had given his life to Jesus Christ. He said that he promised the Lord that, if He would help him, he would never be an embarrassment to Him again. He told me that he had been sober for 8 months. This

286

layman in the small village of Villa de Garcia became a very close friend, and like a brother to me. In fact, Virginia and I became very close to this man and his family. He became a strong witness for Christ in his community. Every time I would make a trip to Mexico, if I was anywhere near the Monterrey area, I would include a trip out to Villa de Garcia to see this family.

Several months after the trip, when Lupe had told me of his conversion, I was there with another mission team. We were going to help them with their VBS, along with some other evangelism efforts.

There was a planned baptism service and a Mexican version of a Baptist covered dish meal, under the bridge at the river in Villa de Garcia. As we were preparing to leave Monterrey to drive out to Villa de Garcia, our SBC missionary stopped by my motel room to talk to me about the baptism service. He told me that the pastor of the mission had not yet completed the ordination process with the local Baptist Association; therefore, he would not be able to administer the act of baptism. He told me I should take some extra clothes because he thought they were going to ask me to administer the baptism. Lupe and four others from the Baptist Mission in Villa de Garcia were being baptized that day. On the way out to the baptism service, I had the missionary go over the Spanish words spoken during a baptism service, so that those being baptized would know what had been said. I was asked to conduct that baptism service, and on that day I had the privilege of baptizing Lupe and four other adults. It was one of the high mark moments of my ministry that I will never forget.

As I have mentioned before, although I grew up in Texas, I had never been to Mexico prior to that first trip after the hurricane. This mission developed into an official three year partnership. I really don't know how many trips I made to Mexico during that time, but besides the mission trips themselves, I would make a pre-trip visit before any trip planned by any of our churches here in the Dogwood Trails area. I would do that to make sure that all preparations were being made and that everyone understood the scope of the mission trip. That was the best way of making sure that the trip would be a success for everyone involved.

Both Dallas and Houston had non-stop flights to Monterrey. Depending on where I could get the best price, I would drive to either Dallas or Houston, and fly directly to Monterrey. After a few trips I became comfortable enough with my limited ability to speak Spanish to make the trips alone. Once I got there, our missionary would coordinate meetings with the churches there. He would be with me when we would discuss the details of upcoming mission trips. Sometimes the purpose of the trip would be to discuss with the churches in Mexico some things that our churches felt they could do and find a church there that had such a need. Most of the time I was there to hear what the needs of the churches there were, and then return home to find churches who could meet that need.

It was amazing how the Holy Spirit led in these meetings. I was very impressed with how the pastors in Mexico came to these meetings with very genuine needs. I was even more amazed when they would help me prioritize the various projects. There was no "me first" attitude. They seemed to realize they were all in this together, and they all seemed to want us to meet the most critical needs first. As has been the case in all mission experiences I have had, I felt like I received far more from the people of Mexico than I was able to give to them. In many ways, the Christians I worked with there gave me a fresh new perspective on my own ministry.

As we were coming to the close of the second year of the three year partnership, we agreed with the leadership in the Monterey area that we would like to climax with a City-Wide Crusade in Monterey. Dexton Shore and I flew to Monterey to do some initial planning with the pastors there. We discussed who we would like to invite to be the evangelist. We soon discovered that we both had the same man on our minds, Rudy Hernandez. When we arrived at the airport in Monterey, we were picked up by our SBC missionary there. As we were leaving the airport, he related to us that Rudy Hernandez was in Monterey and wanted to meet with us while we were there to discuss the possibility of cooperating in a City-Wide Crusade. We just looked at each other and grinned, and we probably both thought, "That is just like God." We did meet with Rudy and the Monterey pastors the next day, and began the planning process for the crusade the following year.

There was one particular trip where we were taking a large group just from FBC, Rusk. Most of the team needed to follow the procedure we had usually done, which meant they left on Saturday, drove to Laredo, spent the night, and then drove on to the mission sight the next day. There was an important vote on the new budget at FBC, Rusk, on that Sunday morning. Therefore, the Chairman of the Budget Committee and I decided to stay for that vote. We sent most of our luggage for the eight-day trip on the vans with the larger group, which was about 35 people. After church on Sunday morning, Larry Sinclair and I were driven to the airport in Houston to fly to Monterey. We did not think about what it would look like flying into the country, going through customs with just a small carry-on bag, when we were staying eight days and then driving out of the country.

When we first began to go to Mexico, we were told to just indicate that we were tourists, because if we indicated we were on a mission trip, we would not be allowed entrance. So Larry and I had done what I had done on every trip and checked that we were tourists. As you can imagine, that did throw up a red flag with the customs agent. Before we knew it, we were sitting in the office of the head of customs there at the airport in Monterey. After much discussion, he finally looked at me and said, "Why don't you tell me why you are really in my country?" I did explain who we were and why we were there. I also told him that I was a minister. Then he said, "So, Reverend, you lied to me." I was about as ashamed of myself as I have ever been. He wanted to know why. I told him that we had been told that we would not be let in if we indicated the real reason we were coming. I know that Larry was as embarrassed as I was. I told him that I would not blame him if he made us go buy a ticket back to Houston and put us on the next plane back. I promised him that I would never lie again about why I was coming into his country, and I would not let any of my groups lie again, even if it meant we never got to come back. I assured him that we were only there to assist his people. He chastised us for a few more minutes, and then let us go.

Let me say something else about that trip. We had a large group from our church, who had trained for months to come on the trip. JoEd and Nancy Anderson had kept an exchange student in their home a few years earlier. During his year in Texas he had become a Christian. Now his sister was staying with them, and she had also become a Christian. We made arrangements to fly the young man from Mexico City to Monterey and his sister rode with our group from Rusk. The two of them served as interpreters for us during the week.

When we got settled into our motel on that Sunday night, I called the local pastor who we were going to work with while we were there. For the first time, there had been poor communication and he had forgotten that we were coming. I got our team together and told them what had happened. I told them that we had two choices: one, we could go home; two, we could make the most of it and let the Lord lead us on a daily basis. They were excited about the second choice. Thankfully, by then we had gone down there enough that we had some good ideas of where to look to let the Lord lead us. I remember one day in particular, the weather was not cooperating for the outdoor activity we had planned. I remembered that, in the middle of downtown Monterey there was a small underground shopping mall. We could make the day a combination of tourist activities and whatever opportunities the Lord opened up for us.

I will never forget some of the images in my mind from that day. There was the young store clerk that I had the opportunity, with the help of an interpreter, to lead to Christ. After she accepted Christ, I gave her a Spanish New Testament. Later I walked back by that store and she was reading the New Testament. I remember seeing JoEd Anderson in the hallway. He had a gang of young people in a circle around him; he and one of our interpreters was sharing the gospel with them. Several of them made professions of faith right there.

290

Later, after the rain stopped, we went outside to a city park beside the river. I watched as our people engaged others with the gospel and would call on our two young interpreters to come close the deal. I noticed a young man sitting by himself. I went over and sat down beside him and began a very limited conversation with him using my little bit of knowledge of Spanish and his limited knowledge of English. When I determined that he might be ready to receive a gospel presentation, I looked around and both of our interpreters were busy. I had a Spanish New Testament that had the gospel presentation in the back in English and Spanish. I also had my testimony that had been translated into Spanish. I let him read my testimony; then we went through the gospel presentation, and he prayed to receive Jesus Christ as his Lord and Savior.

When we got back to the motel that night, there were many stories about how the Lord had worked that day. It was a day, when we started out to do one thing, and the Lord took us in a completely different direction. It was also the last day of our trip, which made for a very memorable trip back to East Texas.

Call to New York

It was not long after that trip to Mexico to plan the crusade that I was shocked to discover that God was calling us to a new ministry in New York State. I will go into the details of that call in a moment, but let me first wrap-up my involvement in Mexico.

I had really become personally attached to the work in Mexico and, more importantly, to the people there. When I realized that the Lord really was calling me to New York, it was almost as hard to leave the work that had been started in Mexico, as it was to leave FBC, Rusk. I felt like I must make one more trip to Monterey to speak to the leadership there face to face about why I would not be around for the conclusion of the things we had planned. I also wanted to reassure them that others would be picking up where I left off, and all that we planned would continue. I met with the pastors from the Monterey area, and they were more understanding than I had hoped they would be. I am sure having Dexton Shore with me helped a lot with their attitude. He and I had been together on every major part of the project from the beginning.

I also wanted to go out to Villa de Garcia to say goodbye to my friend. We found him at work. After we visited for a few minutes, I told him what was going on with me, and that I would probably not see him again until we get to heaven. He then said something to me through my interpreter. I knew that I was in trouble when the interpreter began to weep. He said that he knew that I would be back to see him, because he knew that I loved him, and that love always finds a way. We stood on that street corner in Villa de Garcia, Mexico, and embraced and wept and said goodbye to one another. As circumstances would have it, it turns out that I was right and I have not been able to get back down there. I had hoped that when I retired and moved back to Texas, I might be able to take a trip back down there. However, with all of the unrest around the Mexican border, I have not felt like it was a good idea to try. I will admit that while recounting this story, if I could find out that he was still alive, I might try to find a way to get back to see my friend.

We had just gotten back from vacation. It was the first day of Vacation Bible School. One of my VBS leaders was in my office visiting with me, when I received a phone call from a Pastor in Plattsburgh, New York. He identified himself as Jim Bradley, the pastor of the Bread of Life Baptist Church, in Plattsburgh, New York. He told me that he was also the Moderator of the Adirondack Baptist Association in northern New York, and that their association had been searching for a Director of Missions for two years. He said that they had been given my name. He also told me that the DOM Search Committee had asked him to call me and ask me if I would be willing to pray about becoming their Director of Missions. I told him that I would pray about it, but they needed to know that they were wasting their time, because I was sure I was where I was supposed to be for the foreseeable future. His reply was that it was their time and they could waste it if they wanted to, and I would be receiving a call from the search committee that night. I later told him that if he had not inserted the phrase, "Would you be willing to pray about it," I would have just said no and the conversation would have been over, because I did not have the least bit of interest in leaving where I was.

The lady who was in my office when the conservation started had gotten up and left the office. She was one of the strong prayer warriors in our church. I went and found her to tell her about the conversation so she could be praying about it. She told me that, if she prayed, it would be selfish, because she did not want me to leave. I told her that was alright because I did not want to leave.

When I got home that day, I told my wife about the phone call I had gotten and that I had an uneasy feeling about it all. I did talk with the search committee that night and, almost from the beginning, there was a feeling that this was something that the Lord was doing. I knew that it was not something I was doing, because the desire of my heart was to stay right where I was.

A series of events began to happen that all pointed to our going to New York. The next day, on my way to work, I stopped at the Post Office to pick up the church mail, which I did every day. That day I had gotten some material from the Home Mission Board of the SBC, now the North American Mission Board. The material contained a letter and a booklet. The letter was addressed to all of the Directors of Missions in the USA, and the booklet was about starting new churches.

The next day I went to the Post Office and picked up the mail. In the mail was a copy of a Gospel tract that you could have personalized with your local church information on the back. On the front of the tract there was an outline of the state of New York, and the title of the tract was "How to Get to Heaven from New York." I just sat in my chair and stared at the tract.

The next day I met with the group of men from our church that I had been praying with once a week for about three years. I told them what was going on and the things that had happened during the week. One of the men said that I should not be surprised if the Goodyear Blimp was hovering over the parsonage the next day with a flashing sign that said, "Go to New York."

On the next Sunday the lady I had asked to pray for me came to tell me that the Lord had revealed to her that He was sending me to New York, and that she needed to be willing to let me go. So by this time the Lord had spoken to me through His Word, circumstances, and the church, which are all of the ways I had been teaching to the church with the "Experiencing God" material.

I began to have regular serious conversations with the DOM Search Committee of the Adirondack Baptist Association. There came a time, when they and I agreed, that there was enough indication that this might be of the Lord, and that the only way for all of us to know for sure is for Virginia and me to make a visit there. When the discussions first began, I would become the DOM for both the Adirondack Baptist Association and the Thousand Islands Association, which at one time had been a part of the Adirondack Association. One of the real sticky issues was going to be how much time was spent in each association. As it turned out, I ended up being the DOM for the ABA only. This ended up being a blessing, and it allowed me to concentrate all of my efforts on one territory, which was already quite large anyway.

So a trip was planned for the middle of August of 1991. I had just one major problem. I had just recently gotten back from a time of vacation. I had also used up all of my other personal time on mission trips to Mexico. I had just announced to the church that I would not be gone again the rest of that calendar year. I felt it was impossible for me to be gone another week and another Sunday without some explanation. Everything I had ever been taught and known from my own personal experience was that you did not tell the church you were considering a move this early in the process. However, I felt I must do it and leave the results to the Lord.

As I looked out at the congregation that morning, I saw several families that had been attending the church; I knew they were considering joining the church. So I prayed that if the Lord intended for them to be a part of FBC, Rusk, they would go ahead and join that morning before I made the announcement. When I extended the invitation that morning at the conclusion of the message, three families came forward to join the church and two others came to profess Christ as Savior and Lord.

After the invitation was over, I asked everyone to be seated and I came back to the pulpit to speak to them. I told them that what I was about to do went against everything I knew to be the best thing to do, but that I also believed it was the right thing to do under the circumstances. I told them what had been going on for about a month and that I was now at the point when I felt that Virginia and I must make a trip there in order to give the Lord every opportunity to speak to our hearts. I told them that the desire of my heart was to stay in Rusk the rest of my life, but that I also wanted to make sure that I was being obedient to the will of God for my life. I asked them if they would begin that day to pray with me that I would know the will of God.

I looked down on the front row at those who had joined the church that morning and they had strange looks on their faces. I then told them that I had prayed before the service began that, if the Lord wanted them to be a part of our church, they would join today before I made this announcement. I think most, if not all, of them understood.

I told the church that, if the association and I felt good about moving forward, I would have to become an appointed missionary of the Home Mission Board, now the North American Mission Board. I also told them that the process would take three months, so it would be at least three months before we would know, if we were moving or staying.

That became a very interesting time in the life of the church and the city of Rusk. One of the unexpected pleasant byproducts of the process was that one of the most talked about subjects in town was, "What is the will of God for the pastor of First Baptist Church?" Also, during this time when the church did not know if I was leaving or staying, we had the greatest three months of people being saved and baptized than at any other three month period in my 7 ½ year ministry in Rusk. This goes to prove that it is the Christ, Who is preached, that changes people's lives, and not the one doing the preaching.

In February 2016, we were attending the Annual Board Meeting of Texas Baptist Men. I got into a conversation with a long time ministry friend in Texas Baptist Men. We got to talking about the first ever Experiencing God Weekend, which was held at FBC, Rusk, in the fall of 1991. He remarked to me that the thing he remembered most about that weekend was how freely the subject of me possibly moving to New York was discussed. I asked him if he remembered Claude King saying to the church that there were two ways they could look upon this time in the life of their church. One way of looking on it was that they were losing a pastor they loved. The other way to look upon it was that God had chosen this church to send their pastor as a missionary to northern New York. My friend was very moved by the way the church bought into the idea that they were sending their pastor, rather than they were losing him. Let me say that, for the most part, that is the way the church viewed this time. This made it a very special time.

Without a doubt, the hardest decision we have ever made to leave a church was the one we made when we left Rusk to go to northern New York. We not only left a wonderful church family that we loved dearly; we left to go to the greatest unknown we had ever gone into.

I was originally told that I would be voted on for appointment by the trustees of the Home Mission Board in their October 1991, board meeting. Therefore, I had told my church that I would let them know if I was leaving or staying no later than the first Sunday in November 1991. I received a phone call on the last Friday in October telling me that my paper work had been misplaced and I would not be voted on until the November Board Meeting. I told them that I had promised my church I would give them an answer by the first Sunday in November. Therefore, I was going to take this as a Word from the Lord that I was to stay where I was, and that I was going to announce to the church that, because of the delay, I was staying. I was encouraged not to do that. In a few minutes I got a call back, telling me to go ahead and resign, and that I would be appointed in the November Board Meeting. I asked them if they would delay the beginning of my time with the Mission Board to January 1, 1992, so that I could stay with my church and near my family through the Christmas holidays. So when I was appointed in November 1991, my new ministry was to begin in January 1992.

On the first Sunday of November 1991, I resigned as pastor of FBC, Rusk, Texas, to become the Director of Missions of the Adirondack Baptist Association, in Upstate New York. The deacons and members of FBC, Rusk, were very gracious in allowing me to stay for two months after my resignation. In retrospect, I think it was a very good time of adjustment for me and for the church. I think that the fact that I was going to a new ministry, and especially the fact that I was leaving for missionary service, made the move easier.

The church began to look at the whole situation as an opportunity for them to be more personally involved in missions. Many in the church began to talk in terms of "we are sending our pastor and his wife as missionaries to New York." Therefore, on the last Sunday of December 1991, the church not only had a goodbye reception for us in the afternoon; they also had a Missionary Commissioning Service that night. I will never forget, when we knelt at the front of the sanctuary. The deacons came and laid hands on us; then all who wanted to lay hands on us were invited to do so. There were many of our people who came to pray for us. I particularly remember when my own brother, and then my dad, came and laid hands on me and said words of encouragement. Dad had really struggled with this move because it was so far away, and he was getting on up in years. In that gesture, however, I saw him submit to the Will of God for my life, and that was really a blessing to me.

The moving van was not coming until Thursday of that next week. Monday was January 1, and we went to my brother's and spent the day with family and said goodbye to them. Then we came back to Rusk for two days waiting on moving day. Those two days were gut wrenching. Everywhere we went in town, people, who thought they had seen us for the last time, would come up, grab us, hug us, and begin to weep. At the end of that day, I came home and told Virginia I was not going downtown anymore. Emotionally, I could not take it.

Then on moving day, I looked out at the end of the driveway and the two neighbor children, Jordan and Ramey Beard, were standing there weeping. When I went out to talk to them, the little boy said, "Bro. Jim, you are really leaving, I told them you would not leave us." That family had been very special to us, and they continue to this day to be very special. So, late in the afternoon of January 4, 1992, we pulled out of Rusk, Texas, which had been our home and place of ministry for nearly eight years, and we started our journey to the Adirondack Mountains of New York.

Texas Baptist Men

I don't even know where to begin in describing what the ministry of Texas Baptist Men, and on a more personal level, Bob Dixon and Don Gibson, have meant to me personally and to many parts of my ministry. That was true first as a pastor and then as a Director of Missions. The three of us got to be close when Don Gibson was serving on the staff of the University of Mary Hardin-Baylor.

Dr. Parker, president of UMHB, developed a ministry advisory team. Bob Dixon and I were both asked to serve on this team with Don Gibson. The three of us worked together on various assignments. By then, both of my sons were students at UMHB. We spent much time praying together. Don was also very closely connected to those at LifeWay, who had developed the Life series of discipleship. Our church in Rusk was very involved in that series of discipleship material. Don had led our church in several activities including the first ever Experiencing God Weekend, and a "Solemn Assembly."

I had accepted the call to be the Director of Missions for the Adirondack Baptist Association. I then had been approved to serve as a missionary with what was then the Home Mission Board of the Southern Baptist Convention. It later became the North American Mission Board.

I was sitting at my desk at FBC, Rusk, Texas, when I received a call from Bob Dixon and Don Gibson. They wanted me to know that Texas Baptist Men considered me to be their missionary. Then they told me that, anytime I needed their help, all I had to do was call them and they would do what they could. They meant exactly what they said. Every time I called upon them, during our 12 years in New York, they were right there to be of assistance. This was true for both financial assistance for various projects, and the sending of teams of men and women to serve alongside us. It was a wonderful partnership that the Lord honored in many ways. I am sure I will describe some of those ways as I move through the story of our years in New York.

Let me give you one specific example. One October Friday morning, I received a phone call from one of the laymen who was a member of First Christian Church, Brushton, New York, which was one of our churches. John Edwards told me that they had an urgent need. They had just been given an old recreation building that had belonged to the Village of Brushton. They had decided that it was worth accepting and remodeling into a Christian Life Center for the church. However, the roof needed to be replaced immediately so that they could then work on remodeling it through the winter months. He told me that they needed 10-12 men to work with their men for about two weeks, so that they could get the roof finished before the snow started falling. I told him I would do what I could. I called a layman with Texas Baptist Men, who was a member of First Baptist Church, Dallas, Texas. I called him Friday night and told him about the need. He said he thought he could put a team together and wanted to know how soon they needed to be there. I told him that they needed to be there Monday, if that was possible. He told me he would call Bob Dixon, Executive Director of TBM; then he would call me back. In less than an hour, he called me back. He told me that Bob had told him to put the team together and that he would raise the money for the plane tickets. He wanted to know if I could arrange to pick them up in Montreal, Canada, sometime Monday. He also told me that he already knew of one man and his wife who were going to drive up in their RV, so they could stay as long as they were needed.

The building team from Texas did arrive on Monday and began to work alongside the men from the church. Two weeks later the roof of the building was covered. That was only the beginning of getting that building ready to be used for the glory of God, but for many years now it has been used for the glory of God.

Just Making the Move to New York was an Altogether Different Experience.

When I moved to a new church, I had experience to fall back on to get me through the early days, while I was getting my feet on the ground. Now I was moving into a new area of responsibility, where I had no previous experience. The first week of January 1992, we moved from Rusk, Texas, to Malone, New York, which is 12 miles south of the Canadian border. When we arrived in Rusk, our picture had already appeared on the front page of the local newspaper. The day we arrived in town, our name was on the sign of a local bank welcoming us to town. I was coming to be the pastor of the largest church in town, so everyone in town knew who we were before we even got there.

On the other hand, the day we drove into Malone, New York, may have been one of the loneliest feelings we had ever had. There were a few people who knew we were coming and knew a little bit about us, but for the most part we really felt alone. This was also the first time that we made a move without either one of our children moving with us. Three days after we arrived, the actual temperature was 30 degrees below zero, and it was snowing. We had to get adjusted to the weather in a hurry. Just learning how to dress to go outside was an interesting learning experience in itself.

We had made a quick trip to northern New York in early December 1991, to find a place to rent. We had less than a week to find a place to rent that we could move into in three weeks. We were told by the association that we could live wherever we felt it best. The other two DOM's that had preceded me had lived near the Malone, New York area. This was as close to being in the geographical center of the association as any. We searched around the Malone area for several days for a place to rent, that would meet our needs and be within our budget, without any success. Finally the real estate agent said that there was one house that might be available. He took us to this very large home. It had seven bedrooms, which included the servant's quarters, and 5 bathrooms. It was a two story house with a full basement and a full attic. The spiral staircase which led to the second floor had 20 steps. There was only one problem. The wind had blown a window open, and it had gotten so cold that all of the radiators had burst. The owner was in the process of having the radiators repaired. We went by and looked at the house and thought it would be fun to live there for a while. The owner agreed to a rent we could afford, and they felt like they could get enough of the radiators repaired that we could move in three weeks.

When we arrived, they were still in the process of repairing radiators. They did have enough of them repaired that most of the downstairs rooms had heat in them. This included one bedroom, one bathroom, the living room, kitchen, and dining room. There was an unexpected advantage to all of the radiators not being repaired before we got there. Virginia got very well acquainted with one of the plumbers and was able to lead him to a saving knowledge of Jesus Christ. Praise God! Several years later after we had moved to a new home, we had to call a plumber to help us with a problem. This same man was sent to work on our problem. When he came in, Virginia recognized him, and he right away recognized her. He said, "Aren't you the one who helped me put Jesus in my heart?" What a blessing to know that, after all those years, he knew that Jesus lived in his heart.

We were able to live in this wonderful old home for nearly 5 months. While we were living there, one man, who we entertained, was a preacher friend who had come to consider the possibility of moving to our area to pastor a church. He was about 6'5" tall. He came down for breakfast the next morning and said that he had just taken the first shower he had ever had where the shower head was taller than him. The house sold in April of that year. We had 6 weeks to find a place to live, but we enjoyed the time we lived in this beautiful old home. We were able to take advantage of its size to entertain a number of people, including a Spring Break Mission Team. The church at Rusk had given us a very generous love gift as a going away gift, and I joked with them that this would probably pay our heating bill for the first winter. It turned out to not be a joke, because our heating bill that first winter was $1,400.00. I do believe that the novelty of living in what could literally be called a historic mansion helped us with the fact that we were in a place so far away from home and family, and had not had the time to develop close friendships.

We had an interesting experience in the early spring. Our son Tom had come to do some youth ministry in the association and stayed with us in this large house. I was showing him around the house; we were down in the basement, when we came upon a skunk, who was sunning himself in a basement window well. He had probably been in our basement all winter. Tom and I took whatever we could find to build a path to the basement door to the outside. We did this hoping that we would not disturb him and make him angry, also hoping he would find his way outside. We were successful in both ventures; two days later he was gone without leaving behind any evidence that he had been there.

Through a set of miraculous events, we were able to purchase a home on Main Street in Malone, which is where we lived the remainder of the 12 years that we spent in the North Country of New York State. You are not supposed to be able to buy a house when you don't even have enough money for the down payment. Through the graciousness of the Baptist Convention of New York, I was able to get a loan from them for the down payment and a local bank approved our loan. We were able to buy the house from a young preacher and his wife. It was not a fancy house, but it met our needs and became our base of operation for almost 12 years. We actually moved into the house three months before we were able to close on the loan. The young preacher and his wife were moving just out of town to a family home he had inherited. We did not find out, until the day we closed on the loan, that he and his wife and children had lived in a tent on their property all summer because his house was not yet ready to move into. I asked him why he did that, and he simply said, "Because you needed a place to live." We were very humbled to find out that they had made such a sacrifice for us.

During the process of considering the move to New York, I met with all of the pastors and the key leaders in the association. There were several things that were determined that they needed from a new Director of Missions. The churches were scattered over a large territory and many of them felt alone and without any support. So, encouraging the pastors was a major need.

Most of the churches needed a new vision, of not just their work, but also the work of the association. So, strengthening and encouraging the churches would be a major role. Giving them a new vision of working together was also important.

Most of the churches in the association were not doing well financially. Helping the churches in the area of stewardship would be vital.

Most, if not all, of the churches needed a new vision for reaching the unsaved in their communities, which was vital. Helping them develop effective evangelism strategies was important to the task.

Also, constantly being sensitive to the opportunity to start new work was just an expected part of the job description. In the early years, however, I felt a greater responsibility to strengthen the existing churches.

As I considered their needs, I came to the conclusion that many of my own pastoral experiences had been preparing me for this new area of ministry. I quickly developed a strong sense of God's call on our lives to move to a new area of ministry. I would never have sought this ministry for myself, but it was a direction in which the Lord was obviously leading me. At the time that I accepted the call to be the DOM for the Adirondack Baptist Association, there were 11 churches and 5 church type missions. Most of the churches were small and struggling in many ways, but at the same time there was a strong sense by the congregations that they were there because God had placed them where they were. Most of them had almost miraculous stories about the way they even came into existence. I was the third DOM in the history of the association. The first DOM had been a pastor in the area prior to the time that the ABA was formed out of a much larger association that had covered all of Northern New York and Western New York. He had come first as a Church Planter and then had moved to the First Christian Church, Brushton, New York, which was a strong, conservative, evangelical church in the area for many years. He accepted the call with the understanding that the church would affiliate with the Baptist Convention of New York and the Southern Baptist Convention. He was a strong Church Planter and he led the Brushton church to sponsor a good number of the missions in the association. It would be fair to say that he just about became a legend among Baptists in Northern New York. Through his influence, the Gospel was shared in many of the small communities and towns across the North Country of New York.

The second DOM was there for about three years, before he moved back south. The association had been searching for a new DOM for about 2 ½ years when they came across my name.

A dear friend of mine, who had known me and my ministry in the early years of Southern Baptist life in the state of Ohio, was leading the music for a revival in one of the ABA churches. I had recently had him lead the music for a revival at FBC, Rusk, Texas. After that revival, he asked me for a copy of my resume. I gave it to him, but told him I had no interest in moving anywhere. He told me that he was considering recommending me to be the Director of Evangelism for the Alaska Baptist Convention. During the time he was in New York, he went to an ABA Pastor's Prayer Meeting. The meeting soon broke out into a discussion of the kind of qualities they felt like they needed in their next DOM, and the kind of DOM experience they hoped he would have. He said as he listened to them, my name kept coming to his heart. So he finally entered the discussion and told them, "I don't think it is a man with a lot of DOM experience that you need. I think it is a man who has been a pastor in places similar to where you serve and has been successful at it. You need a man who understands the kind of struggles each of you are experiencing." Then he said, "I think I know who he is and I have his resume at my house." That is the way the association got my name and then felt led to pursue me. I later teased my friend and told him that he ended up sending me just about as far north in the eastern part of the U.S. as he had originally thought in the western U.S.

One of the things that I discovered quickly was that a lot of people were hoping they would get a carbon copy of their first DOM. They loved him dearly, and he had earned that love. As I have already said, he was as strong a Church Planter as they had in the state of New York during his time. Although I had planted several Southern Baptist churches when I served in the Baptist Convention of Ohio, I was sensing a calling in a different direction

I also think my philosophy of starting churches was and is a bit different; it's not necessarily better, but different. It seemed to me that he found places to start churches and then found churches who would be the sponsor of that mission. Sometimes the sponsor church would not be much, if any, stronger than the new mission. Part of that had to do with Home Mission Board requirements. A new mission could not get financial assistance without a recognized sponsor. However, the general requirements of the HMB on how long a new mission could get financial assistance would run out before that mission was prepared to stand on its own. At that point, the only place for assistance was a sponsoring church and a small association, neither of which was strong enough financially to step in and provide the financial support needed. It is my philosophy that churches start churches. Associations, State Conventions, and National Conventions come alongside churches assisting them in the ministry the Lord has given them. Sometimes it can be a fine line in areas where the ministry of the convention is not very strong, and there is a genuine desire to have a strong evangelistic witness in the area.

I learned that I had to find my own identity with the ABA churches and with the ministry of the association. I think you could say that I came to have a three-pronged approach to my ministry. One was to strengthen the association itself and seek the day when it would be more stable financially. Another was to do what I could to help strengthen the existing churches and encourage their pastors. The last was probably the one that became very dear to my heart. It is what I referred to as the special ministry opportunities within the territory of the association. Those special ministry opportunities included:

- Campus Ministry to the 13 Colleges and Universities within the territory of the Association;
- Prison Ministry to at least 11 State and Federal Correctional Institutions;
- Resort Ministry to the many resort facilities in the association territory (Ski Lodges, numerous winter recreation opportunities, and summer resorts that were located all over the Adirondack Mountains area.)
- The Olympic Training facility in Lake Placid, New York, which was the only Winter Olympic Sports Facility in the United States when we first moved to New York, in January 1992.

Winter in the Adirondacks

One of my pastors said to me, "We do have summer here; it usually arrives around July 4th, and if we have a particularly good summer, it will still be here July 5th." There were times when there seemed to be more truth than fiction in that statement. We were introduced to winter weather quickly. We moved into our home in Malone, New York, the first week in January 1992. Shortly after we moved in, the temperature dropped to well below zero.

I attended my first official function of the association the second week of January. There was a Baptist Men's Breakfast and work day at the Bread of Life Baptist Church, Plattsburgh, NY. The Bread of Life Church had purchased property and was in the process of building their first building. The basic structure had been completed, but no doors or windows had been installed. The heating unit had been placed in the attic, and they were beginning to run the duct work. On that day, the plan was to have a simple breakfast, a short prayer meeting, and then we were going to pull electrical wiring throughout the building in preparation for the electricity to be installed. When I arrived on the scene, there was a small group of men standing outside the back of the building huddled around a campfire built out of scrap building material. The actual temperature was -5 degrees, but there was another phrase I became acquainted with quickly. The wind chill factor was -30. I had worn my warmest winter clothes that I had brought with me when we moved. I was standing there beside the pastor, and I told him that I was freezing. He immediately told the group that we would be back in a few minutes, and he took me to his car. He then took me a few miles away to a Military Surplus store to buy me something warm to wear. We found me a pair of 100% wool overalls that were on sale for $90.00. That was probably the best $90.00 I spent during the entire 12 years we were in New York. I put them on over my clothes and we went back to the church to participate in the work.

There was a slight problem with the work day. The electrical wiring was inside flexible metal conduit, and it came in large rolls. It was so cold that the wiring and the conduit were frozen. Every time you would start to unroll the wire it would literally break off in 10" – 12" pieces. Therefore, my first Association Men's Meeting ended rather abruptly, and we all went home. We had to wait until spring to have another meeting at that church, so we could run all of the electrical wiring. However, all was not lost in attending that meeting. I was able to buy those heavy 100% wool overalls. I literally wore them almost every morning during the snow season. My routine every morning, after it had snowed the night before, was to spend 1 – 2 hours clearing our driveway so that we could get out and go during the day. At times it seemed like it snowed every night. At times I wore those overalls on the Bobsled and Ski mountains, as we were volunteering at various events. I may not have had the best looking outerwear on the mountains, but I was warm. It did not take me long to discover that warmth was more important than fashion.

Soon after we moved to New York, The Southern Baptist Convention approved some major changes, which had major impact on the two mission boards. The Foreign Mission Board became the International Mission Board, and the Home Mission Board, for which I was employed, became the North American Mission Board. Many changes were soon to take effect in a rapid fire sequence.

Cleaning House

One of the things that I have learned over the years is that, for lack of a better word, there is a certain amount of house cleaning that must be done before anything very positive can take place in your ministry. In almost every move I have made, I found that there were some things left unsettled by the previous leadership that had to be addressed and resolved, if you were going to make any progress. Let me just say that I am sure there were unsettled issues that I also left for those who followed me.

For example, in one new place of service, I had not been there long before one of the deacons came to visit me. He said that he had come to help me. Then he told me that he had come to tell me who in the church I could trust and who I could not. Before he could go any further, I stopped him and told him I did not want to hear the names. He then repeated that he had just come to help me, and that he was trying to help me avoid some future grief. I told him that I did not want to hear it, because in most situations there are those who did not get along very well with the former leadership that got along really well with the new leadership. I told him that I thought every member of the church deserved to start on the same footing with the new pastor, and that I was going to treat everyone as trustworthy, until they proved to me differently. Since I did not let him give me the list, I am speculating that his name was not on it, and it probably should have been.

In another situation I found that, as I was visiting church members as their new pastor, I got a peculiar reaction from some of them. I had been there nearly a year before I discovered that the former pastor sent a letter to all of those that he considered were no longer supporting the church. He sent the letter as he was making

312

preparations to move to a new place of service. The theme of the letter was that, because of their inactivity, he and the deacons were discussing whether or not to recommend to the church that their names be withdrawn from the church roll. The letter said, since he was moving, they had decided that it would be best to wait until the next pastor arrived to deal with this matter. The way that I discovered the letter was that it was shown to me by one of the recipients of the letter. I asked them if I could make a copy of it, and they agreed.

You may be surprised to know that, when I showed this letter to the deacons, they had never seen it and had never discussed it with the former pastor. It was then understandable why some church members were uncomfortable when I visited them. They were waiting for the axe to fall. We were able to recover some of these members, but some never returned. At least we knew the real reason why.

When I came to the Adirondacks as Director of Missions, I discovered the same thing to be true of an association as it is with a church. There were issues that were never dealt with in the association that I had to pretty much discover for myself. I will mention three of them.

Ticonderoga, New York

I had not been in New York long before our State Missions Director told me that he had not gotten the Monthly Mission Report from the mission that was located in Ticonderoga, which was at the far southeastern boundary of the association. This report is one that is required by the Home Mission Board (now NAMB), from every missionary that is receiving funding from them. We also did not have much information from them in our association files. In early March of 1992, Jim Bradley, pastor of Bread of Life Baptist Church, Plattsburgh, New York, drove with me to Ticonderoga to visit with the pastor. All we knew was that the church was operating out of the pastor's home. Ticonderoga is 100 miles southeast of where I lived in Malone, New York. I drove to Plattsburgh and picked up Jim and we drove down the "Northway." We found the address we were looking for, but all we found was an empty house. I don't remember how we got it, but somehow we got the name and address of one of the church members.

We were surprised to discover that the pastor had resigned and had moved back south. He told me that they had not decided what to do as a small congregation. I made arrangements with him for me to come back and preach for them and answer any questions they might have. He warned me that I would be coming into a hostile environment, and that the people did not have a very good taste in their mouths, because of the way their pastor was treated by Southern Baptists. When I got back home, I dug up all of the information I could find, to prepare me for my next trip.

It was mid March 1992. We started back to "The Northway" about 5:00 P.M., and all of the snow was gone. We stopped at a McDonalds and ate a hamburger and fries. We got back in the car and started out again. Before we could get to the Northway, I mentioned to Jim that we had some snowflakes on the windshield. He said that he hoped this was not the late winter snow storm they usually got. By the time we got to the Northway, it was snowing so hard I could hardly see the hood of my car. I then became familiar with another North Country phrase. Jim asked me if this was my first "whiteout," meaning that it is snowing so hard that you cannot see where you are going. He also told me that, probably, the worst thing I could do was pull over and stop. First, you do not know what you are pulling over onto; second, someone behind you might not see you and ram into you. An 18-wheeler had just passed me. I decided to get into his tire tracks and follow him.

Normally it would be an hour's drive to Jim's house from where I got on the Northway. It took us two and one half hours to get to his home, where his wife Sylvia was nervously awaiting our arrival. Jim and Sylvia, and my wife Virginia did everything they could to get me to spend the night. However, I felt that it was important for me to get home; after all, it was only a little over an hour drive home. So at 9:45 P.M., this novice to a late winter snow storm left Plattsburgh for Malone, New York. At 1:45 A.M., I finally rolled into my driveway. I pulled into a huge snow drift in the driveway and got stuck. I was at least home, and getting the car unstuck could wait until daylight. I was so thankful to get home that night. The Lord really does take care of those who don't know how to take care of themselves. My bed never felt better than it did that night. I did learn a valuable lesson for my next 11 plus years in the North Country; have a healthy respect for a late winter snow storm. Virginia and I went back to Ticonderoga a few weeks later. We had a couple from Rusk visiting with us, and they went with us. As it turns out, they were very helpful. Both of them had been very involved in SBC missions all of their adult lives. They were able to share some things about the way Southern Baptists do missions that were very helpful.

In my searching, I discovered some unfortunate language used in their discussions with one another, about the work the pastor was doing. Because he was receiving financial aid from the State and National Conventions, he was required to send in a monthly report, which described his activities for the month. It was basically the same form that I, also, had to send in each month. In my opinion, the form was weak at best, but at the time it was the only way the senders of the money had to know how the money was being spent. It asked such questions as, "How many hours did you spend this month in evangelistic witnessing?" "How many did you baptize?" "What was your average Sunday School attendance?" Unfortunately someone at the State Convention office had responded to one of his monthly reports in a poor fashion. He wrote him a letter that said, "We paid you $300.00 last month for every hour you spent in evangelistic visitation. That is a pretty good hourly wage, if you can get it."

Needless to say, the group was angry with me before they ever met me, and all of the explaining I tried to do had no effect on them. They were convinced, as one layman put it, "The only things Southern Baptists are interested in are nickels and noses." My efforts, to try to explain that the reason for the monthly report was so that we could know that we were being good stewards of the Lord's money, were not heard. As a result, we left a bad taste in the mouth of members of a community, and we lost all of the time, effort, and money that had been poured into that project. This bad experience taught me several things about starting new work in non-traditional Baptist areas. One of the biggest lessons was that, there is not one formula that fits all for starting new churches. I preached this to anyone who would listen, the whole 12 years we served in the North Country. I don't think many were willing to listen. My constant request was, "Come and see, before you decide this will work where I am."

One other observation about the effort to start a new work in Ticonderoga was the location of the facility. The mission was meeting in the home where the Pastor and his family lived. When you walked out onto the front porch, what you saw right across the street was a huge Catholic Church. I know that facilities do not reach people, but I also believe that facilities can send a message that we may not have been intending to send. I believe the Lord deserves the very best we have. When we are the largest non-catholic denomination in the

United States, I believe we can do better than that when we establish houses of worship to our Lord.

I don't know where the fault lies, with this particular church start effort. I do know that a lot of SBC mission dollars were spent and enough effort was put into it to move a young preacher and his family there to serve as pastor. I don't know whatever happened to that young pastor; my hope is that he was able to reevaluate his ministry and move on. Hopefully, he is in productive ministry somewhere today.

Moriah, New York

When I came to the Adirondack Baptist Association, our finances were very limited; so I tried to watch our income and outgo very carefully in the early months of my ministry there. Because it was the winter heating season of the year, I soon noticed that every month we were paying a large heating bill in a place called Moriah. I asked my secretary about it and was told that we had a mission in Moriah. There was also a house where the pastor lived and where services were held. I asked why we were getting the bill for the heat instead of the sponsoring church, and was told the sponsoring church could not afford it, so the association had been paying the bill for several years. I asked if we knew anything about how the mission was doing and was told no. I did discover that the first pastor of the mission had resigned, and a "pastor" from Florida showed up at an association meeting looking for a place to preach. One of the pastors recommended that they let him move into the house in Moriah. That apparently was all we knew about him or how things were going since he had moved into the house.

I called the Missions Chairman of our association and told him the situation, and asked him if he would make a trip with me to Moriah. This was another place that was almost 100 miles from where I lived. We drove to Moriah in the spring of 1992. We met the "pastor" of the mission, who was living in our house. I put the word pastor in quotation marks because I think that it was a stretch to call him pastor of anything. I think you will see what I mean. When we asked him about his work, he was very evasive. He did not have any Sunday School or church member records. He did say that he had 7 adult ladies who were attending the church with some degree of regularity, but he could not recall any of their names. We asked about the church financial records; he told us that none of the ladies could afford to give anything. We asked about his own giving records, and he did not have them available for us. We made an appointment with him to come back in two weeks. During that time he was to secure the names and addresses of the ladies who were attending, and he was to go to the bank and get a bank statement of the mission's financial condition. As we left, we noticed that there was a van parked in the garage with the name of the sponsoring church, Lake Placid Baptist Church, on the side. The church had given the old van to the mission, but the title was still in the name of the church.

When we returned, he had not done any of the things that we had asked him to do. He still could not come up with any names of anyone attending services, and he did not produce any records. I told him that, in being good stewards of the Lord's money, we could no longer support him, and we asked him to move. He refused and said we could not make him move. This was now in May 1992, and we told him we wanted him out by August 1. He was very adamant that we could not make him move.

I talked to a lawyer and discovered that, by New York law, we had to give him a 3-month written notice. He suggested that I do that; then he told me that I also needed to know that, by New York law, we could not kick him out on the street. We could, however, warn him that we were not required to pay his utility bills. I did write him a letter and gave him a three-month notice to vacate the house. I also included in the letter that after August 1, 1992, we would no longer be responsible for any of the utilities on the house, until after he moved. I went back in July to see if I could find out what his plans were, and discovered that he had moved out, and that the old van was also gone. I told the Lake Placid Church about the van and they were not concerned about it.

A couple of months later, the pastor at Lake Placid resigned and the church called me as their interim pastor. In the spring of 1993, the church clerk from Lake Placid came to me with a certified letter from the city of Atlanta, Georgia. Apparently, the preacher who had lived in the house in Moriah had decided to take the van, because he did not have a car, and drive back to Florida. He got as far as Atlanta, Georgia, and it died on him. He walked off and left it on the side of the

Interstate. From the license plate, the van was traced back to the Lake Placid Baptist Church. The City of Atlanta had contracted with a towing and salvage company to get it off of the highway. The company wanted $900.00 in storage fees, and if it was not picked up in three days they were going to sell it. The church clerk asked me what to do and I told her to send them a letter telling them to sell it, because it was stolen from us and we were not coming after it. That is what she did, and so ends that saga in the history of Moriah. But praise God, as Paul Harvey would say there is a "rest of the story" and we will get to that later.

Waddington, New York

Waddington, New York, is another one of those unfinished stories I inherited that did not seem to be important enough for anyone to tell me about beforehand. Probably no one thought that it would be that big of a deal, and end up consuming as much of my time as it did. Waddington, New York, sits on the banks of the St. Lawrence River, at the top of the state of New York, just across the river from Canada. When I arrived on the scene, the association had a fairly large sum of money in an account known as the Waddington account. When I asked the treasurer about this account, I discovered that a large section of land had been given to the association by an individual who lived in Waddington. Some of the property had been sold and some was still owned by the association. In the early days of my ministry there, the treasurer was borrowing money almost monthly from that account to pay the association's part of my salary. I became concerned about that, and told the treasurer we must stop doing that. He reluctantly did that, but feared that he could not pay all of my salary. I told him that at some point that money would run out anyway if we kept doing it. By doing the right thing with that money, which was to save it for mission causes, we were still able to pay the association's portion of my salary.

After owning the property for several years and not doing anything with it, we began to get an annual tax bill because we were not using it for religious purposes. Because we had no immediate prospect of using it for religious purposes, we contacted a realtor and put it up for sale. We sold one of the house-size lots rather quickly and for a good amount of money because it was the only house-size lot left in Waddington that had waterfront on the back of the lot. Shortly after we put it up for sale, I got a nasty letter from the son of the man who gave us the property. He demanded that we return all of the unsold property and the money from the properties we had sold. He said we received the property from his father under false pretenses, because we said that we wanted it to build a church.

I wrote him back and told him I was not there when the transaction took place, but I would look into it and get back to him. I did look into it and found out some interesting information. Apparently he had told the city that if they would run city water and sewage to this property that he would build a sub-division there. Then they would be able to recoup their cost from sewer and water bills. After the city had fulfilled their part of the bargain, and had run the water and sewer to the property, he had a falling out with some of the city fathers. It was known that he told them that he would give the property to someone so they would never be able to collect taxes. Shortly thereafter, he gave the property to us. Because of the challenge by the son of the man who made the original transaction, I had to spend an enormous amount of time at the county courthouse, digging through records that were now almost 30 years old. I guess I learned a lot about real estate laws in New York, and how they particularly related to non-profit organizations. I also learned who the right people were to talk to in local government in New York. Without a doubt, that was valuable information I was able to use in working with our churches and missions in securing property. I learned another good lesson about starting a new mission. There must first of all be someone God has given a vision. That is usually a church and some people who live in the area who have an interest in starting a work there. Let me give you an example. We were trying to start a work in what was known as the Champlain Valley, which was located on the eastern border of our association, near Lake Champlain. Very soon, a woman and her children who lived in the area began to attend our church. She was a native New Yorker, and even a native of the Adirondacks. She was from Canton, New York, which is located on the western border of the association, but still a part of the Adirondack region.

One day she and I were talking about some of the needs of the mission if it was going to grow. She said, "We have to start reaching some local people." To which I replied that she was local. She then said, "I married a local and moved here 32 years ago, but I am from Canton and that is not part of the Champlain Valley." Then she said that we would not be looked upon with any credibility until we started reaching some local Champlain Valley people. Needless to say, we began to focus attention on reaching local people, and praise God; we were able to reach some. It was alright if the pastor was not "local," as long as we had "locals" who were part of the congregation. That concept was not true everywhere, but it was true in many places.

I have found, over the years, that when I was willing to embrace the place where I served as home, I was accepted. I remember coming into the office one morning right after the Christmas season. Virginia and I had just gotten back from visiting family in Texas and Oklahoma. A lady from one of our churches came into the office and asked me how our trip went. I told her that it was good, but that it is always good to get back home. She replied, "That sounds so good." I asked her what she meant and she said, "It sounds so good to hear you call this place home." I told her that, all of our marriage, our attitude has been that wherever our place of ministry is, that is our home. I explained that we both had places where we grew up and it was good to go back there and visit, but that was no longer home. She walked away with a smile on her face. I suspect that in her heart she knew that we were New Yorkers. I can certainly agree that there is some advantage to the Lord calling someone and then sending them back to their homeland. But the important thing is the call, not where we were born. We remained in the Adirondacks 12 years because of the call, and chances are, we would have been there even longer except for me reaching mandatory retirement age.

Early in our ministry in the Adirondacks it became apparent that the primary emphasis of the Board would be changing and the primary emphasis of the North American Mission Board would be to place most of its resources into the effort to reach the highly populated areas of North America. Therefore, those of us, who had been hired by the former Home Mission Board to serve in the town and country areas of the United States, began to feel a great deal of discomfort about our job security. In fact, The Town and Country Division of the Mission Division of NAMB was soon to be no longer a specific division at NAMB. Those who had that responsibility, lost their jobs in the reorganization, and we soon had supervisors who had too many irons in the fire. You see, although the Adirondack Baptist Association had the largest territory of any association in the State Convention, we also had the smallest population.

On the other hand, I still knew that the Lord had called me to the North Country of New York, and I continued to do my job the best way I knew how. In the doing of that job, I confess that I did not always go about things in a way that made some at NAMB feel good about me. It took me a while to learn the team concept. My nature had always been such that, when I saw something that needed to be done, and had prayed about it, I generally would do it. I soon learned that I was working with a team who were there to help me accomplish what God had put me there to do. I will admit that it took me a while to learn that we were working as a team. The more I learned how to work the National, State, and Association Team, the better my job went. I learned how to be a lobbyist for my Lord for the place where He had placed me. I knew that if I did not speak up for them, no one would.

If I were asked the question, "What is the one thing you wished that your pastors and your churches knew about you?" my answer would be that I wished they knew how hard I tried to make the system that was in place work for them. I think of one mission pastor in particular, who felt like I failed him. If he only knew how far I pushed the envelope for him and his family, maybe he would have understood. I am sure that the problem was probably largely mine in that I did not express it the right way when I told him I had done all I could do. But praise God, I know that the Lord knows I did my best. I confess that my best left a lot to be desired sometimes, but I am glad that I know that I did all I knew to do.

A Fishing Trip and So Much More

My second year in New York, my brother Bobby and I began talking about taking a trip to Canada to fish. He would fly into Ottawa and I would drive up from Malone to pick him up. Then we would drive north of Ottawa to fish for Walleye. At that time, I was Interim Pastor of the Lake Placid Baptist Church. One of the church members at Lake Placid heard about the trip and volunteered his boat and his vehicle to pull the boat.

I got some brochures at the Canadian border and began to look for a place. I found a place about two hours north of Ottawa, Cobden Lake, in Cobden, Ontario, Canada. I rented us a cabin on the lake, and we made our first trip together to Canada fishing.

We were catching some fish, but we were not catching the Walleye (Pickerel). As fate would have it, we were having trouble with the boat motor running as smoothly as it should. We took it into a boat repair shop to be fixed. While we were there, we asked the owner about the best place to fish for Walleye. When he found out where we had been fishing, he said that we were fishing the wrong side of the Ottawa River. He told us that we needed to be over in Quebec Province, and that the best place to go was a little town called Portage du Fort. He told us how to get over there, and we drove over that afternoon. Portage du Fort is a small town that sits beside the Ottawa River and there is a Power Plant Dam there, which provides electrical power for all of the area including the city of Ottawa, which is about an hour and a half downstream. In years past, the logging industry would float their logs down river and there was a log chute on the dam, which would propel the logs on down the river.

There was one little store in town; we went in to see if we could get some information about how to fish the river. The owner of the store pointed out a lady who was shopping and said, "If you want to know how to fish this river, you need to talk to her. Her husband knows more than anyone about fishing this river." Keep in mind that we were talking to these folks in Canada with a very distinct Texas accent, which meant we were a novelty to everyone who talked to us. This actually turned out to be to our advantage. We approached the lady who we later discovered was Wanda. After we had talked with her a few minutes, she pointed out the door of the store to her house down the road. She said, "My husband is sitting on the patio, if you will come to the house, I am sure he would be glad to talk to you." We drove down the street and met Sterling for the first time. I had no idea when we walked up on that patio that I would be meeting a man who would become one of my dearest friends. He was one of the most jovial and friendly men I had ever met. We talked to him about what we were doing in Canada and how much we would love to catch some Walleye. This was on a Wednesday; he said that he would not have a day off until Friday, which was the day before we were to leave. He called his wife out on the porch and told her to call their nephew and tell him he was bringing a couple of "Yanks" to his house, who needed to know where to fish. He put us in his truck and drove two blocks to his nephew's house, where we met Darrell for the first time.

Darrell talked to us for a little while. He said, if we would come back about noon the next day, he would take us fishing. We asked him what kind of lures we needed to get. He got out his tackle box and showed us what we needed. Then he told us not to buy any because he had all we needed. We got back in Sterling's truck, drove back to his house, visited with him a little while longer, then got back in our vehicle, and drove back to our cabin. As we drove back, we looked at one another in amazement at what we had just experienced. We both agreed that, if this was an example of Canadian hospitality, it was at least equal to, if not better than, Southern hospitality.

The next day we pulled our boat out of the lake where we were staying, and drove back across the river to meet Darrell at his house at noon. He already had his boat hooked up. He told us how to fish, and then told us to just follow him everywhere he went. After we had been fishing about 30 minutes, he motioned for us to pull alongside him. He pointed to a sandy beach, told us to put our boat there, and get in the boat with him. We fished till nearly dark and caught lots of fish. When we pulled our boats out of the water, he told us that his dad was at Sterling's house, and they would be very disappointed, if we did not stop by and visit with them. We did stop by and visit with them. Sterling told us that he had the day off the next day and, if we would come back, he would take us fishing. He did not have to twist our arms, and we did go back the next day to go fishing with him.

When we were finished fishing, he told us he wanted us to meet a man who owned a house on the river that would rent it to us the next year, if we wanted to come back. We did meet the man and made arrangements to come back the next year. We left Canada with lots of fish and some new found friends. We were all set to return the same time the next year, and at the last minute my brother had to cancel because of a job interview. We put the word out to family to see if anyone could join us at the last minute. Virginia's sister Pat and her husband Darl, a retired Delta Airlines pilot, said they could come. They flew into Montreal and we picked them up and drove over to Portage du Fort. Darl and I had a great week of fishing with Sterling, and Virginia and her sister spent the week antique shopping.

The cabin where we stayed was adequate but it had some issues that left a lot to be desired. During the week, Sterling introduced us to another man who had a three bedroom house on another location on the river. We made arrangements to rent that place the next year, during the week of Memorial Day. That became an annual trip for Virginia and I, and various couples would go with us. Dr. J.B. Graham and his wife Areta went with us on several occasions. He was the Executive Director of the Baptist Convention of New York. While he and I fished, usually with Sterling; Areta and Virginia shopped. We had a wonderful time.

On one occasion, Sterling and I went out to fish. Remember that this is the last week in May. We would go early, and go up next to the dam to fish until they opened the locks. Then we would move, because the water was so swift coming through the locks. On this particular day, it was unusually cold, but neither one of us said anything to the other. When the locks finally opened, we headed downstream to our next fishing location. This one was very close to the house where we were staying. I asked Sterling if he wanted to take a break and go to the house and get some coffee; he nodded yes. When we got into the house, I asked him if he was cold. He said he was freezing. I agreed that I was also cold. He said he had never been that cold while Ice Fishing in the winter. We decided to go to a local café for breakfast before we went back fishing. Over the years we laughed about how cold we were but neither one was going to be the first to admit it. I guess that is what you call being a "macho man" to a fault.

During one of those early years, I asked Sterling if he knew that he was a Christian, and was going to heaven when he died. He assured me that he was, and talked about all of the things he had done in the church since he was a boy. This was not the right time to pursue it any further. Another year when we arrived for our annual visit, I found out that Sterling had had a heart attack. I fussed at him for not letting me know. I reminded him that I only lived a four hour drive away. He promised me that, if there was a next time, he would call me. That was in late May of that year. In July, I got a phone call from Wanda on a Sunday morning telling me that he had a very serious heart attack the day before and he told her to call me so that he would not get in trouble with me again. I asked if it was critical enough that I needed to come right then, and she said no. Because I had preaching assignments that day, I told her to tell him I would come early the next morning. On Monday morning I drove to the hospital in Pembroke, Ontario, to visit my friend. He was in the ICU, waiting for his doctor to get him admitted to the Heart Institute in Ottawa. I sat down by his bed and we visited for a little while. Then I asked him if he knew that I loved him. He said that, if he didn't before, he did now. I told him that because I loved him I needed to ask him a question that I had asked him once before. I told him that all of us are going to die some day. Then I asked him, if that had happened Saturday night, did he know that he would have gone to heaven? He said, "I think so." I asked him what he was basing that on and once again he began to talk about all of the good things he had done. I agreed with him that he was a good man, and he had done a lot of good things. Then I asked him, "Would we not have to agree that God the Father was at the very least cruel, to allow Jesus to go to the cross, if we could somehow work our way into heaven?" He said that he had never thought about it that way. It was just a matter of minutes before we were praying, and Sterling asked Jesus Christ to become his Savior and Lord. I received word a couple of years ago that he had another heart attack and went home to be with the Lord.

Because of our relationship with Sterling and Wanda, we were local residents of Portage du Fort, Quebec, Canada, one week a year. During our early years in New York, Quebec Province tried several times to withdraw from Canada and become a nation of their own. It never did happen, but emotions ran very high on each side of the issue. I remember one year that the vote only failed by a vote of 48% to 52%. The strong feelings for withdrawing from Canada came primarily from the cities of Montreal and Quebec City, which are both located on the eastern side of the Province. Sterling felt very strongly about not withdrawing and he had a lot of Canadian flags on his large patio, which also wrapped around one side of his house. He would do that just to irritate his friends who were in favor of withdrawing and becoming their own nation.

That morning that he and I both got so cold that we finally came in to warm up, we ended up going to have breakfast at a café owned by one of his "Chums." I ordered one of my favorite breakfast meals (a stack of pancakes and two eggs over easy on the side). When the order came, I slid the eggs onto the pancakes, and let the egg yellow run over the top of the pancakes, before I put on the syrup. The owner looked at what I was doing, and said that it was very strange. I asked him if that was the first time he had ever seen someone do that, and he said no. Then he grinned and said that he saw it done about a year before, by someone who looked a lot like me.

When Sterling would introduce me to someone new, he would always say, "This Yank came up here a few years ago and asked me to show him my favorite pickerel fishing spots. He said that I could show them to him because he would never be back." Then he would laugh and say, "I showed him all of my favorite fishing spots and he has been back every year." About that time I would join into the story and say, "Sterling is not upset because I come every year; he is upset because I have learned to catch them about as good as he does."

In early December of 2003, just a few weeks before we were to move back to Texas, we made plans to meet Sterling and Wanda at a genuine Tex/Mex Café in Ottawa. It had genuine Tex/Mex Mexican food and great Texas Bar-B-Que. The owner of the café had been a football player with the Ottawa Rough Riders of the Canadian Pro Football League. He was a native of Texas, and had played college football at Baylor University. After he retired, he built two Tex/Mex – Bar-B-Que Cafes in Ottawa and just stayed there. After our meal, we stood out in the parking lot and said our goodbyes to each other. Sterling told me that I would never be back. I assured him that we would be back, but he was convinced we would not be back. I was glad it was dark in that parking lot, because the two of us were trying to hold back the tears as we said goodbye. We came back for the Ironman USA, Lake Placid in 2004 and 2005. Both times we made arrangements to drive up to Canada to visit Sterling and Wanda. On the second trip, Sterling had made arrangements for us to stay at a local motel/restaurant and had made arrangements that he was paying the bill.

I will never forget my Canadian friend. From the first time I met him, until the last time, he was as friendly as anyone I have ever met. It was one of those relationships that just clicked from the first time we greeted one another. He also really enjoyed my brother Bobby and my brother-in-law Darl. He treated all of us like lifelong friends. He was a man who loved his home and local surroundings, and was very content. In fact, he literally lived all of his life in his mother and dad's home, which he inherited after they died.

Praise God for a fishing trip that became so much more, and for the assurance that my friend is waiting for me on the other side. God usually has more in mind that He wants to do with us and through us. I get a warm feeling all over every time I think about my Canadian friend.

Unexpected Joy

I have only been asked one time to serve on a national SBC Committee. During the time that Paige Patterson was president of the SBC, he called me and asked me if I would serve as one of the two representatives on the Committee on Committees from New York. I agreed to do that. The only thing that committee does is meet and recommend the other committees to be elected by the SBC.

At the beginning of our first session, we were all asked to introduce ourselves and tell where we were from. At the first break in our meeting, a man by the name of Jim Tatum, from Florida, introduced himself to me, and said he would like to tell me his story. He told me that he had been successful in the Real Estate business. He said that he was attending a Missions Conference in Brazil, when the Lord told him to go home, sell his real estate business, start a men's suit business, and clothe His preachers. Then he told me that he had been doing that ever since. He then asked me, "Would you let me buy new suits for all of your pastors?" I began to weep. I told him that some of my pastors had probably never owned a new suit. This was in June of that year. With the help of the pastors' wives I got all of the measurements I needed and sent them to him. The plan was to present them to each pastor at our Pastors and Wives Christmas Dinner. He had hoped to be able to come, but was unable to attend the dinner. He had the suits shipped, and at the Christmas Dinner each wife presented her husband with a new suit. It was an awesome experience. We took video to send to him. One wife was weeping when she thanked him for enabling her to give her husband his very first new suit.

During that next year, I began to wonder what I could do for our pastors' wives, who made incredible sacrifices in order for their husbands to be able to do what they did. I called Don Gibson, with Texas Baptist Men. I told him I wanted to do something special for our pastors' wives. I asked him if he thought there would be enough Texas Baptist Men couples who would be willing to give a $100.00 Christmas gift to one of our pastors so that they could give it to their wives. Without hesitation he said yes and they did. So at the next Christmas Dinner, each pastor was able to give his wife a Christmas card with $100.00 in it, with the understanding that they were to spend it on just themselves. As you can imagine, that too, was a joyous occasion.

Summer Revival Crusade

For a couple of years I had been talking to our Association about an Association-Wide Evangelistic Crusade. The biggest problem with a crusade at one location was the size of the association's territory and the miles most people would have to travel to come to the services. I began to talk to them about the possibility of having the crusade in three different locations over a three week period of time. After much prayer, the association's leadership recommended that we have a three week Evangelistic Crusade in three locations in the association. The three crusades would all begin on Sunday night and go through Wednesday night.

The first crusade would start on Sunday night in Potsdam, New York, in one of the auditoriums at Potsdam State University. This would be for the churches on the east side of the association. We would give the evangelistic team a break the latter part of the week; then we would move to the Tri-Lakes area of the Adirondacks (Lake Placid, Saranac Lake, and Tupper Lake) for the second week. We would start on Sunday night at the Saranac Lake Baptist Church. That crusade was held on the front lawn of the church. Once again the crusade was from Sunday night through Wednesday night. Once again we gave the evangelistic team a few days of rest, and then we moved to Malone, New York, where I was able to secure the grandstand of the county fairgrounds. A new stage had just been built at the grandstand for the various performances that are held there during the county fair. Our crusade became the first way that the new stage was used. This crusade was primarily for the northern and eastern section of the association.

The Jim Bob Griffin Music Evangelism family had been members of our church in Rusk. We had talked to them on several occasions about coming for a revival. One of their daughters and son-in-law and their sons were still with them at that time. So we had the Griffins and the Easleys as our Music Evangelistic team. They recommended Evangelist William Blackburn, from Alabama, to be our Evangelist. The Lord used this team in a remarkable way.

When I first met with the association's leadership to discuss the possibility of having an Association Evangelistic Crusade, I told them that if they would trust me that I knew what I was doing. We could have a great crusade. I told them that I had received some valuable training on how to do a crusade, and how to do it right. I told them that I had been given all of the preparation material we would need, and was trained on how to use it. I told them that it would take us at least a year to get ready, if we were going to do it right. We would need to form an Organization Committee that would have representatives from the three different areas of the association. I told them that they needed to make sure they got the lay people in our churches involved in the preparation.

We were able to put together a Crusade Preparation Committee that was willing to be trained to do their job and were willing to work. The year of preparation was a demonstration of what can be accomplished when God's people are willing to work for the glory of God. I remember, in particular, the young woman who was in charge of publicity. We had selected a crusade theme from some options provided by the Evangelism Division of the North American Mission Board. By selecting one of their themes, they already had promotion material we could use, which included some TV spots that we could use and include our local information.

The young woman who was in charge of publicity for the crusade was a member of our church in Potsdam. Her family owned four furniture stores in the North Country, and she did all of the advertising for the family business. She had sent the advertising sales person from one of the major TV stations that covered most of the territory of our association to visit with me about the various options. I did not know, until we started this process, that the cost of TV commercial time is

335

based on the volume of business you do with them. While the sales person and I were discussing the possible things we could afford, she called my office and talked to the TV salesman. After talking with her, he told me that she wanted the two of us to meet her at one of their stores. We stopped our meeting and both of us drove to her store to meet with her. What she wanted was for our advertising to be done under the contract her stores had with his TV station. He did not like that, but she insisted, and reminded him of how much business her company did with them. He finally agreed. Because of the volume of business her stores did with this TV station, we were able to get three weeks of TV spots for under $1,000.00. We were able to pick the times of day and the cable stations on which the commercials would appear. He could even tell us who we would be reaching at various times of the day, and on which channels we would reach them.

I can say that all of those who accepted a responsibility in preparation for the crusade did their job and did it well. As the time approached for the July 1998 crusade to begin, the excitement was growing among our churches and our pastors. Something like this had never been done, which always makes you wonder if you have done everything you could to get ready. It was actually easier on me after we got started, because if there was anything we did not do, we had to just go with what we had done, and trust the Lord for the results.

When the time came, the people had worked on getting ready. The people had been praying for months. The pastors in the three locations were coming together to pray on a regular basis at the crusade sites, for the Holy Spirit to be poured out on that place. Then when the time came, the people came to the crusade services. When they came, many of them brought unchurched people with them. Probably the site that most appealed to people just dropping in off of the street was the County Fair Grounds in Malone. I think there were a couple of reasons for that. One was that it was getting close to time for the Annual Fair and people were curious about what was going on at the Fair Grounds. Two, the new and greatly improved stage for the grandstand area had been under construction all summer, and I think people were curious about what it looked like. Another appeal was the Griffin family. You might be surprised to know how popular Country and Western music is in the North Country of New York. The Southern Gospel style of music of the Griffin family fit right in with what the people enjoyed in music.

Another thing that we were very careful in doing was in training counselors to deal with those who responded to the Gospel invitation. If those who came indicated a church preference, we would send their information to that church, whether it was Southern Baptist or not. If they did not indicate a preference, we would send the information to the closest Southern Baptist Church to where they lived.

The Griffin family singers were received very well. Their music was outstanding. Their spirit was just as I expected it to be. William Blackburn did a great job of presenting the simple Gospel of Jesus Christ. The Lord blessed, and before the three weeks were over, there were 252 public decisions recorded and 232 of those were professions of faith in Jesus Christ. The revival team worked hard, but the Sunday – Wednesday night revival schedule we planned, gave them the time to refresh each week. I praise God for these people being willing to come and spend nearly a month with us. They allowed the Lord to use them in an awesome way.

One of our churches had some land that included a large open field; there was a Creek that ran through the back of the property. We planned an Association-Wide Picnic on the Friday after the last week of crusades. Some men dammed up a section of the creek for a place to baptize. We encouraged, as many as would, to bring people with them, who had been saved during the crusade, to be baptized in the creek. Quite a few were baptized on that day. One man, who I knew from playing golf with him, had come to me one night after the service at the crusade in Malone. He told me that he had been saved watching a Billy Graham Crusade. He wanted to know if I would baptize him at the picnic. He was a Presbyterian and wanted to be baptized by immersion. His pastor was a dear friend of mine and a

337

part of the group of pastors that prayed together every Thursday morning. I talked with his pastor and received his blessing. After that, I agreed to baptize my friend at the picnic. We had a wonderful time of fellowship that concluded with a concert by the Griffin family.

Resort Ministry

I am sure that there were some who viewed my lack of whole-hearted support for the Church Planting Strategy as a negative, when they measured the success of my ministry in the Adirondacks. I also think that there were some who came to appreciate the uniqueness of the many resort areas in the Adirondacks and began to see them as ministry opportunities that must not be overlooked. I believe that the first DOM for the Adirondacks had a unique gift for church planting, which was much needed during his time of ministry.

I believe the Lord gave me a vision for special ministries and challenging the churches to disciple the believers they already had. We stressed the importance of evangelism and church planting, which were a part of the bigger picture of what I believed the Lord wanted the association to do.

I began to challenge our churches to realize that we could not overlook the thousands of people who visited our territory almost year round. There were people who owned mountain cottages in the Adirondacks who spent most of 3 – 4 months every summer in the Adirondacks. One of the largest yearly financial supporters of one of our churches only lived in the area 3 - 4 months in their mountain cottage. There is also another whole culture of people who were involved in the winter sports activities and came during the winter months.

Because of the decision I made, I sometimes felt like an outsider with some of the other DOMs, and some of the State Convention Staff. However, I never felt that way with our Executive Director, Dr. J.B. Graham. I could always talk to him. We did not always agree, and sometimes he would have to "reel me in" a little bit. But he always did it in love. The way we conducted business, allowed us to have a very good personal relationship.

Dr. and Mrs. J.B. Graham

When our Executive Director Dr. Quinn Pugh retired, because I was serving as the First Vice President of the Convention and also serving on the Executive Committee, I became a member of the Search Committee for the new Executive Director.

This committee had prayed and searched long and hard. After Dr. Graham came on the scene as our Interim Executive Director, it soon became apparent to many of us on the committee that he was God's man to lead the Baptist Convention of New York, at a very critical juncture in her history. After a real struggle in his own heart, Dr. Graham finally realized that it was, in fact, the Lord's will for him to take on this responsibility. Let me tell you what I mean by a real struggle. He had not only declined our offer to submit his name for the position of Executive Director of the Convention; he had also resigned as Interim Director, and was on his way back to Georgia. He pulled off to the side of the road and told his wife he believed he had made a mistake in turning down the job. I think she agreed with him. He said that he was going to call the chairman of the search committee, and if the offer was still good, he was going to accept. I remember the joy in my heart, as a member of the search committee, when I heard of his decision. He was the right man at the right time to lead our convention back to where it needed to be.

Because of our relationship, his wife Areta and my wife Virginia became very close friends. I invited them to go to Canada with us in the spring of the year on our annual Walleye Fishing Trip. While Dr. Graham and I fished, Areta and Virginia shopped. Areta bought a small fishing trophy that we passed back and forth, depending on who caught the biggest fish. I think the trophy has spent more time on my mantle, but he will probably disagree with that.

341

Since we are in an election year, and we would love to find someone who is honest in the observations they make, I just got up from my computer and walked into the den to see if the trophy is, in fact, at present on my mantle. I am happy to announce that, at least at this time (spring 2016), the trophy is in my possession.

Seriously, although the Grahams have retired in Georgia and are now fully retired, and we retired in Texas, and I am not yet fully retired, we remain close friends. Some of the joys, of the Christian faith, are the relationships that are developed that last for a lifetime. Just last fall we got a call from the Grahams. They wanted to know if we were going to be home on the Tuesday night and Wednesday before Thanksgiving. They were going to be driving from Colorado to Houston and would make the very out of the way trip over to East Texas if we were going to be home. Fortunately for us we were, and we got to spend some quality time with our dear friends. We had done something similar a few years ago when we were going to North Carolina for our grandson's wedding. True friendship is worth making sacrifices to keep alive. Thank you to the Graham's for being faithful ministry partners and great friends.

The Bronx Connection

During the time that I served as First Vice President of the New York Convention, Dr. Sam Simpson was serving as President of the Convention. Because of the positions that we held, we both served on the Executive Committee of the Convention and the Executive Director Search Committee. Dr. Simpson was affectionately known as the "Bishop of the Bronx." He was pastor of two churches in the Bronx. The Bronx Baptist Church was located in the old downtown section of the Bronx; the other church was the Wake Eden Baptist Church, which is located in the suburban section of the Bronx. Dr. Simpson and his wife Lola are natives of Jamaica. There is a large Jamaican population in New York; therefore, there were many Jamaicans in his churches.

He felt that he needed to introduce the First Vice President of the Convention to his churches. So he invited me to come and preach at both churches on Thanksgiving weekend. Our son Tom and his family came as well and we all stayed in a house they owned at the Wake Eden Church.

His Sunday schedule was that Wake Eden would have their preaching service first followed by Sunday School. The Bronx Church would have Sunday School first and begin their worship with music until the pastor got there.

My son Tom and my wife Virginia sang at both churches that day, and I preached at both churches. That first weekend we were there, began a love affair between the Goforth family and the Wake Eden Church and Bronx Baptist Church. Over the years we found many reasons to go to New York City, and the trips would usually include trips to those two churches. I remember one time when we were there; we had just finished the second service at the Bronx Church, and we were going to

343

drive back to the North Country from there. Mrs. Lola Simpson said that we must eat before we leave, and we were to follow them to the restaurant. They took us to a Jamaican Restaurant. We had never eaten Jamaican food; therefore, she told the owner she wanted him to bring us samples of everything on the menu. She told us that would help us know, the next time, what we liked best.

One trip we made to the Bronx was during baseball season. I have a story that most people would not believe about New York City. I had never been to Yankee Stadium. We were there at a time when the Yankees were home and playing that night. I went down to Yankee Stadium in the afternoon to buy tickets. There was a man standing on the corner across the street from the stadium who had two tickets for sale. He said they were behind the first base dugout, five rows up from the field. I asked him how much he wanted for them. They had a face value of $20.00 and he sold them to me for $20.00 each. I bought them and was skeptical if they were real tickets. We came back about an hour before the game and were looking for a place to park. I saw one parking area out in the median of the road right across from the stadium. I pulled in and there were no parking meters. There was a tall African American man walking back and forth on the median. He told me to go and enjoy the game and he would keep an eye on my car. I walked over to him, handed him a $5.00 bill, and told him that, if my car was still in one piece when we got back, I would give him another one. We walked across the street with the tickets I was unsure about. Our tickets were good, and at our first ballgame in Yankee Stadium, we sat five rows up from the field just even with first base. After the game, we went back to the car. The man was still there and our car was undamaged. So for $50.00, we parked our car, walked a block to the stadium, and sat in some of the best seats in the stadium.

On another trip, Dr. Simpson had me meet briefly with the deacons at Wake Eden on Saturday. The next morning he had the Chairman of the Deacons introduce me before I preached. In his introduction he told the church that after meeting with me the day before they had decided that when Dr. Simpson retired they were going to call me as pastor. When I got up, I told them that, if that was an offer, I accepted. That became a standing joke between Dr. Sam and me. The truth is that I retired from the Mission Board, before he retired. We had a special brother in the Lord relationship. He went home to be with the Lord a couple of years ago, and left behind a wonderful legacy of love for two churches and the Bronx, New York.

When I think about those two churches, I am reminded of a humorous and at the same time humbling experience. The first time I was there, they had me listed in the bulletin as Dr. Jim Goforth. A few weeks later, I was talking to the church secretary at the Wake Eden Church, who kept referring to me as Dr. Goforth. I corrected her and told her that I wasn't even a practical nurse, and there was no need to call me Dr. Goforth. She said, "OK," and continued to call me Dr. Goforth; so I just quit correcting her. I have determined that this has come out of the desire in most African American Churches I have known, to show as much respect as possible to their ministers. So I guess you could say I have a BA, from Howard Payne University, a Master of Theology from New Orleans Seminary, and a Doctorate from The Wake Eden and Bronx Baptist Churches. Our lives were greatly enriched by our relationship with Dr. and Mrs. Sam Simpson, and the Wake Eden and Bronx Baptist Churches.

The first actual ministry activity that I did, after we moved to New York, was to see how many pastors might be interested in going through the Experiencing God study. I mentioned it at an associational meeting. I had several pastors and lay people express an interest. I set up three different study times in three locations in the association. One study was held on Monday morning, another was held on Monday night, and the third was on Tuesday night. We began this six week study in February 1992, which was my first winter in the North Country of New York. There were a total of 34 pastors and lay people who attended these three groups. These people became the ones the Lord would use to take this study throughout the association and beyond.

We were only a few weeks into the study, and on a particular Tuesday in February; it snowed hard all day. My Tuesday night group met in Saranac Lake, at the Saranac Lake Baptist Church. This was about 40 miles south of where I lived; I also had other group members who were traveling the same distance. I called one of my pastors to ask him if he thought I should cancel the meeting that night. He thought about it for a bit, and then said that, if I started getting the reputation of cancelling meetings in the winter because of the weather, everyone would expect that every time there was bad weather, I was going to cancel the meeting and the winter association meetings would be poorly attended. I thought about it seriously all afternoon and decided not to cancel the meeting. Virginia and I drove up to Saranac Lake in a hard snow storm. When we got there, the only ones there were Virginia and I and the other pastor and his wife who also had to drive 50 miles. When I called the local pastor, he said they had just assumed I would cancel the meeting that night. As it turned out, I would get the reputation as one who did not cancel meetings every time the weather was bad.

The next day the pastor I had called to ask his advice called to ask me what I had done. When I told him, he told me that he had worried all night that we would have a serious accident, and it would be his fault. As it turned out, it really was good advice. I became known as the DOM who did not cancel meetings. In 12 years in the North Country, I cancelled one meeting. It was after I had been there almost 10 years. It was a Semi-Annual Association Meeting, which was scheduled for the third Saturday in April. When I woke up that morning, it was snowing and had been snowing most of the night. After spending an hour cleaning my driveway, I wasn't even close to being finished. I went inside and told Virginia to begin calling our pastors and cancelling the meeting. We always had a representative from our State Convention that would attend our Annual and Semi-Annual Meetings. Our State Convention office is in Syracuse, New York. Even in good weather it was a 3 – 4 hour drive from Syracuse to our area of the state. I knew that our State Missions Director was scheduled to come. I guess I just assumed he would call before he tried to drive that distance. I made the wrong assumption. He drove all the way to the church where the meeting was to be held. Then he drove nearby to the pastors home before he discovered the meeting had been cancelled. Later he told me that, before he left the house that morning, his wife suggested he call me to see if the meeting had been cancelled. He said that he told her, "Jim never cancels a meeting." He said when he got to Watertown, about 100 miles away, he started to call me, but then he said to himself, "Jim never cancels a meeting." Come to think of it, that may be part of the reason that when the association gave us a going-away party on the Friday night after Thanksgiving 1991, over 300 people came from all over the association in a driving snow storm. I had told my wife the crowd would be very small that night because of the weather. I never claimed to be a prophet.

When we moved to New York, the Baptist Convention of New York had just started a five year partnership with the North Carolina Baptist Convention. BCNY Associations were encouraged to establish partnerships with North Carolina Baptist Associations. I was able to make the connections to make several worthwhile partnerships with associations in North Carolina. I will have more to say about those partnerships later. Because of those partnerships, I was able to take Experiencing God Weekend teams from our association to North Carolina churches to share the Experiencing God Weekends.

One morning I received a call from a friend of mine at the Sunday School Board (now LifeWay). He wanted me to know that I would probably be receiving a call from a pastor of a World Wide Church of God in Montreal. He said the pastor wanted information about implementing Experiencing God in his church. He told me that he thought the man was serious and that he told him that there was a man who lived very near him, who could help him as much as he could. A couple of days later I received a call from Montreal, Canada, which was only 70 miles from where I lived. The caller identified himself as Dennis Alexander. He told me that he was pastor of two World Wide Church of God churches in Canada. He told me that he was trying to get some information on the Experiencing God material in order to determine if it was something that would be profitable for his churches. He told me that he had called the Sunday School Board to see if he could get some help from them. The man he talked to in Nashville told him that there was a man who lived near him who could probably help him. I told him that I would be glad to do whatever I could to help him. We made arrangements for him to drive to Malone, New York, and we met for breakfast to discuss Experiencing God.

Dennis and I met on the assigned morning and not only did we have a long discussion about Experiencing God, but a personal friendship was also established between the two of us. What I suggested to him was that he set a time for an Experiencing God Weekend that would start on Friday night and go through Sunday noon. He thought that would be a good idea and wanted to know what it would cost them for us to come and conduct the weekend. I told him that it would not cost him anything. I told him that all he would need to do would be to have a place for our team members to stay and provide our meals while we were there. He began to weep. He explained to me that he was weeping because, over the years, the World Wide Church of God had been very critical of Southern Baptists. Now we were willing to come and help him without any charge. (By the way, the time frame for this meeting was just a few years after the leadership of the World Wide Church of God admitted to their churches that they had been purposely misleading them for years, and that much of their doctrine had no basis in Scripture.)

He told me that their churches in Canada owned a camp and that we could hold the weekend there. That sounded like a perfect setting and did turn out to be perfect. I told him that it would take him about 3 months to properly prepare his two churches for the weekend. We set a date a little over 3 months away. He began preparing his churches and I began putting a team together. We scheduled the weekend for late in the spring, after the weather had warmed up and the snow was gone.

Dennis was pastor of a church in Montreal and another smaller church type mission in Cornwall, Ontario, Canada. The church in Cornwall was just across the St. Lawrence River from New York. On the weekend scheduled for the Experiencing God Weekend, he cancelled regular services in both of his churches and encouraged all who would, from both congregations, to attend. We met at their camp and retreat center. This may have been the best location for an Experiencing God Weekend I have ever had. The camp was located in a quiet, beautiful setting and yet it had all of the facilities that we needed. Because they owned the camp, we did not have to deal with third parties for any of our needs, and there was adequate housing for everyone. A large number of members from both congregations, including Youth and Adults, came and, because of the setting, they were pretty much committed for the whole weekend.

I brought a team of about 15 members from our association. There was a good mixture of ministers and their wives and lay people on our team. If you are not familiar with the way an Experiencing God Weekend works, there is a mixture of large group teaching time and small group times to discuss the concepts that have been taught. There are personal testimonies from the team members that are mixed into both settings. Virginia led the small group times for the Youth while our other team members led the Adult small groups.

We had an unusual thing happen with the make-up of our team. We had an unsaved man who came with his wife. I will share more about him at another time. I asked his wife to give her testimony during one of the large group settings. During her testimony, she talked about how difficult it had been for her to do the things she wanted to do for the Lord because of her "heathen husband." Later in a small group setting, one of the participants began to ask her husband questions. Finally this unsaved husband said, "I don't know how to answer you; I am that 'heathen husband' that lady was talking about."

When we came to Sunday morning, I closed the weekend with a message from God's Word. The content of the message went beyond the scope of a typical closing message for an Experiencing God Weekend. As the weekend progressed, I sensed that the Lord was doing more than just introducing these two congregations to some new discipleship material. Normally we close the weekends by asking people to commit to being a part of an Experiencing God small group study. Before the message, I told the pastor that I sensed that the Lord might be doing some other things and I asked him how he felt about me having an altar call at the close of the message. He told me to do whatever I felt led to do.

I had learned a lot of things about the participants during the course of the weekend. For example, the young lady that was the Music Minister for the Montreal Church had been a student at the World Wide Church of God University in Texas. She was a senior and student body president at the time the church began to admit that much of their doctrine was heresy (her words). She told me about how betrayed they all felt, and how humiliated they felt. Another layman in the church had said to me that he felt like he had been lied to by his spiritual leaders for 20 years; now he was trying to sort all of that out.

When I completed the message, I just said that I felt like there were some who needed to do some serious business with God. Therefore, the time was now theirs to do whatever they needed to do. The response was immediate and as genuine as I have ever seen. I asked our people to just hang around and to be available to counsel and pray with people. Some were being saved, others were on their faces before God at the altar, weeping and confessing sin. Others were going to one another, weeping and restoring relationships; then you could see others just sitting and quietly doing business with God. This went on for over an hour. When it was finally wrapped up, we had our final meal together; then with many embraces and tears, we made our way to our vehicles to go back to New York. All of us on the team knew that we had had an encounter with God that we would never forget.

Little did we know that, what God was up to that day, was not over. The "heathen husband" was saved later that night in his home. I will tell you the rest of the story in another setting.

We maintained a close friendship with this World Wide Church of God pastor during the rest of our time in New York. I think that it was a relationship that was special to both of us.

One of the early opportunities I had, during my time in New York, came my way because of my involvement in Experiencing God. I was preaching a revival in a church in Tennessee, in September 1992. I received a call from Jeanette Nichols with Texas Baptist Men. She said she had three questions she wanted to ask me. First, did I have a current passport? Second, did I have a particular week open in November? I said yes to both questions. Then she said she had one more question. She wanted to know if I would be willing to go to Belgium and pinch hit for Henry Blackaby. I told her that they couldn't possibly think I was qualified for such a task. She said she had been told to try to get me to go before she called anyone else. The assignment was to go to the Annual Meeting of our Foreign Missionaries in Belgium. I was to lead them through an introduction to Experiencing God during the day, and preach in a worship service in the evening each night during the week. With a great deal of fear and trembling, I agreed to do so. I took one of my young pastors with me on this trip. He helped me with the Experiencing God material, and I asked him to preach one night. We flew into Brussels, where we met one of our SBC missionaries. We traveled with this couple to a remodeled 17th century castle that had been converted into an absolutely lovely conference center. It was a wonderful week with our missionaries in Belgium.

My pastor friend and I enjoyed getting acquainted with the culture of Belgium. The first night, the missionaries we stayed with took us out to dinner. They asked if we wanted Belgium food or American, and we told them Belgium food. They took us to a nice Belgium cuisine restaurant for dinner. We learned a couple of things that night; one was that neither one of us were very fond of raw or barely cooked fish. We both ordered smoked salmon. I think what they did with the salmon steaks was to wave them over the smoke a couple of times. The second thing that we learned was that Belgium waiters were not very happy serving Americans; the reason being that we are too impatient. They said that we did not take the time to enjoy a good meal. Our missionaries told us that the difference in the cultures was that Americans might go out to dinner and a movie; where Europeans would most likely do one or the other. Therefore, if they were going out to dinner, that event alone would consume the whole evening. When we got to the conference center, the meals were wonderful and very rich in flavor. We also really enjoyed stopping at Waffle Stands and getting hot "Belgium Waffles." They were absolutely wonderful, and fresh out of the waffle iron. They would almost melt in your mouth, and were very high in sugar content.

I had a really interesting personal experience that was related to my invitation to pinch hit for Henry Blackaby. My first impressions were of how unworthy I was to try to fill such large shoes. For several weeks leading up to this trip, those feelings dominated my heart. Then Satan used another tactic to try to keep me off balance in my preparation for the trip. The next feeling I had was, "You must really be better than you thought, if they are asking you to pinch hit for such an outstanding man." As you can imagine, those thoughts really kept me bogged down and unable to hear the Lord, as I was making preparation for the trip. Getting ready to introduce them to the Experiencing God material was not hard. I had already done that many times. It was getting my heart right, so that, in presenting the material, my heart was in tune with the Lord. I also needed my heart to be in tune with the Lord in order to prepare the evening messages.

Finally one day the Lord spoke clearly to me that I was not unworthy nor was I any more special than anyone else. Then He told me that the truth was, His intention all along was, that this was to be my assignment and not Henry Blackaby's. During that time with the Lord, He gave me the message that I was to preach the first night. It was about how to deal with the spiritual battles in your life. After we returned home from that trip, I received a phone call from one of the missionaries thanking me for the message of the first night. She said that she had come to the conference with all kinds of spiritual battles going on in her heart and the message of that first night helped her to deal with them. She also told me that when her family got back to their field of service after the conference, they discovered that some new battles had developed while they were gone. She said that because of that first message she had the spiritual tools she needed to deal with the new battles as well.

The lesson learned, that we all should apply to ourselves, is that God has assignments for us that no one else can fulfill but us, even though they are probably much more qualified than we are. If all of us could always keep that in mind, we would more likely be ready for the assignments that the Lord has for us.

This was my first experience traveling in Europe. I had flown into European airports before, but had not had any travel experiences in

Europe. I had no idea at the time that one day my oldest son would live in Europe (Germany), and pastor an English speaking church there.

From Heathen Husband to Man of God

I met Marina Bolster when I was supply preaching at the Bangor Baptist Church. She was a member of the church. The first time I met her was after the service. She was leaving quickly after the service was over. She told me that her husband was not a Christian, and if she did not come home immediately after the service was over in order to fix his Sunday dinner, she would have trouble all afternoon. He would not have anything to do with Christianity and the church. She could not even have a Christian book where he could see it. When her pastor came to visit him, he threatened to physically throw him out of his house, if he did not leave on his own, and he was big enough to do just that.

Marina had gotten involved with our North Country Resort Ministry. When it was announced that Lake Placid would be the location of the first ever Winter Goodwill Games, Marina's husband Dick made contact with those in charge in Lake Placid to offer his services as a volunteer. Dick worked for the telephone company, and had served as a volunteer for the 1980 Winter Olympics in Lake Placid. Dick knew that the volunteers were given some real nice winter coats to wear. He really wanted a jacket, and really assumed that because he had volunteered for the Olympics, they would be glad to get him. However, when he called, he was told that they did not need any more volunteers.

When Marina came home that day, Dick told his wife that he was not going to be able to be a volunteer for the Goodwill Games. Marina then told him that she was going as a volunteer with our ministry. Dick asked her if she thought we would let him go with us and be one of our volunteers. She told him she did not think so, but she would ask. She called my wife Virginia and told her about him wanting to

355

come with us. Virginia told her to tell him he could go. Marina did tell Dick that he could go, but he needed to know that he would be around Christians all week and would actually sleep in the church. Then she told him that she better not here him cuss in the church. He told her he could fake anything for a week in order to get one of the jackets.

Apparently Dick spent the week watching to see if any of the Christians messed up during the week, so that he could say that they did not practice what they preached. Praise God, all of our volunteers conducted themselves in a way that left no room for criticism. He later said that he saw two men have a very minor disagreement and later come back and seek one another's forgiveness.

Shortly after the Goodwill Games were over, I began to put the team together for the Experiencing God Weekend in Canada. I invited Marina to go, and a few days later she called to say that Dick wanted to go with us. I told her he could go. He did go and spent that week-end with a room full of Christians who were studying the Experiencing God material. He had to listen to his wife refer to him as her "Heathen Husband." We got home from that weekend in Canada about 6:00 P.M.; about 10:00 P.M. we got a call from Dick and Marina. Dick said that he had followed his wife around the house for two hours wanting to talk to her and she was busy doing laundry and other things. He said that he finally grabbed her and said, "Woman would you stop long enough to tell me how to be saved?" That night his wife got the privilege of leading him to Christ, and he gave his life to Christ.

Dick became a major factor in our North Country Ministry. He and Marina also became people we could call on to participate in Experiencing God Weekends. Dick had an interesting experience as a volunteer at the Bobsled Gold Cup World Championship. There was a VIP tent about halfway up the mountain. It was my responsibility to have a volunteer at the entrance to the VIP tent. That volunteer would check the credentials of everyone who tried to enter the tent. If they did not have the proper credentials, our volunteer was instructed not to let them inside. I had assigned Dick to check credentials at the VIP tent. Now you need to keep in mind that Dick is a large man. He is probably about 6'5'' and weighs almost 300 pounds. I happened to see Dick having a long conversation with the man who was the Director of all of the Olympic Training Center facilities. This man's first name is Jim. The problem was that Jim had left his credentials on his desk and Dick did not know him and was not going to let him inside the VIP tent. I went over and told him it was alright to let this man into the tent. When Jim went inside the tent, I told Dick that he had just kept the biggest VIP of all out of the VIP tent. He was embarrassed. I told him that he was just doing what we had told him to do. I then went inside the tent and apologized to Jim for what had happened. He told me that he was just glad to see that the volunteers were doing their jobs properly. Later that day I saw Dick engaged in conversation with someone else. I heard the man ask him why he was doing what he was doing. Dick said, "I am glad you asked, last year I came down here to get a jacket and I got Jesus. Let me tell you what Jesus has done for me."

Over the next few years, Dick and I became the closest of friends. He retired from the phone company during this time, which made him available almost anytime I needed him. We volunteered in all kinds of weather, doing whatever was needed to be done, but always waiting for someone to ask us that important question, "Why are you doing what you are doing?" That was our invitation to share Jesus with them. Marina shared with me that she and Dick were going to a Semi-Annual Association Meeting about a year after Dick was saved. She said that Dick asked her what they did at this meeting and she told him, "I don't know, you never would let me go before." Dick and Marina also became very involved in Experiencing God Weekends. They have traveled much of New England on these weekends. Most of the time, they have gone with Texas Baptist Men's Teams.

Ministers' Prayer Group

I have indicated already that I learned very early in my ministry that there is real value in seeking to cooperate with ministers of other religious persuasions. Therefore, over the years it was my practice to seek out local Interdenominational Ministerial Associations, and determine if they are a group that I can find common ground for cooperation. When we moved to Malone, New York, this was the first time I had moved into a community where I was not the pastor of one of the local churches. Therefore, it took a little effort for me to discover the local Ministerial Association, when and where they met, and introduce myself to them. I discovered that the local Ministerial Association in Malone was actually made up of pastors all over the northern part of Franklin County. I attended one meeting in May of 1992, and discovered that they did not meet in the summer. During the summer I decided I would attend their meetings, if I was invited to them. I went all summer without hearing from them, and I was somewhat relieved, because I had decided that I really did not have time to be involved. Then in August, I ran into a local Presbyterian pastor. We struck up a conversation and he invited me to the first meeting of the fall, which was going to be the next week.

In the early months of that fall, I went to all of the monthly meetings and came away feeling that we were accomplishing absolutely nothing. Then we had a chaplain of one of our local prisons begin to attend. He was a Muslim Imam. I noticed that everyone was working hard at not talking about things that would be offensive to this Muslim Imam. Toward the end of 1992, the Imam did not attend the meeting. At that meeting, plans were being made for the Annual Community Christmas Service. Someone said that we would have to be careful about using Scripture in the service that might offend the Muslim Community.

After that meeting, one of the Methodist pastors called me. He said that he needed to ask me a question. He said that he got the feeling that I had decided, because of the things that were discussed, that I was probably not going to attend any more meetings. I told him that he was right, and that I felt I did not want to spend my time at meetings, where the ministers felt like they had to apologize for being Christian. He said that he hoped I would reconsider, because the Ministerial Association needed a voice like mine. I told him I would pray about it. The Lord did lead me to attend the next meeting.

That Methodist pastor and I became close friends. About a year later he called me and invited me to lunch. We met for lunch the next day. During that meal he told me that he had a two-fold reason for meeting with me. First, he told me that he would soon be moving to a new place of service. Second, he was leaving to move to Central New York to pastor a United Church. A United Church is where more than one denomination in a small town have come together to bear the expense, so that they can still have a full-time pastor in the community. He said that his church would be Methodist, Baptist, and Presbyterian. He said that they met together for worship, but that each church still maintained its own belief system and ways of doing church. He said that with the Baptist group, he knew he would be asked to immerse those who were being baptized, and he had never done that before. He wanted me to teach him how to do a Baptist baptism. I told him I would be glad to do that, but I had a warning for him. He wanted to know about the warning. I told him that once he baptized someone "the right way," he would never be satisfied doing it any other way. He got a kick out of that.

At the next meeting I spoke up and said that it was offensive to me that we would even consider the possibility of having a Community Christmas Service, celebrating the birth of Christ, without using Scripture concerning the Son of God, the Savior of the world. I asked if we had any kind of statement about who we were as a Ministerial Association. A committee was formed to write such a document and I was asked to be on that committee. We ended up with a document that basically stated that we were unashamedly a Christian Ministerial Association, and we would not apologize for that. After the meeting when we adopted that statement, we put an article about the Ministerial Association in the paper. That article included a statement about who we were, a Christian Ministerial Association.

I suppose in the year 2016, we would be harshly criticized for making a public statement about being specifically a Christian Ministerial Association. My response to that would be, let others be whoever their hearts dictate them to be, but do not tell me that I cannot be who I am. This is, for me, a deep conviction that is based on what I believe about the Bible, and what the Bible teaches me about Jesus Christ, the Son of God, Who died on the cross for my sins. This same Bible teaches me that Jesus is the only way to eternal life in heaven. There are those who believe that anyone, who takes the position I just took, is wrong. They have the right to believe that I am wrong about what the Bible teaches, however, they need to know that, if I am wrong, I am sincerely wrong; I cannot back away from the deep conviction of my heart.

Through my involvement in the local Ministerial Association, I developed a close relationship with Rev. John Werley, who was pastor of the First Congregational Church of Malone. The beautiful First Congregational Church was located just two blocks up Main Street from my home. The building itself had a great history. During the Civil War, this church was the last stop in Northeastern New York for the "Underground Railroad" for slaves who were headed to safety in Canada. The tunnel ran from the river up to the basement of the church, and it is still there. They would come up that tunnel into the church basement in the morning and stay there and rest throughout the day. Church members would provide them food for the day; then when night came, they would go back to the river bed to travel the last 12 miles into Canada.

Rev. Werley described himself as the only remaining conservative Congregational pastor in the State of New York. He and I had a common concern to see the church experience genuine revival. We decided to send out a letter to all of the pastors in northern Franklin County, and invite them to a time of prayer for real revival. We sent out 36 invitations, and we had 16 pastors who came to that first prayer meeting. We were very encouraged by the turnout. At first we decided to meet once a month. We soon discovered that we really needed to meet more often. Before long we were meeting every Thursday morning. We were a very interesting group. The makeup of our group included Baptist, Methodist, Presbyterian, Pentecostal, Non-Denominational, Congregational, and eventually, we had a Roman Catholic Priest join our group. Our only agenda was praying that revival would breakout in at least one of our churches, and we really did not care where it started. We just wanted to see the power of the Holy Spirit break out in our area. The group met regularly throughout the last 8 years of my ministry in the North Country.

When we retired and moved, this prayer group continued to meet, praying for revival. After we had been back in Texas about a year, I got a call reminding me that the next week the prayer group would celebrate its 10th Anniversary. They wanted me to join them in a conference call to participate in the prayer meeting that Thursday. There was one thing that allowed us to stay together for such a long time. We obviously had a number of theological differences, however, we all believed that Jesus Christ was and is the answer to all of the problems of mankind. We agreed that we would keep our focus on Jesus Christ. Every Thursday morning, when we came together to pray, we left our theological differences at home. We concentrated on the one thing or rather the one person we all had in common, Jesus Christ. The Holy Spirit was able to create a bond in that mixture of belief systems and personalities that was something that only the Lord could do.

Fairly early in our process, we were in the middle of our prayer meeting, when the Lord convicted me of an attitude in my heart. I had heard about some practices that were reported to be happening in the Pentecostal church. The conviction from the Lord was so heavy on my heart that I stopped praying and reached over and touched the knee of the pastor of that church. I told him about the critical spirit that I had about things I heard were happening in his church, yet I never had approached him to talk to him about it. I asked him to forgive me of my critical spirit. Praise God, he did forgive me, and a new bond was created between the two of us.

There was a defining moment for me personally and for us as a prayer group one Thursday morning. I was going through a very personal stressful time, so much so that the Administrative Committee had agreed that they needed to give me some time to get away. Virginia and I had made plans to go and spend five weeks with her sister and our brother-in-law, in Miami. I was in one of our prayer meetings shortly before we were to leave on our trip. If you remember, I mentioned that we had a Catholic Priest that showed up one Thursday morning and became a vital member of our group. On this particular Thursday morning, I was apparently having another pity party. That day we were meeting in the fellowship hall of one of the Methodist churches in Malone. In the midst of my feeling sorry for myself, the Catholic Priest slammed his hand down on the table and shouted, "Jim, I have heard enough. Is God in charge or not? If He is in charge, then you need to just trust Him and quit this whining." The room became very quiet. You could feel the tension as the others were wondering how the Southern Baptist was going to respond to being spiritually disciplined by the Catholic Priest. I looked at him for a moment, and then I told him that he was absolutely right. I thanked him for having enough courage to rebuke me in love. Needless to say, we had a great prayer meeting that day. That moment also opened up the avenue for all of us to be spiritually accountable to one another.

We did a number of meaningful things which included an annual retreat with our wives. The various things we did together became a strong support system for us and our wives. We were able to have outdoor worship services in the City Park, which was located right in the middle of town.

The first outdoor worship service that we had was on a Sunday evening in the summer. We asked each church to gather their church members at their church, and then we marched together from all parts of town to converge on the City Park. Some of the churches, that were not in Malone, went to one of the Malone church buildings and joined with that church to converge on City Park. The groups sang gospel songs and quoted Scripture as they went. Because the City Park was on Highway 11, Main Street, eventually all of the groups became two groups merging together from the East and the West. The people of Malone and surrounding areas were amazed at the unity of Spirit that was being demonstrated by this group of pastors who came from such a variety of backgrounds.

One year, at our annual Maples Conference on Revival, I asked this pastor's prayer group to come and introduce themselves and share their perspective about how the time we spent each week praying together had impacted their own lives and ministries. When one of the Methodist pastors introduced himself, he said, "I am the token liberal in this group."

Maples Conference on Revival

In the fall of 1992, I got a call from Don Gibson with Texas Baptist Men. He wanted to know if the Adirondack Baptist Association would be interested in hosting a Conference on Prayer and Spiritual Awakening sponsored by the office of Prayer and Spiritual Awakening at the Home Mission Board. Henry Blackaby was the Director of this ministry at the Home Mission Board. He was looking for a place in the Northeast to conduct this conference in the fall of 1993. Don told me that all we had to do was provide the location and Henry Blackaby's office would pay all of the expenses for the conference. We were more than happy to host this conference.

We began communication with Henry Blackaby's office to make the arrangements needed for the conference in the fall of 1993. The Bread of Life Baptist Church in Plattsburgh, New York, agreed to be the host for the conference. We began to send information throughout New York and the entire Northeast, inviting pastors and churches to attend this conference. The conference was well received and very well attended. We even had a pastor of one of our Southern Baptist Asian Churches, from New Jersey, leave after church Sunday night and drive all night, so that they could be there for the start of the conference on Monday.

During one of the afternoon sessions there was a question and answer session with those who were speakers on the program. One of those speakers was Bob Dixon, Director of Texas Baptist Men. I asked Bob to tell us about the annual Cedars Conference sponsored by Texas Baptist Men. After his answer, I asked him if he thought it was possible for us to use this conference as a springboard for an annual conference on revival for the Northeast USA. He not only said he thought it was possible, he actually named the conference. He suggested that we hold it in the fall foliage season of the year and call it the Maples Conference.

Just that quickly, the idea of an annual conference on revival sponsored by the Adirondack Baptist Association, The Office of Prayer and Spiritual Awakening of the Home Mission Board, and Texas Baptist Men, became more than an idea. This became a remarkable relationship that provided a quality conference and a time for the pastors and their wives to get away from the daily grind and be refreshed both physically and spiritually. Our small churches could not afford to send their pastor to such a quality conference. We made an early decision that we would not charge pastors and their wives to attend the conference. The last 11 years of our ministry in the Adirondacks we conducted this conference annually. We were able to do this without charging our pastors and their wives anything. There were various groups that helped make this possible. The Day Foundation, based in Georgia, and Texas Baptist Men were two of the major groups that sent me money almost every year for scholarships, so that any pastor and his wife could attend. There were other Christian foundations that believed in what we were trying to do that also provided funds, so that no pastor and his wife would have to stay at home because they could not afford to come.

Sometimes I did not have the money until the very day the conference began; however, I never turned away any pastor and his wife. We simply trusted that the Lord would provide for our needs. One of the most significant ways the Lord met our needs was in the very last Maples Conference before I retired.

We had decided to move downstate a bit to the Word of Life Conference Center in Schroon Lake, NY. I went to the business office of Word of Life to find out how much we were going to owe when we checked out the next day. The amount was almost $1,500.00, and we only had one more session left when we would take an offering for the expenses. We would be taking this offering from the same people who had been giving all week. The group was smaller that year than it had been in the past. When I took the offering that morning, I told the

365

group how much we needed and asked for them to give what they could. I was fully expecting to have to pay the balance myself. The offering we took did not come close to what we needed. I went to the business office the next morning expecting to have to make arrangements to pay the balance. When I went to the business office, I discovered that the bill had been paid in full. I went away from the conference amazed at how the Lord had once again provided for all of our needs.

That year there was a pastor and his wife from Central America who attended. Several months later I discovered that this pastor was a member of one of the wealthiest families in his country. I still don't know for sure where the money came from to pay that bill, but I have a feeling that the Lord sent a family from Central America to help meet our needs.

In 1994, the year after the conference that was sponsored by the Office of Prayer and Spiritual Awakening, of the Home Mission Board, we had our first Maples Conference. Although the Maples Conference on Revival was officially sponsored by The Adirondack Baptist Association, it was done in cooperation with the Office of Prayer and Spiritual Awakening (Henry Blackaby and Ron Owens), and Texas Baptist Men. We decided to have that first official Maples Conference in Malone, New York, and the historic First Congregational Church allowed us to use their facility. There was a beautiful Bed and Breakfast, down the side street from the church, and we secured that as the place for those on the program to stay. It was literally in walking distance from the church. This church is where my friend John Werley, who helped me start the Minister's Prayer Group, was the pastor.

In cooperation with Don Gibson and the Renewal section of Texas Baptist Men, we planned a simultaneous Lay Renewal Weekend. Texas Baptist Men would provide the teams for the churches that agreed to participate. Most of our churches agreed to participate in the Renewal Weekend prior to the Maples Conference that would begin on Monday night and go through Wednesday noon. Don Gibson enlisted one team of 8 from the Men's Ministry of the North Carolina Baptist Convention.

Just a few weeks before the weekend was to take place, the church where the team from North Carolina was to go, backed out. The 8 team members had already bought non-refundable plane tickets. Don Gibson called me and asked me if there was somewhere else they could go. Because most of our churches were already committed, I did not have many options. I told him I had one place that was not really a church or a mission at the moment, but we hoped it would be. He said that he was sure this group would be willing to come to that place.

You remember Moriah, New York, that I listed as unsettled issues that I had to deal with in the early days of our ministry in New York? That mission closed down, but they had a house that was actually owned by the sponsoring church, Lake Placid Baptist Church. John and Peggy Clarke were members of Lake Placid Baptist Church and were living in the house that Southern Baptists had bought for the 1980 Winter Olympics. The Lake Placid Church was getting ready to call a pastor and needed that house for the pastor and his family. I was the Interim Pastor at Lake Placid at the time. After getting approval from the church, I went to John and Peggy and talked to them about living in the house in Moriah. John immediately said to me that he was not going to start a church. I told him I did not expect him to do that. Peggy told me that she was not going to start a church without John. I told them that we just needed someone living in the house. I had a feeling that Peggy might start a ladies' Home Bible Study, which she did. I told them that I would be pleased if they just changed the image of who Southern Baptists are in the minds of their neighbors.

I called them and asked them if they would be willing to host this Lay Renewal team from North Carolina and invite some of their neighbors to attend. They were not real excited about it, but did agree to do so. I saw them on Wednesday before the weekend was to start on Friday night and they told me that no one had agreed to attend. They thought they should cancel. I asked them if they had considered that the Lord had put this together just to encourage them. They did agree to go ahead with the weekend.

The Lay Renewal Weekend is designed with a format where each church comes together on Sunday night to share what the weekend has meant to them. We had asked our churches if they would all come together in Malone, at the Congregational Church on Sunday night for a joint sharing service. That church will seat 500 people and our churches filled it up that Sunday night. When the group from Moriah got there, they were on cloud nine. It had been just John and Peggy and the team from North Carolina Friday night and Saturday. However, 44 people from the community showed up Sunday morning. John came to me and told me I was going to have to find someone to preach to them the next Sunday, because he had told them that, if they came back, he would have a preacher there. I told him we would figure out something. Somewhere in the midst of that sharing service, which went on for almost 3 hours, I saw John and some of the men from North Carolina get up and go out somewhere. Later they came back. When it was John's time to share, he told about all that had gone on and how they really did not think they should even try to have the weekend. Then he told about the locals who had shown up on Sunday morning. Then he told us that in a room in the back, the Lord had just called him to preach, and he would be the one preaching to those that would come back. The Moriah Baptist Mission was reborn that weekend and is still in existence today.

For a year before that conference in Malone, I had been having some severe health problems in my abdomen. Every time I would eat, within just a few minutes after eating, I would experience severe pain on the left side of my abdomen. It had been determined that I needed surgery and that I probably needed to have half of my stomach removed. As it got closer to the time for the Maples Conference, I told the doctor I wanted to wait until after the conference was over. He agreed, but also said that he wanted to set up an appointment with a surgeon in Burlington, Vermont, to get his opinion about what needed to be done.

When the time for the conference came, I was helping Don Miller get settled in his room at the Bed and Breakfast. After we got to his room, Don told me he wanted to talk to me. He told me that he believed that the Lord wanted him to pray for me to be healed. I don't know of anyone I would have rather had pray for me than Don Miller. We knelt beside the bed and he prayed a very simple prayer. He prayed, "Dear Lord, would you set Jim free from the problem he is having?" In that moment, I felt a tingling in the area of my stomach where the pain would always start every time I ate. Later that day I ate an Italian hoagie with everything on it, and I had no pain. I believed that the Lord had healed me. The next day I asked Claude King if he thought I should share my experience with those attending the conference. He said that he had been praying "that the Lord would heal me before or during the conference, so that He could get the glory." So he encouraged me to share my experience. I did and I do believe that the Lord was honored in it. The next time I visited my doctor, he told me he never did get a report from the doctor in Burlington about my condition. I told him that was because I canceled the appointment. Then I told him what had happened to me. He then told me that he believed in divine healing.

Maples and Howard Johnson Lodge and Conference Center – Lake Placid

After the second year of the Maples Conference, we made a decision to move Maples to Lake Placid. We did that because it gave us more lodging options for those who would come, and we were having the conference in the fall foliage season, which made Lake Placid an even more attractive place. One of the problems, however, was that the "Leaf Lookers" season, which is what the locals called the people who came to the mountains during this time of the year, was one of the busiest seasons of the year. This meant that the room rates were higher than any other time of the year. I had met the events coordinator at the Holiday Inn through one of the members of the Lake Placid Baptist Church. He had helped me with room rates for a state-wide event which was held in Lake Placid. I found out that he had moved to a similar position with the Howard Johnson Motor Lodge and Conference Center, which was located on the west side of town right on the main drag.

I went to Lake Placid to talk to him and his boss about having our conference there. They had a large building that sat up on a hill, which was their conference center. It had a large indoor swimming pool and enclosed recreation area, with three floors of rooms, and a conference room that would seat three hundred that was on a mezzanine level overlooking the pool area. During the fall foliage season, their normal room rate was $120.00 per night. When I explained to him what we were trying to do, he let me have the rooms for $60.00 per night. The first year we were there was a huge success. Howard Johnsons went out of their way to make our stay comfortable. It was a perfect setting for the Maples Conference.

The management of Howard Johnson was amazing in their dealings with me. They would let me hold a certain number of rooms with no guarantee from me until right up until time for the conference to begin. This was even more amazing because the time of year was the highest demand of the year for rooms. When the time for the conference came, they would literally turn over all of the facilities in the conference center to us. It was like a match made in heaven. It was just the perfect place for us to have our conference, and for those who participated, it was a perfect place to relax and enjoy the surroundings, while being blessed by the conference.

The morning after that Maples Conference had ended, Ron Owens and I met for breakfast to discuss the future. Don Gibson had told me before he left town that if we decided to continue, Texas Baptist Men were willing to continue their support. Ron and I agreed that the Lord had demonstrated that this was something that should continue as long as the Lord was blessing it. One of the things that I discovered was that, we could get the really quality speakers that everybody wanted to come to our conference, if they knew that their time was not going to be wasted, and if we planned far enough in advance. The best way for them to know that their time was not going to be wasted was, if someone that they knew and had confidence in their judgment invited them. What we decided that morning was that he and Don Gibson and I would work together on the program personalities for the next year. When that was settled, Ron and Don would make the contacts to secure those who would be on the program. I would then be responsible for making all of the local arrangements. These two men also did a great deal in pointing me in the right direction to raise the money for the scholarships for pastors and their wives.

One of our goals was to provide a quality conference to these pastors of small churches in the Northeast. Most of these men were in churches so small they would never be able to send them to a conference with the kind of quality that the Lord gave to the Maples Conference. It was amazing to me year after year, the speakers that were willing to pay their own way to come and participate in the

371

Maples Conference on Revival. We would take an offering during the conference. Most of this was used to pay the travel for a few speakers who were not in a position to pay their own travel. No one got love offerings or fees for their service. I think I may have said this before, but I will say it one more time. We did this for 11 years and did not use any money out of the association's budget. God provided, as only He could.

When you consider the fact that I really did not have a clue what I was getting into, there were amazingly few flaws along the way. As you can imagine, there were some, but the Lord was able to overcome those on our behalf. When I look back on the Maples Conference, there were two men that the Lord used that, without them the good things that happened over the years would not have happened. I have already mentioned them, but I want to say a very special thank you to Don Gibson and Ron Owens. What wonderful men of God that He gave me, who had the patience to work with someone like me for the greater good.

There were some humorous incidents along the way. I remember one year Henry and Marilyn Blackaby were flying into Montreal, Canada, on Sunday night. Montreal is about a two hour drive from Lake Placid. Virginia and I drove to Montreal to pick them up. We came back across the border about 10:30 P.M. I knew that the Blackabys were natives of Canada, but they had been in the U.S. so long, I assumed they had become U.S. citizens. The Border Patrol officer asked me where I had been. I told him that we had been to Montreal to pick up our friends from Atlanta, Georgia. He wanted to know if everyone in the car was a U.S. citizen. I told him yes. Henry was sitting in the front seat beside me and the ladies were in the back seat. When I drove off, Marilyn spoke up and said, "Henry, I can't believe you let Jim do that." His response to her was, "Jim was doing so well I did not want to interrupt him." I looked at Henry and said, "You mean after all these years you never have become a U.S. citizen?" He said, "No, the need has never arisen." I then jokingly asked him if he had a Green Card. Then I said, "Here we are on our way to a conference on revival, and my main speaker has just allowed me to lie for him." Henry then said, "I have time to seek forgiveness before we get to Lake Placid." Henry Blackaby is a wonderful proclaimer of God's truths. He also has a great sense of humor.

Ron Owens, who was a vital cog in the success of Maples, is also a Canadian. I think both men really enjoyed being involved in something that was really significant, and also close to their Homeland. Ron and Patricia Owens became dear friends of ours. It was our honor to have them in our home on numerous occasions, and I am grateful that we have been able to maintain that relationship with them during these years since New York. As fate would have it, our home in Texas has been a good stopping off place for them, as they had reasons to travel to east and southeast Texas. They are one of the most talented couples I have ever met in my life.

By the way, one of the humorous stories that came from Maples was about a man called "Joe Gimforth." A dear friend of Ron and Patricia came with them to Maples one year to be one of the speakers. On the plane, she asked Ron, "What is the name of that DOM in New York?" Apparently she caught him half asleep. He stammered around a bit, and managed to get all of the letters right, but got them a little bit misplaced. Instead of Jim Goforth, it came out, "Joe Gimforth." That became one of the sidelight stories of that conference. And with some "friends" it has stuck over the years.

You also need to know that although there was no love offering for the speakers, we did not allow them to leave the North Country empty handed. I always gave the program personalities some fresh New York Maple Syrup that had been made somewhere in the Adirondacks. I really think the reason I was able to get some of them to come back so often was, so that they could replenish their supply of maple syrup. They also got to spend a week in some of God's most beautiful creation, the Adirondack Mountains, in the fall foliage season.

Partnerships

As I have already mentioned, when we first moved to the North Country of New York, the Adirondack Baptist Association and the Baptist Convention of New York had just recently established a five year State to State Partnership with the North Carolina Baptist Convention. One of the things that the North Carolina Association Directors of Missions did was that they invited the DOMs from New York to come to their Annual DOM Retreat, which was held on the campus of Wingate College. The retreat was free for us and our wives. All we had to do was pay our travel expenses to get there. This turned out to be a real blessing for those of us from New York. It also gave us an opportunity to get acquainted with DOMs in North Carolina and develop Association to Association partnerships. I was able to establish relationships and partnerships with several DOMs and their associations in North Carolina.

From that first retreat, several DOMs in the area just south of Raleigh/Durham, North Carolina, invited me to come and speak in their Annual Association Meetings in the fall of the year. I went and spoke to four Annual Meetings in about a day and a half. In the first meeting the schedule was so close that I literally spoke in one meeting and a driver was waiting for me as I walked off the platform to take me to the next meeting.

I had an interesting experience as I was making my way to the car. One of the pastors stopped me on my way to the car. He thanked me for my presentation. Then he said, "I suspect that you and I have a lot of differences theologically, but when it comes to missions and evangelism, I suspect that our hearts are very close. In that spirit, I would like to give you this. Use it as the Lord leads you." He handed me an envelope, shook my hand and walked away. After I got in the car, I opened the envelope and there was a check for $1,000.00.

Before I left on this trip, the wife of a family that had come with us from East Texas to pastor one of our new missions came to visit me. They had come at great personal and financial sacrifice. She told me that she did not have the money to buy winter coats for her children, and she did not know what she was going to do. I told her that the Lord had called them there and that He was going to supply their need. When I returned from my trip to North Carolina, we invited that family over for dinner. The Lord had told me to give half of that $1,000.00 to this family for clothes for their children and the other half to another pastor and his family who had a great need. It was a real delight to show this family how the Lord had met their need in a way they would never have imagined.

That church in North Carolina ended up becoming particularly involved with our church in Lake Placid and with our ministry to the Olympic Training Center. Over several years I was handed other $1,000.00 checks from that church, to use "as the Lord led me."

One of the North Carolina Associations invited me to bring a team of my pastors to come and speak in individual churches in their association. My son Tom had come to work with us by that time and to help restart the ministry to the Olympic Training Center. I took him and three other pastors and we spoke in many of the churches in that association. Out of that trip, many relationships were developed with individual churches, as I was able to link them with churches in our association.

On that trip, I spoke at the First Baptist Church, Lillington, North Carolina. That speaking engagement opened up a wonderful relationship between that church and our association. It also developed a strong personal relationship between a family in that church and Virginia and me. That relationship was a real blessing to us throughout our ministry in New York. On purpose, I am not calling many names, so that I don't have to try to get their permission in the writing of this book. However, I am going to call the name of the Earl Esslinger family from First Baptist Church, Lillington, North Carolina.

When I spoke at FBC, Lillington, North Carolina, that church became particularly interested in a new mission which had been started in Chateaugay, New York. This is a small town 12 miles east of Malone, New York, where I lived, where we had the association office, and where the Shiloh Baptist Church was located. Virginia and I knew that we would not actually be able to attend the church much where we were members, but we believe that when it is at all possible, it is best to be a member where you live. When we joined, I told the church we would probably not be there much, but we promised to send our tithe.

The Shiloh Church had already begun the mission in Chateaugay, in the home of one of their church members. The mission had been in existence for several months, but had not yet called a pastor. There was a young dentist in Rusk, who had been called to preach during my ministry in Rusk. When the Lord called us to the Adirondack Baptist Association, they began to feel that the Lord might be calling them to go with us. This dentist and his wife went with us in December of 1991, when we went to New York to find a place to live. While we were on that trip, they met with the group and the mission called him as their pastor. He told them that it would take them at least six months to go home and sell his dental practice and the new house that he was building. I told the mission I would serve as their Interim Pastor during this time. So when we returned from our house hunting experience, this young dentist and his wife came back to make plans to move just 10 miles south of the Canadian border.

The next summer, a group from the FBC, Lillington, North Carolina, came to Chateaugay to lead the mission in a VBS. A picnic was held in the city park the day before VBS was to begin. Mrs. Esslinger was serving a hotdog to a 12 year old girl. The girl asked what they did at Vacation Bible School. Mrs. Esslinger told her that they studied about Jesus. The 12 year old girl asked her, "Who is Jesus?" When she walked away, Mrs. Esslinger said that if she had not heard it with her own ears, she would never have believed that a 12 year old in the United States would say that she had never heard of Jesus.

As I have already said, the Esslingers became dear friends of ours and treated us as if we were their own. One year, Earl called me and asked us to come and visit them and just spend some time relaxing. It came at a time when we really needed some time to relax and get away from everything. So a few weeks later we drove to North Carolina to spend some time with them. At dinner that night, Earl said he had something he wanted to share with us and if we wanted to do it, we could, and if not that was fine.

He said that Myrtle Beach, South Carolina, was only a short drive from there and that he had already made arrangements with the Holiday Inn for us to stay there at his expense. Because of the time of year, it was the tourist off season in Myrtle Beach, but he said, "I still think you will find lots of things you will enjoy doing." He told me that the Holiday Inn was booked on his account, and then he gave me his American Express card and told me to pay for everything else with that. Needless to say, we were overwhelmed. The next day we loaded back up and headed for Myrtle Beach. We found that the Holiday Inn was ready for our arrival. Earl had already made arrangements at the first golf course he wanted me to play, and then I played a different one every day. Virginia shopped each day while I was playing golf and we ate at some wonderful places each night.

After spending the week in Myrtle Beach, we drove back to North Carolina and spent the weekend with the Esslinger family before we headed back to the North Country. The Esslingers were one of those wonderful families that the Lord put in our lives that kept us going during our 12 years in missions in the North Country of New York.

Special Ministries

Let me list these special ministry opportunities first and I will come back to them. Within the territory of the association, there were 13 Colleges and Universities with no ministries on any of these campuses. There were 11 State and Federal Prisons and a ministry at only one prison. Needless to say, there were resort areas all over our association and not one church had a ministry of any kind to any of these areas. One of the favorite spots to vacation for those who lived in Eastern Canada was the Adirondack Mountains. Eastern Canada was one of the least evangelized nations in the world; yet we had no ministry to any of these resort areas where they came every year.

A ministry that became an immediate burden on my heart was the Olympic Training Center. The Winter Olympics of 1980 in Lake Placid, New York, was the first time Southern Baptists got involved in Olympic Ministry. Our church in Lake Placid was started as a direct result of the ministry in 1980; yet we had no ministry there.

I had a moment one day that would define my ministry. I was driving through the association territory. I drove through a very small community, which was very typical of the Adirondacks. I remember thinking, "I guess this place is too small to start a church." As soon as that thought went through my mind, the Lord spoke to my heart and He said, "I love the few just like I love the millions. I died for the few, just like I died for the millions. I have brought you here so that Southern Baptists will not forget about the few." That became a part of my message anytime I could get someone to listen. That is still true today. God loves the few as much as He loves the millions, and He died for the few just like He died for the millions.

As I look back on that experience concerning the few, I can see how the Lord was already preparing me for what may be the last official

378

place of service I will ever have. I am now into my tenth year of service in a small rural church in East Texas. I am grateful today, for the lessons learned about serving the few for the glory of God. In the first week of October 2015, I was preaching a Senior Adult revival at the FBC, of Center, Texas. I had a lady come up to me and ask me why I was serving in such a small church, after all of the experiences I had had. I told her it was because the Lord had placed me there. It was the very next Friday night that one of the players on the Alto High School Football team died on the field during the game. When that happened, I knew why I was there. I was there to minister to the few.

4-H Camp Overlook

One other thing that I feel very good about is the Youth and Children's Camp ministry. The association had been blessed to have an arrangement with a 4-H Camp to use their facilities for two weeks in August, after their camping season was over. This had been a long-standing agreement long before we moved to the association. There were a good number of adults who had been a part of the association from its beginning, and had also been part of the camp ministry from its beginning. They gave themselves tirelessly to that effort.

They did everything they could to keep the cost of camp affordable, so that families could afford to send their children to camp. They did such things as, bringing fresh foods right out of their gardens to cook, so that the cost for food would be small. The programs were also usually conducted by local people, in order that the overall cost of the camp could be kept low.

Unfortunately, by the time I arrived on the scene, participation had fallen off to 30 – 40 campers each week. Along with the help of many associational leaders, we were able to begin to make some changes that encouraged more and more campers to want to come to camp. We developed a policy that no camper would stay away because they could not afford to come. Every year we would make it possible for campers to come to camp, in spite of the fact that they could not afford to come.

The last several years the camp was at maximum capacity with a total of 130 – 140 campers each week and a total including staff of about 170. The most significant thing about the camp ministry was that every year there were more people saved than any other activity in the association. Usually anywhere from 30 – 50 professions of faith were recorded every year. We have been retired since January 1,

2004. It has been a great source of joy to see how well the camp continues to minister. It has been a blessing to see that many young adults, who grew up in the camp, are now taking leadership roles in the operation of the camp.

Something that I think became very significant about our camps was the size of the youth and children's groups in most of our churches. In most of our churches the youth and children's groups were fairly small because of the size of the churches and the towns where most of them are located. Once a year they were able to come together and have a large church children's group for one week. Then as they got older, they were able to come to youth camp and for one week have a really large youth group that related to one another 24 hours a day for a week. Many of those same youth were excited when they turned 17 and got to come back as counselors. I was surprised to discover that many of those young counselors demanded more from their campers than the older counselors did. Those young counselors also looked forward to being able to join in the fun and games the adults had each night after lights out for the campers.

Without a doubt, one of the highlights of camp each week was the bonfire on the last night of camp. After all of the activities for the week had been concluded, the campers gathered around the bonfire, and sang some of the music that had been a blessing to them during the week. Then the campers would begin to step forward and share what the Lord had done in their lives during the week. For some of the campers, they had their first experience of sharing what the Lord was doing in their lives around that bonfire. Everyone went to bed on Thursday night with a warm feeling in their hearts because of what they had just experienced around the bonfire.

A few years before I retired, the owners of the camp came to me and wanted to know if I would object to them sending a request to our churches to take an offering for a new Dining Hall, with additional dorm space. This facility was really needed. I told him that I had no objection, but he needed to know that most of our churches were small and what he would receive would be small. Then I asked him how he would feel if I could get the labor for the new building, free of charge. He was shocked and found it too good to be true. I was talking about Texas Baptist Retired Builders. I called Texas Baptist Men and they agreed to do it. Over a period of time the 4-H Camp Directors believed that it could be done.

Several weeks later I got a call and was asked to meet with the Directors of the Camp and the architect for the new building. They had a list of the various projects that would be involved in building this new facility. They wanted me to check off the various parts of the construction I felt that the retired builders could do. After I finished, he sat there with a calculator and estimated the cost of labor for those things. They had received a matching funds offer from the State of New York. If they could raise $250,000.00, the State would match that with an additional $250,000.00. The donated labor could be counted as donated money and what the TBM builders would do would exceed that amount. To make a long story short, today at Camp Overlook 4-H Camp, there stands a beautiful Dining Hall and Dorm. It was built primarily by Texas Baptist Retired Builders. One large porch is dedicated to the Adirondack Baptist Association and Texas Baptist Men. The impact these retired builders made on the North Country of New York for Christ was huge.

Getting the churches of the association involved in these various special ministries was probably one of the hallmarks of whatever legacy I may have left after the 12 years that we were there had come and gone.

Church Planting vs Strengthening Churches

Because of the strong emphasis to plant churches that began to develop in every meeting I attended, I had to determine where I was, and where the Lord wanted me to be in relation to the ministry He had given to me. There were two things I knew. NAMB was probably not going to fund a fully appointed Church Planter Strategist for our association. The second thing was that, if I gave the time required to be a Church Planter Strategist, most of the other things the Lord was leading me to do would suffer. I did not quit supporting the planting of churches; however, it was and is my philosophy that associations do not start churches. Churches start churches. It was my role, to assist the churches in looking out beyond themselves, not only for other church starts, but also for other ministries that would also draw men, women, boys, and girls to Jesus Christ. Therefore, in my working with BCNY and NAMB, I had to begin to try to cast my vision for the ways we could most effectively reach the North Country for Jesus Christ.

When you have a plan where weak churches become sponsoring churches, just so the new start can be recognized as a real church start, you have almost guaranteed failure, because the support system is not there. I believed in planting new churches, as the Lord leads you to do so; however, you don't start them just to be able to say that you have started X number of churches.

One of my early primary goals in the life of the association was to strengthen the churches, and to do whatever I could to strengthen and encourage the pastors. I spent a lot of my time in the early days, just getting acquainted with our congregations. This was an interesting experience in itself, considering that we moved to the North Country of New York the first week in January 1992. As I was getting familiar with our churches, I was also learning how to move about in the winter weather, which proved to be vital to what I did. Usually every day included a considerable amount of driving.

Most of our pastors introduced me to their churches by inviting me to come and spend a Sunday with them and preach for them. They would also ask Virginia to sing for them. One of my early, very vivid experiences of getting introduced to winter in the Adirondacks was the first Sunday in February 1992.

I had been invited to come and preach in one of our small missions almost 100 miles from where we lived, right in the heart of the Adirondack Mountains. Virginia and I left home early that Sunday morning to make our way through the mountains in the snow, one month after we had moved to New York. When we arrived at the church about 2 ½ hours later, we discovered that the church heating system had run out of fuel oil during the night, and there was no heat in the building. The temperature was well below zero outside, and needless to say, it was freezing inside. Six people from the church showed up that morning. One of them went home and got a propane heater out of their attic that they had not used in years and brought it to the church and lit it and set it in front of Virginia and me to try to keep us warm. It immediately started smoking and I did not know if I was going to freeze to death or die from the fumes.

I remember vividly the conversation I had with the Lord that morning during the service. First, I said, "Lord, do you know where I am?" Then I said, "Lord, do you understand that, if I was back in Rusk, I would be preaching to about 500 people this morning, instead of just 6?" I got a quick reply. The Lord said, "Yes, I know where you are, and yes, I understand that if you were in Rusk you would be preaching to far more people today. I also understand that, if you were in Rusk right now, you would be outside of my will for your life."

In that moment I remember a feeling coming over me of being right in the center of the will of God for my life. Suddenly, nothing else mattered. It did not matter how cold it was, or how much smoke was in the room, or how few people were there to hear me preach. It only mattered that I was where God had placed me, doing what he had called me to do. The best place in the world to be is right in the middle of God's will for your life. That experience, on that cold Sunday morning, became a watershed moment for me that carried me through many difficult experiences over the next 12 years. It was on that day that, without a doubt, I got my marching orders from the Lord to serve the Adirondack Baptist Association as their Association Missionary. For the most part I can honestly say that I was able to spend the next 12 years serving this association with great joy in my heart.

Probably one of the hardest things I had to learn to deal with was the loneliness that came with the job. I soon learned that, when you belonged to everyone, sometimes you did not belong to anyone. As a pastor, I had been used to being very involved in the lives of the members of my church. As a DOM, with 16 small congregations spread out over a very large territory, it was almost impossible to have that kind of involvement in the lives of the people.

However, I was able to find those kinds of relationships, when I served as interim pastor of our various churches. During the 12 years we were in the North Country, I served almost all of our churches as interim pastor at least once and several of them more than once. This allowed me to become close to most of the active lay people in our churches. Because it would take longer than normal for churches to find a new pastor, I had the opportunity to become closer to the lay people in the churches than DOMs in traditionally stronger Southern Baptist Associations. The role of the DOM in areas where Southern Baptist work is relatively new is quite a bit different than it would be in a more traditional Southern Baptist area. There was a very close connection between the Home Mission Board (now the North American Mission Board), the State Convention, and the local association. During the time we ministered in New York, the churches and missions of the Baptist Convention of New York received more financial support from the North American Mission Board than any other State Convention other than California. Therefore, there was a very close connection between the association, the state convention, and our national agencies. This meant that our local churches were much more dependent on state and national agencies. They received financial aid and other sources of help that were necessary for them to continue to exist.

I soon discovered that one of the most important roles I played in the life of our churches was to be a resource person. What I mean by that is, discovering what our small congregations needed to continue to exist and have viable ministries in their communities, then finding those resources. I discovered that the Lord had actually gifted me to do that in ways that even surprised me. I became an advocate for our churches to anyone who would listen.

This statement will probably offend some preachers, but I am going to say it anyway. I also became the defender of the faith for our churches, when some preacher would come in and take advantage of them. I remember a particular instance, when one of our churches had a visiting preacher who would come in and preach on Sunday. He wanted to be considered as their pastor, but he was unwilling to move into the community. He wanted the church to elect a couple of the deacons as elders, to take care of the pastoral work during the week, and let him just come and preach on Sunday. I strongly advised the church not to do this, and they did listen to me. There came a time that his preaching came close to heresy, and certainly contradicted Baptist Doctrine. I met with the church leadership and pointed out the things that he was preaching that seemed to violate scripture, and they decided they needed to find someone else to preach until the Lord provided them a new pastor.

Heat or Sunday School Literature?

Let me share with you a really neat experience that I had with the Sunday School Board, now LifeWay Christian Services. I found that one of the strongest supporters of my ministry was LifeWay. I found them to be pro-active in their efforts to help churches and missions in non-traditional Southern Baptist areas. I don't know if they still do it, but during the time I was a DOM, LifeWay brought the DOMs in every five years to give them an update on what was available from them to assist our churches in their ministries. Of all of the meetings I attended, this was one I always looked forward to attending. It was always very helpful, and I always left believing that they really wanted to assist me in my ministry.

One of the issues that some of our small congregations faced during the winter was whether to spend their money on fuel oil to heat their buildings, or buy Sunday School literature. Obviously, they were making the decision to keep their buildings heated and going without Sunday School literature for six months. I called a lady at the Sunday School Board that I had gotten to know. I asked her if there was any way these churches could receive a discount on their literature during the winter months. She said that she did not think so, but she would see if anything could be done and call me back. A few days later she called me back. She told me that trying to give them a discount would not work. However, she said that they would like to provide Sunday School literature free of charge to these churches for the winter months. They just needed to promise to order it themselves during the other months of the year. She told me that she would leave it up to me as to which churches really needed the help and that they could order anything on the order form that they felt like they needed. I just wept as she gave me this information, and she wept and told me that she was doing what she was doing because of a calling from God, not just because it was a job. For several years, several of our smaller congregations were able to have Sunday School literature during the winter months, because of this arrangement.

Why do I love being a Southern Baptist? This is one of the examples. There are support systems built into the way we work that are designed to assist our churches. Are we perfect? Absolutely not! For lack of a better term though, I still believe being a part of the Southern Baptist Convention is the best game in town.

New Church Starts

One of the things that I did a lot in the early days, was spend a lot of time driving through the Adirondacks getting acquainted with the territory and trying to determine the places where there might be the need to start a new church. I remember one day in particular. I have already shared this experience, but I will share it again because it had so much to do with the way I viewed my work. As I was just driving through the Adirondacks, I drove through a community that was so small that I remember thinking that it was too small for us to try to do anything there. No sooner had that thought gone through my mind than the Lord spoke to my heart. This is what he said to me. "Jim, you need to know that I love the few just as much as I love the millions; I died for the few just like I died for the millions. I brought you here so that Southern Baptists would not forget about the few." I knew in that moment that I had been commissioned to minister to the few.

Not long after that, I was attending a meeting at our State Convention headquarters in Syracuse, NY. The meeting was for the DOMs in our state, some of the convention staff and a man from the Home Mission Board (NAMB). Our DOMs from the metropolitan areas of our state, and the person from HMB, were discussing some of their strategies for reaching the cities. I listened for a while and then I asked the man from HMB a question. I asked what the SBC strategy for reaching the small towns was. Then I said, "If you have one, it is one of the best kept secrets in the SBC." He admitted that they did not have one. For some reason, I felt justified in putting him on the spot; however, a few hours later the Lord put me on the spot. I was driving home, when the Lord asked me what my strategy was. The truth was, I did not have one. I was waiting for someone to get one for me. Then the Lord said to me that I did not need anyone but Him to help me develop a strategy for reaching my territory. After repenting for my attitude, and calling my friend at HMB to apologize to him for my actions, I began to work on the plans that the Lord gave me. Part of that was to recognize that some communities were too small to ever develop a self-supporting church. Therefore, we had to think of innovative ways we could get people in small communities involved in some kind of Bible Study and then find ways to connect them to a church in a larger community.

One of the new church starts, where we had the opportunity to have personal involvement, came in a very unusual way. My wife Virginia had gone to Ohio for a World Missions Conference. The family that hosted her had an elderly parent who was a minister in Champlain, New York. He was trying to retire and move back to Ohio to be closer to his family. He was an independent Baptist preacher. He had a small congregation that he wanted to turn over to someone. Virginia got his name and phone number. When she came home, I called him and went over and visited with him and his wife, and he invited us to come to a service at his home the next Sunday. He gave me time to explain to the people what it would mean to become a mission in a Southern Baptist Association. The people expressed an interest in working with us, and the pastor indicated a willingness to give us the few assets they had, which included a small checking account.

It was early December, and we were leaving for three weeks to come back to Texas for Christmas. I told him I would call him when we got back. When we got back from our trip, I tried to call him and discovered that his phone had been disconnected. We called the preacher in Ohio that had given us his name. He told us that they had sold their home quickly and had already moved back to Ohio. I called him and got the phone number of one of the ladies who had been a member of his church. I called her and arranged for Virginia and me to come and visit. During our conversation with her, she expressed an interest in having a Weekday Bible Study in her home.

In January of 1999, we began driving to her home in Champlain, NY, once a week to lead a Bible Study for a group of ladies. Most of these ladies had one thing in common; their husbands were not Christians.

It was about a 50 mile drive one way from our home in Malone to Champlain. After several weeks they began to tell us about others that they knew who they thought might be interested in a new church. We began to talk about finding a time and a place where we could meet, and they would invite their friends to this meeting.

The Bread of Life Baptist Church, in Plattsburgh, NY, was our nearest Southern Baptist Church. They agreed to sponsor this new mission. One of their deacons lived in the general area of the new mission. He agreed to an initial meeting in his home and later agreed to host a Thursday night Bible Study and Prayer Meeting. There were 19 people who showed up for this meeting. The purpose was to discover how much interest there was in starting a new mission. There was great interest expressed. Therefore, we began by driving there every Thursday night for Bible Study and Prayer. There was a very consistent group who came every week. It was not long before they began to express interest in having Sunday services. I began to look around and found a VFW hall that was willing to rent space to us on Sunday morning. The first service was held on April 4, 1999. The name Living Water Baptist Chapel was suggested and approved by everyone and so the Living Water Baptist Chapel was born. I served as their pastor for nearly a year along with my other responsibilities.

One Thanksgiving season we were having a Thanksgiving Dinner. One of the ladies in the mission came to me to tell me that she was bringing a friend to church the next day. She wanted me to know that this young woman had a nose ring, a tongue stud, and her ears were filled with various kinds of earrings. She wanted me to know that she was very sensitive about people staring at her, and so she was encouraging me to do whatever I had to do to not stare at her. The young lady did show up the next morning at the VFW hall, where we were meeting. The Lord did an amazing thing while I was preaching that morning. The Holy Spirit took hold of her heart and she hung on every word I was saying. This was true in spite of the fact that there were crying children all around her. When I gave the invitation, she was saved that morning. Virginia and I began to meet her once a week for lunch and disciple her. She worked at a tattoo parlor, and she needed to keep the job because that was all she knew how to do at the time. One day she said to me, "Since I got saved I don't do any tattoos below the waist." She was such a delight to disciple, because she was just so honest with her feelings. Her salvation was one of the great joys of our involvement in the starting of the Living Water Baptist Chapel.

We met in several locations in the area that were not actually in Champlain. Finally a little building that had been a pharmacy became available on the main road leading into Champlain, and we rented it. One of the men in the church became our Adult Sunday School Teacher. Later the Lord called him to preach. When it came time for me to move on to other things, he became the first pastor.

There is an interesting side story. Southern Baptists had attempted to start a work in Champlain two times, but both of those efforts failed. One of the attempts actually had the name Living Water Baptist Chapel. When we had our 35th Anniversary Association Meeting, I updated a history of the association that the first DOM had written and we gave it out at the Annual Meeting. When I got home from that meeting, I got a call from the pastor at Living Water. He was almost in tears. He had been reading the early history of the association. There was a story about the first effort that was made to start a church in the Champlain area. There was a story about a man and his wife that were won to the Lord on the steps of an apartment complex. He almost shouted into the phone, "I was that man." That first effort failed but he and his wife were saved. When he joined our mission, he was not even aware it was the same group. Now 20 years later this layman that was saved on the steps of an apartment complex was pastor of a church with the same name that was thriving. God is so good!

Now the church has purchased land just one mile south of the Canadian border and a building has been constructed. More than 10 years later, this man is still pastor of the Living Water Baptist Church, in Champlain, New York. God works in strange and mysterious ways to accomplish His purposes. As I look back on the way that congregation began, I realize that only the Lord could have worked out all of the circumstances which caused all of this to take place. Before the Lord worked out all of these details, I had driven through Champlain on numerous occasions and wondered if Southern Baptists would ever have another opportunity to minister to this community. I had to drive through it every time I drove over to the airport in Burlington, Vermont, which was more often than you might think. This is just another example of the fact that God's ways are, most of the time, not our ways.

My wife could have been assigned to any number of families for that World Missions Conference in Ohio. However, God had far more in mind than just her speaking on missions in Ohio. He had a larger plan of beginning a new mission in the northeast corner of the state of New York. Perhaps a lesson that should be learned from this experience is that, in whatever we are doing, we should have our spiritual eyes and ears open for something else the Lord may have in mind.

Here Comes the Judge

Early one January, I was visiting with four ladies, who were the only active members left in their church. This church was located in a small town in the middle of the Adirondack Mountains. During that meeting, one of the ladies said to me through her tears, "Bro. Jim, please don't close our church." I reminded her that I did not have the authority to close their church, even if that was what I wanted to do. She said that she knew that, but she said, "If you don't help us, we are going to die." I told them that the first thing they were going to have to do was tell their pastor, who was allowing the church to die around him, that he was going to have to go. I told them that if they would do that, I would do what I could to help them. They agreed that they needed to do that and told him exactly that a few days later. They gave him time to find a place to move, and he agreed to do so.

Let me interject a thought here. One of the most frustrating parts of my job in the association was how little some of our congregations knew about how to go about calling a pastor. It was not one or two, but several of our congregations that seemed to have no training in finding a pastor. Here is an unfortunate truth; it seems there are a limitless number of men out there who declare that they are preachers of the gospel. These men seem to be perfectly willing to prey on small congregations where the lay people are very good people, but just have no understanding of how to find a pastor. If these churches have any means whatsoever to provide any kind of financial support, these men seem to be able to find them and take advantage of their goodness without providing them any real spiritual leadership. Then I was expected to come in and save the day. This congregation had a man like that and I could not help them until they were willing to help themselves. Part of helping themselves meant telling their pastor he had to go. Then they could have a chance of starting over. In this case, I did not have much hope that the congregation would survive.

In a few days I got a call from a friend of mine, Judge Bennie Boles, from Center, Texas. He told me that he had been driving home from leading an Experiencing God Weekend in the Houston area, and the Lord spoke to him and told him to call me and tell me he was willing to come to the Adirondacks for the summer. He said I told the Lord I had already been to the Adirondacks and I would really prefer to go somewhere else. He said that the Lord told him that unless he was obedient about calling me, He was not going to let him do anything else. I told him that I would pray about it; I was sure the Lord would show me where He wanted him to go. The more I prayed about it, the more I became convinced that the Lord wanted Bennie and his wife to spend the summer with this small church in Newton Falls, New York.

During the time I was praying about where they were to go, Bennie called me back. He wanted to know if I had found them a place. He said he was really getting concerned that the Lord would not use him again. I assured him there would be a place of service for them, and I would know soon where it would be. Shortly after that, I was able to share with the small group at Newton Falls that I had a couple who was willing to come and spend the summer with them, and help them get back on their feet. One of the things that made this place attractive as a place of ministry for Judge Boles and his wife was that the church had a parsonage they could provide for them, which would give them a place to live at no expense to them. The Lord blessed the union of Bennie & Anita Boles and the church at Newton Falls. As a result of that summer of ministry, the church was revived and later they called a pastor who led them to a new day of reaching new people in their area.

That same summer, our church in Lake Placid had just been through a very difficult time. They had lost their pastor through an unfortunate circumstance. Because of the Maples Conference, the church had come to have a lot of respect for Claude King. I made arrangements for Claude to come and spend some days with the church, with an emphasis on spiritual healing. The church responded well to his teaching. At his suggestion, the Lake Placid Baptist Church called a friend of Claude King's dad as their Interim Pastor. His name was Laddie Adams. He was retired from the Oklahoma Baptist Convention. He and his wife also spent that summer in the North Country. The Lord used him in an amazing way to bring healing to the church and prepare them for the coming of a new pastor.

I had the joy of watching the Lord use two retired men and their wives to be a blessing to two of our congregations. One was a retired Minister and his wife and the other a retired Judge who was also a lay preacher and his wife. It is amazing the way the Lord can use people when they are willing to be used.

Special Ministries – The Olympic Training Center – Lake Placid, New York

As I have already indicated, early in my time in New York, the Lord had indicated to me that He was putting me in a position where He was going to bring the world to me, and I needed to get ready to minister to them.

Not long after we moved to the North Country of New York, I was driving down Main Street in Lake Placid. I saw a group of athletes walking down the street. They had their team uniforms on with the word France written on the leg of the uniforms. My heart skipped a beat as I thought about the possibilities. Sometime later we were in Lake Placid overnight for an event. We stayed in the house that the SBC had purchased as a ministry center for the 1980 Winter Olympics. I needed some winter boots; so I walked down to a shoe store on Main Street to purchase a pair of boots. As I was standing in line to pay for my boots, there were three people in line in front of me. One was from France, one was from Italy, and one was from Russia. I remember the overwhelming impression I got from the Lord. He spoke to my heart and said, "I am bringing the world to you, you need to get ready to minister to them." Needless to say these experiences made a great impression on me about the priority of establishing a ministry to the Olympic Training Center.

At the 1980 Winter Olympics in Lake Placid, New York, was the first time that Southern Baptists were involved in ministry to an Olympic Event. At that time, the SBC Home Mission Board bought a house in Lake Placid as a place to house volunteers, and a place to start a church plant. They appointed a man to direct the ministry for the Olympics and to use that as the starting point for a new church plant and the development of a Resort Ministry to the Olympic Training

Center. This all developed after the Olympics were over and everything moved along well for a period of time. Unfortunately, problems developed and the pastor/resort minister had to leave, and for whatever reason, everyone lost interest in ministry to the Olympic Training Center.

On the other hand, the Olympic Training Center there in Lake Placid flourished. It became the place where most of the Winter Olympic caliber athletes came to train, and athletes started coming from all over the world to train there. Some of the best coaches in all winter sports came to live there and train winter sports athletes year round. They had even established the National Sports Academy in Lake Placid. This was a boarding school where students, who seemed to have abilities in the winter sports events, came and went to school while they were trained in the various winter sports. I saw this and saw that Southern Baptists were doing nothing about developing a ministry to these athletes.

I approached our State Convention leadership and found little if any enthusiasm for the effort. I was told by one state leader that, if I could get backing in what was then the Home Mission Board, he would support me. I made arrangements to fly to Atlanta and meet with the Resort Ministry Director at HMB. He said he wanted me to meet the man who had actually orchestrated the ministry to the 1980 Winter Olympics in Lake Placid. When he introduced me to him, he told him that they finally had a DOM in the Adirondack Association that was interested in Resort Ministry, and he greeted me with a big smile and handshake.

They asked me what they could do to help me. I told them that I needed help in knowing what I was doing, and that I needed a Resort Minister assigned to Lake Placid. I was told they were the only ones who could get that done. For the next two hours they took me through all kinds of training material and gave me books to read that they had written. When I pressed them about a Resort Minister, they said they did not have any money in their budget for me. I asked them about the next year's budget, and they told me it was already fixed and there was nothing in it they could earmark for me.

I thanked them for their time and told them I was determined that God wanted this ministry, and I was going to search for His man. When I said that, they said, "Be sure and find someone who meets our guidelines." When they said that I will admit that my attitude probably wasn't what it should have been; so I replied, "Since you don't have any money anyway, I think I will just concentrate on finding God's man."

In the spring of 1992, I invited my son Tom to come up and lead an Association Youth Retreat. During the time he was there with us, I took him to Lake Placid for a visit. Later he said that it was while we were in Lake Placid that he knew that the Lord was calling him to Lake Placid to minister to the youth there. At the end of that year, Tom and his wife, who was expecting their second child, and their young daughter moved to Lake Placid. They moved on faith that the Lord would provide for their financial needs, because we did not have a guaranteed salary for them.

Shortly before Tom and his family moved to Lake Placid, the Lake Placid Church had called a new pastor. I had become aware that SBC National Resort Ministries was having a National Resort Minister's Retreat in Missouri. I was able to make arrangements for the new pastor at Lake Placid, Tom, and myself to attend this conference. This was an important introduction for us to SBC Resort Ministry. We made some contacts at that meeting that later became very important.

Unfortunately, the new pastor at Lake Placid did not stay very long. After he and his family moved on, it was decided to allow Tom and his family to move into the Ministry House in Lake Placid and let that be the base of operations for his ministry. He later started having a Friday night youth come-and-go night, for the youth of Lake Placid at the house. They also allowed a teenage young lady to live with them. She had come to Lake Placid to train for figure skating.

Tom was able to establish a good relationship with the leadership of the National Sports Academy and was able to minister to many of the students who were living and going to school there while they were training for their chosen winter sport. He hosted fellowships and Bible Studies in their home during his time there.

Unfortunately, the amount of funding that was needed for a full-time position never did quite materialize. However, during this time the Lord caused Tom to refocus His calling on his life, and he came to the point of believing that the Lord was calling him to be a Doctor. During their time in Lake Placid our second granddaughter was born. While he was taking the additional courses at the university that were needed for medical school, Tom served as Pastor of one of the churches in our association. He eventually ended up in medical school on Long Island and is now a physician in New York City.

During this time we were able to make some positive connections with the Olympic Regional Development Authority. We were able to provide some volunteers for some events.

Youth Link 2000

The Baptist Convention of New York was holding the Annual State Evangelism Conference in Lake Placid, New York, in the spring of 1997. There was a man there by the name of Charles Snow. He had been selected by the Sunday School Board to be the site director of Youth Link 2000 in Philadelphia. This was going to be held a couple of years later as one of the locations around the United States where Youth Retreats would be held for the Year 2000 Celebration.

Charles and I met and we became almost instant friends. Before he left Lake Placid, he asked me if I would attend a Planning Meeting for Youth Link 2000 in Philadelphia as a representative from the New York Convention. I agreed to attend that meeting which would be held later that year. When I flew into Philadelphia, I discovered that several who had been invited to the meeting flew in at the same time and we rode to the meeting together. One of those was Carol Baker, who I had met at the National Resort Ministers Conference, in Missouri, in the fall of 1993. Bo Martin, who was the new pastor at Lake Placid Baptist Church at that time, and my son Tom, who had already agreed to become the Resort Ministry Director for the association, also attended that conference.

 Carol Baker was now working for NAMB, and was their representative to Philadelphia Youth Link 2000. She asked me if I had ever gotten my Resort Minister and was surprised when I told her I had not. She told me that Jeff Wagner, who had been the Resort Minister in Las Vegas, had just come to NAMB as Resort Ministry Director and that this would be a good time for me to contact him about my need. I did that and it proved successful. I will talk about that later.

During that initial Planning Meeting in Philadelphia, Charles asked me if I would be on the Steering Committee for Philadelphia, which would involve coming to Philadelphia about every three months for about two years. I asked him what he would like for me to do and he asked me to listen to the discussions of the various responsibilities and choose one. Later in the meeting I suggested to him that the best place I would fit was as the Prayer Chairman, which is what I ended up doing.

Most of the members of the Steering Committee lived in or near Philadelphia. Because I did not, I usually had to fly in the day before the meeting, because we would usually start in the morning and meet most of the day. The first time I flew in for one of our meetings, Charles asked me if I wanted to go with him as he negotiated contracts with various vendors for our meeting. After one of those meetings, I asked him if he had heard a particular thing they had said, and he had not. He then asked me if I would be willing to come in early each time and go with him and just sit and listen as he negotiated with various ones. I told him I was willing to do that. We became a good team, and developed a very close friendship.

On one of those trips, we were staying at the Marriot Hotel Downtown, which was going to be the Conference Hotel for Youth Link 2000. Our meeting was going to be on Monday. One of the African American pastors in Philadelphia, who was on the committee, asked me if I would come in on Saturday, so I could preach in his church Sunday morning. I agreed to do that. Charles also came in on Saturday night. We decided to walk downtown to find a place to eat. Believe it or not, in the part of downtown where we were, the only restaurant we could find open was Ruth Chris Steak House. We were eating on a LifeWay credit card. Later we were advised that from now on we should find somewhere else to eat. Oh well.

Because I could see how well planned this event was, I began to promote taking a charter bus of youth and adult sponsors from our churches in the Adirondack Baptist Association to this event. We ended up with about 50 youth and sponsors from ABA to Youth Link 2000, Philadelphia.

I had planned a number of prayer activities leading up to the actual event, plus various prayer opportunities during the actual Youth Link 2000 event. Probably the most meaningful activity was the last one. It took place on New Year's Eve, during the last worship service which led up to a commitment service just before midnight, January 1, 2000. I had asked adults to join me outside the Marriott Hotel, for a Prayer Walk, while the closing worship service was going on inside. As we walked, we were praying for the power of God to be poured out upon that service and upon the people out on the streets, who were celebrating the New Year. The city of Philadelphia celebration of New Year 2000 was just three blocks away from our location. Therefore, when we got outside at 9:30 P.M., the streets were already crowded.

I came out of the main entrance of the Marriott and started my first trip around the city block, praying for the service inside and the people outside. I was wearing a headset, so that I could communicate with Carol Baker inside about what was happening in there. That was for the purpose of keeping me up to date on how to pray for what was going on inside. I got about halfway around the city block on which the Marriott sat and I passed a young lady, probably a 16 or 17 year old teenager. She was wearing a long winter coat. It was very cold in Philadelphia on New Year's Eve. However, her coat was not buttoned, and what she was wearing underneath her coat was advertising that she was available for any man who might want to spend some time with her. My heart broke, as I wondered if her parents knew where she was or even cared where she was. For obvious reasons, I did not feel like I could stop and talk to her. I began to pray for her. I talked to Carol Baker, inside the hotel and asked her to pray for her. I knew that I had two college age girls, who had come with me from Lake Placid, NY, who were also out prayer walking. As soon as I found them, I told them about this young lady and asked them to look for her. They never did find her. I assumed the worst that she must have found a customer before they could get to her

As the time neared midnight, we went back inside, so that we could experience the closing with everyone else. During the commitment service, hundreds of young people in the five locations across the United States came to faith in Christ. Praise God! After this last worship service was over, there was a short break, and then there was a Christian concert for the young people during the first couple of hours of the year 2000.

During that time, Charles Snow decided it would be a good time for the Steering Committee to have a wrap-up meeting. He knew that everyone would be going in separate directions at different times later that day, and there probably would not be another opportunity to have such a meeting. He asked each of us to share at least one experience that we would probably never forget from our time together. When it was my time, among other things, I shared about the young lady I encountered out on the street and asked everyone to pray for her.

After I shared, the young man who was the Youth Chairman shouted, "Praise God!" Then he told about a young woman who had come with him as a sponsor from Michigan. She had only been a Christian for a little over a year, and she had been a prostitute prior to her conversion. He said that during the worship service he noticed that she was not in the service. He said that he was fearful that she had fallen back into her old lifestyle. He said that he got up to go look for her. When he got outside the auditorium, he found her coming up the escalator. He asked her where she had been. She said that shortly after the worship service started, the Lord clearly spoke to her and told her that there was someone outside that needed her help. She said that she got up and went outside, and when she got halfway around the hotel, she found a teenage girl on the street corner advertising herself. She said that she managed to get her away from the crowd and shared the gospel with her, and she trusted Christ as her Savior. She said that she got her name and address and phone number so she could give it to one of the churches in Philadelphia. Then she said, "I put her in a cab and sent her home to her parents."

When this young man finished sharing, Carol Baker spoke up. She said, "I need to tell you how I prayed when Jim called me and told me about this young woman." She said that she prayed to the Lord that surely in our crowd there was someone who could relate to her. She said she prayed, "Lord, if you have someone here who can relate to her, would you send that person out there?"

Needless to say, we all just sat there amazed at all that the Lord had done to bring one young lady to faith in Jesus Christ. What a great God we have and that we have the privilege of serving.

This was a great time in my life. I am so glad that I had an opportunity to be a small part of such a significant event. I praise God that He continues to speak to the hearts of His people who hear and are used of the Lord to plan life-changing events. Such big events are not what keep us going on a daily basis, but they are used of the Lord to change the lives of some who might not be reached any other way.

For me personally, and for our ministry in the Adirondack Baptist Association, not only did I have a wonderful experience with the Youth Link 2000 event, but also I was made aware of the new opportunity of getting some help with our Resort Ministry in our association. The conversation I had with Carol encouraged me to contact Jeff Wagner and renew my efforts to get the help we needed for this very important ministry. The bottom line of my conversations with Jeff was the appointment of Jake Morrow to serve as our US-2 Missionary.

North Country Ministries

Shortly after Jake Morrow arrived on the scene, we sat down to discuss his job, and more particularly, how I expected for the two of us to work together. It was a conversation that was not that much different from similar conversations I had had with staff members of churches where I had served as pastor. One of the things that we knew going in was that we did not have much time for him to get adjusted to the job. His appointment was for a two year period of time. What we were able to get accomplished during those two years would go a long way in helping our appeal for a full-time position to be established.

Jake had two areas of assignment. They were Campus Ministry and Resort Ministry, with Resort Ministry claiming the major amount of his time. We decided that we needed a name for his ministry so that, simply by using that name, it would identify his ministry in the hearts of our people. We threw around several names, none of which appealed to us or described his ministry. Then I mentioned to him that the whole area we served was known all over the state of New York as the North Country. At first we thought about North Country Resort Ministry, but that would not have included the Campus Ministry aspect of his assignment. We finally came up with the name, North Country Ministries, which could include resort and campus ministries and any other ministries that might develop. So we adopted the name North Country Ministries, under the umbrella of the Adirondack Baptist Association.

That name and more importantly that ministry has stuck and is still one of the most viable volunteer ministries in all of northern New York. The Lord has continued to bless the ministry, and has risen up a new generation to continue the servant evangelism, which was at the core of why North Country Ministries was begun.

Servant Evangelism

In almost every ministry move we had made prior to moving to New York, by the very nature of the position to which I was moving, I was already accepted before I got there. Most of the time that move was to pastor a church that already existed and for the most part was accepted by the community. Therefore, I just became another part of the story of the history of that church.

However, when I moved to northern New York, most people knew very little about the Adirondack Baptist Association, and did not have a clue who a Director of Missions was and what he did. After a period of time, some wanted to know if I was like the Arch-Bishop of the diocese.

I learned that my title no longer got me automatic respect and acceptance. Even in the Ministerial Association, they were not quite sure what to do with me. I soon learned that respect and trust was earned. The more I found ways to serve others; the more respect I gained. One of the keys to the volunteer ministry that we performed was to do what we were asked to do, to do it in a timely fashion, and not expect anything in return.

You will read shortly how this kind of spirit enabled us to become such a vital part of the Winter Goodwill Games, which in turn opened the doors for all of the ministry opportunities that continue to exist to this day. A couple of years after the Goodwill Games, I was making a state-wide appeal for volunteers to come and help us with the Bobsled/Luge Gold Cup World Championship.

I was at our State Convention office for a meeting. I had a BSU Director in the State come to ask me a question. He said that he was trying to get a group of volunteers from his BSU to come for this event, but he said he had a problem. He said that one of his senior leadership people had volunteered for the Goodwill Games, and she was telling the students that if they went, all they would be able to do is park cars in the cold and snow, and would not be able to share their faith with anyone. I was able to share with him all of the things that we were now able to do because she and others like her did just exactly that, without complaining to anyone. I told him to let her know that she had helped pave the way in Servant Evangelism, and now we were able to put our gospel tracts right beside the registration material for the athletes from all over the world to read.

When I first began to get the door back open for a Southern Baptist witness in Lake Placid, many saw us as a cult. I even had a writer for the local newspaper accuse us of being a cult. Our response to these accusations was that we kept on serving. "Turning the cheek" part of our Lord's theology has never been one of my greater strengths, but in learning how to be a Servant Evangelist, it became a more and more helpful tool.

There are things that I remember, that at the time did not seem like such a big deal, but they were building blocks for the future of all of the doors that the Lord would either open, or just go ahead and knock down. Early in our volunteer ministry, we were helping with registration and making sure that all of the athletes and coaches got the things that had been prepared for them. We were putting various things in a welcome sack. One of the things was a T-Shirt that had the emblem for that event on it. I was put in charge of them and told to make sure only registered athletes and coaches got one.

When the event was over, and we were cleaning up, I asked the man in charge where he wanted me to take the leftover T-shirts. He wanted to know how many were left over. I told him 2 boxes. He asked me if that would be enough to give to all of my volunteers, and it was. He told me to give them to my volunteers, and thank them for how hard they had worked. He said he had never seen anybody like our group. It was with great joy that I passed out those gifts and words of encouragement to some of our very first volunteers.

I cannot tell you how many times I was able to share the gospel in casual conversation, while doing Servant Evangelism. I believe that genuine Servant Evangelism completely disarms the one who needs to hear the gospel and makes him or her more receptive to the gospel. In fact, I am now convinced that Servant Evangelism is the most effective evangelism we can do. It is what I call earning the right to be heard.

Winter Goodwill Games

Who would have believed that the Lord would use Ted Turner, to help us restart the ministry to the Olympic Training Center? Ted Turner and Turner Sports Network decided to sponsor the Winter Goodwill Games. The location was narrowed to three places in the world, and finally, Lake Placid was chosen as the location. Because of that decision, The Olympic Regional Development Authority and the State of New York, invested a great deal of money and long hours of hard work, to upgrade all of their facilities.

In February of 1999, I met in Lake Placid, New York, with Dr. J.B. Graham, the Executive Director of the Baptist Convention of New York, and Jeff Wagner, the Director of Resort Ministry for the North American Mission Board. We met for dinner one beautiful winter night, to discuss what our response would be to the fact that Lake Placid had been chosen as the location for the first ever, and as it turned out the only, Winter Goodwill Games ever held. This event had the potential of being the biggest event to come to Lake Placid since the 1980 Olympics. I told them that I was not interested in making the effort if it could not be a first class effort. I told them that meant I was going to need financial assistance as well as someone to help me do the work. Both men agreed with me and both men pledged their support.

I talked with Dr. Graham later and he suggested that I needed to go through our Evangelism Director and submit a request to NAMB for a combination Resort Minister – Student Minister. That is what I did.

I received word that our association had been approved for a US-2 Missionary. This is a program for students who have just finished college and desire to spend two years in some kind of mission work in the United States. The young man I got was Jake Morrow, from

Louisiana. Our NAMB Resort Ministry Director, Jeff Wagner, told me that he thought I was getting the cream of the crop for that year.

Jake actually moved on the scene a few months early so he could get his feet on the ground before the ministry to the Winter Goodwill Games. He arrived in July of 1999. I took him to Lake Placid for us to meet those who would be in charge of securing volunteers for the Goodwill Games. When we spoke to the one in charge at the Chamber of Commerce, she let us know that they had not started thinking about the Goodwill Games because they were involved in getting ready for the Ironman USA competition. Then she asked if we would be interested in helping with that, which was going to take place in three weeks. She said she still needed a captain for one major venue. We agreed to be the co-captains of that venue. This meant that we had three weeks to discover our responsibilities and make sure everything was in place and everyone had everything they needed during this event. That turned out to be a major factor in opening doors for us into all of the ministries that would follow. In later years, our involvement in Ironman USA, Lake Placid, became huge. I will probably say more about that later.

In the fall of 1999, Jake and I began to make preparations for our involvement in the Winter Goodwill Games. Jake worked very closely with the people in the Chamber of Commerce in Lake Placid and really developed a good relationship with them. We began to send out invitations across the country for volunteers to come and join the volunteers from our association who would participate in the event. We also needed a great deal of financial help. We received help from the Baptist Convention of New York and the North American Mission Board, but we still needed more help. I called my friends at Texas Baptist Men and asked for their assistance. They sent a team of 12 from Texas to prepare all of the meals for our 125 volunteers, and sent enough money for them to buy all of the food to feed our volunteers for the whole week. When they were not cooking, they were working wherever we needed them.

One of the things that our local churches did was to prepare welcome baskets for all of the participants and their coaches from all over the world. Some deacons from First Baptist Church Rusk, Texas, heard what we wanted to do with the baskets. They raised the money and had the baskets shipped from the Basket Factory in Jacksonville, Texas. Our baskets included a variety of fruits and homemade cookies, which really went over big. We were also able to put gospel tracts in the baskets. It was a joyous day when a large group of our local people met at one of our churches and put together all of the baskets. We had to rent a large U-Haul trailer to carry them all to Lake Placid. Then we took them to the various hotels for them to distribute as the athletes arrived.

NAMB sent two experienced Resort Ministers to help us. One was from California and the other from Colorado. We would have been lost without them. Steve Hoekstra from Colorado was particularly helpful. The event planners in Lake Placid were all new to an event of this magnitude. None of them had been around when the planning was done for the Winter Olympics of 1980. At the last minute they realized that they did not have enough volunteers assigned to the various locations. Steve Hoekstra, from Colorado, asked them to tell him what they needed. He and Jake stayed up all night and rearranged our volunteer schedule so that our volunteers could meet their needs. It was absolutely amazing the way our volunteers worked. We had 125 volunteers and they did the work of 250 people. Some of them would go out early in the morning, usually to an outdoor assignment of parking cars or crowd control, and come back in the middle of the afternoon. They would get something to eat, try to get warm, rest a little while and then go back and work until about 11:00 P.M.

At the beginning of the week, a major thing happened which made a lasting impression on many people about our willingness to serve others. On Monday before the games began on Wednesday, I was asked to take a mini-van and six drivers to Albany to pick up athletes who were flying in for the games. Other vans had been rented in

Albany so they could drive the athletes to Lake Placid. Jake went to Montreal, Canada, to do the same thing. When I left Lake Placid, I was asked to look up a certain young man by the name of Eric, when I got to Albany. He was coordinating travel from Albany to Lake Placid. By the time I got to Albany, a full-blown blizzard had blown across northern New York and really most of the East Coast.

When I got to the airport in Albany, I told our drivers to just hang around until I found out what was going on. When I found Eric, he was on the phone with the people in Lake Placid who had sent me there. They were both in a panic mode because of all of the flight delays and how they were going to come up with a plan to get all of the athletes to Lake Placid when their planes finally arrived. When he got off of the phone, I told him he needed to calm down because I was there to help him and I intended to do just that. One of the things that he was in a panic about was that because of the flight delays, he did not have enough drivers there. What I found out that day was that when a "World Class" athlete comes in, you do not tell him or her to sit and wait until the van is full to take them where they need to go. I don't know how many athletes I put in a 7-passenger van that day by themselves with the driver and sent them on.

Eric was concerned that my drivers might get bent out of shape because they had to sit around for hours to pick someone up, as we were not for sure their planes would really get in. I assured him that my drivers would be fine. He also did not know if he had enough drivers. I told him that I also had that covered for him. I told him that I had 12 volunteers flying in from Texas and I was sure many of them would be willing to hang around the airport and drive a van.

When he found out these folks were flying in from Texas, he wanted to know who was paying their airfare. I told him that they had all paid their own way to come, and that they were going to sleep on sleeping bags at the church when they got there. He was absolutely amazed. Then he said to me, "People don't do that. People don't do something without expecting to get something in return." I assured him that we did, and then he wanted to know, why? At that moment the Lord gave me an answer that I would never have been smart enough to give on my own. I said, "When Jesus Christ was on this earth, more than anything else, He served people. We are His followers and we are just trying to be like Him." Then I said, "Eric, you need to relax. We are going to serve you today and everything will be okay." He agreed to trust me and we went to work figuring out how to get everybody to Lake Placid, which was a trip of 100 miles, in a blizzard.

One by one I sent the men, who had come with me, back to Lake Placid. Most of them went with one athlete and a coach. When the group from Texas got there, I told them what was going on. There were 8 men and 4 women. We had rented a 15 passenger van to take them to Lake Placid. All of the men volunteered. I asked one of them to go ahead with the women and drive that van. The other 7 men stayed and one by one drove a van with one or more athletes in it to Lake Placid. All of these men from Texas drove 100 miles in a blizzard to a place in the Adirondack Mountains they had never been before.

Eric kept asking me when I was going back. I told him I would stay until the last plane got in and I would take those athletes to Lake Placid. The last plane in that night had the team of skaters from Japan. We left Albany about 10:30 P.M., and arrived in Lake Placid at 2:45 A.M. When we got to Lake Placid, only one lane of the road that goes through town was open. The other lane had snow up to the window of the van. I got to the home where Virginia and I were staying about 3:15 A.M. I slept for a few hours, got up and had some breakfast and then drove back to Albany. When I got there, Eric was shocked that I had come back.

There was not as much new snow Tuesday, but there was still all of the snow from the day before. So again that day, I spent the day getting drivers and vans and athletes together for the trip to Lake Placid. The planes were a little more on schedule that day. I had a really interesting experience that night. I had gotten acquainted with four young personal staff members of Ted Turner. About 8:30 that night, one of them came to me and wanted to know if I was as tired of airport food as they were. We were waiting on one more plane and it was coming in about two hours later. They invited me to go out to dinner with them. So for more than an hour I got to witness to four of Ted Turner's personal staff members. I got to share Jesus with them and explain to them why we were doing what we were doing.

I had to pick up one more 15 passenger van that we were going to use during the week. I told Eric to go back to his room and I would make sure no one was left behind. The last group to get in was the German downhill ski team. I loaded them up with all of their gear in my van and was about to leave when I noticed that there were two athletes standing on the curb. I told the ski team to make room for them and they said there was not enough room. So I told them I would have to call someone and that we would not be able to leave until they got there. Then they decided there was enough room. As it turns out, it was a German Pairs Figure Skating couple. We left Albany about 11:00 P.M. and arrived in Lake Placid about 2:00 A.M. the next morning. Needless to say, I was worn out, but that experience built bridges with the leadership in Lake Placid that is still drawing dividends.

On the first day of the event, we were asked if we could send someone to one of the hotels in Lake Placid. We sent one of the ladies from the team from Texas. When she finished her day, she told the man she was working for that she would not be able to come back the next day because she had to take her turn in the kitchen. That upset him, and he spent much of the rest of the day trying to talk to someone at the church so that he could get her back the next day. I happened to be at the church late that night when he called again. He was obviously very upset. He wanted to speak to someone in charge. I told him that he had gotten the right person. He was so upset that he used some profanity with me. He explained to me that his job for the Games was to make sure that all of the 300 U.S. and Foreign Press people got where they needed to be, when they needed to be there. He then explained that he had placed the lady we had sent him in charge of that; she had done a great job, and then could not come back the next day because she had to take her turn cooking. After I got him calmed down, I assured him that she would be back the next morning, and as long as he needed her. She ended up doing that same assignment all week. So this lady who came, simply willing to serve by cooking for other volunteers, ended up with the assignment of making sure all of the reporters from around the world were where they needed to be, when they needed to be there. Of course, she got a chance to share her faith with many of them. I went down the next morning to meet the man who had called me the night before to make sure that he was really calmed down. We had a great conversation and he apologized for his language the night before. Then he said he needed to tell me something else. He said that not only was this lady a great help to him, but that my drivers were the only ones that were there on time and did not have some kind of accident in the difficult driving conditions.

After the Games were over, I received the following letter from him:

John David Kristoff
Washington, DC

24 February 2000

Dear Reverend Goforth,

I want to thank you for your outstanding support, cooperation, and kindness during the 2000 Winter Goodwill Games.

The effective and successful management and operation of the transportation shuttle system for the international media depended directly on the support of your volunteers. Without exaggeration, a full 80% of the drivers that participated in the system were visiting members of the Baptist Mission.

Your volunteers worked long hours. In many cases drivers willingly drove double shifts to fill in for local "no shows." Your volunteers quickly grasped the importance of attention to detail and control when operating in adverse weather conditions.

In my professional career as the former Director of Transportation for Central and South America and later as the USSOUTHCOM Logistics Representative for the Panama Canal Treaty implementation, I have worked with men and women of accomplishment and rank. As a private International Transportation Consultant I have worked with citizens in every major city in the United States and Europe. It takes a great deal to humble me – but last week I met my match. The volunteers of the Baptist Mission operated with the precision of the best VIP Marine Military Escort, the friendliness of the seasoned State Department "Meet and greet" staff, and the versatility of a crack infantry unit. Please share my sincere thanks with your members.

Sincerely yours,
John D. Kristoff

I spent most of the rest of the week driving around to the various venues, making sure that our volunteers were all in place and had everything they needed. On Friday I received a call telling me that I needed to come back to the church immediately. One of the interesting things that was happening, as the Games progressed was the story about our volunteers. One of the things I learned quickly was that our volunteers were the only true volunteers there. Meaning that we were the only ones who were not getting something in return for their volunteer service, and that is just the way we wanted it.

When I got back to the church, I discovered that the reporter for the CBS TV affiliate in Burlington, Vermont, was there covering the games and was waiting to interview me on camera, about our volunteers. He had heard about our group and the wonderful way they were serving wherever they were asked to serve, and most of the time that meant outside in the very cold weather. He was particularly interested in the story of the 12 who had paid their own way to come from Texas. During the course of the interview, he also asked me why we were doing what we were doing. I gave him the same answer I gave Eric at the airport on Monday. "When Jesus was on this earth, he spent most of His time serving others, and we are His children and we are just trying to be like Him." He then asked where he could find some of our volunteers. I told him that there were a few in the church, but that he would find most of them at the various venues parking cars and working crowd control.

On Saturday, the lead front page story in the local newspaper was about our volunteers, and the report of the Games was in the bottom corner of the front page. God was using the amazing story of the hard work of our volunteers to make a lasting impression on many people. You would have to have been there to understand how difficult it was for them. They did all of the unglamorous jobs that no one else was willing to do. They would get up early and have breakfast and the first crews would be on the job by 7 – 8 A.M. Late morning replacement crews would go out so that the early morning crew could come in, have lunch, get warm, rest for a few hours, and be ready to go back out about 4 P.M. to work until about 11 P.M. They would then come back to the church to sleep on pews or sleeping bags on the floor. There were very few complaints, and when there was a bump in the road, everyone just seemed to adjust and move forward.

Our volunteers were comprised of people from our Adirondack Baptist Association churches, BSU teams from some of the Universities in New York, lay people from parts of the Baptist Convention of New York, and lay people and church staff members from all over the U.S. As I have already said, we had 125 volunteers and they did the work of about 250 people.

The Games were over on Sunday night. Jake Morrow told me that someone from Turner Sports had asked us to come by the arena on Monday morning where they had their headquarters. I was told to bring a trailer. So I rented a U-Haul trailer and went over there. The man I was told to find, had the words "Remote Director, Turner Sports Network" on his jacket. He thanked me for all the work our people had done. Then he said, "That young man Jake of yours is a star." He had all kinds of equipment and supplies they had brought that they did not want to take back to Atlanta. I loaded up a U-Haul trailer of

419

supplies that they gave me. He once again thanked me for all we had done. Then he said, "This event would not have happened without you, and your people, and I just wanted you to know that we know that." He said that he had never met a group quite like ours. I told him we were able to do what we did by the grace of our God, and that all the glory goes to him.

As I was leaving the arena, I saw the CBS TV reporter. We spoke briefly and he told me that I should be sure and watch the 6:00 P.M. news that day. We got home late afternoon that day, and I remembered what the reporter had told me. So we turned to the CBS TV Station out of Burlington, Vermont, which covered all of the North Country. Toward the end of the half hour, they did a report on the Winter Goodwill Games and went to a commercial without a word about our group. Then after the commercial break the News Anchor said, "Where does a small place like Lake Placid find enough volunteers to put on a world class event? This week they found that the answer was the Baptist Church." They then began showing footage of our volunteers as they were working at the various event sites. In one location, they were in the middle of interviewing one of our volunteers; he looked over his shoulder, apologized to the reporter, and told him he had to get back to work. They also showed some of his interview with me. Then the camera came back to the News Anchor. He said, "Why do people do what this group did all last week?" Then he said, "When we asked the Reverend Goforth of the Adirondack Baptist Association that question, he said, 'When Jesus was on this earth He served people. We are His children and we are just trying to be like Him.'" With that statement, the story was over. I just sat there in my chair and wept. I sat there and thought how, only the Lord, could give me something so simple and yet so profound to say, and then end up using it in such a powerful way.

The Lord was able to open doors for us through the Winter Goodwill Games that we had not been able to unlock any other way. Every time I think about that experience, I praise God for the way He put everything together. I praise God for every volunteer and for the way they responded to every situation. The Lord brought Jake Morrow alongside me at just the right time, and was able to use him in a wonderful way.

As I reflect back on the Winter Goodwill Games, I am absolutely amazed at the things that were accomplished in a short period of time, by a couple of people who really did not know what we were doing. In February 1999, shortly after the announcement was made that Turner Sports Network had selected Lake Placid as the sight for the first ever Winter Goodwill Games, I had a meeting with our State Convention Executive Director, Dr. J.B. Graham, and Jeff Wagner, Resort Ministry Director for the North American Mission Board. Both men agreed that they would give me the full support of Southern Baptists to do what we would do the right way. They both did exactly what they promised they would do.

It was later that spring that I received word that we had been approved for a US-2 Missionary for Resort/College ministry. We were told that the assignment would be for two years, and I would meet my missionary in July. Jake Morrow from Louisiana turned out to be our missionary. He really turned out to be the right man for the right job. He moved to the association in July and we were able to provide living quarters for him upstairs in our office building.

As it turned out, our willingness to help with the summer event in Lake Placid, put us in a good position for future relationships. However it left us with only five months to put everything together for the Goodwill Games. I told Jake to spend as much time as he could with the people in charge in Lake Placid. I then began to work on every network of securing volunteers I could think about. Jake began to visit our local churches to get as many of them involved as possible.

Only the hand of the Lord could have brought everything together that had to happen to make our ministry to that event successful. The reason that I have spent so much time describing what happened with one event was because of the significance that event had on jump-starting the North Country Ministry.

Because Lake Placid had to repair and rebuild many of its Winter Sports Venues in order to have the Goodwill Games, Lake Placid got back on the map for world class winter sports events again. Lake Placid once again was on the circuit of the World Cup Winter Sports Events. They completely rebuilt the Bobsled/Luge track and it became one of the fastest and best in the world. The Ski Jump Facility was given a surface with a texture that made it possible to actually ski jump in the summer. Some improvements were also made to the Olympic Downhill Ski Facility at Whiteface Mountain.

The new Bobsled/Luge Track put Lake Placid back on the world schedule for World Cup events. The World Cup is like a tournament and each team that wins is awarded points for how well they do at each event, and all of that is to qualify them for the World Cup Gold Cup Championship at the end of the season. I became very well acquainted with those from the Olympic Regional Development Authority who ran the Bobsled/Luge Facility. I went to them and offered to take all of the responsibility for the parking facility and making sure that the fans got from the parking lots to the facility. They were happy to turn that over to me and it allowed me to become close to them.

There was a special opportunity that we had at the Bobsled World Cup Championship. They set up a registration cabin for all the athletes and coaches from all over the world, just outside the entrance to the facility. They had to have one of their officials there, but they allowed us to provide the volunteers who worked with the officials. My wife Virginia coordinated those volunteers and was actually there most of the time. One of her jobs was to make sure they got their credentials and all of the other information they needed. They allowed us to place gospel tracts and scriptures right beside the material they had to pick up and our volunteers were able to call attention to those gospel materials.

One of the things that would happen with a lot of local volunteers is that they would show up and get the give-aways, like the uniform jackets that were given to the volunteers to identify them. They would stay for a little while; then they would leave. That meant that we usually ended up doing more things than we started out doing. At the World Cup Championship Bobsled event they came to me and asked me to get two other adults and come with them. We went into a trailer, where we were given quick instructions on how to be an "escort." Escorts were the ones who would go to the finish line and attach themselves to the Gold, Silver, and Bronze Medal winners. There was a statement we had to get them to sign and then they had one hour to get to the place where they had to take a mandatory drug test. I was assigned the Gold Medal winners. The four-man team from Germany won the gold medal. While I was trying to get their attention to get them to sign the form so that we could get their drug test over, the whole team and their coaches acted like they could not speak English. I was standing out there in -43 degree temperature freezing to death and chasing the Germans around the platforms. Finally I approached the captain of the team and told him I was getting ready to record the time and sign the paper and he would have one hour to get to the drug test or lose his gold medal. Suddenly everyone could speak English.

Over a two week period of time, I got to know the two-man and four-man German Bobsled team very well. The same tall blonde young German was captain of both teams. I got the opportunity to share the gospel with him while we were waiting for his drug test. As I was sharing with him, I was reminded that the Lord had promised me that He had put me in a place where He would bring the world to me.

Every event depended upon dependable volunteers. Because we had now proved ourselves, North Country Ministries became the number one supplier of volunteers that could be counted on to show up and do their job the way it was supposed to be done. We maintained the policy that we did not accept perks for doing our work. This created a relationship with the folks in charge of all of the events in Lake Placid that continues to exist to this day.

The marks of our volunteers were:

- We showed up on time for our assignments.
- We did not complain about what we were asked to do.
- We stayed as long as we were expected to stay.
- We did what we were told to do.
- We did not expect nor did we ask for favors for doing our job. (There were events where we were expected to wear the uniform jackets that were provided, and we did accept them and were allowed to keep them.)

As Jake's two year time was coming to an end, the ministry had proven so successful that NAMB was considering giving us a full-time resort minister. Because Jake had done such a good job, I offered him the new position. He prayed seriously about it, and came to me and told me that as much as he would like to accept the position, he felt he needed to go on and get started on his seminary training. I could not disagree.

Shortly after that, Virginia and I had gone to Syracuse for a BCNY Board meeting. We spent the night with Dr. and Mrs. Graham. During dinner we talked about the new Resort Minister position. Suddenly Mrs. Graham said, "I know who it should be." She then began to tell us about Derek Spain, a young man they had known all of his life. He was a Youth Minister at a large church in Georgia. He and their son Jon had been best friends growing up. The bottom line is that Derek turned out to be the Pastor/Resort Minister of the Lake Placid Baptist Church. Through Derek's efforts, he got the church involved again in a ministry they should have been involved in all along. Derek also developed a strong relationship with the local people of Lake Placid. It was my pleasure to work alongside him as we saw the ministry grow and the opportunities to minister to the world grow by leaps and bounds. Because of the connection made with winter sports people, Derek was actually chosen to be one of the official chaplains at the 2010 Winter Olympics in Vancouver, British Columbia, Canada.

At the same time, Derek was leading the church to become stronger than it had ever been. He had only been in Lake Placid a short while, when he led the Lake Placid Church in a major remodeling and new building project. I remember the first time I was at the church and he was showing me the plans that had been drawn up. He said that the Lord had told them to do this and that they were not going to borrow any money. They would pay for it as they went forward. I did not tell him, but I was somewhat skeptical. The following summer, I was standing in the hole that had been dug for the lower level of the project. One of the church members was with me. I remarked about how amazing this was. The church member said to me, "A year ago, no one but our pastor believed this was possible, but he was so convinced that the Lord had told him to do it, that we decided to follow him."

The Lord left him there for several years before he moved back to Georgia. While he was there, he trained a young man to continue the Resort Ministry, and it continues to this day.

The Lord gave me the vision for reaching the world with the Gospel without leaving the United States, and He allowed me to stay long enough to see that vision become a reality. I had the opportunity to be a part of the ministry to these various world class events for the last three years of my ministry before retiring from NAMB.

ESPN Great Outdoor Games

The ESPN Great Outdoor Games decided to return to Lake Placid the second year. By then, Jake had become well known with the Chamber of Commerce people in Lake Placid. He came to me and told me that he had promised them that we would provide 100 volunteers. I told him he better get busy recruiting or he was going to be very busy. I think we did get real close to the number he promised.

Do you remember the name Eric at the airport in Albany at the beginning of the Winter Goodwill Games? What I did not know was that he actually worked for ESPN. He saw me the first day of the Great Outdoor Games. He said, "Jim, why am I not surprised you are here?"

The next summer ESPN had signed a three-year contract with Lake Placid to host the Great Outdoor Games. So for three years we had the opportunity to provide volunteers for this televised event, which featured a wide variety of outdoor sporting activities, such as: Fishing Events, Sporting Dog Events, Target Events, and Timber Events. Participants came from all over North America and around the world. Someone who was in charge of one of the activities approached my wife one day and told her that he had been told about the "Baptist volunteers" and how amazing they were. He told her that he did not believe what he had been told, but the truth was we were even better than he had been told to expect us to be. All of this just kept giving us the opportunity to give God the glory for what he was doing in our lives.

I had an interesting experience the first year we provided a large group of volunteers for the Great Outdoor Games. I was in charge of the Target Shooting Venue, which was held at the Horse Show grounds. They were about to begin bow and arrow target shooting. Suddenly someone noticed that they had allowed cars for another venue to be parked right behind the targets. It would not be a problem unless someone missed his target. It was decided that the cars must be moved. We knew where the owners were, because they had parked there and been driven to the Dog Retrieval Venue. I got the description of all of the cars and then had to go from person to person finding the owners. One of the problems was this venue required complete silence, so that the dogs could hear the commands from their owners. They tried to kick me out twice, but I finally found all of the owners so that we could get them over to move their cars, so that our event could begin. One man was adamant that he was not going to give up his front row seat. I told him that if his car was not moved, we would not be responsible for any damage to his car. He finally decided to trust me and give me his car keys and look me up after the event.

Because of our involvement in Ministry to the Olympic Training Center, we spent a lot of time in Lake Placid over the years, which meant there were many times that we needed to stay overnight. There were times when the ministry house met that need, but there were many times when staying there was not practical for one reason or another. The second year we were in the North Country, I served as Interim Pastor of the Lake Placid Baptist Church. On one particular Sunday no one had invited us to join them for lunch after church. We went out for lunch and then came back to the church to rest before the evening service. When one of the ladies came in for the evening service and discovered that we had gone out to eat and then spent the afternoon at the church, she fussed at us for not coming to their house. She then told me that the former pastor would just drop in and eat with them without being invited. I told her that would not happen with me. If she wanted us to come for a meal, she would have to invite us, which she did for the next Sunday. That prompted her and some other ladies to make a schedule of who was going to take us home for lunch and give us a place to rest for the afternoon.

The home of Phil and Claire Thayer did in fact become a home away from home for us when we needed it. We did come to believe we were part of their family and could drop in whenever we needed to do that. Phil and I both loved golf; we played together quite often. One day in particular, it was already in the month of May, but it was cold when we teed off. We decided to play anyway. It started snowing on us on the third hole. You're right; we played 18 holes of golf that day. The local pro at Craig Wood Golf Course called us his all-weather golfers.

The Golf Pro was a close friend of my friend Phil. He decided that he was not going to charge me when I played there. Most of the time I would go with Phil, who was a member and I was allowed to play as his guest, when I played with him. However, the Pro told me to feel free to come and play any time I was in Lake Placid and had time to play golf.

Other families in Lake Placid also invited us into their homes and provided us a place to stay when we needed to be there for several days. The Appletons had a small cabin behind their house that was available to us whenever we needed it. We made some lifelong friends while there.

Interim Pastor

In the guidelines of my job description, I was allowed to be the Interim Pastor of one of our churches for up to three months. Any period of time beyond three months would have to be approved by the Steering Committee of the Association, at the request of the pastorless church. That permission would be given for three months at a time. Most of the time, I was needed for more than three months because the process of calling a pastor usually took a year to two years. Most of the time, I would stay a maximum of six months. I would then help them make other arrangements until they could call a pastor. Every situation was dependent on the specific needs of that particular congregation.

Recently we have had a young lady, who grew up in one of our churches in New York, attend our church in Texas. She and her husband have purchased property and moved to East Texas. The first time she attended our church here, she told everyone I had been her pastor. As I thought about it, when she was a child growing up, her church was without a pastor about half of the 12 years I was in New York. Every time they were without a pastor, I was her interim pastor. So I was actually her pastor more than anyone else. The first time they were without a pastor after I became DOM, they never did call me as their interim; they just kept asking me to come back and preach week after week. The next time they were without a pastor, one of the deacons said that they should probably go ahead and call me as interim this time, if that was ok with me. Each interim situation was different, because the make-up of the congregations was so different. Some needed stronger leadership than others. Some just basically needed someone who was always going to be there to preach for them, so that they did not have to worry about that. It was the interim relationships that allowed me to have that pastor-to-people relationship I knew I was going to miss when I left the position of pastor to take this association position.

For example, the first time I was interim pastor at Lake Placid, I found out that one of the girls in the church played on the High School Basketball Team. I got the schedule of the home games and we started going to her games. Her family was unusually impressed that I would drive 45 miles in the winter to go to her games. I did not think anything about it, because it was the kind of thing I did as a pastor. I found out later that their former pastor had never attended the activities of the youth in his church. So they were very surprised when I began doing it. Later this same family had a son who started playing Ice Hockey. I really enjoyed going to those games and learning some things about this sport.

Long Pond

I cannot close the time in New York without talking about a beautiful place and two people who became dear friends. It was the second summer we were in New York, when I got a call from Pastor Bruce Aubrey of the First Christian Church, Brushton, New York. Pastor Bruce had been the Chairman of the DOM Search Committee when I was called to the Adirondacks. He had just accepted the call of a church in the Syracuse area. He had made arrangements with Jim and Anne Price to lead an Experiencing God group in their home that summer. He wanted me to go to the first meeting of this home discipleship group. He would only be able to lead the first couple of sessions before he would have to move. He wanted me to meet this family and take over the group after he was gone. I was glad to do that.

Jim and Anne were natives of the North Country, who spent most of the year in south Florida. They spent the summer and early fall on Anne Price's family estate in the Adirondacks, about 10 miles south of Malone, where we lived. This was a large estate just inside the Adirondack State Park, which had a couple of lakes on the property. We had a wonderful time with that discipleship group that summer and getting to know Jim and Anne Price. We became instant friends. During the time we were in New York, they treated us like family. In fact they always celebrated their anniversary in early September, before returning to Florida for the winter. They always went on a short trip somewhere and after a couple of years of becoming friends, they would invite us to go with them. We usually went to some location in Canada that was easy driving distance from where we lived.

Their estate is known as Long Pond. Their home looks out over the larger of the two lakes on the property. They also had a guest cabin which also looks out on the lake. The larger of the two lakes was stocked with small mouth bass and northern pike. They found out that I liked to fish. After we developed our strong friendship, I had an open invitation to come and fish anytime. Anytime the cabin was empty, we had an open invitation to come and spend the night or spend the week. It was only about a 20 minute drive from their place to my office, so sometimes in the summer we would go and spend the week, and I would drive back and forth to work.

I wanted to mention this because in many ways the Prices and Long Pond became a haven of rest for us. I don't know how many times we sat at their dinner table and ate the fresh vegetables that were grown in their garden every summer. Because it is such a large place, they had a year round caretaker, who lived in another house on the property. Having someone there year round meant they did not have to worry about the property during the months they were in Florida. One of the duties of the caretaker was to plant a large garden and care for it. I remember one summer evening; we must have eaten two dozen ears of corn that had just come out of the garden that day.

I don't even know how to adequately describe how beautiful Long Pond is. Watching the sun go down over the lake and the mountain was breath taking. Waking up to the sounds of the loons on the lake in the morning was so peaceful. Jim and I developed a very close friendship, and had many long conversations that were quite interesting, since we both had strong opinions about the things we believed. There were some very personal ways that they ministered to us that I will not mention, but they know and the Lord knows what a blessing they were to us. Virginia and I felt like they were God's gift to us. We have not been able to see them much since we retired, but our love for them and appreciation for them will always be with us.

Jim and Anne were Presbyterians except for the time in the summer when they came back to Long Pond. They were involved in our churches. Anne is one of the most mission-minded persons I have ever known. Therefore, she would get involved in any mission activities I had going on, to go along with the other projects she had. She got several of our churches involved in Franklin Graham's Operation Christmas Child, putting together shoe boxes to go to children all over the world.

We had a remarkable experience one year. One of our churches had called a new pastor who had just finished Southwestern Seminary. His wife had worked for a Christian radio station in Fort Worth. That radio station had been involved in sending shoes to orphans in Russia. When they moved to New York, she challenged our churches to get involved in this ministry. Anne Price had grown up in the Malone, New York, area. There was a shoe manufacturing company in the North Country. She had gone to school with the manager of the plant. When she heard about the shoes to orphans in Russia, she called her friend. She then called me and told me that I needed to meet her at the shoe plant.

I visited with this plant manager who told me that he had some children's house slippers that he could give us. I told him we would give him a statement of donation to our association. They had lost a contract with a company and had these house slippers that they could not sell to anyone else. Anne and I made arrangements to meet him at his warehouse. We got to this large warehouse and went in to look at these slippers. There were rows and rows of shelves filled with shoe boxes. They were cartoon character house slippers. He then told us that he had 20,000 pairs of brand new, never out of the box, slippers that he was going to give us. We were astonished. We told him it would take us a few days to make transportation arrangements, but we would get back to him quickly. One of the men in one of our churches worked for a trucking company. His boss loaned us two 18 wheelers, and he and a truck driving friend drove the slippers along with the shoes that our churches had collected, to Philadelphia to be put on a ship and sent to orphanages in Russia.

I guess this was one of the most amazing stories of giving to missions that I have ever known. It happened because of Anne's mission spirit and the willingness of a young pastor's wife to challenge our churches to do something we had never done before. Can't you just imagine the smiles that came on the faces of all of those orphans in Russia? Those smiles came because of the love of Jesus Christ, for "all the children of the world." You never know what one simple phone call can lead to, when you are doing it for the Lord.

Yes, Long Pond and Jim and Anne Price were very special to us. And by the way, over the years, I caught some really nice fish out of that lake.

Saying Goodbye

Saying goodbye to a group of people that the Lord has called me to serve has never been easy for me, even in places where it has been very difficult to serve. Regardless of how difficult a circumstance might have become, in every place the Lord has given me the opportunity to serve, there have been those who have been willing to get on board with me and stick with me, no matter what might come. I know that I have mentioned this before, but it is worth mentioning again in this context. Shortly after I moved to New York, my son Jim asked me the question, "Was there ever a move I made that, looking back, I felt like I made the wrong decision?" My answer to him was, "You can't look back and start second guessing your decisions." I told him that what I knew for sure was, at the time I made each decision, I believed I was making it in obedience to the will of God for my life. So down through the years, when we have said goodbye, though it was a hard decision to make most of the time, it was a decision made based on a belief that we were being obedient to the Lord's will.

When we said goodbye in Rusk, I thought that was the most difficult time I would ever experience. It was an extremely emotional time. I had really believed I was going to be in Rusk for the rest of my ministry, and then retire there. Then God stepped in with a plan that I would never have imagined, as He sent us to the Adirondack Mountain Region of the State of New York, to be the Director of Missions.

For 12 years we served in this beautiful part of God's creation. I had never been a DOM or desired to be one. I loved being the pastor of a local church. One of my goals was to do everything I could, to be a pastor to the pastors of our churches. To do that required a great deal of travel, because of the vastness of our territory. Sometimes it took more effort than I thought it would, to get pastors to let down their barriers, and let me in to who they really were. That is probably because many pastors develop a built-in system of protection from criticism, "The less you know about me, the less you will have to criticize."

I really did miss being a pastor more than I thought I would. However, during the 12 years we served the ABA, I had the privilege of serving most of our churches as Interim Pastor, and some of them more than once. To most of our churches, they looked upon me somewhat like a second pastor, even when they had a pastor. Part of that was probably because so many of them came out of the Catholic Church, and had been used to the Bishop having authority over their Priest. Part of it probably had to do with the fact that, when nearly all of our churches were started, they were receiving some kind of help from the Southern Baptist Convention and the Baptist Convention of New York. That help had to begin with approval from the local Director of Missions.

It was announced at the Annual Meeting in the fall of 2003 that I would retire at the end of the year. That meeting was in mid-October, so for the remainder of the year, Virginia and I went on a farewell tour of the association. Every Sunday we were in a different church. I would preach and Virginia would sing, and there would be some kind of farewell gestures. The pastor and his wife of one of our missions even planned to be away the Sunday we were there so that, "We won't get in the way of the people saying goodbye."

I knew that there was some kind of "going-away party" that was being planned. It ended up being on the Friday night after Thanksgiving, because that was the only Friday night they could get everybody there that they wanted to be there. I had already told Virginia that I would be surprised if there was much of a turn out on Thanksgiving weekend. On that Friday morning it started snowing, and it snowed all day long. The meeting was held at the Recreation Center of the First Christian Church, Brushton, New York. Because of the snow, I was sure that the attendance would be small. Some of the churches had to travel more than two hours one way to get there. All of our churches were represented but two. One of those two we had been in the Sunday before and they had a really big farewell time for us there, because they realized that most of them would not be able to be there on Friday night. The other church literally got snowed in and could not come. There were over 300 in attendance that night, who had driven from all over the Adirondacks in a snow storm to say goodbye to us.

They had the program well planned. The only thing they asked us to do was to sing "The King Is Coming" one more time. We were glad to do that; although I got more emotional than I usually do while singing. The meal and program started at 6:00 P.M. They finished up about 9:00 P.M. After the program was over, they asked us to come and sit in two chairs in front of the stage. Then they told the people that, if anyone had a personal word for us, they could come by and share it. That began a little after 9:00 P.M. We said goodbye to the last person at 11:30 P.M.

Oh, and by the way, those little congregations gave us a love offering of $3,000.00. We were overwhelmed. They really left no stone unturned in making sure that they said goodbye in a good way. They had already had a Resolution of Appreciation of our Ministry adopted at the Annual Meeting of the Baptist Convention of New York.

Our state Executive Director, Dr. Graham and his wife Areta attended this farewell party. They had already made plans to spend the night with us and drive home the next day. When we got to the house and were discussing what had happened that night, they too were amazed. Dr. Graham looked at me and said, "Well Jim, you should know now how your 12 years were received by the people that really mattered."

We have not been back to the Adirondacks in many years. If the Lord allows, we plan to go back this summer of 2016. Our son Tom will be a participant in the Ironman competition. It is with great fondness that I remember our years in the North Country of New York. The people received us well, and the Lord blessed our efforts, even when we didn't know what we were doing.

I have not even begun to touch the many experiences that we had during our twelve years of ministry in the North Country of New York. There were also many fun and exciting experiences. May I say that, for the most part, the pastors of the churches in the Adirondack Association made incredible sacrifices to be where they were, serving the churches to which they had been called. Because of them and some incredibly dedicated lay people, the churches and the association were able to survive some very tough days.

I also need to say that without the support of the Baptist Convention of New York and the North American Mission Board, we could not have survived. As a matter of fact, without the faithful members of the churches all across the Southern Baptist Convention, we could not have survived. Praise God for the churches of the Southern Baptist Convention who believe in missions and give faithfully so that our national and international missionaries can do the work the Lord has called them to do, and they can do it without having to spend half of their time raising financial support for their work.

Coming Back to Rusk

Probably, if one of our sons had been in a situation where we knew that he was going to be there from now on, we would have considered moving close to one of them. However, our older son Jim was a pastor in St. Louis, Missouri. I knew that the chances of him being in the same place from now on were slim to none. As I write these words, he is in fact in his fourth year in Germany as pastor of an English speaking, primarily U.S. Military church. We have been there twice and hope to go again, but that is not somewhere we want to live in retirement.

Our son Tom was still in Medical School on Long Island, New York, when we moved back. At that point in time he had no idea where he would be living when he finished Medical School. As it turns out he has had a medical practice in New York City, ever since he finished Medical School. We are not big city people and our retirement income would have made it difficult to try to retire in New York City. So we go and visit him from time to time.

Not living near one of our children meant determining where we would live. My dad asked me a few months before he passed away, if I thought I would like to live in his home after he died. I told him that I loved the house; I just didn't like where it was located. It was just off I-45 north of the Woodlands and south of Conroe. Over the years we have come to love living in small towns. We loved Rusk when we were here.

On one visit back to Texas, we drove from Conroe up to Rusk to attend services on Sunday morning. After the service I talked to the pastor, Bro. Lee Welch. I told him that we were thinking about retiring back in Rusk, but I did not want to be a former pastor who might create problems for the pastor. I asked him if he would pray about it and let me know. His response was that he did not have to pray about it; he wanted me to move back. I told him I would accept that answer, if he would promise that he would pray about it and if the Lord told him something different, he would let me know. He promised to do that.

JoEd Anderson Realtors began helping us try to find a home. After about a year of looking over the internet, we finally found the home we wanted to look at more seriously. It turned out to be the home of a former deacon of FBC, Rusk, and good friends of ours, Tony and Lois Murray. I flew to Oklahoma City and rented a car and picked up Virginia, who was visiting her parents in Shawnee, OK. We drove to Rusk on Friday and went out to dinner with JoEd and Nancy Anderson. That happened to be Rusk High School graduation night, and so we went to that event with them. We saw a lot of old friends that night. One in particular, seemed to know that something was going on more than just a visit. Vicki Beard, who has been like a daughter to me since she lost her parents, really pressed me on why we were there. I finally told her that I would tell her something later.

We met Tony and Lois Murray on Saturday morning and agreed to buy their home. Those of you who know their home, know that it is a wonderful home. We never dreamed that we would own such a magnificent home. We signed the contract in May 2003, and closed on the loan in July 2003. All of our friends in New York were amazed at how easily and quickly we closed on the loan and the house became ours. When we bought our home in New York, it took three months for the loan to be approved and to close on the loan. We signed the contract here on a Saturday; I flew back to New York on

Monday. On Tuesday, in a five minute conversation with Charles Hassell at Citizens Bank, our loan was approved. I thanked Charles for his quick response and his reply was, "We are honored that you have chosen to retire here." That sure did sound good.

After we got back to JoEd's office that Saturday morning, I called Vicki Beard. Her son Jordan answered the phone. Jordan has been like a grandson to us. His grandparents Doug and Sally Jordan passed away before he was born, and his parents had moved into their home next door to the FBC pastor's home. I asked to speak to his mother but she was gone. I told him to give her a message about the question she asked me the night before. I told him to tell her we had bought Tony Murray's house, and we were moving back to Rusk when I retired from the Home Mission Board. He wanted to know when that would be and I told him August 2004.

Through an unusual set of circumstances, we were actually able to retire at the end of 2003. We decided that it would be best to do whatever things we wanted to do to the house before we moved in, rather than after we arrived with all of our furniture. So shortly after we closed on the loan and the home was actually ours, I told Virginia to fly to Texas and take as long as she needed, to do the things that needed to be done. Her sister and brother-in-law Pat and Darl Henderson, from Miami, Florida, met her in Dallas. They drove to Rusk and lived in the house, while they were working on various projects. While they were there, Virginia made arrangements for several things to be done after they were gone, and before we would move in January 2004.

By the way, I need to say that one of the reasons that it was so easy for the bank to make a loan to us was because we paid cash for 80% of the cost of the home. The reason I wanted to mention that is because that was possible because of the inheritance I had received from my parents. In fact, if you were to come into our home through the front door, you would see a plaque that acknowledges that this home was made possible because of the generosity of Carl and Frances Goforth. The first time my brother came up to see me, we

441

were standing in the front yard when he said, "Dad and Mother would be pleased with the way you spent your inheritance."

The Move

When we moved from Rusk to Malone, New York, it was January 1992. When we arrived in Malone, the temperature was -5 degrees. When the moving van got there two days later, it was snowing and -30 degrees. One of the movers did not even have a pair of gloves. I went to K-Mart and bought him a pair of gloves.

When we moved from Malone to Rusk, Texas, it was January 2004. Atlas Moving Company sent a crew from Atlanta, Georgia, to move us. On moving day the actual temperature was -34 degrees. It was so cold that his diesel fuel was as thick as molasses. I had to call a diesel mechanic I knew, to help him get his truck started. Our home in Malone was a two-story with a full attic and a full basement. So the movers had three flights of stairs to deal with all day, plus the cold weather. About halfway through the day, I told the movers I had some good news for them. I told them that they were moving this furniture to Texas and the house they would be moving things into did not have any stairs. They grinned and said that was good news. However, I don't think it was much help at the moment.

Finding Where You Fit In

Someone needs to write a book about how you find out where you fit in when you retire. One week you have the responsibilities of the kind of work you have been doing for years; the next week you are not responsible for anything but you and your household. For me I had a blessing. That blessing was in the form of the pastor of First Baptist Church, Rusk, Bro. Lee Welch. Bro. Lee immediately accepted me back in town, but also welcomed me as a friend. He would call me and invite me to go places with him. He did an excellent job of making it clear that there was no jealousy about a former pastor being back in town. In fact it was just the opposite; he went out of his way to make it clear he was happy I was back in town.

Shortly after we moved back, Bro. Lee told me about a group of men that met for breakfast every morning and invited me to join them. This group was an interesting and diverse group of men to say the least. I had a lot in common with some of them; I had absolutely nothing in common with the others. This made for some very interesting conversations about almost anything and everything. As you can imagine, with such a group, there was always a lot of wisdom involved in our discussion. Most of it may have been classified by others as misguided wisdom, but make no mistake, we were very clear and determined about things, particularly those things we really knew nothing about.

I will give you an example of some of the very important things that we discussed, and something that almost came about that would have really put Rusk on the World Sports Stage. In 2009 when I was putting together a group of volunteers to go to Vancouver for the 2010 Winter Olympics, it seemed to create unusual interest in at least some members of the breakfast group in winter sporting events. As

444

the Games began, some began to watch to find an event that would match the skills of our breakfast group. One was found. Soon some serious discussions began about forming the Rusk Curling Team. Since most of us already walked pretty close to the floor, we felt this would be a natural for us. I am not sure what happened, but for some reason our hopes to participate in the Winter Olympics never quite materialized. We also never could figure out why CNN did not come and interview the "Whataburger Club" during election years in order to get the pulse of East Texas. I guess our wealth of information was just a well kept secret. That was probably because we were all too humble to toot our own horns; although I will say that some local politicians were known to suddenly show up for breakfast during election years. I will not mention any names, but some contribute articles to the local newspaper on a regular basis. One local politician was accused of taking his old campaign cards and having the dates changed to match the next election. I will also not mention that name either, because I may find that I will get arrested on some trumped up charge. I can't believe I just said that.

I remember the first December we were back; Bro. Lee and I had just finished breakfast on Friday morning with the breakfast group. He asked me what I had planned for the rest of the morning. I told him I had no plans. He asked me if I would like to drive to Tyler with him. I told him that I would be glad to go to Tyler with him. We made a stop at the LifeWay store. He took me over to the Bible section of the store to look at the new Holman Standard Bible. While we were looking at them, he asked me if I had one. I told him no. He then told me that he wanted me to pick one out, and that it was his Christmas gift to me.

I think, without a doubt, it became a very strong testimony in Rusk that Bro. Lee and I got along so well. I am very grateful to him for the way he received me and welcomed me back into the life of FBC, Rusk, Texas. We were asked by numerous people in Rusk why we chose to retire here. Our answer was easy. We chose to retire here because of the people. It was just as simple as that. Twelve years later, we can honestly say that we made the right decision for us.

That spring of 2004, I was asked to be the Annie Armstrong Offering speaker and share about our work in New York. One of the things I shared was about the North Country Ministry, and I showed some pictures of our ministry to the Ironman competition. After the presentation that night, Jason Hoffman came to tell me that he had not finalized any plans for their summer youth trip. He wanted to know if I thought I could arrange for them to go to New York for Ironman week. I told him I was sure I could, because I was going back myself to help run the ministry to Ironman at least one more time. Jason did decide to make that the summer mission trip, and there were 70 Youth and Adults from Rusk who made the journey from Rusk to the Adirondacks. Coach Mahaffy wanted to go, but he had the problem of needing to be back to get ready for fall football the very next week after the race. So he flew into Albany and rented a car and drove up to Lake Placid. The group from Rusk did a great job all week long. They did everything they were asked to do, without complaining.

One of my memories about that week happened on race day. Our ministry operated a run aid station during the last stage of the race, which was the 26.2 mile run. It was late afternoon and one of the athletes stopped and asked me if I had a towel and some Vaseline. I told him I did, and I encouraged him to sit down while I went to get it. When I got back and gave it to him, he took off his artificial leg; wiped the sweat off the stump of his leg; wiped the sweat out of the inside of his artificial leg; spread the Vaseline over his leg and inside his artificial leg; then put the leg back on. He then asked me if I had a real 7-Up I could get him. I got him the 7-Up; he wiped his brow, thanked me, and got back in the race. Keep in mind that he had already done the 2.4 mile swim, and the 112 mile bike ride, and was halfway through the 26.2 mile run. Coach Mahaffy was standing beside me, and observed what I have just described. I asked him how sympathetic he was going to be next week when his football players complained about running wind sprints. Coach Mahaffy said, "Not nearly as sympathetic as I might have been five minutes ago."

It is good to know that you have been obedient to the Lord in the decisions you make, and that you are trying to be who He wants you to be. A few years ago I was shopping in Brookshire Brothers Grocery Store in Rusk. I was toward the back of the store, and I saw a young man working who was a recent High School graduate and a member of FBC, Rusk, Texas. I spoke to him briefly; then I moved on down the aisle. As I walked away, I heard him call out to me. I stopped, and he was walking toward me. He reminded me that the scriptures call on us to let our light shine before men so that Christ can be glorified. He said, "I just want you to know that your light shines brightly in Rusk, Texas." I walked away with the Lord having just given me all that I needed to keep on, keeping on. I am sure I did not deserve the praise, but it was great to know that, something I had said or done, had encouraged a young man to keep on serving Christ.

Twelve years after moving back to Rusk, Virginia and I still agree that the Lord led us to plant our lives in our retirement years in this place. Pretty much the whole community has welcomed us back with open and loving arms. We could not ask to be treated better than we have been here.

It has been particularly rewarding to see many of the couples, who were young couples in the church when we were here as pastor, as they have accepted strong leadership positions in the church. It is also good to see many who were teenagers in the church when we were here before, who are very active young families in the church today.

Processing Difficult Information

My first experience of processing difficult information was when I was a college student and my dad had been diagnosed with throat cancer. I have a very clear memory of my dad setting me down in the living room of our family home, and talking to me about his cancer. He said, "I want you to know that I am fine, and if I don't make it, I am fine. However, I want you to promise me that, if something happens to me, as my oldest son, you will take care of your mother." As I fought back the tears, I made him that promise. Praise God; I never did have to keep that promise. Dad not only survived, but also thrived, as he lived another 41 years. We actually lost our mother before we lost him.

There have been many difficult moments since the day I had that conversation with my dad. However, once again, on February 27, 2015, I had a similar feeling, but more severe. Virginia and I had gone to her doctor's office to get the report on a biopsy she had done earlier in the week. I watched as the doctor with his nurse entered the room to talk to us. As I looked at him, I knew we were not going to get a good report. He fumbled around for a moment; then just said, "There is no easy way to say this. You have cancer." As I looked at my wife of 51 years, I felt like we had both just been kicked in the stomach. I have decided to jump ahead and write these thoughts down while they are fresh in my mind.

I have been in the ministry in an active capacity for 54 years. I have been through difficult times with many people. I have been with many people when they got bad news either about themselves or about a family member. But just in case you did not know, it is a whole different ballgame when it is you or your own family. I remember Virginia and me driving to College Station, Texas, where my dad and mother had been taken after a terrible head-on automobile accident.

From the information my brother had given me, I did not really know whether either one of them would be alive when we got there. I said to Virginia, "We are about to find out, if everything I have been preaching for the last 25 years, really works." My mother died two weeks later, and dad was in the hospital for 55 days. I am here to tell you that the gospel works.

However, I say again that, when something happens to the one who has become so much a part of who you are, you feel like you have been kicked in the stomach. There was not near the same feeling in my gut, when I was told 6 years ago that I had a low grade prostate cancer. That was so much easier to handle than to sit next to my wife and wonder what she was feeling in the deepest recesses of her heart. I think we were both in a daze as we walked out of the clinic. Then began the process of telling our family and closest friends about the news we had received. That, in itself, is an emotional roller coaster as you relive those moments over and over again.

What were those feelings about that came so quickly? They certainly were not feelings of despair. Our Lord is sufficient for every circumstance, and nothing catches Him by surprise. However, I do remember the thoughts going through my mind of all of the people I had seen suffer with cancer of one kind or another. It is not a pleasant thought to think that your life partner might have to experience that kind of suffering. Yet I know that none of us are exempt from anything this world may throw at us. We just know that, as believers in Jesus Christ, we are able to endure all things, through His strength in us. As a new day has dawned, and we have had time to process things, I think we are both better and we are moving forward in arranging treatment.

I had a three-fold prayer this morning: First, I prayed that, if it could be the Lord's will, he would just touch her and heal her. We know that He can do that. Second, if it is not His will to heal her, that He would direct us to the right medical people who will do the right things to bring healing. Third, I prayed that, during this process, we will know the peace of our Lord and Savior, Jesus Christ, and that we will bring honor and glory to His Name by the way we conduct ourselves.

The Journey Begins

The Lord has led us to MD Anderson Hospital in Houston, Texas. So here we are on March 16, 2015, to begin the journey on the treatment of Virginia's Breast Cancer diagnosis. She will have several tests this morning; then tomorrow morning we will come back for a consultation with a surgeon.

We are confident that the Lord has led us to the right place for her treatment. We are ready to find out the extent of the problem and develop a game plan for her treatment. We still believe that the Lord could see fit to just touch her and heal her. If that is not His will, we believe that we have come to the best place we could possibly find, in order for her to receive the best possible treatment.

So at this point, we are waiting on the Lord, believing that we will be better because of this experience. We are praying that the Lord will be glorified in all that we do throughout this process. We pray that we will be stronger because of this experience and that God's Kingdom on this earth will be advanced because of this experience.

I pray that our church will experience revival because of what the Lord is doing. I pray that revival will break out throughout southern Cherokee County, because of this experience. I pray this morning that, as this journey begins, my personal faith in my Lord and Savior Jesus Christ will become stronger than it has ever been. I pray that I will be open to whatever it is that the Lord is preparing to teach me. So, dear Lord, as the journey begins, I pray that my personal love relationship with you will become stronger than it has ever been.

The appointments with the two surgeons went very well, and she was scheduled for surgery the middle of April. We came home from that first visit feeling like we had made exactly the right decision about treatment for Virginia's cancer. Her surgery was set for the middle of April. We came back to Houston for her surgery, only to discover that they had neglected to tell her that some vitamin supplements she was taking were also blood thinners; so the surgery had to be rescheduled for the next week.

She had her surgery on April 23, 2015, and has done extremely well. We have since gotten the report that they were able to get all of the cancer, and that it had not spread. She will begin radiation therapy in June for four weeks. It still appears that she will not have to have chemotherapy, for which we praise God. After the radiation, her Oncologist will begin hormone therapy with prescription medicine.

We are praising God that everything is going so well, and we are convinced it is because so many people are praying for her. At one time we figured that we had people in at least 5 countries and 14 states praying for her. Virginia completed her radiation therapy on July 3, 2015. The doctors are amazed at how well she has done with everything. She has begun to take medication and is having no ill effects from that. She appears to be back to her normal self, and we continue to praise God for what He has done for her. We are so grateful for the many people who have prayed for her and are continuing to pray for her. We believe that, through the combination of prayer and medical science, she has been healed. Sometimes that is the way the Lord chooses to work, and we praise Him for both. I thank God for those who have chosen the medical profession as a career and have taken the time to prepare themselves for the task. I am also thankful for God's amazing grace and for caring Christians who lift others up to the throne of God in prayer.

Later in the year of 2015, I had someone ask me how Virginia was doing. The question, at first, caught me off guard. She has done so well that I had almost forgotten that she has had breast cancer. So I said, "Oh, you are asking how she is doing with the breast cancer issue." Then I told him that things had gone so amazingly well, that I had almost forgotten all about it. Think about that for a moment; a battle with breast cancer had gone so amazingly well that in less than a year, it is almost out of both of our minds.

Were it not for the occasional notes we get from M.D. Anderson Hospital, and the medication she takes by mouth, we probably really would have forgotten about it by now. She has done so well, it even amazes her doctors. Praise God! You think maybe He had a hand in all that? We know that He did. Does God answer prayer? We know that He does. Does He always answer it the way we would like? No, or I would be free of all back pain. Is there a reason that prayer has not been answered? Yes, but I don't know what it is. Will I understand someday? Yes, but it may not be until I get to Heaven.

It is now February 2016; I am still laboring over getting this book finished. Hopefully I have resolved in my heart that I will finish it sometime this spring of 2016. I have mentioned the date, because Virginia and I are rejoicing over the fact that this year has gone by so quickly, and it appears that one year later she is cancer free. Not only does it appear that she is cancer free, but she has had none of the after effects of the various treatments and medication that can and most of the time do happen. Part of that blessing is due to the fact that she did not have to have any chemotherapy and she only had four weeks of radiation treatment.

I have also mentioned the date because a year later, at almost the exact same time of the year that we discovered Virginia's breast cancer, our next door neighbor Penny Reynolds has discovered that she now has almost exactly the same cancer Virginia had one year ago. Penny's treatments are going very well and she has been able to maintain a really good attitude. We are really grateful for the friendship that we have with Roy and Penny.

About a year after we moved back to Rusk, I was out on the side of my house. A car pulled into the driveway of the home next door to us that looked just like the owner's car. The owners had recently moved to Georgia. I went over because I thought it was them. It was not them. It was Roy and Penny Reynolds from Fort Worth. They were on their way back to Fort Worth and were looking for a small town where they could retire. They happened to see this house and wanted to look inside, but the realtor was out of town. The realtor was my friend JoEd Anderson. The owners had given us a key to the house just in case someone needed to get in when they were away. I told them I had a key if they wanted to see the house. They looked at the house and immediately fell in love with it and the neighborhood. Shortly thereafter, Roy and Penny Reynolds bought the house, and before long they were our new neighbors.

We soon discovered that Roy grew up in Plattsburgh, New York, which was just 50 miles from where we lived in Malone, New York, for 12 years. One of the churches I served in the Adirondack Baptist Association was located in Plattsburgh. I spent a great deal of time and energy in and around Plattsburgh, and at one point in time, I came very close to resigning as the DOM of the ABA and becoming pastor of the Bread of Life Baptist Church in Plattsburgh. One year after we moved back here, the Lord moved a man and his wife next door, who grew up in a place that was very familiar to me.

Roy and Penny have become like brother and sister to us. We look after their place when they are gone, and they look after ours when we are gone. They have the best of both worlds with our dog. They can enjoy him as much as they want, and then walk away when they have had enough. They have the benefit of "Rusty" being the watch dog for both places. Our relationship with one another is very special. There is a bond and love for one another that is very special.

It is ironic that this time last year they were our encouragers and the ones whose shoulders we could cry on; now, just one year later, the roles are reversed. I guess it is our payback time for all the encouragement they were to us last year. I pray that we will be as faithful to them, as they were to us, and that the results for Penny will be the same as it was for Virginia.

It is April 2016, and Penny has begun her chemotherapy treatments. She is doing as well as a person can do while taking these very difficult treatments. Again let me say that we have come to love this couple more than words can describe. It is a very special relationship that the Lord has given us.

Someone in Rusk had four cemetery plots to sell; Roy and Penny bought them at a very inexpensive price. We have agreed to buy two of them from them. Penny and I have joked that we will leave instructions to bury us on the inside and bury Roy and Virginia on the outside, so that they won't disturb the whole cemetery by talking all the time. Somehow they did not get the humor in that.

In all seriousness, I cannot express how much the people of Rusk, Texas, mean to Virginia and me. Everyone has been so kind to us. I may write another book, if I ever get this one finished, "Treat Your Current Pastor Like You Treat Your Former Pastor." If most churches would do that, it just might be that some of their former pastors would be their current pastor for a longer period of time. However, since I have already told you that the reason we moved back to Rusk was because of the people, that would certainly imply that we were treated very well by most of the people, and we were.

What Do You Do When the Doctors Don't Have the Answer, and God Chooses Not to Heal in a Miraculous Way?

That is something I have been dealing with personally for almost 10 years now, and more specifically, for the last three years. Ten years ago, we were involved in an automobile accident involving an on-coming vehicle, where the driver had gone to sleep at the wheel. We were extremely fortunate that we were not more seriously injured at the time and actually that one or both of us were not killed.

The injuries that I received caused damage to my spine, which was already inflamed by arthritis. This eventually led to back surgery in May of 2012. However, the surgery did little, if anything, to resolve the very serious back pain. It may have even contributed to the continuing pain that I have experienced. I could go on and on about the various treatments I have had with the hope of gaining relief, but that is really not what I think the Lord wants me to share, or that you would even be interested in reading. The truth is that there are far too many who have endured way more than me, for you to be interested in my "poor me" story.

The question is the one that I have already raised, "What do you do when the doctors don't have the answer, and God chooses not to heal in a miraculous way?" At least for now, He has chosen not to heal. The lack of healing on God's part is not because others have or have not been praying for Him to heal me. I also do not believe that it is a lack of faith on my part that He can heal, because I have been healed at least twice in the past by the Lord as His people prayed for my healing.

In the 1970's, I was pastor of the First Baptist Church, Pickerington, Ohio. I had gone to be the first pastor of this congregation when it was a mission with three members. We had been there for a few years. The mission had purchased property and had built its first building. During the winter, I had come into the house through the garage. I was carrying an 80 pound bag of water softener salt on my shoulder. I stepped into the house, opened the door to the basement, and started down the stairs with the bag of salt to put into the water softener. My foot slipped on the first step of the staircase. I grabbed the stair rail to keep from falling down the stairs. That movement caused all of the weight of my body, plus the bag of salt, to shift to one side, and I went straight down on that knee.

The result of that fall was that the cartilage in that knee was torn. Through some tests, it was determined that I needed surgery and would be on crutches for 3 – 6 months. That determination was made at the beginning of the summer. The day I was to have surgery, one of the young ladies of my church called me before I went to the hospital. She called to tell me that she and another lady in the church had stayed up all night praying for me to be healed, because we had too much going on that summer for me to be hobbling around on crutches. I told her I appreciated her prayers and then went on to the hospital. The day before the surgery I had gone to play golf with my preacher golfing buddies. By the third hole, I was in so much pain that one of them had to go back to the club house to get a golf cart to come get me and take me to my car. That was on a Monday. I went into the hospital on Tuesday to have the surgery on Wednesday morning. When the surgeon opened up my knee, he could not find anything wrong. My knee was completely repaired. He sewed me up and sent me home. On Friday of that same week, I walked 18 holes of golf with my preacher golfing buddies. Thank God for two young women who believed that the Lord could and would heal their pastor, because the church had too much ministry going on for him to be a cripple for 3 – 6 months.

I went to see the surgeon the next week. He was baffled about what had happened to me. He told me that he was absolutely sure I needed surgery. He then said that he did not know what had happened. I told him that some young ladies in my church could tell him what happened. Then he said, "I guess you are going to talk about that 'Jesus stuff.'" He told me he did not believe in that kind of stuff. I told him, until he could come up with a better answer, then that was the one I was going to believe. Praise God, Who is able to demonstrate His power to an unbelieving world.

I am writing these thoughts down on July 29, 2015, more than three years after the surgery that I had hoped would take the back pain away. Not only is the pain not gone, but in some ways it may be worse. For more than three years, many Christian friends have prayed for me, and a pain doctor is doing everything he knows to do to help me deal with the pain, and make life more bearable.

As I honestly reflect on what my attitude has been during this time, I have to admit that it has been that the next procedure is going to be the one that is going to put my life back to normal. For me, that would be a life of little or no back pain. I keep saying, "If I just was not in so much pain, I could do all of the things I need to do." I can tell you that coming to the place where you accept that you cannot do what you once could do physically has been one of the most difficult struggles of my life. The truth is that in another month I will be 76 years of age; I cannot do what I used to do physically whether there was back pain or not.

The issue now is, if my back is never better, will I live my life in a way that will bring honor and glory to my Lord and Savior Jesus Christ? If I know my heart, that is what I want. I believe that, in the last few days, I have begun to face that question. I am in the process of living this out; so I don't know the outcome yet. I do know that God is able to accomplish His purposes in my life, if I will allow that to happen.

It is now December 28, 2015. In regards to my back, the pain is still as real and severe at times as it has ever been. I recently brought the devotional for the monthly fellowship meeting of the Senior Adults of FBC, Rusk, Texas. Many in this group were the active leaders of the church when I was the pastor from 1984 – 1992. Some of them still hold leadership positions in the church. I probably get more genuinely concerned questions from them, than any other group, about how I am doing physically. Maybe part of the reason for that is because many of them are dealing with aches and pains of their own that seem to come with "old age."

I told them that I was making a determined decision not to have the rest of my life defined by my "back pain." Therefore, when they ask me how I am doing, and I reply, "I'm alright." they should not look at me like I am being less than honest with them. What I mean by, "I'm alright" is that in my spirit and mind, "I'm alright." Then I say to them, "Don't ask me how my back is, because that is a whole other story that you don't have time to hear, and probably don't want to hear anyway."

Also in 2015, I have injured one of my vocal chords. For a good portion of the year, I have barely been able to speak louder than a whisper, which is an interesting set of circumstances for a preacher and a husband. I am currently taking vocal therapy and am hopeful that in 2016 the outcome of this issue is going to be better than the issues with my back.

As an example of my determination to move on with my life with the Lord's help, I am currently finishing up my annual Preaching Planning Retreat. I have not actually gone off and done the intense planning for 3-4 days that I have done for years, because it is very intense and physically taxing. During these planning retreats, I will spend 15-18 hours a day in prayer, pouring over the Scriptures, and seeking God's direction for my preaching schedule for the next year. I am coming to the close of that very intense time of planning, which has required many hours over my computer, using my well-rehearsed, "hunt and peck" system of typing.

When I return home tomorrow, I will be going on a "Deer Hunting" trip. This is also something I have not done for over two years, while I have been waiting for my back pain to get better. If I should get a trophy deer, maybe my wife will be so sympathetic to my back pain, that it will not become an issue to have the head and antlers mounted. I have always wanted a "Deer Mount" of my own. Since I have mentioned the Preaching Planning Retreat, let me say that I am very excited that, if this plan is carried out, I will still be preaching 4 months past my 77th birthday.

Let me tell you how this planning retreat became a part of my ministry routine. Sometime during the 1970's, I was attending the annual Pastor's Conference sponsored by the Baptist General Convention of Ohio. It was held at the State Convention Camp Ground in Seneca Lake, Ohio. I was having lunch in the dining hall with a fellow pastor from the Columbus, Ohio, area. His name was Jim Effird. Jim told me about how he would come to the camp during the offseason each year. He would stay in one of the camp motel rooms and spend the week planning his preaching for the coming year. I remember thinking how hard that must be. While I was thinking about how hard it must be, he told me that I should try it. He even offered that I could come at the same time he was there the first year, if that would help me get started.

Instead of admitting that I did not want to do it because it sounded like too much work, I took a much more "spiritual" approach. I told him that I liked to be free from week to week to allow the Holy Spirit to lead me wherever He wanted me to go. Jim Effird replied to me, "Jim, I am sorry that the God you know only knows what is going to take place one week at a time. Mine is much bigger than that; He knows what is going on well into the future." Frankly, his answer made me angry, although I tried not to show it. That was the end of the conversation, but the seed was planted in my heart and mind. Several years later, after he had already gone to Heaven, I had the opportunity to tell his wife how he ministered to me, even though he died without knowing it.

It was several years later, after we had moved from Ohio, to Rockdale, Texas, to pastor FBC, Rockdale, that I had my first Preaching Planning Retreat. We had purchased a small camping trailer before we left Ohio. We moved from Medway, Ohio, to Rockdale, Texas, in the summer of 1981. In the fall of 1981, I pulled my trailer onto some remote property owned by one of my deacons. In November 1981, I sat at the dining table of that little camper and planned my preaching for 1982.

I was not prepared for what would happen during the course of that year. In August of 1982, I had finished preaching and greeting people after the service. I had gone back to my office to prepare to go home. When I came out of my office, there was one of our young men standing in the hall waiting for me. He said, "Pastor, that sermon you preached today was as if you knew everything that happened to me this week." He told me a little bit about the week, and we prayed together. Then I told him the Lord had put that sermon on my heart for that day the previous November. Then I said, "Isn't it great that last November God knew what was going to happen to you the next August, and led me to preach a sermon that would meet your need?"

Needless to say, I have looked forward to that retreat every year since that time. This is now 34 years of Preaching Planning Retreats. Although the last couple of years have not been as intense as they should be, I am happy that I have gotten back on track. I am also happy to say that this is one really good tradition my son James, Jr. has picked up and has also been doing for a number of years.

It is now May 5, 2016; this will probably be the last time I try to give a time frame update, because at some time I need to wrap this up. Virginia has just had her three month check up with her cancer doctor, and the report continues to be that she is doing great. Praise God! On May 10, 2016, my pain doctor will try one more procedure to try to ease the pain in my back. This continues to be one of the biggest tests, on a daily basis, that I have ever experienced. I pray that I will honor my Lord with the way that I conduct myself.

Discipleship Prayer Study

At the end of April 2005, I had just completed a 10 month period as Interim Pastor of FBC, Alto, Texas. Bro. Lee Welch, Pastor at FBC, Rusk, had to be away and he asked me to preach for him on Sunday night. I preached that night on prayer. The next day Virginia and I drove to Shreveport, Louisiana, to visit Jason and Melonie Hoffman and their premature baby girl at the hospital. While we were in the waiting room with Jason, he told me that my message of the night before was really timely. Then he said that the church really needed to go through some good prayer material. I told him about Don Miller's 10 hour seminar, "Spending Time with the Master in Prayer." I told him I had the material and could either get Don Miller to lead it or lead it myself. He was excited about it.

On the way back to Rusk that day, the Lord began to speak to me about taking this 10 hour seminar and developing it into a ten week Discipleship Study. I called Don Gibson the next day, and told him what the Lord seemed to be putting on my heart about taking Don Miller's Prayer Seminar and developing it into a 10 week discipleship study. He agreed to pray about it and said he would get back to me soon. He did get back to me in a couple of days and said that he had a real good feeling about it. I then communicated with Don Miller what I believed the Lord was doing and he agreed with me.

I had actually had all of the material for over a year, because over a year before, Don Miller had called me and asked me if I would come to Fort Worth to spend some time with him. So in the spring of 2004, I drove to Fort Worth to spend the day with Don and Libby Miller. Don took me out in the back yard to his prayer arbor, where he went every morning when he was home and the weather permitted. I had heard him talk about his prayer arbor; it was a two seat swing. He had me sit to his left. He told me that he always sat where he was sitting because it reflected that he was sitting at the right hand of God, waiting to do His bidding. He pointed out four large trees that were in his back yard. They all had a name. They were all named after one of his children. He told me that he planted each one of them when one of his children was born so that he would be reminded to pray for that child every day.

Don then told me about how the writing of the prayer seminar, "Spending Time with The Master in Prayer," came about. He said he was reading in scripture one day how Jesus chastised his disciples because they could not spend one hour in prayer with Him. He said that it broke his heart that those who were closest to the Lord could not spend one hour in prayer with Him. He said that he told the Lord that, if He would show him how, he would teach His church how to spend one hour in prayer."

Don then told me that he had invited me to Fort Worth, because he wanted me to know how the Lord gave him the Prayer Seminar. Then he said, "I want to give it to you, and I want you to do with it whatever the Lord leads you to do." I was overwhelmed at what I had just heard, and at the same time I knew that he would not be doing it, if he had not had a word from the Lord. We went back in the house and he told his wife Libby to get me a copy of everything that went with the prayer seminar. Then he told her to get one of the Hour Glasses that he would use in his presentations. That afternoon, as I left Fort Worth to drive back to Rusk, I did so with some precious cargo that was unexpected when I made the journey to Fort Worth that morning.

My first impression of why I had the material was that, because of Don Miller's age and health, he was going to start recommending me to churches to lead the Prayer Seminar. As it turned out, that was not the case. I believe I was given the material and told to do whatever the Lord led me to do with it, in order to develop it into a 10 week Discipleship Study.

I asked Larry Sinclair to develop a daily activity guide to go along with the study. I asked Jason Hoffman to take the material and develop a teaching PowerPoint. Then I sat down to take the teaching material from each of the 5 two-hour teaching sessions of the seminar and develop them into a 10 week Discipleship Study.

Don Gibson is remarkably gifted in taking material and dividing it up in such a way that an overview of the material can be presented to a church in a renewal type weekend setting. So he took the work that we did and developed the "Spending Time with The Master Weekend." That material was originally designed to be presented to the FBC, Rusk, Texas. Since then, it has been presented to churches all over the world. I really under-estimated the time it was going to take me to complete the breaking down of the material from a 10 hour seminar to a 10 week Discipleship Study. Therefore, when we had the first "Spending Time with The Master Discipleship Study Weekend" at Rusk in the fall of 2005, we really did not have everything completed. We had enough complete that the leadership at Rusk wanted to go ahead with the weekend.

Shortly after we had completed the material, I was asked to come to the Annual Board Meeting of Texas Baptist Men to do a brief overview. I asked Jason Hoffman to go with me. I told him on the way to Dallas that I was very nervous about the presentation. After the presentation, as we were driving back home, Jason said he understood why I was so nervous. He said that he did not realize that Don Miller was going to be there that night. I just grinned and nodded my head in agreement. The next year, I was invited back to the Adirondacks to what turned out to be the last Maples Conference, to teach the full weekend presentation. Don Miller was there as one of the preachers for the week. He sat through my entire presentation of his material. When it was over, he told me he was very pleased with what the Lord had led me to do.

I had the opportunity a couple of years ago to take a team and go to our son Jim's church in Germany and present the Spending Time with The Master in Prayer Weekend. The church where he is pastor is an

English-speaking, primarily U.S. Military church. It was a wonderful weekend. One of the highlights for me was the first night, in a small group. The question had been asked, "What do you hope to accomplish this weekend?" Everyone was giving some of the very typical answers; then we got to one airman. He said, "I hope I learn how to pray." The rest of us sat there stunned at his honesty. The next day, in the same small group, the question had been asked, "How can we pray for you?" The same airman said, "Pray that I will become the spiritual leader of my home. I am tired of my wife and children being the spiritual leaders." This time we really sat there stunned at the honesty of this young man.

Since then I have heard from my son that this young man came to realize that he had never been saved. He has been saved and baptized. He is becoming the spiritual leader of his home.

Lake Community Baptist Church
Dogwood City, Texas

In May of 2005, I received a phone call from the Lake Community Baptist Church, Dogwood City, Texas, which is located on Highway 155 south of Tyler, Texas, in the Lake Palestine, region. I was asked if I would consider becoming their pastor. I agreed to come and preach for them, talk with them, and pray with them about it. As it turned out, I did agree to become their pastor, and began that assignment in July 2005. I agreed to be there on Sunday morning and night, Wednesday, and to be in the office on Monday and Wednesday. It was a 40 mile trip one way from my house to the church. The church had gone down significantly in attendance. Shortly after we arrived, attendance began to pick up, the Lord began to bless the ministry, and people were being saved. When we got ready to baptize for the first time, there was a huge amount of cleaning that had to be done to the baptistery, because it had been so long since it had been used.

In August 2005, I led them to have a Sunday – Wednesday revival. I did the preaching and we invited our dear friends Jim Bob and Louverl Griffin to do the music. I had the privilege of serving as the Griffin's pastor when I was the pastor at Rusk. I suggested to Jim Bob that the theme of the last night of the revival be "Heaven," and that they sing about heaven and I would preach about heaven. At the conclusion of the service that night, I told the people that if everything we teach

467

and preach about heaven is true, we make way too big a deal over grieving over the death of a Christian. Then I told them, "If I am driving over here for services sometime, and I am in an auto accident and killed, it is alright to grieve for a while. However, you should not still be in great grief six months later. You should be rejoicing in where I have gone." That was on Wednesday night. The very next Sunday night, the driver of an oncoming pickup truck, which was pulling his electrical contracting trailer, went to sleep at the wheel. I had to go to the ditch so that the blow to our car would be a side blow rather than a head on collision. Needless to say, we did not make it to church that night. The next Sunday some of the people said to me that I needed to be a little more careful about the illustrations I use.

I soon discovered that the 80 mile round trip, four times a week, was a little more than I had bargained for and that they really needed someone who lived closer to the church field. As I began to pray about what the Lord would have me to do, a minister friend talked to me about the Camp Ground Baptist Church, Alto, Texas. As I prayed about it and talked to the leadership of the church, it soon became apparent that the Lord wanted me there. So the first of November 2006, I announced my resignation to the Lake Community Baptist Church and accepted the call of the Camp Ground Baptist Church.

Camp Ground Baptist Church, Alto, Texas

On the Sunday before Thanksgiving 2006, I began my responsibilities as pastor of Camp Ground Baptist Church in Alto, Texas. Almost a year before I retired from the North American Mission Board, I had a meeting with the Steering Committee of the Adirondack Baptist Association. During that meeting, I was asked this question, "If the Lord were to let you do what you really want to do before your ministry is over, what would it be?" I looked at them and told them that I did not want to hurt anyone's feelings, but it would not be what I was presently doing. I told them, "If the Lord lets me do what I really want to do, I will pastor a little church somewhere that will let me love on them, and they will love on us."

I am now moving toward my 10th Anniversary as the pastor of Camp Ground Baptist Church, and for almost 10 years, the Lord has been allowing me to live out my dream. This church has been sharing the gospel now for 117 years and counting. This is, by the way, my longest tenure in one church, although I did serve the Adirondack Baptist Association for 12 years. In more ways than I can describe, they have demonstrated their love for us, and I believe that they know that I love them. The Lord has blessed in more ways than I can mention. We have built two additional buildings. First, we built a Pre-school building directly behind the original building. Second, we built a Fellowship Hall building right beside the Sanctuary. We spent $125,000.00 on these two buildings and only had to borrow

$40,000.00, in order to complete the second building. As of the first of May 2016, we only owe a little over $15, 000.00 on the loan.

Birth of Dogwood Trails Baptist Association

I had been the pastor of Camp Ground Baptist Church less than a year, when in August 2007, Lee Welch and I received a phone call from our Director of Missions, Dr. Mike Smith. He wanted to meet us for dinner in Jacksonville, Texas. At that dinner he let us know that the Southern Baptists of Texas Convention had offered him a job as Director of Church Relations and that he had accepted. He also wanted us to know that he would be leaving in two weeks, which would be just a month before the meeting of the three associations that made up the Dogwood Trails Baptist Area. The reason he needed to share this information with Bro. Lee was because he was Chairman of the Area Committee. The reason he needed to share the information with me was because he wanted to recommend to the Area Committee, Olin Boles and me as Co-DOMs. Olin was also a retired DOM who lived within the territory of the Dogwood Trails Baptist Area. He told me that Olin had already agreed to do the job, if I would also agree. I felt like I could accept this responsibility and continue to serve Camp Ground Baptist Church. I did agree, with fear and trembling, because there was such a short period of time to get ready for three annual meetings.

Just getting ready for an annual meeting is a large task. I knew that, because I had done that for 12 years in New York. However, this time there was going to be a final vote on the three associations: Saline, Cherokee, and Henderson merging into one, and the Dogwood Trails Baptist Area would become the Dogwood Trails Baptist Association. There were many concerns, particularly among the long time lay members of the various churches of the three associations, that they were going to lose their identity.

Shortly after the Area Committee elected Olin Boles and me to serve as Co-DOMs, he and I met to discuss how we would divide the work load. Two major things needed to happen. We were going to need a new constitution and by-laws. We were also going to need a plan to show how everything would work without some losing their sense of identity. Olin agreed to work on the constitution, and I told him that, believe it or not, I already had a plan on how to make things work.

When I was in New York, we originally had 10 associations. NAMB and the State Convention let us know that some mergers were going to take place and we would go from 10 associations to 6. This meant that the neighboring association to mine would join with us to make one association that would literally cover the entire top of the State of New York. This meant going to meetings was going to be very tough and time consuming. In an effort to make this merger work, I spent a great deal of time dividing the new territory into five different regions. The only time we would ask everyone to come together in one location would be at the annual meeting. I spent many long hours working on this plan, all to no avail. In the end the other association decided to make a go of it on their own, which meant that they would be assigned a DOM, who could spend very little time with them. I told Olin that I still had that plan in written form, and I thought I could make some minor adjustments to it so that the three associations could see how they would still be three distinct regions, who were part of one association. Olin and I spent the month before the three Annual Meetings having question and answer sessions on how things would work, and why it would be beneficial and more effective to have one association instead of three.

October and the three Annual Meetings finally came. There was pretty close to record attendance at all three meetings. There was lively discussion, but at all three meetings the vote to merge into one association passed with a very clear majority. Another issue that made this a somewhat tense time was that a majority of the churches had already aligned themselves with the Southern Baptists of Texas Convention, and those churches who were still part of the Baptist

General Convention of Texas were concerned that they were going to be looked down upon. We were able to convince enough of them that this was not true, that it did not create a big negative vote concerning the merger of the three associations into one.

All of this was accomplished while there was not a full-time Director of Missions. Olin and I served for a full year as Co-DOMs. I was also a member of the DOM Search Committee, as was Lee Welch. One day Bro. Lee, Jason Hoffman, and I were driving to a trustee meeting at Piney Woods Baptist Camp. I asked Lee if he realized that at some point he was going to have to resign from the DOM Search Committee. He asked me why. I told him it was because he was going to be the next DOM. He laughed and said that was a job he was certain he would never do. I told him to be careful about making such a statement, because I knew another pastor of FBC, Rusk, who had made a similar statement, and ended up spending 12 years as a DOM. Jason caught what I was saying and laughed.

After going through the interview process with several men, there did come the time when the rest of the committee asked Bro. Lee to resign from the committee and submit his resume. I remember the meeting when the committee voted on Lee. One of the committee members was real big on us following the letter of the law on the process we had adopted at the beginning of our proceedings. At this particular meeting I suggested that we needed to move Bro. Lee's name to the top of the list and vote on considering him before we went any further with anyone else. This one member of the committee spoke up and said that, if we did that, we would be violating the process we had all agreed upon. I responded by saying that I was so sure that Lee was the man for the job, that I could not honestly look at anyone else until he was resolved one way or the other. Then I asked if an unofficial poll could be taken. I said that, if I was the only one that felt the way I did, I would agree to back off and go with the process. The chairman of the committee took an unofficial straw poll of the committee, and everyone in the room but this one man agreed with me. When he saw this, He also agreed to scrap the procedure and consider Lee Welch to be our next DOM. We then voted to invite Bro. Lee and Marolyn to an interview, and as they say, the rest is history.

At the first Annual Meeting of the Dogwood Trails Baptist Association, which was held at the Southside Baptist Church, in Palestine, Texas, Bro. Lee was elected the first DOM of the newly formed association. At this meeting he was installed as our Executive Director and there was a reception in honor of him and Marolyn.

2010 Winter Olympics – Vancouver, British Columbia, Canada

Early in the year 2009, while serving as Co-DOM, I was also the Missions Committee Chairman for the association. I decided to look into the possibility of taking a team from East Texas to the Winter Olympics in Vancouver, Canada. The more I looked into it, the more it looked like something that we could do. I checked with the Resort Ministry Director I knew at NAMB, Jeff Wagner, and got the name and how to get in touch with the person they had hired to do the preparation work for the ministry to the 2010 Olympics. I found out that there would be two different training weeks in August 2009. I picked out one of those weeks, flew from Tyler, to Houston, to Seattle, to Vancouver, and rented me a car in Vancouver. It was a good week of gathering the information I would need in order to train the team from here that would go.

There were 12 people from our association that went. We stayed in a Christian Camp facility along with about 100 other volunteers. We had about an hour train ride into the city every day and that same train ride back at night. We were assigned to a train station location where people would get off of the train and catch a bus to the Olympic Ice Skating facility. At our station, we had free hot chocolate and water. We also had a table filled with gospel tracts. There were also gospel trading pens. "Trading Pens" at an Olympic or International Sporting Event is a really big deal. Sometimes people would have the time to stop and let us explain what our "More Than Gold" trading pen meant. Other times we just had to give it to them and hope they would read the card that was attached to it that explained the meaning.

One day, during the middle of the day, a young woman came up to me. She had one of our "More Than Gold" pens in her hand. She said, "You gave me this pen." She had a camera in her other hand and wanted to know if someone would take our picture. I found Virginia and got her to come over and take a picture of us. She had gotten off of the train there because she lived near that train station. I asked her if she needed to talk and she said that she did. She and I pulled off to the side and she began to weep. She and her husband were having problems. She thought he was going to leave her and their children.

I found out that her background was "First Nation" which is the same thing as "Native American" in the U.S. This of course meant that her religious background was cult religions. As we talked, it was like the little space where we were standing became "Holy Ground," and in just a matter of minutes she was inviting Jesus Christ into her heart. Her name is Crystal. I am convinced that the Lord sent me to Vancouver just for that encounter with Crystal. Two days later she came by our aid station with her husband and children so that we could meet them. Virginia and I communicated with her for a long time after we got home from this trip. Praise God for the opportunity to be involved in her life!!!

Summer Olympics 2012 – London, England

After the good experience of taking a team of volunteers from East Texas to the Winter Olympics in 2010, I decided to offer the opportunity to take a team to London, for the 2012 Summer Olympics. We ended up with a team from East Texas of 15 that went to London. They were involved in a variety of ministries that mainly were supportive of ministries that were being conducted by local church groups in the greater London area during the time that the Olympics were in progress. Once again we stayed at a Christian Retreat Center. It was a very comfortable place to stay. The biggest problem was the long train ride every day to get to our places of service. Sometimes we had to rush to catch a train back to our sleeping quarters so that we did not have a long wait for the next train. The long train ride gave us many opportunities to share our faith with others on the train with us. The biggest challenge for sure was making sure we got on the right train when we got to the Tube in London. Getting on the wrong train could and did cause problems in getting to our assignments.

One of my most interesting experiences was while taking a religious census for a local church. I had the opportunity to visit with a man whose family survived the bombings of World War II. He pointed out the spot where one of the bombs landed, and talked to us about how his family survived that time.

Then there was the day we were working with the Victoria Park Baptist Church. We were out in front of the church. Jason Hoffman was over at the corner of the building. He called me over to look at the cornerstone. The date and the name of the preacher were on the stone for the dedication service. The name was Rev. C.H. Spurgeon. I stood there speechless to realize that I was ministering with a church where one of the greatest preachers of all time had preached. It was said about Charles Hadden Spurgeon that, no matter who was in his home on Saturday night at 8:30 P.M., he would excuse himself by saying, "I have to do the most important thing I do all week tomorrow morning. I must get my rest, so I can be at my best." Then he would go to bed.

Ministry to Alto High School Athletes

When I came to Camp Ground Baptist Church, we already had two of the coaches in our church. I have always enjoyed being around the High School Athletic Program wherever I have been. As you know, if you have gotten this far in this book, I have one brother and his career has been built around high school athletics. In fact, when we moved to Rockdale, Texas, my brother was already the Athletic Director and Head Football Coach at Caldwell, Texas, which was only 25 miles away. Someone in Rockdale asked me how my brother and I ended up in the careers we had chosen. I told him that I guess it was because we were both looking for a low profile job.

After I had been pastor at Camp Ground for several months, I went to the high school and met the Athletic Director and Head Football Coach, Keith Gardner. He knew of my brother and my nephew because of his long time involvement in athletics in Texas high schools. I told him that I wanted to support him any way that I could. I told him that, in other places where I had been, I had worked with the coach and fed the football players one day after practice during two-a-day workouts in August. I told him, if he would like for me to, I would be happy to do that for his team when the next season started. He was very receptive to the idea, and told me that I could also speak to the boys at that time. I told him that I would get back to him when the next season rolled around. He was very grateful for my offer of help. In fact he told me that I was the first Anglo pastor that had offered to help him since he had been in Alto. The next August, a tradition was started with the football team. On an agreed upon day, I ordered pizza from Pizza Hut and took it to the field house to feed the team and coaches. Before they ate, I shared a brief devotional with them. There are a number of athletes in Alto who don't remember my name, but they do know me as the "pizza preacher." Over the last several years that has been expanded to include a day with the cheerleaders, and the last couple of years has included the boy's basketball team at the beginning of basketball season. In recent years, I have gotten the Alto Ministerial Association involved in the feeding of the football team and the cheerleaders.

At a point in time, Coach Keith Gardner and his wife Carlynn joined our church as did his son Clint and his wife Amy. I had the privilege of baptizing Clint and Amy's two oldest daughters in the spring of 2016.

Our children and grandchildren all live a great distance from us, and so getting to see them on a regular basis is not possible. Therefore, we have pretty much adopted the children and youth in our church and our community as ours. I learned a long time ago that the way you let children and youth know that they are important to you is to show up at the things that are important to them. Therefore, going to ballgames and other events is a way of showing the young people and their parents that you really care about them.

Since becoming a pastor in the Alto area, our focus has been on events involving the children and youth of Alto. One day I was sitting in the waiting room of my doctor's office, when a man from Alto came in. He saw me and came over and said he appreciated the support I gave to the students in Alto. His son played on the football and basketball teams. I was at an Area Track Meet and a lady came up to me and wanted to know if I had a grandchild on the track team. I told her no. Then she asked me why I came to all of the meets. Before I could say anything, the woman I was talking to said, "Because he loves them."

I really believe that my call to pastor Camp Ground Baptist Church also included giving me an open door to minister to the community of Alto. For the last three years I have also been the President of the Alto Ministerial Association. We do not have as many of the ministers in the Alto area involved in the association as I wish we did, but for those who have chosen to be involved, a very close bond of love and respect has developed. We, as a Ministerial Association, are blessed in that we have a wonderful relationship with the Alto ISD, with both administration and faculty. I was asked one time to come and talk to one of the football players who had made some bad choices. I went to the school and the High School Principal found me an office where I could talk with him in private. After it was over, I told the Principal I appreciated his cooperation. He said, "Anytime, in fact anytime you want to come and just walk the halls, feel free to do so; we are better off when you come around." I was at a football game and visiting with the Alto ISD Superintendent. He encouraged me to come from time to time at lunch time and visit with the students while they are having lunch. I have already mentioned the special times that I have with various groups of students which include bringing a devotional. I am never told what I can and cannot say to them. However, let me say that I have been at this long enough that I know the kind of things that, if I said them, could potentially cause problems for the school officials. Therefore, I stay away from those things.

Snatched from the Gates of Hell

We were on our way to Dallas when I received a text from one of the ladies in our church. She shared with me that the husband of another one of the ladies in our church was in the hospital in Tyler, Texas. I called Katrina Davis and she told me that her husband Jonathan had had a serious seizure during the night and that they were in the hospital in Tyler, Texas. I told her I was on the way to a doctor's visit in Dallas, but that I could turn around and come to Tyler right then.

She encouraged me to go on to my appointment. I told her we would be in Tyler, as soon as possible. Virginia and I arrived in Tyler that afternoon. Jonathan is a native of Alto, and by the time I got there, many of his friends had gathered to show their concern for him and pray for him. We went into the room where we found his wife and parents. Katrina told me about the events of the night before. Everyone, including the medical staff, was greatly concerned about his condition.

I need to say that I have asked Jonathan's permission to share the things I am about to share. I would never share anything this personal that involved someone else without their permission.

I went to visit Jonathan every day that week. He was in a coma-like condition most of the time, and therefore did not know anything about what was going on. His wife and I were both concerned about the fact that Jonathan had never made a profession of faith in Christ as his Savior. I promised the Lord, his wife and myself that, when he woke up, I was going to talk to him about his relationship with the Lord. I had asked the Lord to wake him up so that I could talk to him about his relationship with Jesus Christ

482

We drove to Tyler after church on Sunday. He had now been in the hospital for nearly a week. When we arrived, his wife Katrina met me in the hall and told me that he was awake. She told me that he had told her something when he woke up that she wanted to tell me. He told her that he had seen hell. He described what he had seen in great detail. He said that he was invited into Hell; then he saw a picture of his wife and knew she could not go with him, because she was a Christian. He told them he did not want to go where his wife could not go. When we got to his hospital room, I asked her and my wife to stay in the hall and not let anyone else in so that I could talk to him.

When I went in the room, Jonathan was awake, alert, and knew who I was. We visited a few minutes; he shared with me some of the things that he had shared with his wife. I then shared with him that I had asked the Lord to wake him up so that I could share with him how to become a Christian. The bottom line is that on that Sunday afternoon, Jonathan Davis invited Jesus Christ to be the Savior and Lord of his life. After he trusted Christ as his Savior, I brought his wife and my wife into the room, and he told them what he had just done.

What I have not mentioned is that Jonathan had had a very serious problem with alcoholic drinks most of his adult life, which may have contributed to the medical condition he was experiencing. Everyone who knew him knew about this problem. When the Lord saved Him, He also took that problem away from him. He has had many opportunities to witness to his friends.

Jonathan continues to have health issues, but praise God, his spiritual issue has been permanently healed. Like me and others, Jonathan continues to have health issues that he may live with the rest of his life. The good news is that he does not have to deal with them alone, and one day he will spend eternity in heaven with his wife and all of God's children. Praise God!

Both of his daughters were saved and baptized in our church, and then the Lord gave me the opportunity to lead their Daddy to a saving knowledge of Jesus Christ. This is another example of the extraordinary activity of God where He allows ordinary people to be a part of His activity.

God Is Gracious During Difficult Times

This special relationship I have had with the athletic program has put me in the position to be able to minister to both the athletes and coaches when the unthinkable happened before all of our eyes on a Friday night last fall.

On October 16, 2015, along with a High School Football Stadium full of people, I experienced one of the most difficult experiences I have ever observed. We watched as an Alto High School football player stumbled off the field with the help of two of his coaches. In a matter of minutes it became obvious that something very serious was going on.

I was sitting in my reserved seat which is on the 4th row, right behind the home team bench. The player stumbled off the field and was sitting in front of me with his back to me. I could not see his face; however, I could see the look of horror and disbelief on the faces of the coaches and medical staff who were trying to help him. I have had a very close relationship with the team and the coaches for several years. I sat there for a while trying to decide what I needed to do. Nurses had already come out of the stands, and were administering CPR. When I heard one of the players shout, "Start breathing," I felt I needed to go on the field. Shortly after I arrived at the bench, two African American pastors came to me and we joined hands and began to pray. Players and coaches were kneeling and praying all over the field. The opposing team went to their locker room and the Alto coaches sent their team to the locker room. The coach asked me to go to the locker room with the team. When I got to the locker room, there was a lot of confusion and concern among the team members. I gathered them together to have prayer. Before I prayed, I asked them if they would agree with me that we were going to trust God, whatever happened. They all nodded their heads yes. I prayed with them and then told them to go and sit at their lockers until we knew what had happened. I then went to each one of them and prayed with them individually. One of the players, who is a strong Christian, pointed out one of his teammates he wanted me to question about his salvation. When I got to that young man, I did question him, and he assured me that he was a Christian.

When we heard the life flight chopper arrive, they all ran out to the fence that surrounds the stadium to see what was happening. After the chopper left, I told one of the senior captains that he needed to get his team back inside the locker room. The father of one of the team members had been in the locker room with me. He was also an EMT. When we got back into the locker room, he told them something I did not know. He said that, if there was not some sign of life, they would not have put him in the chopper. They would have taken him in an ambulance instead.

In a few minutes the coaches came in to tell the boys that the game had been called, and they all needed to get a shower and go home. Then he saw me and asked me to lead them in prayer before they left. I dropped to my knees; the whole team and all the coaches gathered around, and I prayed.

When I got back out to the stadium, the people were slowly and quietly leaving. I told my wife that we were leaving to drive to Tyler to the hospital. Shortly after we got to the hospital, it became obvious that the physical condition of Cam'ron Matthews was very critical. As you can imagine, the hallway outside the critical care unit of East Texas Medical Center was filled with family, coaches, teammates, classmates and concerned citizens of Alto. About 2:00 A.M. Saturday morning, I was sitting with some of the coaches, when one of the younger coaches came and sat down beside me. He asked me, "Bro. Jim, what are we going to do?" I told him that we were going to trust the one who could see the bigger picture. The Head Coach was one of those sitting there. I looked at him and the rest of the coaches and said to them, "It is important how we handle this. We need to understand that others will be looking at us to see how we will handle this." Coach Gould agreed with me. We decided to go home a short time later, and we got home about 4:00 A.M. We got a few hours sleep and woke up late morning. We decided to go back to the hospital, and we stayed there all afternoon with probably at least 100 people, which included most of his teammates, his coaches, many of his classmates, and many others who were very concerned.

One of the things that impressed everyone from Alto was that several of the members of the opposing team from Carlisle High School, had come to the hospital both Friday night and again Saturday morning. Some of the local citizens of Alto had called for a prayer vigil at the Alto High School football stadium for 5:00 P.M. Saturday evening. It was at that same time that the doctors finally determined they had done all they could do and Cam'ron Jamell Matthews was pronounced, gone to be with the Lord. The vigil at the stadium was held anyway, and I am told that it was an amazingly awesome experience.

In the aftermath of this tragedy, a number of good things have happened. Several of us pastors and other counselors came to the school on Monday to help with the grieving process with the students. I personally had the opportunity to lead three high school students to the Lord on Monday. I went back to the school on Tuesday to help any way I could. I had been there about two hours when one of the football players came looking for me. He was the same player that had shared with me on Friday night that he knew that he was a Christian. When he sat down to talk to me, he said, "You asked me Friday night if I knew I was going to heaven. When I said yes, I lied, but I want to know." I shared the gospel with him and in a few minutes he was praying to receive Christ as his Lord and Savior.

The memorial service for Cam'ron Jamell Matthews was held the following Saturday. It had to be held at the Rusk High School Coliseum to hold the crowd that attended. It was a sad time, but at the same time it was a time of rejoicing over a young life that had been lived well. Cam'ron was a wonderful Christian young man. The testimony of his young life loomed large that day.

In looking back, let me just say that I was very proud of Head Coach Paul Gould and his coaching staff. I was proud of the way they handled themselves in the midst of this tragedy and in the aftermath of having to continue the football season. One of the lead sports stories in the fall of 2015 was what happened in Alto, Texas, on that Friday night.

I was also very proud of a couple who are members of our church. Coach Clint Gardner and his wife Amy were there for the Matthews family throughout that whole ordeal. They never left their side at the hospital. I also know that they have continued to be there for them in the days and months since that very trying weekend.

We are now just a month away from this school year being over. Everyone has had plenty of life experiences since that Friday night. However, I am sure that for everyone who was in that stadium on that October Friday night, some impressions have been made on them that will always be a part of their life experience.

This should awaken us to the reality that it really is true that we can be living our lives with everything seemingly going well one moment, and then the next moment we are facing our eternal destiny. I pray that as time goes on, many more will come to know Christ as their Savior because of the testimony of the life of Cam'ron Matthews.

Head Coach Paul Gould and my wife and I had a conversation on the Thursday after the tragic event about all of the things that had been going on since the tragic death of Cam'ron Matthews. Coach Gould told us about an experience that he had the day before with one of his players who seemed to be having as hard a time as anyone dealing with the loss of his teammate and close friend. He said that he took him into the equipment room to talk to him in a place where they could be alone. He said that, after his player had been crying for some time, he suddenly noticed that the young man was smiling. He asked him why he was smiling and the young man pointed at a bag and said, "Cam's name." The coach looked down and his player was pointing at their "12th Man" bag. At the beginning of the year, the coach had pulled down one of the equipment bags used by one of the players from the previous year. It is a bag they take to every game which has extra equipment in it.

The bag he had pulled down to use as the "12th Man" bag for this year was the equipment bag the player who had died the previous week had used, and it still had his number and name on it. The grieving player said, "Look, Coach, Cam will be going with us to all of the games after all." The Coach told me that he was sure that it was divine intervention that caused him to choose that particular bag. He was very grateful for how much it had helped his player.

When I accepted the role as pastor of Camp Ground Baptist Church, I had no particular vision of some kind of outstanding growth in the church. I just wanted to be faithful to the Lord and to them. God did bless and we had some amazing growth. In the spring and summer of 2013, over a period of two and a half months, 15 teenagers and young adults were saved and most of them were baptized. For various reasons, many of those are now attending church somewhere else. Over the last couple of years the attendance has dropped off quite a bit. I have felt like at times that maybe they would be better off if I would step aside and give them the chance to call a younger pastor. So far they don't seem to want that to happen. At this point I am doing my best to be faithful to them in proclaiming God's Word, and ministering to them as much as I am physically able. Because of my back condition, I am not physically able to do the things I could do. My prayer is that I will not be one of those pastors who does not know when it is time to step aside and let someone else take over. However, I also pray that I will remain faithful in service to the Lord, as long as His hand is on my ministry.

I am going through an interesting experience in these latter years of active ministry. Our church is not growing in attendance, in fact we are losing ground in attendance. There is a small group that is staying faithful and I have given them every opportunity to say it was time for me to move on. In fact, I have even tried to make that decision for them and they continue to encourage me that they believe I need to stay.

Certainly from an age and health point of view, I could easily say that it is time to call it quits. The problem is that, so far, I have not gotten freedom from the Lord to do that. Will that time come? Without a doubt, it will come at a time when it is not only best for me, but also best for the church.

I am blessed that the Lord has allowed me to serve this little group of people as their pastor. I receive unconditional love from them. When they say, "Bro. Jim, I love you." I not only hear their words, I look in their eyes and see their love. "Dear Lord, help me to be faithful to you and to this group of people for as long as you lead me to stay."

I am so grateful for those families who have remained faithful to the ministry of this church, which has had a long and rich history in the southern part of Cherokee County. I am particularly grateful for those young children and teen-agers who have decided to remain an active part of the ministry of the church. It is an encouragement to me each Sunday morning when I look out and see those young families and their children and youth who regularly attend the services.

Thank you, Camp Ground Baptist Church, for allowing me the privilege of serving as your pastor. Thank you for taking me into your hearts.

Finish Well

A few years ago, a dear friend of mine, a deacon at FBC, Rusk, and a retired Minister of Education, George Nielsen, went home to be with the Lord. George and his wife Tommie had been strong supporters of my ministry when I was pastor at FBC, Rusk. We had gone on several mission trips together. When he passed away, his granddaughter Meredith Sinclair Goz, who now lives in Russia with her husband Misha, could not come home for the funeral. They have been serving all of their married life with Campus Crusade for Christ in Russia, which is Misha's home.

Because she could not come to the funeral, Meredith sent a tribute to her grandfather that she had written. It was very moving, and also very true. She concluded by saying that her grandfather finished well, and he did. I have thought about that many times, and I don't know much more that you could ask than for someone who knew you really well to say, "You finished well."

I started this project with a great deal of fear and trembling, not really believing that my story is all that significant. Frankly, I am still convinced that my story is not any more significant than anyone else's story. I am just an ordinary man, but along the way the Lord has allowed me to meet some very extraordinary people, and be involved in some pretty extraordinary activities. That was not because I was any better than anyone else; it was simply because I made myself available to the Lord at those times. I can only wonder how many opportunities I missed, because I was not available or was not in the position spiritually for the Lord to use me as He intended. However, it is a feeble waste of time to let Satan get you caught up in "what might have been."

What Really Matters

I have been debating with myself for some time now about how I would bring all of this to a close. The title of the book is "The Meanderings of a One Horse Preacher." Hopefully by now, you know that the book has nothing to do with a horse. Pretty Boy, the horse in the picture, is not mine, although I did have a horse at one time. As I close this book, hopefully there will still be some "Meandering" left in me.

Recently I attended the birthday party of a young man that has been like a grandchild to me all of his life. His name is Jordan Beard. Jordan asked me how I was going to finish the book. I told him I did not know. Now I know.

I want to finish by talking about what matters to me, and what I think really matters in life, at least from my point of view. If I had been asked many years ago what I believed really matters, my answer might have been somewhat different than it is now. There is some real advantage to looking at life, when you know that most of your life has already been lived.

First: In the things that really matter in life, the first thing must be **my relationship to Jesus Christ.** I have already shared with you my salvation experience. I made a decision very young in life, but really did not know what I was doing. Even into years of pastoral ministry, I let pride keep me from acknowledging that I never had really given my heart to Jesus Christ. Then through the influence of a dear pastor friend, I was able to release all of that and give my heart and life to Jesus Christ. Nothing else matters, if you do not know Christ as your Savior and Lord. In all of those years that I struggled with Christ being first in my life, the problem was not in a lack of desire for that to be true. The problem was in a relationship with Christ that was flawed from the beginning.

When I was a six year old boy, I am sure my heart was stirred in the right direction by the things I heard at home, in Sunday School, and church services. However, when the time came that I wanted to make a decision for Christ, apparently too much was taken for granted. You might wonder how I could go so many years without making things right. I also wonder about that sometimes myself. I think, because I grew up in such a strong Christian home, the way my brother and I lived our lives was going to look much like a Christian whether we were or not. It was when I got into college and began studying the Bible in more depth, that it did not make any sense to me that I could remember everything about the night I was baptized, and absolutely nothing about the night I was "saved."

For many years, pride kept me from admitting that I did not really know Christ as my personal Savior. What a wonderful release it was when my dear friend Pat Maloney asked me, "What is really wrong with you?" When I told him that the problem was that I just did not think I was saved, then my dear friend said, "If that is your problem, then get saved. I know you know how, because I have watched you tell hundreds how to be saved." In that moment I was released, and I cried out to God to save me and He did. Praise God!

Second: My brother and I were raised in an atmosphere where **family** mattered. We were not raised by perfect parents, but we were raised by parents who wanted to do the best that they could possibly do for their two sons. That did not just mean having things, although we always had more than enough. It meant teaching us what they believed to be the right things that would make us better men. It meant that they taught us valuable life lessons that we did not really understand at times, until we became adults.

My brother and I were normal brothers. We fussed and fought with one another like most brothers do. However, if someone else was going to fight with one of us, they were probably going to have to fight with both of us. I could tell you many humorous stories about things that we did that caused us problems with our parents. Let me just say that, in doing those things, it seemed I was always the one who did the final thing that really caused problems.

We survived and, I guess more importantly, our parents survived. I can tell you this, my brother and I look back on our childhood, and we never doubt that our parents loved us. We know that they were motivated by wanting to do what was best for us. I think that both of us have tried to live our lives as adults the same way. I am grateful for my brother and his children and grandchildren. Recently my nephew had a very difficult situation that was beyond his control. He handled himself very well. I wrote him and told him how proud I was of him. He wrote me back and said, "Love you, Buddy; it's Carl and Frances helping me. We have a wonderful family. Heaven will be a great reunion." If you do not remember from earlier in the book, Carl and Frances are my parents, his grandparents. Their testimony lives on from heaven. The Lord gave my brother a wonderful, strong, Christian woman for a wife. Over the years she has been a blessing to all of us.

When I was in seminary, the Lord brought Virginia Patterson into my life. It was one of those moments that, literally the first time I saw her, the Lord told me that she was to be my wife. It took a long time for that relationship to develop. Two weeks after that, we met and spent Sunday afternoon together, two weeks later we were engaged, and four months after that we were married. That was 52 years ago. To say that we really did not know one another when we got married would certainly be an understatement, but we did know that the Lord had brought us together. I am not sure that we could even say that we really knew what loving one another was, after only knowing one another for about four and a half months. But again, we knew the Lord had brought us together, and He has nurtured that love for Him and for one another over the years.

The Lord was gracious to us and gave us two sons. James Lonnie Goforth, Jr. was actually born one month before our first anniversary. I had always wanted to name a son after myself, if I had one, and

Virginia was gracious in agreeing to it. Jim was born during my second year in seminary. I look back on those days and wonder how in the world we managed being new parents, me finishing school, working part time, serving as pastor of a church, and Virginia working full-time. Praise God, through His strength, we survived.

Our second son Thomas Bryan was born while we were in Mississippi. This was shortly before we moved to Ohio. Tom was born in May of one year and we moved to Ohio in June of the next year. So 12 of his first 13 years were spent in the state of Ohio.

We are not a perfect family. Our flaws as a family are as real as any family. There were some things that were very important to Virginia and me, as our boys were growing up. One was that we wanted to be careful not to teach them that they could or could not do certain things because their dad was a preacher. If there was not a better reason to give them for what we did not allow them to do than, "Dad is a preacher," we just did not give that reason. We felt like, if it was wrong for our children to do, then it was wrong for any child to do. I am sure that just like I did not always agree with the decisions my dad made for us, my sons also did not agree with some of the decisions we made for them. However, it was our conviction that we were the ones responsible to the Lord for decisions about right and wrong for our children, until they reached the age of responsibility.

I am convinced that one of the things that is wrong with the home in America today is the unwillingness of too many parents to say no to their children. One of the things I learned from dad was that, when he said no, he did not have to give me a reason. "Because I said so," had to be a good enough reason. He did not have to explain himself to me. He was the dad; I was the son, and I was expected to respect that authority. That was a valuable lesson for me to learn and it was one that I passed on to our boys. If I chose to explain to them, I would, but if for some reason I did not choose to explain, then "because I said so" must be good enough.

You are told that if you take that approach with your children, they will grow up not respecting you. The problem with children not respecting their parents is not in the parents not explaining every decision; it is with the inconsistency of the decisions being made.

A major part of being family is understanding that there are God-given roles in the life of all families. When we follow God's guidelines, most of the time all things work out best for everyone in the family.

I am happy to say that, here in the latter years of our lives, Virginia and I have a great relationship with our children. Part of that had to come from learning how to let them be adults, when they became adults. That may have been the hardest learning curve of all, because parents never get over being concerned about their children, and their grandchildren, when they come along.

Let me digress a little bit and talk about a time when our sons had a serious conversation with me. I was celebrating my 70th birthday. Our older son Jim was a pastor in the St. Louis, Missouri, area. Tom was living in New York City. Virginia and I drove up to St. Louis and Tom and Karen flew in from New York City. We spent the weekend together; then celebrated my birthday on Sunday. On Monday, Jim, Tom, and I drove to another part of Missouri, to a Trout Farm/Resort to fish for a few days. On Monday night after dinner, Jim and Tom wanted to talk with me. They told me that they got the impression that I did not care if I lived much longer. I told them they were probably right. Then they told me that my family really did care about how much longer I lived. They talked to me about taking better care of myself.

At the time we had this conversation, I had just turned 70 years of age. I am 5'7 ½" tall, and I weighed 235 pounds. Needless to say, I was extremely over weight. We talked for a good long while that night, and I promised to try to do better. Today is April 30, 2016, I am 76 years old. This morning when I weighed, I weighed 163 pounds. I am very grateful that my sons cared enough about their "old dad" to have that conversation with him. It was the motivation I needed to begin making the right decisions about my health.

I did not go on a diet; I have been on most of the popular ones. I have lost and gained back more weight than I want to imagine. I told my wife that the only way I was going to do it was to develop discipline in my eating habits. It has been a simple formula for me. Rule number one: When my stomach gets full, I quit eating regardless of how much food is still on my plate. Rule number two: Eat three meals per day. Rule number three: No more late night snacks. Rule number four: Quit drinking the huge number of diet drinks I was drinking every day. My doctor son told me that the sodium in the diet drinks was as harmful as the sugar in regular drinks. So when I do drink some kind of cola, I drink the real thing. Rule number five: I eat anything I want to eat, but in smaller portions. Therefore, I never do have cravings for foods I miss.

In my old age, I was headed toward being very heavy and having to increase the size of my clothes almost every year. It was not a pretty picture, as many could testify. I am now convinced that, for very many people, the key to weight control is summed up in one word, "discipline." That is not true for everyone; some have a medical reason why weight control is an issue, and should follow the advice of their doctor. For me, however, it was all about discipline. I realize I am taking a risk talking about this in a book, but it has now been nearly seven years, and I think I have learned something that works for me.

By the way, let me mention one other thing. Gluttony is a sin that the Bible condemns. However, it has become one of the acceptable sins for many Christians. When the Lord convicted me about my sin problem, I confessed it publically to the church where I am pastor. I also gave them permission to chastise me, if they saw continuing evidence of the sin of gluttony in my life. A few months later, at a church fellowship meal, one of my church members called me to task for the amount of food on my plate. He did it in a kind way, and I thanked him for it. People are watching our lives.

Third: My relationship to Christ, to my family, and now **my relationship to my church** sum up the things that I believe really matter in life. I said much about these at the beginning, but I felt a need to close by coming back to the things that molded me into the person I have become.

As I think about church, my heart goes immediately to the local body of believers. The majority of times in the New Testament, when there was discussion about the Ecclesia, it was referring to a local body of believers in Jesus Christ. Therefore, my first thought, when I think about church, is the Market St. Baptist Church on the east side of Houston, Texas. In those days, the church was located on Market St. Road, in a community known as Greens Bayou. In that community, most things centered around three things: the church, the family, and the school. The school almost never planned anything that competed with the normal operations of the churches. Community activities were rarely in conflict with church schedules.

As I think about growing up in that community, I realized that it was not just my parents that helped shape who I became; it was also many other adults who were members of that church, whose values were similar to those of my own parents. I realize that I have just given a lot of attention to the importance of the family. It would seem that I am endorsing putting family activities over church activities.

Let me tell you some important family activities that don't seem to have much priority anymore. I believed that, when my dad, mother, brother, and I got into our car and went to Sunday School, that was a family activity. When we sat together in church until my brother and I were old enough to know how to behave in church, that was a family activity. When we attended almost every extracurricular activity of our church, that was a family activity.

Now it seems that it is just the opposite; any activities, outside the church that we or our children might be involved in, are a good excuse to miss Sunday School, church service, or both. Now we are teaching our children that keeping our commitment to outside of church extracurricular activities is more important than keeping the "10 Commandments." "Remember the Sabbath day to keep it holy." We have become obsessed as a society with teaching our children how to run faster, play ball better, ride a horse better, etc. Our child is going to be the one that becomes a pro in whatever activity it may be, and make a ton of money.

I have been watching the annual NFL draft of college football players the last few days. When you think about how many young men play high school football, and how few of them go on to actually become really good college football players, and finally, how few of that number are considered good enough at having a shot at playing professional football, the numbers are staggering. When you measure that by the amount of time, energy, and money that is invested by so many families for their child to become a star in something, it gives cause to wonder about priorities.

If you then factor in the fact that learning how to do all these things better than the next child does not prepare them for the harsh realities of life, then it is really time to stop and reexamine our priorities. Learning how to do all of these activities, even when they are done really well, will not prepare a child for that first temptation to drink alcohol or take drugs, but Sunday School and church services might. Learning how to do all these activities will not help when trying to decide to be honest or dishonest, but Sunday School and church might. Sunday School and church services might help them make the right decision about whether or not to engage in sexual activity before marriage.

Even as I was writing the above paragraph, images came on the TV of a young man who had won college football's highest award. He was selected in the first round of the NFL draft, and was given every opportunity to be a starting quarterback in the NFL. Because of his choices off the field, he was cut from his football team. Because of poor relationship choices, the images of him on TV were his mug shots as he was being arrested.

Is that story sometimes repeated when parents have done all they could do to provide the right spiritual leadership? Yes it is, but I am convinced that the child has a better chance at making the right decisions as an adult, when there has been a consistent Christian example set for them at home and at church.

The reason that my brother and I did not grow up resenting the amount of time we spent at church was because church was a family activity. When we got to church, we were not just attending church; we were involved in what was happening. A good portion of the time we observed our parents, not just participating in what was happening, but a good portion of the time they were providing leadership in the church.

You might say that was well and good for you, but your boys did not have the same option, because you were always the pastor. That is the very reason that, when we told our boys what we were going to do as a family, we never based that on the fact that I was the pastor, and they had to be there. As they got a little older, if there were meetings I had to attend because of who I was, we would let them decide about attending with us. My argument for what we did is, "The proof is in the pudding." What I mean by that is that we have two sons who are not perfect, but who love the Lord and love His church.

There was one very positive example in Camp Ground Baptist Church, with one of our younger families who have remained faithful to our little church. During a time when a number of other younger families have decided to attend church somewhere else, this family has remained faithful to our church. I recently commented to the wife and mother of their three children how much I appreciated them coming to our church, when so many other churches could offer them so much more. She responded back by saying, "We just love the way our children are loved on here." Most of those who are doing the loving are grandparent or great grandparent age for the children.

A few months ago, the two older girls in this family wanted to talk to me after church. They both wanted me to know that over the last several weeks they both came to know Jesus Christ as their personal Savior and Lord. They came forward the next Sunday to make their decision public before the church, and present themselves as candidates for baptism. We then began to work on a date when all of their extended families could be present to participate in their baptism. During the week before they were to be baptized, I got a note from their mother indicating that they might need some extra pews for them on that Sunday. When that Sunday rolled around, literally half of our church sanctuary was filled with family members and friends who had come to see two elementary age children baptized into the fellowship. This family made, becoming a member of the church, a really big deal for these girls. I suspect the girls were given a memory that day they will never forget.

This is an example of the balance that can be achieved in a family. Their dad and mother both teach and coach in our school. One of the granddads that was present is a retired coach. One of the uncles who attended the baptism service is a former NFL football player. I had told the mother before the service that the message for the day should be particularly helpful for one of their co-workers who had been through a great tragedy in her life. The next Sunday the young mother said she had something she wanted to tell me. She said when she got home from church that Sunday, one of the family members had pulled her aside and said I need to tell you that your pastor's sermon was just for me today. She said she then got everyone's attention and told them she had a question she wanted to ask them, and that she wanted them to answer her very seriously. She then asked them, "How many of you felt like my pastor was preaching directly to you this morning?" She then told me that every adult in the room raised their hand. She said I just wanted you to know that your sermon wasn't just for one person last week.

Other families in our church have also been faithful to bring their children as a family to church every Sunday. We have watched them grow from little children to young people before our eyes. Being in church as a family has made a tremendous difference in the lives of these children and the decisions they have made in their lives. We have seen them, one by one, come to know the Lord as their personal Savior at a young age. Their spiritual lives are more mature than some of the adults who only come occasionally.

Extended Family

Fifty two years ago, I became a part of my extended family, which was a much larger family than I had known. I have one brother. My wife Virginia is one of eight children. The first time I met her family that was still at home, which was about half of the family, it was with the intention of asking for her hand in marriage. My soon to be father-in-law, who had ministered to the Native Americans in Oklahoma, had become the pastor of the Barataria Baptist Church in Lafitte, Louisiana, which was as far south as you could go without getting out of your car and getting into a boat. On a Sunday afternoon after we had become engaged, Virginia and I drove to her parent's home to seek her family's blessing on our marriage. I had instructed Virginia to get her sisters and her brother away from the table, so that I could talk to her dad. When I became aware that the others were not going to leave the table, and that her father ate slower than anyone I had ever seen, I could wait no longer. So I told Bro. Patterson, that Virginia and I wanted to get married and that we would like his blessing. He asked me what we were going to do if he did not give it to us. I told him that we were going to get married anyway, but we would really feel better if we had his blessing. He then said, "Well, I had always hoped she would marry a preacher." Then he went back to eating. I took that as a yes and did not press it any further. Two other daughters were already married, but they had done so while away at school. So we were the first big family wedding. All of her family and mine came to New Orleans for the wedding.

What can I say about Virginia's family? First I would say that they are a very tight knit family. My father-in-law was one of the hardest working men I ever knew. He was unable to go to seminary when he was a young man. Therefore, later he began going to an Extension of Southwestern Seminary, which met at Oklahoma Baptist University in

504

Shawnee, Oklahoma. He graduated from Southwestern Seminary when he was 74 years old. When he was 90 years old he received his Doctor's Degree after taking a correspondence course. My mother-in-law Helen Patterson is one of the most wonderful people I have ever known. We will celebrate her 100th Birthday, September 11, 2016. She is still active in a Native American church and plays the organ for their services. All of the sisters are a unique group of women. Each one had their own individual strengths, including a Professor of Nursing, a Principal, an Administrative Assistant, a Secretary, a Registered Nurse, Banker, and a Chemical Engineer. Their brother John is a Minister of the gospel and a very talented carpenter, as was his father.

The daughter-in-law is a school teacher and the seven sons-in-law, are an interesting group of men. One was in the field of Psychology, one was an Air Force Captain, and then an airline pilot, 3 are seminary graduates (one of which was in Juvenile work), one is a carpenter, and one is a Geologist and has worked in the oilfield industry most of his life. Six of the sons-in-law also have other talents that distinguish them in some way, meaning that they are really good at doing other things, usually creative things with their hands. Then there is the one who can preach, fish and play golf before his back gave out on him.

All of us are men with strong convictions, which has made for some interesting conversations over the years. But I think it would be safe to say that over the years we have come to respect one another for who we are. One of the things we all are is the husband of one of the Patterson girls.

There are a lot of wonderful memories that come to mind when I think of my extended family. One relates to my sister-in-law Dorothy, who is in heaven now with her dad and her husband Jim. We were at their home in Orlando, Florida. I was watching a golf tournament on TV. She came in and began to watch with me, in order to be a gracious hostess. Tiger Woods had come to the tee. She knew him because he had recently moved to Orlando. After he hit his tee shot she said, "He hit that ball in the air." When he got out to his ball on the fairway and hit his second shot she said again, "He hit that ball in

505

the air. How is he ever going to know where it is going, if he keeps hitting it in the air?" It suddenly dawned on me that the only golf she had ever experienced before was miniature golf. But she was doing her best to be a gracious hostess with her brother-in-law.

Then I probably ought to say that one of my favorite spots in all of the world is on the docks behind the house of my brother-in-law and sister-in-law Darl and Pat Henderson. Over the years, I have loved being on that dock or in a boat, fishing for Peacock Bass in the private lake behind their home. I could go there every time I go on vacation and never get bored. Part of it is the fishing and the scenery and part of it is that they are a wonderful host and hostess.

The End

How do you end something, when you did not know what you were doing when you started? Now that it is time to say "The End," you still may not know what you are doing.

I guess the best thing to do is to remind you of why I believe the Lord gave me the freedom to take on this project. As I said at the beginning, I am really a very ordinary person. I have some talents, but none that would just leave everyone breathless. For example, I can sing fairly well, but my wife and two sons are extremely talented vocalists.

As I said, I am just an ordinary man, but for some reason, during my lifetime, the Lord has allowed me to be part of some of His extraordinary activities. Every extraordinary activity that has been part of my life has related to the activity of God as He was doing Kingdom business in this world.

In relating my story, I have tried to do it in somewhat of a chronological fashion, and then trust the Lord to bring things to my mind that needed to be said. This has been a project that has taken me more than two years. I am grateful to those who encouraged me to do it. They know who they are, and without their encouragement I probably would never have given the Lord a chance to say that it was something that needed to be done.

My prayer is that some other ordinary person will read this book and be challenged to believe that, if he or she will make him or herself available, God can do extraordinary Kingdom work in their lives.

Thank you Lord, for keeping after me until it was done!!!

The End

P.S.: I am still alive, so I praise God for whatever else He allows me to join with Him in His Kingdom activity.

Postlude

"Follow Me and I will make you fishers of men" – Mark 1:17. These words or similar words are the ones that Jesus Christ used as He called the first 12 in an unbelieving world. These were ordinary men. Most of them were fishermen by trade. One was a tax collector and even one ended up being a traitor to the cause of Christ. Listen to what Jesus said to this group of men when He called them: "...go to the lost sheep of the house of Israel. As you go, announce this: The Kingdom of God has come. Heal the sick, raise the dead, cleanse those with skin diseases, and drive out demons." These ordinary men were used of God to take the gospel to the known world of their day. Down through history, ordinary men and women have been used of God to make a difference in the world in which they lived.

General Dwight D. Eisenhower

He was born in Denison, Texas, and grew up in Abilene, Kansas. He was raised in a Mennonite family and worked in the family creamery. He would eventually become the Supreme Commander of all of the Allied forces during World War II. Later he became the 34th President of the United States.

Corrie ten Boom

She grew up in a Dutch Christian family. Her family began hiding Jews from the Nazis during World War II. She and her family began what became known as the "Hiding Place," which saved the lives of untold numbers of Jews.

Billy Sunday

Billy Sunday was a professional Baseball player in the early days of professional baseball. The following was said about Billy Sunday after his conversion to Christianity: "Following his conversion, Sunday denounced drinking, swearing, and gambling, and he changed his behavior, which was recognized by teammates and fans." Shortly thereafter, Sunday began preaching at churches and the YMCA. Sunday turned down a new baseball contract to go to work for the YMCA for $83.00 per month. He soon became the most popular evangelist of his day.

Dwight L. Moody

Moody had a fifth grade level of formal education. His father died when he was very young. He worked in his uncle's shoe store to help his family with income. As a young adult he started a Sunday School class in Chicago, which later became the Moody Memorial Church. Later he became one of the best known Evangelists in the United States and also in London.

Mordecai Ham

He was a little known Baptist Evangelist. He is best known as the evangelist who was preaching the night that a young Billy Graham gave his life to Christ. Billy Graham went on to become the best known Evangelist the world has ever known. Billy Graham went on to preach to over 215 million people.

You might be saying, "But these people were more than ordinary people." However, I would submit to you that they all came from humble, normal, ordinary families, who went on to be involved in some of God's extraordinary activity.

I indicated that one of those who encouraged me to tell my story was Henry Blackaby. He did so by tapping me on the chest and saying, "Jim, there is a story in there that needs to come out. I would say to you that everyone has a story.

Every one of us is created uniquely by God, and every one of us can use our own uniqueness to become all that the Lord wants us to be. My prayer is that someone will read this book and realize that "the Lord can use me in extraordinary ways to advance His Kingdom." Your story is important to the Lord and is important for the world to hear.

Made in the USA
Monee, IL
25 January 2021

58616279R00282